Successful Sport Management

Successful Sport Management

Third Edition

Edited by

Herb Appenzeller

Tom Appenzeller

Carolina Academic Press / Durham, North Carolina

Library of Congress Cataloging-in-Publication Data

Successful sport management / edited by Herb Appenzeller, Tom Appenzeller.
    p. cm.
  Includes index.
  ISBN 978-1-59460-420-1 (alk. paper)
  1. Sports administration--United States. I. Appenzeller, Herb. II. Appenzeller,
Thomas.
  GV713.S83 2008
  796.06'9--dc22
                                              2008028705

Carolina Academic Press
700 Kent Street
Durham, North Carolina 27701
Telephone 919/489-7486
Fax 919/493-5668
E-mail: cap@cap-press.com
www.cap-press.com

Printed in the United States of America.

Dedication

Successful Sport Management, Third Edition, is dedicated to Dr. Guy Lewis, a pioneer in sport administration at the University of Massachusetts and the University of South Carolina. His colleagues describe him as an outstanding author, administrator, visionary, mentor, leader and scholar. His contributions to the sport industry are recognized nationally and internationally and his accomplishments have led sport administration programs into the 21st century.

Herb Appenzeller
Tom Appenzeller

Contents

Part 9 Career Opportunities

Foreword

Herb and Tom Appenzeller have produced what amounts to the complete encyclopedia of sport management. In the ever-expanding world of sport management, this book provides critical information about the various components of our profession. *Successful Sport Management* keeps abreast of the evolving roles of technology and web-based influences while continuing to build upon its foundation of management concepts throughout the sports industry. The book's contributors, who have been active in their respective fields, relate their vast experience and knowledge.

Whether the reader is considering a sports management career, a graduate preparing for that first career opportunity, or individuals who have made this profession their life's work, this book is an invaluable resource. The student considering a sport management career will discover a broad array of opportunities available in this profession. For the person just entering the field, the book is a comprehensive resource. Seasoned veterans will be amazed by the breadth and depth of the material which provides an opportunity for continual professional growth.

Through this book, I expanded my knowledge and plan to refer to it often in my day-to-day management of a collegiate athletic department.

Ron Wellman
Director of Athletics
Wake Forest University

Acknowledgments

Many things have changed since we published the second edition of *Successful Sport Management* in 2000. In the past eight years, we have left the information age and entered the conceptual age—with its emphasis on social responsibility. Many people have helped us provide up-to-date information for the revised book, and we are grateful for their assistance. It is impossible to list all the contributors to this book, but we hope they realize how important they are and how grateful we are for their help.

We thank the previous authors for updating their chapters and the new authors who have joined us in this important venture. We appreciate the unanimous support of our former students who willingly joined us in our desire to spotlight their careers in the sport industry. We have been privileged to work with such outstanding students, who now have successful careers in the sport industry.

Furthermore, we appreciate the efforts of Ann Terrill Appenzeller, who has contributed countless hours in editing, contacting potential authors, gathering material, typing, and many other tasks that make a good book even better. Her help was invaluable, and we are grateful for her efforts in our behalf.

We especially thank all the authors who made the book strong and relevant by their excellent chapters.

As always, we thank Dr. Keith Sipe and Linda Lacy for their vision and encouragement to publish the third edition.

Herb Appenzeller
Tom Appenzeller

Introduction

Sport management started at Ohio University in 1966 and experienced unprecedented growth among college students. The program became popular among students, but one element was lacking—structured information necessary for the new curriculum. Most professors depended on articles in magazines and periodicals for material to meet the needs of the new program for the sport industry.

In 1985, Dr. Guy Lewis and Dr. Herb Appenzeller decided to fill the void by inviting 21 individuals with expertise and experience in various areas of sport management to share their knowledge in a book designed for students in the field and for the professors who taught in the new major. All of the 21 individuals agreed to provide material in their areas of expertise, and the first edition of *Successful Sport Management* became a reality. The textbook was well received by sport management personnel, and several outstanding books were published to provide valuable information for people interested in the sport industry.

In 2000 the second edition of *Successful Sport Management* was revised and updated, and new chapters were included to meet the changing emphasis of sport management.

The third edition, with 31 authors and 14 former students who are in the sport industry, provide up-to-date information for the Conceptual Age, which is characterized by today's emphasis on social responsibility. A unique feature of the third edition is that the textbook can be used for all levels, undergraduate and graduate, of sport management programs. Each of the 33 chapters can stand on its own, and the book has material for those who are attempting to conduct a job search and need advice concerning resumes, interviews, networking, and other valuable tips of the trade. We advise all students to keep the book handy during their student days and for the future when they are practitioners in the sport industry. This text will provide valuable practical information for years to come.

Herb Appenzeller
Tom Appenzeller

Part 1

Personnel Management

Ultimately, sport leaders for the 21st Century must radiate optimism and facilitate solutions that enhance the role of sport in society and satisfactorily address the diverse needs of employees, participants and customers within this great industry.

David K. Scott, 2007

Chapter 1

The Changing Role of the Sport Administrator

Herb Appenzeller

For many years, the sport administrator had coaching responsibilities as well as administrative duties. Many college and university presidents believed that the combination of duties for the sport administrator needed to be changed. These critics of the dual position advocated separate responsibilities for the sport administrator, and some university systems in various states adopted a policy of prohibiting dual roles for the sport administrator. The Board of Governors of the University System of North Carolina adopted a policy in 1970 that separated the duties of the sport administrator. This action became a trend in many states and dramatically changed the job description of the administrator. Today, dual positions on the major university level are a rarity, and practically no sport administrator is expected to assume dual positions.

In the 21st Century, men and women who choose to be administrators now enter the field with a background and training in sport administration. Many earn master's or doctorate degrees with emphasis on business administration. In 2008, over 200 universities specialize in sport administration. These men and women represent a new breed of administrators schooled in finance, athletic fund-raising, marketing, time management, personnel management, legal affairs, risk management, public relations, and other areas that were previously neglected.

Authorities in the field of sport administration observe that the job of today's sport administrator is complex because of the expansion of sport programs amid decreasing budgets. In addition, they predict that technology is playing a major role in the sport industry and will help the administrator manage a successful program. (*Successful Sport Management*, 2000)

For example, Dr. Todd Seidler and Dr. David Scott, professors of Sport Administration at the University of New Mexico predict:

> New procedures, design ideas, or tools that may allow for an increase in efficiency or productivity of staff can be invaluable and may prove to be the difference between success and failure. (*Managing Sport*, 2003)

Seidler and Scott identify trends and innovations available for the sport administrator in Chapter 2 and Chapter 3 of this text. Undoubtedly, technological advances are the keys to the modern sport administrator, and the late Mark McCormack, CEO of International Management Group (IMG), agreed that technology is important in today's world of e-mails, Palm Pilots and BlackBerries, laptops, digital communicators, the World Wide Web, cell phones, and instant messaging. However, McCormack issued a warning to today's sport administrators when he wrote:

> Technology is wonderful and seductive. But it is also insidious, especially if it chips away at the appreciation of the value of constant human contact—because without these moments of face to face exchanges we lose a vital regulator in our lives. (*Staying Street Smart in the Internet Age*, 2000)

He added:

> Remember this ... no matter how tempting it is to hide behind technology, there's more to be gained by looking into another person's face than staring at a screen. (*Staying Street Smart in the Internet Age*, 2000)

Nido R. Qubein, the outstanding president of High Point University and an internationally known speaker, consultant, and author, supports McCormick's position on technology for administrators. Qubein firmly believes that computers will never replace people. In an article in *BizLife* (December 2007), the dynamic leader wrote:

> Computers are wonderful tools for performing calculations, accumulating data and facilitating communications. But they are incapable of original thought and original action.

Furthermore, Qubein believes sport management leaders need to be creative in order to be agents of change. He concludes:

> Creative people make use of computers. But computers will never be able to lead or inspire—or to duplicate the accomplishments of creative people. (*BizLife*, December 2007)

During my long tenure as the sport administrator at Guilford College, my job description was typical of today's responsibilities as a sport administrator. It included the following:

- supervising the coaching staff and teams
- supervising the budget and system of requisitions
- working cooperatively with coaches in scheduling their sports to utilize coordination of travel and facilities
- issuing contracts for home contests
- planning the Hall of Fame banquet
- checking on the eligibility of all athletes and maintaining records
- checking on physical examinations of athletes and maintaining records
- checking on the insurance coverage of all athletes
- being responsible for crowd behavior and intercollegiate events
- acting as fund-raiser for the booster club and athletics program
- scheduling booster club meetings and acting as an ex officio member of every booster club committee
- working cooperatively with the director of sport studies and the director of intramurals and club sports to coordinate programs as well as sport medicine
- supervising the athletic advisory council as an advisor to its monthly meetings

- acting as an ex-officio member of the faculty athletics committee
- supervising the sports information director
- maintaining a program of publications with the various groups that involve the athletics program along with the sports information director
- attending professional meetings, workshops, and clinics
- encouraging the professional growth of staff members
- conducting weekly athletics staff meetings
- closely supervising all sports programs

In the following chapters of Part I of the text, leadership in a technological world will be featured. The chapters should answer many questions for the aspiring sport administrator as well as for those already in the sport industry.

Chapter 2

Leadership for Modern Sport Organizations

David K. Scott

Introduction

The world and the organizations and institutions within it are profoundly changing. Corporations, private businesses, education, and even individuals are now exposed to both global communication and global competition. Sport organizations are currently operating within an environment that changes rapidly and provides challenges and complexities very different from those in previous years. These changes require different thinking and different preparation in order for leaders of modern organizations to be effective.

It has been said that the long-term, successful performance of any organization is ultimately the responsibility of leadership. However, as has been suggested in recent years by a number of management scholars and practitioners, there appears to be a dearth of truly effective leadership in many of our business and service organizations as well as in our governmental systems. Can the same be said about sport organizations? Although the answer probably depends on who is being asked, several other questions might need to be considered. For example, what is meant by "effective" leadership in sport? Are organizational outcomes such as winning, maximum attendance, and profits the sole indicator of good leadership? How important is employee or athlete satisfaction as an outcome of leadership? To what extent do external groups have to be satisfied with leadership? What are the core values of sport organizations relative to their products and/or participants and to entertainment in general?

These are just a few examples of questions that must be addressed by current and future sport leaders as they assume roles of leadership for sport organizations in the 21st century.

The goal of this chapter is to provide the reader with insight for answering questions such as the ones stated above. The chapter will address elements of leadership that can be applied to both (a) individual organization leadership in sport and (b) the broad leadership challenges within the sport industry. These two components of leadership will be referred to subsequently as "micro-leadership" (personal, small group/team, and departmental leadership) and "macro-leadership" (sport industry leadership), respectively. The sections to follow will broadly define *leadership* and identify what are considered leadership "essentials." In addition, subsequent sections will address leadership and organizational effectiveness, problem solving through a multiframe perspective, managing sport organization culture, and leadership development. The chapter will conclude with future considerations for leadership in a rapidly changing sport industry.

Leadership Challenges in Sport

From a "micro-leadership" perspective, sport administrators, team owners, general managers, coaches, and others in decision-making roles of authority face a number of challenges. Financial issues, personnel problems, crisis management, public relations, and pressure from external constituents can create an overabundance of daily leadership problems. These issues often consume the business, and sometimes personal, lives of sport leaders and require tremendous leadership commitment.

From a "macro-leadership" perspective, there are a number of issues that also represent significant challenges for the sport industry in general. Some of the recent concerns that call for effective leadership intervention include issues of gender equity, use of performance-enhancing drugs, decline in sportsmanship, athlete crime, overcommercialization of sport, and professional ethics. These all represent broad leadership challenges that will likely require collaboration of leaders in sport, business, education, and possibly the government.

Defining Leadership for Sport Organizations

It is evident in the literature that *leadership* has a multitude of definitions. What most of these definitions have in common is that leadership involves vision and the ability to influence or motivate people toward goal attainment. In modern organizations, the goals attained are considered acceptable if they are positive and mutually beneficial for the leader, the group members, and the overall organization.

In addition, there are several other descriptors of leadership that are helpful in framing the leadership phenomenon. Leadership implies that there are one or more followers. Leadership provides direction and support. Leadership creates change. Leadership is rooted in principles, morality, and ethics.

From a sport perspective, it appears that all of the above characteristics of leadership are useful in defining what sport leadership is, or what it should be. In addition, leadership in sport organizations can come from many levels. For example, in competitive sports, one can see the leadership impact that owners, general managers, athletic directors, coaches, and even athletes can have on their organizations. While ultimate leadership accountability in a sport organization rests with upper management, it should be recognized that leadership can come from "within" and must not always be from "above" in the organizational hierarchy.

There are also other factors involved in describing leadership that should be considered. For example, leaders are expected to produce desired outcomes. However, leadership is often proposed as a "process" and evaluated as an "outcome." For example, in competitive sport organizations, newly appointed leaders (e.g., head coaches, athletic administrators, and general managers) must develop effective leadership and organizational "processes" that will produce desired results. Depending on a multitude of circumstances, these processes may take a few years to develop. However, when a team is placed under new leadership, fans and boosters generally expect the team to win and produce positive financial results very quickly. Thus, the focus on reaching successful "outcomes" as defined by external constituents may preclude the development of the necessary leadership processes to produce long-term results. Often, as evidenced by the turnover of head coaches each year, if winning and/or revenue production does not occur to a satisfactory level in the desired time frame, sport organizations often decide to change leadership, and the cycle begins again. Thus, another way to describe leadership is that leaders not only provide vision, motivation, and positive influence but that they also are expected to produce desired results while satisfying constituents within a defined time frame. Moreover, leadership is commonly associated with personal and/or organizational change and is often most visible in times of organizational crisis.

With all of the above definitions and descriptors of leadership in mind, what does it take to be an effective sport leader? In order to be effective at developing vision, influencing people, achieving goals, managing change, and leading an organization through crisis situations, several traits, behaviors, and outcomes are critical to effective leadership. These essential elements, identified in the next section, are the foundation for further development of both "micro-leadership" and "macro-leadership" in sport.

Leadership Essentials for Sport Managers

The leadership phenomenon has been studied for decades and has evolved from purely trait theory to more modern situational, transformational, and values-based theories. These theories have collectively produced a number of characteristics that, whether naturally occurring or developed, are generally recognized as important for a leader to possess. For example, a leader must be internally motivated, must demonstrate self-confidence, and must have cognitive ability. Moreover, for the sake of credibility, a leader must be honest and must have knowledge and/or experience related to the enterprise being led. In addition, several "abilities" are essential to overall leadership effectiveness. These will be discussed in some detail below. However, before proceeding, it is interesting to know what characteristics have reduced leadership effectiveness. The Hagberg Consulting Group (1998), in studies of U.S. corporations, recognized a number of behaviors that reduce the effectiveness of company presidents. Included are (a) poor communication of the vision, (b) excessive dominance of employees and intolerance of disagreement, (c) self-centeredness, (d) failure to build alignment with goals, (e) lack of emphasis on teamwork, (e) arrogance and egotism, and (f) ignoring conflict. Individuals in sport leadership positions demonstrating one or more of these characteristics are undermining their influence on others and ultimately losing their credibility and effectiveness.

As previously mentioned, however, a number of leadership essentials continually resurface in the literature regarding what *is* necessary for a leader to be truly effective. Each of these is addressed in the following discussion.

Ability to Obtain the Trust and Respect of Individuals and Groups

Trust and respect may likely be the most critical components of leadership. While trust and respect may be the result of an individual's personal charisma, previous performance, and physical or career longevity, a number of other traits and behaviors are essential for the development of individual and group trust and respect. These behaviors can generally be associated with values-based or principle-centered leadership. Bennis and Goldsmith (1997) recognize that vision, empathy, consistency, and integrity are the essential components of building and maintaining the trust and respect of followers. Within these components, a leader who can create inspiring visions, "walk in the shoes" of followers, demonstrate consistency of purpose and action, and demonstrate integrity through ethical decision making is doing what is necessary to develop long-term trust and respect.

Ability to Adapt to Various Situations or Contingencies

Leaders of sport organizations have to make difficult decisions regarding policy, personnel, resource distribution, strategy, and a multitude of other short-term and long-term challenges. Contingency leadership theory suggests that the "situation" within which a decision must be made will dictate how a leader should approach a problem. This means that a leader may have to adapt to a new situation or change his or her personal leadership preference in order to produce the desired results. In competitive sport organizations, situations may change on a daily basis, and one's ability to adapt to these situations is critical to effective leadership.

However, an issue that must be addressed regarding situational leadership is its occasional conflict with the trust-building component of consistency. A leadership oxymoron is for a leader to be adaptable to various situations while also demonstrating consistency of behavior. For example, in situations where eligibility rules or team policy have been violated, leaders in charge must take situational factors into consideration while also being concerned about how inconsistent decisions may affect the trust of group members. Although there is no easy answer for this dilemma, it may be that the best approach is to demonstrate *consistency in the process* of reaching a decision that is in the best interest of the individual or groups most affected. However, at the macro-leadership level in sport, the ability to demonstrate situational adaptability requires concern for a broader constituency. Decisions that must often be made by league commissioners and executive directors of state, national, and international governing bodies must take into account the impact of the decision on the entire association and/or industry as a whole.

Ability to Develop Vision and Clarify a Path

The ability to move beyond what "is" and visualize "what could be" is essential to leadership. Additionally, the ability to clear a path and remove obstacles for those who follow is the "action leadership" necessary to be truly an architect of change. A number of sport leaders, both present and past, have demonstrated these essentials. However, it should be noted that their decisions and what they stand for are, or were not, always universally popular. While the following sport leaders certainly do not make up an all inclusive list, individuals such as Branch Rickey, credited with racial integration in sport; Donna Lopiano, executive director of the Women's Sport Foundation; David Stern, currently at the helm of the NBA; the late Mark McCormack, founder and first president of the International Management Group (IMG); and Billie Jean King, former tennis star and advocate of women's rights in sport have demonstrated what vision can do for the industry.

Motivation and Inspiration of Followers

Leaders are able to motivate and inspire followers to achieve and often surpass the goals of the organization. This is frequently accomplished through the leader's personal charisma. However, the effective use of a combination of transactional and transformational leadership appears to be the right formula for success. Transactional leaders are able to motivate through the appropriate use of tangible rewards. Transformational leaders demonstrate the ability to move people beyond self-interest toward a higher level of group or organizational commitment. In many cases, transformational leaders may even move followers to a higher level of moral reasoning. Transformational leaders are effective not only because of their personal charisma but also because of their ability to intellectually stimulate followers while providing proper individual consideration (Bass, 1990).

Ability to Achieve Results

We live in a results-oriented world. Nowhere is this more evident than in the sport industry. Although many great things happen during the *process* of leadership, ultimately people want to see results. Thus, effective leaders are able to produce desired outcomes in a time frame appropriate to organizational expectations and realities. (This aspect of leadership will be discussed in more detail in the section below.) However, too often, people in leadership positions become so focused on outcomes that they are willing to compromise the fundamental principles of honesty, integrity, and trust that form the foundation of true leadership. This dilemma might be referred to as "bottom-line morality." In other words, both strategic organizational constituents and society in general are often willing to overlook how an outcome was achieved if the end result provides the notoriety and/or revenue expected. Consequently, we see such by-products as unethical business practices, athletic programs occasionally on probation, compromise of athlete safety and health, and acceptance of what many would consider intolerable behavior from administrators, coaches, athletes, and fans.

Ideas and Suggestions

- Good leaders give people the tools they need to be successful.
- Leaders need the authority to get things done, but leadership is not synonymous with authority.
- Effective leaders are willing to share power with those who help implement the plan.

Leadership and Organizational Effectiveness in Sport

Five primary components of determining organizational effectiveness have been identified in the organizational studies literature (Cameron, 1980; Connolly, Conlon, & Deutsch, 1980; and Quinn & Rohrbaugh, 1981). These components, relative to sport organizations, are also discussed in detail by Slack (1997). For in-depth information regarding these measures of effectiveness, the reader is referred to the above sources. The purpose here, however, is to briefly recognize these areas of organizational effectiveness and provide an overview of how they pertain to sport organization leadership. The areas of effectiveness are as follows:

1. *Goal Attainment*—based on how well an organization achieves specific outcomes that are agreed upon by its members.
2. *Use of Systems Resources*—based on an organization's ability to acquire scarce resources or "inputs" from its environment.
3. *Internal Process*—based on the internal function, flow of information, and human interaction factors such as trust, loyalty, and teamwork in the organization.
4. *Satisfaction of Strategic Constituents*—based on an organization's ability to satisfy its numerous stakeholders as well as its ability to satisfy other affiliated organizations (i.e., media, sponsors, etc.), which can help it achieve its outcomes.
5. *Competing Values*—based on the idea that no single approach to determining organizational effectiveness is wholly appropriate. Also, effectiveness is subjective and often paradoxical. For example, in competitive sport organizations, winning a championship may be seen as effective; however, there may have been compromises in the "means" through which the championship was obtained.

In sport organizations, all of these areas of effectiveness should be of concern to a leader. Additionally, it should be noted that there is some overlap, and even conflict, in some of the areas. For example, goal attainment can be viewed both internally and externally. In competitive sport organizations, achievement of internal organizational goals may or may not be what is expected from strategic constituents. As a result, leadership performance is often evaluated by entities whose expectations may not be realistic. From this perspective, a sport leader must have "tough skin" and must perhaps be willing to evaluate personal performance based on internal organizational expectations and self-evaluation. Also, goal attainment often depends on an organization's ability to acquire the necessary resources. For example, it is unrealistic to expect a championship season from a sport team when personnel, funding, and media support is inadequate.

Relative to goal attainment, competitive sport organizations strive for championships, optimal attendance, satisfied customers, and, ultimately, increased revenue. These are all outcome-based measures that give some degree of objectivity to how well an organization is performing regarding both internal and external expectations. As discussed previously, effective leaders achieve results. Consequently, subpar performance relative to outcome-based measures is often attributed to poor leadership. While a number of factors other than leadership may contribute to organizational outcomes, leaders are ultimately held accountable and must be willing to accept the responsibility. In order to fulfill this responsibility and be more effective in the area of goal attainment, sport leaders need to do a good job of identifying what is truly realistic, provide the necessary structure (including policies and procedures), and develop strategies that provide goal clarity and reduce or remove obstacles along the way.

Concomitantly, it is important for a sport organization leader to demonstrate the ability to obtain resources and motivate and manage people within the organization. In a recent study of Canadian intercollegiate athletic departments

(Danylchuk & Chelladurai, 1999), financial management, leadership (including supervision, motivation, inspiration, and counseling of coaches/staff), and revenue generation were among the activities perceived to be both most important and most time-consuming as indicated by athletic directors.

For sport organizations, resources can include finances, personnel, facilities, equipment, and even time. Obtaining these resources is often a considerable obstacle to overcome in a highly competitive sport industry. Each level of sport is faced with its own challenge in this regard. Competition for entertainment dollars, financing of product development, balancing payroll, securing adequate media attention, and acquiring quality personnel are examples of resource-oriented challenges that must be addressed by sport leaders.

Managing internal process is also a critical leadership function for sport leaders in achieving organizational effectiveness. Internal process includes the components human resource management, motivation, effective communications, group dynamics, and team building. These areas seem natural for "people-oriented" leaders but may be quite unnatural for authority- and power-oriented leaders. While perhaps somewhat idealistic, it is suggested here that truly effective leadership exists only when people within a sport organization are motivated, are empowered, trust one another, and are committed to each other and their leaders. As a result, sport organization employees or athletes find true satisfaction, personal growth, and perhaps the most meaningful long-term impact of leadership.

Effective sport leaders must also be fully aware of the strategic constituents that will determine, and sometimes define, the organization's effectiveness. Depending on the level of competitive sport or the segment of the sport industry involved, all sport organizations must satisfy both internal and external constituents to some degree. This requirement may present a values-based or ethical dilemma for sport leaders. For example, are athletes the primary constituents who must be satisfied in school sports? If so, should athletes ultimately determine whether or not their leader or leaders are considered effective? With the billions of dollars in television revenue provided to professional leagues, who has the most influence on determining whether or not a league organization is effective? Does the same question exist regarding a $1,000,000 donor to a collegiate athletic department?

These are valid questions that challenge leaders to "do the right thing." Certainly, sport leaders must recognize and must be able to effectively manage the political issues associated with the satisfaction of constituents. These tasks may be accomplished through strategic public relations, improved personal communication, and the demonstration of "strong will" in protecting the integrity of the organization. In this regard, effective sport leaders must also identify their role expectations and be able to maintain a principle-centered approach to managing the satisfaction of constituents. Otherwise, the outside individual or group having the most influence on an organization at any given time will ultimately determine whether or not its leader is effective.

Finally, effective sport leaders must recognize and deal with the "competing-values" approach to measuring effectiveness. Although more complicated than presented here, the competing-values model (Quinn, 1988) generally suggests that organizational effectiveness depends on the focus of the organization and whether outcomes to measure effectiveness are based on means or ends. In this sense, organizations that want to be successful in a highly competitive sport industry will likely have a predominant external focus that involves adaptability, productivity, goal setting, and maximum output. On the other hand, an organization with an internal focus will concentrate on such values as human commitment, internal communication, training, and group morale. However, these values often "compete" with one another—which is especially true in intercollegiate sport organizations where a dilemma often exists between a sport's entertainment value, its value relative to visibility and image enhancement for the university, and its educational or developmental value for athletes. In these cases, what is considered effective by the head coach may be different from what is considered effective by the college president, the athletic director, the marketing director, or the alumni.

In modern sport organizations, leaders should be aware of all these areas of organizational effectiveness. In addition, they should consider the many ways in which their leadership can influence positive outcomes relative to each of the areas. Overemphasis or underemphasis on one or more of the areas can result in catastrophe. Thus, achieving a balance is critical. While a daunting leadership challenge, it appears to be what may likely determine long-term leadership and organizational success.

Multiframe Leadership and Problem Solving

All of the leadership challenges and measures of organizational effectiveness discussed in the previous section require that modern sport leaders be versatile. Problems are often complex and are not easily solved with simple solutions. For example, what are the solutions to the problem of increased criminal behavior by some athletes in collegiate and professional sports? Certainly, while not the norm for most athletes, the resulting negative image reflected upon competitive sport programs creates both a micro- and a macro-leadership dilemma.

In addressing a problem such as the one described above, leaders must often look beyond what appears on the surface to be the problem. Often, because of personality, background, or experience, a leader will tend to look at a problem through only one lens. This may result in a unidimensional approach that ultimately causes the leader to overlook more effective solutions. In addition, various situations or contexts within which problems occur often require a leader to initially "frame" a problem before immediately proceeding to a solution.

Bolman and Deal (1991) present a multidimensional "framing" approach to organizational leadership that allows a leader to determine appropriate tactics for solving various organizational, and perhaps even industry. problems. Although Bolman and Deal's work was not written in the sport context, the fundamental principles involved are easily applied to leadership issues in sport organizations. The frames identified by Bolman and Deal were (a) structural, (b) human resource, (c) political, and (d) symbolic. The following description of these frames should help readers recognize not only their own predisposition toward one or more frames but also how the frames relate to most, if not all, of the areas of organizational effectiveness discussed in the previous section.

Frames of Reference
(Bolman & Deal, 1991)

1. The *structural frame* emphasizes the traditional bureaucracy with a well-defined chain of command, clear division of labor, and specific role responsibilities. Attainment of goals is of utmost priority, and leaders ensure that policies and procedures are clearly understood and followed. Structural leaders are sometimes considered taskmasters.
2. The *human resource frame* focuses primarily on meeting human needs in organizations. In this frame, leaders are sensitive to relationships and feelings and seek to lead through facilitation and empowerment. Seeking an optimal fit between the organization and each individual member is a fundamental concern.
3. The *political frame* recognizes that conflict is inevitable and that competition for scarce resources is a central feature of organizations. Political leaders need to be skillful negotiators who create coalitions, build power bases, and negotiate compromises. In the political frame, interests of powerful constituents may displace organizational goals.
4. The *symbolic frame* is rooted in the values and culture of the organization. This frame attempts to give "meaning" to organizational events. Symbolic leaders recognize and promote myth, ritual, ceremonies, and other symbolic expressions of the organization. Symbolism often defines what is acceptable and assists in establishing the organizational norms.

A brief summary of each of the frames and of how they appear to relate to the categories of organizational effectiveness is presented in Figure 1.

Bolman and Deal (1991) suggest that individuals usually have a predisposition and demonstrate personal characteristics in one or two of the above frames. However, they also suggest that leaders with the capacity to be multidimensional have the potential to be more effective.

Returning to the problem of athlete crime that was identified in the first paragraph of this section, one can see how "framing" the problem results in a variety of potential solutions. For example, structural framing would identify the problem as one that stands in the way of overall goal attainment. A structurally oriented sport leader would likely address the problem through strict policies and procedures that are unambiguous and would provide just punishments for involvement in criminal behavior.

However, framing the problem from a human resource perspective, it would be common to want to know *why* an athlete was involved in a crime. What was the situation? Were there extenuating circumstances that may have contributed to the criminal behavior? In this frame, the leader might recognize that the individual or individuals involved need counseling and, if at all possible, an opportunity to learn from their mistakes and be reconnected to the group.

From a political frame perspective, it might be that pressures brought on by external constituents to produce a winning team resulted in compromises in the athlete selection process. In addition, how the problem is dealt with once it has happened may be influenced by the "power position" of the interested constituents. In this frame, the leader is tested with making a value decision and must

| | **Figure 1** | |
Leadership Frame	Frame Descriptions	Related Measure of Organizational Effectiveness
STRUCTURAL	Coordination and control are essential to effectiveness. Emphasis on goal attainment and policies/procedures. Leaders stress accountability and are outcome oriented.	GOAL ATTAINMENT
HUMAN RESOURCE	Organizations exist to serve human needs. Facilitation and empowerment are important to success. Leaders are supportive and concerned for group members.	INTERNAL PROCESS
POLITICAL	Conflict is inevitable due to competition for scarce resources. Solutions emerge from negotiation and bargaining. Leaders develop coalitions and gain support from people with influence.	STRATEGIC CONSTITUENTS & SYSTEM RESOURCES
SYMBOLIC	Shared values create an optimal culture. Symbols, rites, and rituals convey organizational norms and expectations. Leaders inspire through charisma.	INTERNAL PROCESS & COMPETING VALUES

Leadership frame information based on information contained in Bolman, L. G., & Deal, T.E. (1991). *Reframing organizations: Artistry, choice, and leadership*. San Francisco: Jossey-Bass. Organizational effectiveness information based on Cameron, K. S. (1980). Critical questions in assessing organizational effectiveness. *Organizational Dynamics, 9,* 66–80.

ultimately do what he or she thinks is right on the basis of principles and the best interest of the organization.

Finally, the symbolic frame might suggest that a decline in overall organizational or societal values contributed to the problem. In this sense, a new "meaning" is needed of what it takes to be a "successful" athlete, role model, and productive citizen. Leaders must then identify the symbols, rituals, and rewards necessary to establish more desirable behavioral norms.

Hopefully the above examples, although addressing one specific problem, have indicated how the multiple-frame approach to leadership and problem solving could be beneficial for sport leaders in all aspects of the sport industry. All organizations eventually encounter problems that are rooted in one or more of the frames discussed in this section. As indicated previously, the leadership challenge is to successfully "frame" the problem and develop an appropriate solution strategy. Leaders must remember, however, that this challenge often requires them to think from a different perspective and to be more versatile in their leadership approach.

Managing Sport Organizational Culture

Organizational culture is generally defined as the widely shared beliefs, values, and assumptions that exist at the core of an organization (Schein, 1996). Culture is not always easy to identify from external observation, but it pervades an organization and ultimately defines the norms and expectations of organizational members. In addition, several researchers from business and education have suggested that a strong positive culture is what separates the most effective organizations from those that are less effective and that leadership has a strong impact on the culture within an organization. In fact, it has also been argued (Schein, 1985) that there may be no single more important leadership responsibility than the management of culture. Certainly, in sport organizations, having everyone share a common belief system and work together toward achieving a unified goal is critical to long-term success.

Although a variety of leadership styles can be effective, one that appears to have a strong impact on the development of a positive organizational culture is transformational leadership. Transformational leaders are inspirational and empowering. According to Robbins (1997), "Transformational leaders inspire followers to transcend their own self-interests for the good of the organization" (p. 151). Weese (1995) suggests that transformational leaders in recreational organizations influence a culture of "excellence and continual improvement."

The prevailing culture in an organization can often be traced to its founder or someone with strong influence on the organization. Several major league franchises, for example, have individuals in their past that established cultures which have perpetuated to some degree in their absence.

In sport organizations, one can look at the various symbols and rituals associated with a sport enterprise and get some hints of what it purports to be its values. If indeed these values are widely shared and consistently reinforced within the organization, there is evidence of a strong culture centered on the values. For example, the innovative, controversial, and sometimes brash nature of Nike and its leader Phil Knight provide insight into the culture that likely exists in the company. That the Penn State Nittany Lions football players do not have names on their jerseys symbolizes "team-oriented" values. Mission statements, slogans, signs on the wall, etc., in sport-related manufacturing and retail organizations tell employees and customers something about the existing or desired culture of the business.

However, observable signs of a culture do not mean that it actually exists or that it is strong and positive. The leadership challenge related to organizational culture that must be addressed by sport administrators, sport business owners, managers, and coaches deals with *how* culture can be managed. To address this issue, a sport leader must first understand that there are three cultural situations to consider: (a) creating a culture, (b) changing a culture, and (c) managing a culture. In new organizations without any history, culture must be created. In established organizations, the leader must recognize when the current culture is inadequate for effective performance and must go about the arduous process of changing the existing culture. Finally, leaders must also recognize when things are going very well relative to an organization's performance (both internal process and outcomes) and must do what is necessary to effectively manage the existing culture.

In order to be an effective culture manager in a sport organization, a leader must first define the culture as it currently exists. This may be quite evident from a surface evaluation, especially in cases where culture is weak and performance is inadequate. Franchises in disarray, athletic programs that have experienced excessive turnover, and newly formed businesses struggling to get off the ground are examples of situations where the lack of culture may be contributing to poor organizational performance.

In newly formed organizations, desired values for the infant culture should be developed through collaboration and empowerment of organizational members. In most cases, such development is also required when a leader attempts to change a culture. In cases where the existing culture is somewhat unclear, close examination of internal processes and the use of individual interviews or questionnaires may help the leader determine if the desired values are indeed widely shared. If it is determined that a change of culture is necessary, the leader must develop a vision for the new culture and identify essential steps necessary to proceed. Most important, the leader must put a system into place that supports the desired culture by consistently rewarding individuals for behaviors congruent with the ideal organizational values.

Generally, the most challenging culture management situation exists when a leader attempts to change a culture where things are going well and organizational members have been in their positions for a long time. For example, a sport organization may have a number of managers who have been running their respective departments for years and are somewhat resistant to change. However, in a rapidly changing marketplace, it may be necessary for a leader to establish new values and ways of doing things in order for the sport organization to remain competitive. In this situation, it is critical for the leader to provide opportunities for organizational members to express their concerns and then to provide the security necessary for them to test new ideas.

Overall, as previously mentioned, culture management may be the most challenging, yet critical, component of sport organization leadership. In addition, although not discussed in detail here, one must be aware of the many subcultures that often exist under the umbrella of a larger culture. For example, athletic departments are divided into numerous program areas that all have their own cultures. Sporting goods manufacturers have various departments which all may have unique subcultures operating within them. The leadership challenge in these situations is to have central values crucial to overall organizational performance while allowing some degree of uniqueness in each program area.

In conclusion, there are a number of components of culture management that a sport leader should consider when guiding an organization. Establishing a distinct vision, collaborating with group members, setting and communicating clear objectives, allowing participation in decision making, providing principled leadership, and establishing proper and timely reward systems are keys to successful culture development (Scott, 1997).

Ideas and Suggestions

Strong culture organizations have *core values* that are readily identified by group members and that provide the rationale for decision making. Sport leaders should consider the following relative to core values:

- Establish your core values through a participative process. Get your employees or athletes involved.

- Develop no more than three-to-five core values.

- Arrange the values so that everyone knows what comes 1st, 2nd, etc.

- Teach the core values to all new members of the organization. Don't just hand them a policy book.

- Make decisions (even the tough ones) consistent with the core values.

- Reinforce the core values when rewarding individuals for exceptional performance.

Adapted from K. Blanchard, "Gung Ho" Leadership Seminar, 1999.

Leadership Development

Now that several of the facets of effective leadership have been discussed, what about the development and training of current and future sport leaders? Who should be responsible and what factors should be considered?

Ultimately, the responsibility for leadership training lies within the individual currently preparing for a leadership position. Becoming a more effective leader generally requires a commitment to improving one's knowledge and awareness of personal leadership styles and behaviors and how they can be enhanced.

It is quite likely that numerous leaders in the sport industry acquired their leadership skills through modeling or trial and error. While many have well-developed, and possibly "natural" leadership abilities, it has been determined that leadership skills can be improved through education and training. For students of sport management, leadership courses that examine current issues, theories, and applications relative to sport organizations and the sport industry should be required. Current leaders in the field should be willing to take the initiative to improve their knowledge and skills relative to leadership. This might be done through self-evaluation, consultation with professional leadership consultants, and/or in-house workshops conducted by other sport or community leaders. In addition, current leaders should not be afraid to obtain objective feedback from organizational members regarding their own leadership performance.

Thus, regardless of the leadership training and development avenues available, sport managers must first acknowledge their own need for personal leadership development and then make a commitment to improve their knowledge, skills, and behaviors in order to be effective in the complex and rapidly changing sport organizations of today and the future.

Sport Leadership for the Future

Many challenges face sport leaders in the first decade of the new century and beyond. As mentioned previously, these challenges are both micro and macro in nature. Each individual sport organization has its unique problems that require careful planning, intervention, and as discussed previously, culture management by its leaders. At the macro-leadership level, individuals and groups with influence on the overall sport industry face issues that may ultimately affect the delivery and impact of sport in the United States and worldwide.

Furthermore, some of what we see happening in our sport organizations and in society in general can be disturbing for current and future leaders. It is quite possible that the challenges appear so intimidating they may actually prevent people with exceptional leadership ability from pursuing positions where they feel pressure to compromise their principles, health, and/or life balance. If such compromise occurs, true leadership will be noticeably absent, and problems will worsen.

With these things in mind, what will it take for a sport leader to be successful in the future? In addition to the traits, behaviors, and leadership concerns addressed in previous sections of this chapter, sport leaders should be aware of some of the current thought regarding leadership for today's and tomorrow's world.

Organizational leadership in previous decades has often been characterized as authoritarian and outcome-based. In this frame of reference, leaders were sometimes considered power mongers that had the political clout and/or positional authority to influence, or perhaps coerce, people to work toward goals not always understood. In some organizations, this same approach to leadership exists today. Although in some cases productive, and occasionally required, purely positional and authoritarian leadership can be detrimental to important organizational outcomes such as trust, work satisfaction, and morale. If these critical factors of overall success are disregarded, the organization's long-term performance will ultimately suffer, and a significant change in culture will be required to keep the organization afloat.

John C. Maxwell and Stephen Covey, both recognized authorities on leadership, have recently addressed the issue discussed in the preceding paragraph. Their thoughts on leadership development provide important insights for individuals assuming leadership roles in the future. In *Developing the Leader Within You* (2005), Maxwell points out that leadership is developed in stages, or levels. As Maxwell (2005) explains, the first level of leadership is simply positional, whereby people follow the leader because such action is a requirement. In the second stage of development, leaders have qualities and skills that result in people following them because they "want to." In the third stage of development, leaders have achieved effective results, and people follow them because of what the leaders have done for the organization or team. In the fourth stage of development, people follow the leader because of what he or she has done for them personally. In the final stage of development, leaders have achieved the highest level of leadership maturity and influence, whereby people follow them because of what the leaders represent to a broader society.

This last stage of development coincides with an important contention of Covey (2004) in *The 8th Habit*. Covey contends that the most effective leaders of the future will need to develop "moral authority" in addition to "formal authority." Covey defines *moral authority* as the gaining of influence through servanthood, service, and contribution. Covey (2004) asks: "Why does moral authority exponentially increase the effectiveness of formal authority and power" (p. 301)? Covey goes on to indicate:

> [P]eople are super-sensitive to even the slightest nuance of either "throwing one's weight around" or the use of patience, kindness, empathy and gentle persuasion. Such character strength activates others' consciences and creates emotional identification with the leader and cause or principles he or she stands for. Then when formal authority or position power is also used, people follow for the right reasons, out of genuine commitment rather than out of fear. (p. 301–302)

As suggested by the above authors, truly effective long-term and influential leadership is developed over time, with utmost commitment and concern for serving people and organizations. Secretan (1999) suggests:

> [T]he new-story leaders who will guide the greatest organizations on Earth during the next thousand years are those who will achieve exceptional goals while honoring people at the same time—every step of the way. New-story leaders understand that the process of leadership—how you get there, how you treat people—is equally, if not more important. (p. 16)

While there are many leadership values, such as those discussed in this section, that appear to be universal, it should be recognized that these values and the extent to which they are accepted may not be the same in all cultures. From an international perspective, the relationship of leaders and followers varies across countries. For example, Champoux (2000) indicates that "people in countries with values that specify strongly hierarchical relationships in organizations react more positively to directive approaches than to participative approaches" (p. 231) Thus, cultural influences on leadership should also be taken into consideration as individuals develop their leadership potential in a global market.

In the present and future business environment, sport managers must be prepared for leadership occurring in a society that is moving and changing rapidly. However, it is important for these leaders to recognize that they are ultimately serving the individuals that make up their organizations. Phrases such as "leading from behind," "turning the pyramid upside down," "leading through service," and "principle-centered or value-based leadership" have been used in recent years. These phrases recognize not only that leaders are not always up front when they issue directives but also that leadership is a value-based, people-serving process that ultimately produces results through vision, empowerment, and support.

What is apparent from the leadership literature in the last decade is that in the new century, leadership for sport, as well as for other organizations, requires (a) courage, (b) commitment, and (c) accountability. These three traits unfortunately appear to be somewhat problematic in our society. Sport leaders will not only need to discover and develop these traits within themselves; they will also need to be effective models of the traits for their followers. Furthermore, sport leaders will need to realize that extraordinary organizational and industry achievements do not happen without the dedication and work of many people. The leaders of the future will not only need to provide insightful direction; they will also need to be actively engaged as facilitators and supporters. Ultimately, sport leaders in the 21st century must radiate optimism and facilitate solutions that enhance the role of sport in society and satisfactorily address the diverse needs of employees, participants, and customers within this great industry.

References

Bass, B. M. (1990). From transactional to transformational leadership: Learning to share the vision. *Organizational Dynamic, 18,* 19–31.

Bennis, W., & Goldsmith J. (1997). *Learning to lead.* Reading, MA: Perseus Books.

Blanchard, K. (1999, October). Gung-Ho Leadership Seminar, Lessons in Leadership Series. Public presentation, Albuquerque.

Bolman L. G., & Deal, T. E. (1991). *Reframing organizations: Artistry, choice, and leadership.* San Francisco: Jossey-Bass.

Cameron, K. S. (1980). Critical questions in assessing organizational effectiveness. *Organizational Dynamics, 9,* 66–80.

Champoux, J. E. (2000). *Organizational behavior: Essential tenets for a new millennium.* New York: South-Western College Publishing.

Connolly, T., Conlon, E. M., & Deutsch, S. J. (1980). Organizational effectiveness: A multiple constituency approach. *Academy of Management Review, 5,* 211–218.

Covey, S. (2004). *The 8th Habit.* New York: Free Press.

Danylchuk K. E., & Chelladurai, P. (1999). The nature of managerial work in Canadian intercollegiate athletics. *Journal of Sport Management, 13,* (2), 148–165.

Hagberg Consulting Group (1998). How leadership effectiveness is reduced. Retrieved August 6, 1999, from Leadership Development Web site: http://www.leadership-development.com/.

Maxwell, J. C. (2005). *Developing the leader within you.* Nashville, TN: Thomas Nelson, Inc. Robbins, S. P. (1997). *Essentials of organizational behavior* (5th ed.). Upper Saddle River, NJ: Prentice Hall.

Quinn, R. E. (1988). *Beyond rational management.* San Francisco: Jossey-Bass.

Quinn, R. E., & Rohrbaugh, J. (1981). A competing values approach to organizational effectiveness. *Public Productivity Review, 5,* 122–140.

Schein, E. H. (1985). *Organizational culture and leadership.* San Francisco: Jossey-Bass.

Schein, E. H. (1996). Culture: The missing concept in organization studies. *Administrative Science Quarterly, 41,* 229–240.

Scott, D. K. (1997). Managing organizational culture in intercollegiate athletic organizations. *Quest, 49,* (4), 403–415.

Secretan, L. (1999, December). Spirit at work: Changing the world with growing companies. *IW Growing Companies.*

Slack, T. (1997). *Understanding sport organizations.* Champaign, IL: Human Kinetics.

Weese, W. J. (1995). Leadership and organizational culture: An investigation of Big Ten and Mid-American conference campus recreation administrators. *Journal of Sport Management, 9,* 119–134.

Chapter 3

Technology for the Sport Manager

Todd L. Seidler
David K. Scott

The field of Sport Management is changing rapidly. As more people participate, as media-exposure increases, as revenue escalates, and as more emphasis is placed on the bottom line, the essential job functions of sport managers continually change. More knowledge of issues related to sport finance, law, marketing, sponsorship, organization and leadership, facility design and management, and others is required to manage the sport programs of today. Sport organizations are constantly being asked to do more with less and are being held to more stringent fiscal requirements. As a result, sport managers must work smarter and become more efficient. It is essential for managers of sport and recreation programs to keep up with the latest trends and innovations in the field. New procedures, design ideas, or tools that may allow for an increase in efficiency or productivity of staff can be invaluable and may prove to be the difference between organizational success and failure.

Perhaps the most important of these trends and innovations are advances in electronic technology and the increasing use of computer applications in daily operations. Computer technology is advancing rapidly. Faster, more powerful, and less expensive computers, as well as related hardware and specialized software applications are being introduced almost daily. Computers, used properly, are tremendous tools and can have a positive impact on cost reductions through increased staff efficiency and productivity as well as increasing revenue generation. Not only can computers help with the streamlining of daily operations, but they can also provide almost immediate access to updated information—functions which can enhance the decision-making process. Computers can assume many of the day-to-day operational tasks, thereby freeing up staff for other responsibilities for finding their way into such diverse applications as marketing, communication, public relations, recruiting, automated building-control systems, security, and access-control and energy-management systems. From simple word processors, spreadsheets, and database programs to specially designed computer and software packages developed for specific management applications, the options are increasing rapidly. This chapter presents a selection of these trends and innovations and briefly describes what potential impact they may have on today's sport manager. It is by no means a comprehensive look at technology and computer use in sport management but merely an overview of several areas sport managers should be aware of today. Many of the more widely used applications such as e-mail and mail-merge programs will not be discussed here. The focus will be placed on some of the more recent methods of using this new technology. Every sport manager needs to become familiar with how computers and related technology can be beneficial to their operations. The following are a few examples of how this technology can be used in various capacities related to sport management.

Marketing and Sponsorship

Virtual Signage

The use of virtual signage is increasing quickly in the world of sport. Recent computer technology allows a sport marketer to digitally place a company logo or advertisement into a television picture and make it appear real. A grass field, a blank wall, the side of a building, the bottom of a pool—any television picture can now be made to look as if a sponsor's logo were painted on it. For example, virtual signage is often used in baseball. The wall behind home plate is typically a solid, dark color so that the white ball can be seen against this backdrop. To the fans in the stands and the players on the field, it is only a blank wall. For those viewing the game at home, however, computer technicians can insert a sponsor's logo with such realism that viewers cannot distinguish the difference between it and a real one. Another advantage is that different logos or messages can be inserted for different viewing areas. Take the broadcast of a match in the World Cup Tournament. A different sponsor's logo can be inserted for each different region or country receiving the broadcast. Instead of event marketers having to sell one huge sponsorship package to a company that wants to gain exposure worldwide, it is now possible to provide opportunities for many smaller sponsors to have their message seen only in the area important to them.

Technology and Ticketing

Nowhere is the technology revolution more evident than in the event-ticketing industry. In what seems like overnight technological advances, ticketing for sport events has gone from "standing in line at the ticket window" to fully automated electronic-ticketing services. These advances now provide sport venues with the equivalent of a 24-hour open box office. In fact, it is now a virtual requirement for a sport organization to have a webmaster on staff to manage the integration of the organization or team Web site with its Internet ticket-distribution provider.

Currently, any individual with access to a computer and the Internet can place online orders for tickets to almost every professional sport event as well as most major collegiate sport events. The tickets can generally be purchased several weeks in advance and paid for through online credit card transactions. At the present time, processing fees are relatively small, and it is likely that most customers appreciate the convenience of not having to stand in line. The actual tickets can be received in the mail, picked up at Will Call on game day, or even printed out on the customer's home printer.

Several advances, including new software developments and insightful business agreements, have been responsible for changing the face of event ticketing. For example, in early 1999, Paciolan Systems, Inc. (PSI) made a move toward enhanced customer service by establishing an agreement with Ticketmaster that would allow PSI customers to expand their ticket-distribution network. This agreement allows venues using the PSI system to interface with the global network of Ticketmaster's Internet site. Similar agreements have been developed with various sport organizations and the Tickets.com Network.

In addition, other recent software developments (e.g., CyberSEATS(tm)) provide customers with the opportunity not only to select their seats online but also to see the view of the court or playing field from those seats. Another approach that has surfaced recently offers automated ticketing to consumers through a "ticket machine." ETM, a ticket solution company, has introduced electronic ticket machines (similar to ATM machines) complete with interactive touch screens and graphic, video, and audio capabilities. These machines can be placed in strategic, high traffic locations and can provide sport organizations the opportunity to communicate directly with potential customers.

Advances in ticket-distribution technology, such as the ones mentioned in the preceding paragraphs, have optimized customer service for many professional and collegiate sport organizations. As more people purchase home computers and utilize the Web, it is likely that online ticket sales will continue to grow. User friendliness and consumer satisfaction with at least this part of the sport-entertainment experience is certainly enhanced by these recent technological developments. It is now possible for an individual to pay online for a "ticket" to a sport event and then be able to print out a verification and seat number that can be punched in on a keypad or scanned for admission at the gate.

Technology Enhanced Web Services

Recent development of enormous revenue-producing potential is occurring in intercollegiate athletics with technology enhanced Web services such as audio and video streaming available to paid subscribers. With more people having the bandwidth to support this technology and more advertisers interested in reaching large numbers of fans through a Web site, the technology now allows intercollegiate athletic departments a new source of revenue. It has been estimated (College finds new revenue source online, 2007) that the newest online technology has the potential to create multimedia channels on college Web sites capable of generating over $1 million per year. Marketing and advertising potential is also enhanced with this online approach, which may provide almost limitless possibilities for college athletic departments to maximize revenue streams.

Mobile TV

One of the emerging technologies with potential for marketing specifically to sports fans involves mobile TV. An example of this service in 2007 is V Cast Mobile TV by Verizon Wireless. This service provides sports fans with the opportunity to obtain up-to-date scores and view live television broadcasts on their cell phones, including real-time game and event broadcasts and sports talk shows. Sport programming channels recently available with specific interest to sports fans include ESPN Mobile TV and Fox Mobile. According to industry specialists, there is great marketing potential in mobile TV using sports as a vehicle. One of the primary advantages, according to industry analyst John Gaunnt (Medford, 2007), is that people's full attention is likely to be engaged on the little telephone screen as opposed to regular television. Another unique feature of mobile TV is that the technology allows customers access to live sports programming anywhere within the cell phone-provider service area.

Conjoint Analysis, Data Mining, and Knowledge Discovery in Sport

The power and speed of many desktop computers now allows enhanced methods of market analysis in sport that were previously unattainable. For example, large volumes of customer data can be collected online or through hand-held palm computers and can be transferred instantly to a database for statistical analysis and/or data mining. The following paragraphs briefly discuss some of the ways that this technology is impacting, and will continue to impact, sport marketing.

In the marketing of competitive sports, there are a number of uncontrollable aspects of the "product." However, such things as ticket price, parking services, facility design, security, and general customer relations have various attributes that can be manipulated. One approach that can be used by marketers to better understand and predict what consumers choose as the best combination of attributes for a product is a statistical procedure known as conjoint analysis. Although this procedure has been around for approximately 20 years, only recently has software been developed that will allow mathematical analysis of large numbers of subjects with hundreds of combinations of product attributes. For example, a professional team might want to study what their fans prefer relative to types of game promotions, half-time entertainment, styles of seating, concession offerings, and various arena or stadium amenities. A sample of subjects can be chosen, and a variety of methods (e.g., questionnaires, prop-cards, attribute rankings, and virtual experiences) can be used to collect data for conjoint analysis (Green, Krieger, & Vavra, 1997). With recent advances in technology, information can also be collected from consumers through the use of online surveys and/or hand-held palm computers. The resulting analysis of the data can provide insight into what the most preferred combinations of attributes are for a particular product. This information can then be used to develop the "controllable" aspects of a sport product that are most likely to satisfy existing fans and attract new customers.

Another approach that has potential to increase knowledge relative to customer-satisfaction management is "data mining." Recently, data mining has been introduced as an inductive process that uses a variety of data-analysis tools to discover patterns and relationships in data that may be used to make valid predictions (Edelstein, 1999). While the collection and organization of data has become a common administrative tool for most sport organizations, actually using the data for strategic decision making is not as common.

In sport organizations, data are housed in various database software programs and provide sport managers with what is hopefully an efficient way to manage large amounts of information. In the mid- to late-1990s, technological advances in data management have made it possible to uncover significant information contained in data that might otherwise be unknown. In addition, advancements in on-board memory and processor speeds now allow many computers the ability to process information that can range into terabytes (1 trillion bytes) of data. A recent application of data mining involves the use of "association analysis" to identify relationships among items or services that are purchased by customers

(Liu and Yap, 2001). Sport organizations ranging from a sporting goods retail business to a professional team could use data mining methods to predict what products and services would likely be purchased together and could build targeted marketing campaigns accordingly.

From a sport-business perspective, the information uncovered through data mining has the potential to increase revenues and reduce costs by contributing to insightful decision making at the management level. Currently, data-mining applications provide both simple and complex statistical computations and may require the use of a consultant or in-house specialist to set up and prepare data for mining as well as analyzing the results.

The applications of data mining and knowledge discovery in several aspects of sport business are numerous. However, it may be that sport-marketing departments have the most direct benefit. For example, a collegiate athletic department can collect information from season ticket holders, boosters, students, and even fans at the game regarding such things as seating preferences, ticket packages, preferred merchandise, facility offerings, and so forth. This information can be systematically entered into a database that can be "mined" through the use of a data-mining software program. The program can examine patterns in the data and identify categories of consumers relative to their demographic profiles and their product preferences. This information can then be used to target future market segments and develop or enhance products to fit their desires. In this sense, data mining allows a sport-marketing department to answer market-research questions and build both demographic and psychographic profiles of current and potential consumers. Ultimately, this may allow marketing and promotional efforts to be directed toward the most likely consumers of the sport product. Although marketing departments in collegiate and professional sports are, or should be, identifying their most likely target customers, data mining can uncover patterns in enormous amounts of data collected over several months or years. This can allow the marketing department to make strategic decisions based on patterns in the data that provide predictive information about potential customers.

Another example of how data mining could be used is to classify likely donors for collegiate athletics fund-raising programs. This could be accomplished by obtaining some relatively simple information from alumni, boosters, season ticket holders, and fans. Then, using data-mining "decision tree models," which generally split into yes/no branches for each criterion, the department could analyze results and focus specialized fund-raising efforts on those individuals and/or businesses who fall into different prospect categories (see Figure 1). Data mining can also be used in athlete-recruitment efforts and will be discussed in the next section.

Data mining is relatively new and is being used by more and more corporations to assist in decision support and customer-relationship management. It appears that amateur, professional, and commercial sport organizations can also benefit greatly from this technological advance. A recent example of new data-management and mining technology that has received increased interest across professional sport leagues was recently developed by StratBridge, Inc. This company has designed data-management and analysis software that can assist teams in determining ticket-sales patterns, that can predict attendance, and that can allow teams to develop promotions and ticket packages to maximize sales (Lombardo, 2007). According to Lombardo, StratBridge is currently doing business with over 100 franchises in the NHL, MLB, NFL, MLS, AFL, and minor league baseball.

Figure 1

Data Mining Decision Tree for Athletics Fundraising

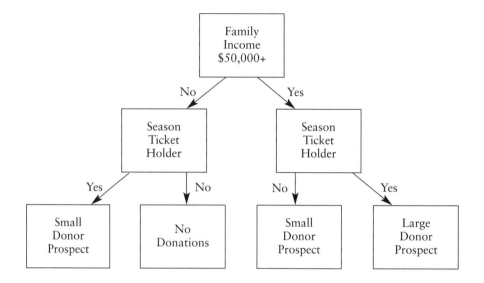

Facilities

Access Control

Controlling access to sport, recreation, and fitness facilities is often an important duty of facility managers. Legal liability, deterrence of vandalism and theft, and member safety and satisfaction are few of the reasons it is necessary to deny access to those who do not belong. A properly designed and equipped facility, along with the use of computer controls and a well-trained staff, can make access control relatively easy to deal with (Seidler, 1999).

When designing a facility, it is often advantageous to plan for one control point through which everyone entering or leaving the building must pass. This control point is usually staffed during open hours so the appropriate fee is paid, the ID card is checked, or permission is given to those eligible to enter. If a higher degree of control is desired, a door, gate, or turnstile can also be used.

In the last several years, many computer software programs have become available to help with access control. If the clientele, such as those in a club, school, or corporate setting, are issued ID cards, systems with magnetic-strip, integrated-circuit, or bar-code readers can be used to quickly check a person's status. In systems designed for high traffic flow, the computer is often connected directly to a turnstile. If, after scanning the ID, the computer determines that the person should be accepted for entry, it can send a signal to release the turnstile and allow the person to enter. However, this system of access control does not prevent an unauthorized person from using someone else's ID. For increased security, picture IDs are desirable to ensure that the person using the card is the legal owner. Other systems of access control include software programs that display a picture of the patron on a computer monitor. This photo can then be compared to the person requesting entry. More sophisticated systems can actually scan a patron's fingerprint, palm print, or retina and compare it to those in the computer memory. These systems are typically used where high security is a priority. They can also be used to track each member's attendance and provide information for marketing or retention programs. Furthermore, they can determine patrons' attendance habits and set staffing levels to provide services at the proper times of the day.

The need for heightened security at high-profile sporting events has been increasing in recent years. After the attacks on the World Trade Center in 2001, the need for a very high level of security became a necessity for many facilities. Threats of explosive, chemical, and biological attacks on venues with the potential for massive casualties have forced managers of such facilities to use the latest in high technology to ensure patrons' safety. One such system uses "facial recognition" software to identify people as potential threats. The system uses strategically placed high-resolution cameras that can scan and photograph the faces of the crowds nearing or entering a facility. The software then creates a map of each individual's face and compares it with those in a particular databank, a process which usually takes less than a second. The databank may consist of known terrorists or criminals. If a facial map matches a file in memory, the system alerts security personnel who can then follow or confront the individual. These systems are also now being installed in airport terminals.

Another aspect of access control that is improving with advances in technology is the replacement of standard door locks and keys. Systems now exist that place an electronic card reader at each door. Instead of a key, each authorized person is issued a card that can be passed through any of the card readers. With "proximity cards," a card only has to come within a few feet of the reader in order to be verified. A central computer then receives the information from the card and compares it with the information stored in memory. The computer determines if the person who was issued that card is authorized to open that particular door and either unlocks it or refuses access. There are many advantages to this type of system. The computer can be programmed to allow access only to certain areas of the facility for each individual card holder. A part-time employee may have a card that works only on a few particular doors, while the facility manager's card can be programmed to open them all, like a master key. Also, the computer may be programmed so that certain cards only work during specified hours.

In the case of regular locks, if someone loses a key, it is often necessary to re-key many or all of the locks in the building. New keys must then be issued to everyone, often at great expense. With the card system, if someone loses an access card, that card can simply be turned off on the computer, and a new card can be issued to the owner. The old card becomes useless.

Another feature of the card-access system is that each time someone uses a card to open a door, the usage is recorded on the computer. For example, computer records may show not only that a certain door was opened on Sunday morning at 12:21 but also whose card was used and if the person went in or out through the door. This information can be extremely valuable for facility security. The system can also be connected to the fire alarm and programmed to automatically unlock any or all of the doors when the alarm is triggered. Though it may be initially more expensive to install the card-reader system than standard locks, the system will usually pay for itself in increased efficiency, convenience, and long-term cost.

Security

Another innovation in facility security that is seeing increased usage is Closed Circuit Television (CCTV) systems. A well-designed system can allow a supervisor in one location to visually monitor many diverse locations, both inside and outside the facility. Often these supervisors are equipped with a two-way radio in order to stay in constant communication with attendants on duty throughout the facility. If a problem is spotted on the CCTV monitor, the supervisor can order an attendant to respond immediately. The cameras are often connected to video tape recorders so that if an incident occurs, security personnel can examine the tape at a later date. These video images can then be used to identify suspects in incidents and can also be used as evidence if a criminal act occurs.

Both black-and-white and color monitors are available for CCTV systems. Color is nice, but many users still prefer black-and-white for improved clarity, especially in low-light situations. For security in dark areas, infrared night-vision cameras are also available.

The newer systems often use digital cameras and recorders and are integrated into the facility's alarm system. These offer several advantages over the older video-tape systems. Tapeless digital recorders save images on a hard drive instead of video tape. Thus, a user can go directly to a given date and time to view an image instead of having to rewind and search for the correct spot on the tape. Exact copies can be made without any loss of quality, as occurs with tape. Also, the system can be hooked up to the Internet and can be controlled from a distance. For example, if the alarm system at a recreation center identifies a problem in the middle of the night when the building is closed, a message can be sent to the facility manager's computer at home. The computer sounds an alarm, and the facility manger can go online and direct the system to activate the camera covering the area concerned. The facility manager can then see what the problem is without going back to the facility. The manager can then reset the alarm if there is no problem, contact the police or fire department if necessary, or take other needed action. A properly planned system may allow for a smaller staff than would otherwise be required while actually increasing supervisory coverage of the facility. Such systems also reduce the number of false alarms that the police have to deal with.

Online Video Conferencing

Another advance in technology that is becoming more commonplace is the use of online video conferencing (OVC). With the advent of digital video, OVC is rapidly finding new uses for sport managers. It is now possible to hold meetings by computer in "real time" with several other people, each located at a different site almost anywhere in the world. With broadband, high-speed Internet connections, a video camera at each terminal can transmit to each of the other participants with only an extremely brief delay. Using OVC is like making a conference call by telephone but with the advantage of seeing the others involved and without the corresponding long-distance charges.

Another aspect of this technology makes use of recorded video that can be accessed by computer from almost anywhere. For example, this kind of technology may be used if an athletics administrator has a question about the interpretation of a league rule. The administrator may go to the league's Web site and select a video on the particular rule in question. The video would then be played online, hopefully answering the administrator's question without the administrator having to talk to anyone. This process could be a real time-saver for both the administrator and the staff in the league office.

Online Video Conferencing can be very useful in many situations by saving time and travel expenses. The downside to its use is the lack of intimate contact and socialization among participants. As our technological capacity continues to increase, this disadvantage is bound to become more of an issue in our society.

Planning for High Tech Applications

It is extremely important to consider all future needs and desires in planning a new facility. It is much easier and less expensive to plan a new facility with the necessary accommodations to support future trends and high-tech applications than it is to add them to an existing structure.

One of the primary considerations in planning facilities for the future is to design an easy method of connecting all of the associated computers, networks, sensors, switches, lights, and so forth, which may be needed later. Even if these high-tech systems are not installed at the time of construction, planners should realize that they are becoming more important every year. If, in a few years they need to be added, planning now for ease of installation will save many headaches and much money in the future. These systems are usually connected by wires and electrical or fiber-optic cables. Designing and constructing the pathways, such as tunnels, conduits, and access panels, costs little up front and will make the eventual installation simple and inexpensive.

One recent example of a technically advanced public-assembly building is the Portland Rose Garden. Owned and operated by Paul Allen, cofounder of Microsoft with Bill Gates and owner of the Portland Trail Blazers of the NBA, the facility is controlled by a command center that operates and monitors the building's lights and security and event cameras. All of the doors and elevators are operated by a card-key system in an effort to make the facility keyless.

Events are planned and tracked on an Event Manifest by using Microsoft Word to access and produce a computer-assisted-design (CAD) drawing for setting up an event. All management personnel have a computer on their desk, and e-mail, rather than paper, is used extensively. There are no menu boards at concessions since TV monitors flash the menus, promote upcoming events, and show the game or event activities in progress. Even the suite holders can use the Internet to order food and drinks ahead of the event. The Rose Garden is even perfecting an automated crew-calling system to schedule the over 200 employees needed for an event. The program will enable the computer to call all part-time employees and leave a message regarding their schedule and also to receive incoming calls confirming an employee's availability to work a designated event. The program will save a lot of management time and, when perfected, will make the Rose Garden truly a facility at the peak of the information and technology curve.

Conclusion

The job of managing sport and recreational programs is becoming increasingly complex. With budgets being reduced, customer preferences constantly changing, innovations in technology, and many other factors affecting the job, it is becoming more difficult to maintain, much less improve, service and productivity. Not many professions demand such knowledge in so many diverse areas. Many jobs in sport and recreation management are changing rapidly. The continued advances in the use of technology in sport may also lead to the need for new positions in sport organizations. It will soon be commonplace to see job titles such as Webmaster, Director of Technology, or Data Analyst to complement traditional sport-management positions.

Continued education for sport and recreation managers is becoming more important every year. Recognizing the need to stay up-to-date with the changes in the field is the first step in remaining competitive. Joining professional organizations, subscribing to professional journals, attending appropriate conferences, and networking and communicating with other sport managers are all effective methods of keeping up with the latest information in the field.

As we continue in the new millennium, computer technology will continue to create new opportunities for sport managers to operate their programs more efficiently while communicating with, and marketing their programs and services to, a knowledgeable and demanding world. Keeping up with and making use of the latest ideas and skills makes good sense for today's managers of sport and recreation programs. To borrow from one of the successful advertising campaigns from Nike, "There is no finish line."

References and Suggested Reading

College finds new revenue source online. (2007, September 12). *eSchool News online*. http://www.eschoolnewsonline/news/showstoryts.cfm?Articleid=7361.

Dysart, J. (1999). HR recruiters build interactivity into Web sites. *HR Magazine, 44* (3), 106–110.

Edelstein, H. (1999). *Introduction to data mining and knowledge discovery*. Potomac, NY: Two Crows Corp.

Fielitz, L. R. (2000). Using the Internet for athletic recruiting. *JOPERD, 71* (2), 13–15.

Green, P. E., Krieger, A. M., & Vavra, T. G. (1997). Evaluating new products. *Marketing Research* (Winter), 12–21.

Linio, R. (1995). Technology and marching orders. *Facility Manager, 11* (6).

Liu, S., & Yap, J. (2001). Beyond intuition. *DB2 Magazine, 6* (4), 10–13.

Lombardo, J. (2007). Tech firm helps clubs get more out of data. *Sports Business Journal, 23* (10), 17–19.

Popke, M. (2001). Setting their sites. *Athletic Business, 25* (11), 45–53.

Ross, C. M., & Young, S. J. (2001). Smooth operators. *Athletic Business, 24* (8), 79–84.

Seidler, T. (1999). Planning facilities for safety and risk management. In T. Sawyer, (Ed.), *Facilities planning for physical activity and sport: Guidelines for development* (9th ed., pp. 65–73). AAHPERD. Dubuque, IA: Kendall-Hunt.

Stotlar, D., & Walker, M. (1997). *Sports facility management*. Boston: Jones and Bartlett.

Medford, C. (2007, August 29). Will mobile TV fumble college football again? *Red Herring*. http://www.redherring.com/Home/22671.

Chapter 4

The Academic Curriculum and Experiential Learning

Dennis Johnson

The development, the revision, and the standardization of a sport management curriculum have been continuing for the past several decades. The first signs of the development of this academic field appear to have occurred when Walter O'-Malley, of the Brooklyn Dodgers, encouraged James Mason, then of the University of Miami (Florida), to develop a sport administration academic program (Gillentine & Crowe, 2005)—that is, a program that would prepare students and potential employees to administer facilities and personnel, advertise and market sport/recreational programs, and organize and deliver sporting/recreation events. Although sporting events and the management and promotion of those events have continued throughout history, this chapter will focus on the professional preparation of sport managers. Specifically, experiential learning and the internship process will be discussed.

Significant sport events such as the early Olympics and grand facility structures such as the Coliseum date back to the times of the ancient Greeks and Romans. With these came the need for people to organize and run the events and manage the facilities. In this country, people in the early 1800s were promoting prizefighting events; in the 1890s, sporting goods manufacturers began to hire professional advertising agencies. By the mid-1920s, the organizations in the sport industry were well established (Miller, Stoldt, & Comfort, 2005). In the early 1990s, the sporting industry was worth over $324 billion dollars, and today it is the fourth-largest growth industry in the United States ("By the Numbers," 2003).

The first professional preparation/sport management academic programs were a mixture of physical education courses with an administration course. The most often referenced first official sport management curriculum was the 1966 Ohio University graduate program in Sport Administration created by James Mason. Although there is some discussion regarding the first undergraduate program, it is believed that the first university to implement a sport administration degree at the undergraduate level was Biscayne College (now known as St. Thomas University) in Florida (Masterlexis, Barr, & Hums, 2005). Since that time, over 300 colleges and universities have been offering some form of a sport management/administration degree in a department or school related to physical education, recreation, and/or business (Letter, 2007).

Sport Management Curriculum Issues

The early sport administration/management programs were often comprised of physical education courses. For instance, students would take the typical physical education courses in exercise physiology, other science courses, motor learning, measurement, and methods. A course in history or sociology might also be included. Then an administration course would be added that focused on sport management and/or administration. In many instances, this degree was developed and offered as a means for colleges and universities to offset declining enrollment (Parkhouse, 2001). The issue of offering only physical education courses for completion of a sport management degree remains a major concern in today's world of sport management programming.

This point of contention was revived in a recent special report in the *Wall Street Journal* (Helyar, 2006). Helyer cited the often-heard comments that sport business programs were not, or were not often, offering training in a business school setting or in business courses. He indicated that sport management programs were not accredited and therefore were not a likely a path to career success in the sport industry. Furthermore, Helyar supported the thesis that sport management programs were simply a cash cow for colleges and universities.

In the recent past, efforts have been made to address this issue and to determine what tools a student might need to become a successful sport manager. There is a concerted effort to move away from the traditional physical education courses. Two professional organizations, the National Association of Sport and Physical Education (NASPE) and the North American Society for Sport Management (NASSM), have been dedicated to the development of a sport management curriculum and officially approved program standards. In the mid-1980s the NASPE and the NASSM combined efforts in a task force to establish formal sport management program approval standards.

In 1989, the Sport Management Task Force established ten content areas for undergraduate study. Those content areas included the following: sociocultural dimensions, management and leadership in sport, ethics in sport management, marketing in sport, communication in sport, budget and finance in sport, legal aspects of sport, economics in sport, governance in sport, and field experiences in sport management. The task force created a Sport Management Program Review Council to review higher education programs in sport management for program approval (NASPE/NASSM Joint Task Force on Sport Management Curriculum and Accreditation, 1993). This event created a move toward standardization of curriculum and credible professional preparation.

The Sport Management Curriculum Today

The program approval process is continuing, and as of the spring of 2005, the council has approved 33 undergraduate programs which meet the curriculum standards. It has also sanctioned 26 graduate degree programs and four doctoral programs. However, that number accounts for approximately only 28.6 percent of the over 220 sport management programs existing today (Gillentine & Crowe, 2005).

In the spring of 2007, the NASSM and the NASPE reported that the organizations were entering into an agreement with an accrediting organization unaffiliated with the member organizations. The accrediting agency would become responsible for evaluating the curriculum of higher education sport management programs. At press time, the Commission on Sport Management Accreditation has developed an Accreditation Manual containing standards that have been developed for preparing for a self-study. The manual can be accessed on the NASSM Web site, www.nassm.com; however, it can only be viewed after one obtains membership in the NASSM.

The Commission on Sport Management Accreditation Manual (NASPE/NASSM Joint Task Force on Sport Management Curriculum and Accreditation, 2007) addresses not only the curriculum but the entire program. Qualified faculty, resources dedicated to the program, scholarly activities, professional development, internal and external relationships are only a few of the many standards that are to be evaluated. The curriculum is evaluated on an "outcomes-based" assessment. The sport management student who graduates from an accredited program is expected to be professionally competent in the following key Common Professional Component (CPC) areas:

A. Social, psychological, and international foundations of sport
B. Management
    a. Sport management principles
    b. Sport leadership
    c. Sport operations/management/event and venue management
    d. Sport governance
C. Ethics in sport management
D. Sport marketing
E. Finance/Accounting/Economics
    a. Principles of sport finance
    b. Accounting
    c. Economics of sport
F. Legal aspects of sport
G. Integrative experiences, such as
    a. Strategic management/policy
    b. Internship
    c. Capstone experience (an experience that enables a student to demonstrate the capacity to synthesize and apply knowledge, such as a thesis, project, comprehensive examination, or course) (NASPE/NASSM Joint Task Force on Sport Management Curriculum and Accreditation, 2007, p. 14)

Higher education sport management programs that successfully complete the accreditation process will eliminate the concern that students are not prepared for a career in sport management. In the future, employers can be assured that students from these programs were not the products of a slightly altered physical education curriculum.

Experience Is the Best Teacher: Experiential Learning

There is concern in the "real world" today regarding the ability of college graduates to match theory learned in the higher education classrooms to the actual practice related to the job skills needed for successful employment. Recent

Figure 1	
KOLBS EXPERIENTIAL LEARNING CYCLE	**WINGATE UNIVERSITY 5K EXPEREINCE**
Stage 1: Concrete Experience	Organization and operation of the actual 5k race
Stage 2: Reflective Observation	Watching/working the race and writing the reflection paper
Stage 3: Abstract Conceptualization	May not occur in class; the students use their reflections as they see and engage in other "real-world" experiences to form new ideas
Stage 4: Active Experimentation	Can occur at any time; most often seen as the students organize and put on the spring triathlon two years later as juniors or seniors and/or in their internship

graduates are seen to possess adequate technical skills and professional attitudes, but they struggle when it comes time to apply those theories to real-world situations (Paranto & Champagne, 1996). In fact two-thirds of corporate employers feel that recent college graduates are viewed as incompetent (Van Horn, 1995). Therefore, gaining "real world" or integrative experience as part of a curriculum is essential.

Hesser (1990) notes that experiential learning can be a liberating experience; however, the "learning through doing" model is not a novel concept. Dewey, Lewin, and Piaget all have documented theories on the topic. Kolb (1984) combines the work of his predecessors into a four-stage experiential learning cycle. He posits that a learner proceeds through four stages. He believes that learning is a social process that begins with some form of an actual experience. Second, the learner reflects on the experience. Then he or she begins to make generalizations regarding that experience to other events/experiences. The cycle ends with active experimentation with changed practices based on the previous considerations and events.

An example of this model can be seen in the Wingate University Sport Management program. All students enrolled in the basic introduction course of their freshman year are required to plan, organize, advertise, and deliver a homecoming 5K race on campus. The students operate as a business organization, compete with divisions assigned various specific tasks and division leaders, and they are charged with making a profit that can be used for their future professional development. Students are required to evaluate their classmates who were in their divisions and to write a reflective paper regarding the actual experience. Figure 1 demonstrates how Wingate University student learning relates to the Kolb Experiential Learning Cycle.

Skills that employers deem important are a willingness to learn, the ability to read and write, proper oral communication skills, the ability to think creatively and critically, personal management, organizational effectiveness, and leadership (McCormick, 1993). Life experiences, field experiences, and/or practicums related to the above-mentioned skills form the underpinning of a student's total educational experience and preparation for the workforce. In sum, experiences such as these allow for collaboration, development of personal initiative, and integration of theory to practice.

Professional Development

The ability of an intern or employee to adapt and adjust is a continuing requirement as the electronic age advances in the 21st century. With all of the changes in the global marketplace, flexibility and the ability to adapt are essential and are more important now than ever (Herr, Cramer, & Niles, 2004). Therefore, young professionals must make a commitment to becoming lifelong learners, which according to Kolb (1984), begins with the social process. There is no better time for a student to start than the first year of college.

Students should attempt to increase learning experiences and to become involved in the student-major clubs in their colleges or universities and/or in student organizations at the state level (e.g., a state chapter of the American Alliance for Health, Physical Education, Recreation and Dance [AAHPERD]), at the regional level, and at the national level (e.g., the AAHPERD and the NASSM). Membership and/or serving in leadership capacities in these organizations not only increases learning but also helps to build networks that may be useful in the future for obtaining internships and/or employment. Students should also consider making research presentations at these organizations' conferences. Involvement, membership, and leadership in these student organizations and events will produce material that can be used to build a résumé as one begins to search for an internship or employment. The following example is a case in point.

Case Study: Michael Hemphill

Michael Hemphill, a former student in the Wingate University Sport Management Program became involved in a variety of professional activities during his sophomore year. He initially became involved in organizations and events on campus and later in the state of North Carolina in order to meet the professional development requirements for his Sport Management degree (see Figure 2). Early on, Michael was a member and leader of two of the school's student-major clubs (in Business and Sport Sciences). He then became president of the Student Majors Association of the North Carolina chapter of the AAHPERD, where he organized the state's first statewide student leadership summit. He also completed an internship with the NBA's Charlotte Bobcats during his junior year.

Michael's work to complete his professional development requirements for his undergraduate degree helped him create a large network of contacts for possible internships. He was offered a number of internship positions for the summer between his junior and senior years, deciding on a paid internship at the national headquarters for the AAHPERD. Through that internship, where he worked with ESPN to develop its *Play Your Way* program, he was subsequently offered and accepted a fully funded graduate assistantship at a Big Ten university, where he is currently completing a master's degree.

Participation in the early professional development activities has enhanced Mr. Hemphill's learning and has created many opportunities for him. Upon completion of his master's degree, it is very likely that employment opportunities and/or PhD graduate fellowships will be plentiful. In part, these opportunities will arise because of the networks that he began to create as an undergraduate student and that he continues to create because he has become a lifelong learner. A variety of other professional development opportunities that students might utilize can be seen in Figure 2.

Sport Management Internships: What Are They and Why Are They Important?

Cuneen and Sidwell (1998) note that employers are looking for employees who possess more than the techniques related to managing sport. They report that employers also look for students who

(a) possess a good work ethic), (b) are flexible in both their personal and professional schedules, (c) are people-oriented, (d) are able to perform in committee-type work or other group projects, (e) are goal-oriented self-starters who have the ability to close-out tasks absent of supervision, (f) are creative, and (g) are intellectually curious. (p. 12)

Therefore work experience gained while still in college can be an important factor in one's career—especially in the early years following graduation. Students benefit from professional development and real-life work experiences prior to graduation by developing networks, improving self-organization, becoming responsible, developing values, and gaining self-confidence (Casella & Brougham, 1995). Such experiences enable students to develop the above-mentioned skills, to hone their oral and written communication skills, and to begin to integrate theory learned in the classroom with the practical application of a business environment (Gordon 2002). Any work-related jobs, field experiences, practicums, and/or internships will contribute to the learning process.

So just what is an internship? In most cases an internship involves working within an organization for an extended period of time. In the sport management world, a narrowly defined concept of the internship is as follows:

Internships are self-contained for academic credit. They involve actual work in a sport management setting subsequent to the junior year, in which management practices are applied. Final arrangement(s) for the internship are completed by a member of the faculty. The internship is a full-time (40 hr/week) work experience for a minimum of 400 hours. It must be directed and evaluated by a qualified faculty member with appropriate supervision by an on-site professional (NASPE/NASSM Joint Task Force on Sport Management Curriculum and Accreditation, 1993).

Students who are motivated to become sport managers would be well-served to become involved in summer jobs or apprenticeships between their freshman and sophomore years and between their sophomore and junior years in an area in which they hope to become employed. The final academic credit internship should occur sometime after one has completed the third year of study—that is,

---

Figure 2

Professional Development Checksheet

Wingate University
Sport Sciences Department
Professional Growth Requirements
(Revised Fall 2007)

The Wingate University Sport Sciences Department is dedicated to enhancing the professional development of students majoring in Athletic Training, Parks and Recreation Administration, Physical Education Teacher Education, and Sport Management. The department goal is to give students opportunities to engage in practical, "real-world" experiences and to begin networking with professionals in their respective fields.

Therefore, all majors are required to meet the following minimum standards for professional development prior to engaging in an internship or student teaching. Please see opportunities for professional development listed below. All students must earn a minimum of **fifteen points** prior to their senior year. If an activity is not listed on this sheet, you must obtain department approval before it may count as one of your professional growth activities.

Wingate University Campus Professional Club Activities
FR SO JR SR YEAR
— — — — Join the Sport Sciences Student Major Club (1 pt)
— — — — Join the Sport Medicine Club (SMED) (1 pt)
— — — — Join Phi Epsilon Kappa (1 pt)
— — — — Active member in Phi Epsilon Kappa (attend meetings & serve on committees) (1–2 pts)
— — — — Active member in Sport Sciences Major's Club (attend meetings & serve on committees/projects) (1–2 pts)
— — — — Active member in SMED Club (attend meetings & serve on committees/projects) (1–2 pts)
— — — — Serve as an officer in the Sport Sciences Major's Club, SMED Club, &/or Phi Epsilon Kappa

State/National Organization Activities
— — — — Become a member of any state/national organization related to the student's major (1 pt)
— — — — Become an officer of any state/national organization related to the student's major (2 pts)
— — — — Attend a district, regional, or state conference related to the student's major (2 pts)
— — — — Attend a national conference related to the student's major (3 pts)
— — — — Present at a state conference (3 pts)
— — — — Serve as a presider at a state, regional, or national conference (1 pt)
— — — — Present at a national conference (4 pts)

Miscellaneous Activities Related to Sport Sciences (1 pt for each activity)
— — — — Attend/participate in a non-class related workshop/seminar related to Sport Sciences
— — — — Volunteer to work the WU Health Fair
— — — — Volunteer to work the PEK Triathlon
— — — — Volunteer to work the Final Exam 6K
— — — — Volunteer at a WU Athletics Event (when volunteering is not required by a class)
— — — — Support the Sport Sciences Department blood drive
— — — — Lead an ORAC trip
— — — — Work and/or function as a lead person for an intramural event
— — — — Serve as editor and/or a member of the editorial board for the Sport Sciences Newsletter
— — — — Obtain any special sport science-related certifications (e.g., Water Safety Instructor, Certified Strength Training Instructor Certification, CPR/First Aid, Aerobics Instructor, Rated Sport Official, etc.)
— — — — Any other professional activity-pending department approval

Source: Wingate University Sport Sciences Handbook (2007)

either during the summer between the junior and senior year or sometime during one of the semesters of the senior year. All of these experiences will add to a student's ability to reflect, to create abstract generalizations, and to prepare the student for active experimentation (as seen in Figure 1).

Sport Management Internship Process

The Beginning

Parks, Quarterman, and Thibault (2007) suggest that a student begin searching for an internship at least six months before the date of the appointment. This amount of time is needed to locate potential agencies and to decide if an agency/company is in line with a student's career goal. The student can also use this time to prepare résumés and cover letters and to prepare for a possible interview.

To begin the process, a student must locate agencies/companies that offer possible internships. A variety of sources can be utilized to locate internship sites. In today's electronic age, a multitude of Web sites provide listings of internships. Many of them can be found by inserting "sport internships" into a search engine (e.g., Google). Such Web sites include www.monstertrak.com, www.jobsinsports.com, www.hotjobs.com, www.internsearch.com, and www.workinsports.com. Some Web sites require a membership fee to acquire listings, while others offer free listings. In addition, Web-searching professional leagues may indicate internship openings. A sample internship advertisement is shown in Figure 3. A student should note that the advertisement lists specific responsibilities and qualifications for the opening.

Additionally, the process during this period can be utilized to screen a company or agency to assure that the internship is not wasted. An internship that is not well-researched may result with a poor experience due to unclear or misrepresented standards and/or expectations (Hite & Bellizzi, 1986). The section of the advertisement in Figure 3 delineating responsibilities is a good place to start in order to determine the job duties. Students are encouraged to steer clear of agencies/companies that may place them in positions as "go-fers" or to serve as simple clerical staff.

Further investigation or screening should make sure that the internship experience at a particular agency is a good fit for an individuals career and that the internship will "look good on paper" once the experience is completed. Gillentine and Crow (2005) suggest interns should have a "clear picture of all the duties and responsibilities that are expected" (p. 189). They recommend this can be achieved by asking a few simple questions during a possible interview or initial contact; Can I be actively involved and will I receive ongoing feedback? Will I be able to use my education in helping to solve real-world problems? Will I be in a position to integrate my discipline-based knowledge in solving problems and engaging in teamwork? Finally, how might I be able to improve my existing skills? Prior to applying for a specific position, a student should also complete research to determine what the company does, what the market is they serve, and who are the key contact people within the organization.

Selling Yourself — The Cover Letter and Resume: Once a student has located an internship that appears to meet their needs in terms of career interest, it is time to make application. The internship listing will detail how application needs to be

---

Figure 3

Sample Internship Advertisement

Internships: Administration/Human Resources
Human Resources Intern — Houston Rockets (Houston, TX)

JOB ID: 024-07 FULL-TIME INTERNSHIP: 07/08 Season

RESPONSIBILITIES include but are not limited to the following:
  Primary responsibility is to provide additional support to the Human Resources (HR) department on various projects that may include:
  Maintaining employee and project files, updating appropriate documents, and formulating correspondence
  Development of new HR processes and an HR procedures manual
  Continuation of ongoing or the initiation of human resources research and analysis
  Development of an HR Information Kiosk for Intranet access as well as other HR communication systems & tools
  Applicant tracking via database entry and support
  Performance of other related duties as assigned

QUALIFICATIONS:
  College Senior, or recent college graduate with Human Resources Management/Organizational Development or related major
  Meticulous attention to detail and organizational skills
  Excellent interpersonal/communication skills, verbal and written forms
  Able to work in a team environment and demonstrate initiative.
  Ability to handle multiple tasks and prioritize goals.
  Proficient in Microsoft Word, Excel, and Access. Familiar with Microsoft Outlook.

Individuals that exhibit our ONE TEAM PHILOSOPHY of PASSION, COURAGE, ACCOUNTABILITY, CUSTOMER FOCUS, TEAMWORK, FAIRNESS AND PARTICIPATION are welcome to apply!

Closing Date: 2007-07-30

Source: <http://nbateamjobs.teamworkonline.com/teamwork/jobs/jobs/.cfm?supcat=174>
Retrieved July 12, 2007

---

completed. Make sure that you follow directions! If the instructions state that you apply on-line-do so; if it states to apply by mail-do so. However, most often, the student will be required to submit a resume accompanied by a cover letter.

Therefore, prior to the time that a student is ready to begin making application, they must concentrate on developing a well-constructed cover letter and resume. The resume is generally used to describe one's skills and competencies. Although resume formats vary, it is generally accepted that they may include information such as: name, contact information, career goal statement/internship objective, academic background, work experience, related activities, awards, and references. Most colleges and universities employ personnel in some type of Career Planning and Placement Office that will offer aid in developing a resume either in-person or with on-line advice (see the Wingate University sample in Figure 4).

The cover letter is another item that should be constructed with much thought and effort. It is an effective way to motivate employers to examine a student's credentials. Cover letters should be specific and sent to the proper personnel. The

---

Figure 4

Career Planning and Placement Sample

Resume Writing

Quick Tips

- Your resume should be brief, concise, and visually appealing.
- Tailor your resume to fit each job description
- Include essential categories: Contact information, Education, Experience
- List experiences in reverse chronological order
- Incorporate volunteer experience, internships, educational projects, international travel, etc.
- Use an action verb to start each description.
- DO NOT misrepresent yourself! The employer will find out.
- Keep your resume to 1 page and use a standard font.
- Avoid using templates!

*Office of Internships & Career Development * Jefferson Clubhouse*
*careerhelp@wingate.edu * (704) 233-8024*

Source: <http://www.wingate.edu/Studentaffairs/careerdev/Resumes.aspx>
Retrieved July 12, 2007

---

sample cover letter in Figure 5 contains elements that an applicant's cover letter might include.

At the beginning of the letter, the applicant states his/her name, the position for which he/she is interested in applying, and how he/she found out about the position. The candidate summarizes his/her general experiences and accomplishments in the middle two paragraphs, saving specifics for the résumé. Finally, the candidate attempts to align himself/herself with the mission of the company. Whether the cover letter is for a job opening or an internship position, the format is similar.

There are a variety of templates for cover letters, such as the one seen in Figure 4. However, Norman (1992) suggests that candidates author their own templates to indicate their ability to write and to be unique as well as creative. Regardless of whether a student uses a template or one of his/her own creation, the letter should be written, proofread, and rewritten several times. Finally, before the student sends the letter to a prospective employer or internship agent, it should be proofread by an outside source, such as the personnel in the Career Planning and Placement Office at the college or university.

The Interview

The purpose of an interview is to determine whether the student is compatible with the agency/company. The interview also provides a time in which the student can evaluate the organizational culture and climate. Questions should be asked both by the interviewer and the interviewee. Again, there are a variety of resources that are of value in preparing for an interview.

Figure 5

Sample Cover Letter

Cover Letters

Example

Ima Student (USE SAME HEADING FROM YOUR RÉSUMÉ)
100 University Ave.
University Park, NC 20000
(—) ###-####
imastudent@university.edu

Ima Employer
100 Employer Ave.
Office Building, NC 20000

Dear Ima Employer,

My name is Ima Student, and I am interested in applying for the Marketing Representative position in Charlotte, NC, that is posted on the Bank of America Web site.

My background qualifies me for this position in several ways. The communication studies faculty at Wingate University have prepared me to be successful in this field. As part of my graduation requirements, I spent a semester as an Event Intern for Rock Bottom Restaurant in Charlotte. The Rock Bottom marketing team had recently implemented a new signage campaign to advertise their special event capabilities and reach a new market. As the Event Intern, my responsibilities included coordinating assigned special events, working with a marketing team to promote the events through specific mediums as identified by market research. This internship gave me insight into what a career in marketing entails.

In addition to my education and internship experiences, I have multiple other experiences cited on my résumé that exemplify my ability to work collaboratively with people and take a leadership role. I received the President's Award for Leadership at Wingate because of the charity auction I organized to benefit a local nonprofit. As the auction chair, I assumed responsibility for planning and scheduling speakers, negotiating contracts, and supervising promotional campaigns. The auction resulted in raising $50,000 for the charity.

One of the key initiatives Bank of America puts forward in its mission statement is the importance of supporting people and businesses in a specified community. I feel that my experiences coincide with this vision, and I encourage you to contact me for an interview. Thank you for your time and consideration. I look forward to hearing from you soon.

Sincerely,

Ima Student

Copyright 2006—Reprinted by permission of *Wingate University Office of Internships & Career Development, Jefferson Clubhouse, (704) 233-8024.*

*Office of Internships & Career Development * Jefferson Clubhouse*
*careerhelp@wingate.edu * (704) 233-8024*

Source: <http://www.wingate.edu/Studentaffairs/careerdev/Cover_letterexample.aspx>
Retrieved July 12, 2007

There are two notes of caution for students preparing to be interviewed for either an internship or a job. A student should make sure that their answering machine has a professional message, since the potential agency or company will more than likely telephone the student to set up an interview. The chances for securing a job or an internship will be greatly decreased if the student has an obscene or crude answering message. In addition, students should review their pages on networks such as www.MYSPACE.com and www.Facebook.com and eliminate anything that may prove damaging to their professional character (e.g., provocative pictures, pictures of alcohol or drug use, and so forth). This is an electronic age, and those types of networks are being observed, and sometimes used, by employers to determine the hiring of an employee or an intern.

Now on to the actual interview, where a student can expect some basic questions—for example:

- Tell me about yourself.
- What do you consider to be your strengths? Weaknesses?
- What do you know about our organization and why should I hire you?
- How is your previous experience applicable to this position?
- Describe a situation where you had a conflict with another individual and how you handled it.
- Please share a time you demonstrated your problem-solving skills.
- Can you give me an example of your leadership ability?
- Describe a situation where you have demonstrated a great deal of initiative.
- What are two or three things that are most important to you in a job?
- Of what accomplishments are you particularly proud?

These are but a few of the basic questions that students can expect to be asked during the interview (<www.wigate.edu/student_Affairs/ICD/new_interview.htm#3> Retrieved July 12, 2007).

For the interview, the student should dress in a manner suitable for the business world. That means a coat and tie for men and appropriate attire and dress for women. The student should also be prepared to ask questions during the interview. Once the interview has concluded, it is recommended that the student send a letter the next day thanking the person and the agency/company for the opportunity to meet.

The Sport Management Internship Experience

Throughout the internship, the student intern should make every effort to become a productive member of the organization. Each agency/company has a unique organizational culture, and the intern should become acquainted with the behaviors expected. Some of these behaviors are documented in a company manual, while others are unwritten and learned through observation and hearsay.

During the first few days of the experience, the intern would be well served to create a good impression. That is, the student should present a professional image at all times during the internship. Studies on the overall impression a person makes indicate that 55 percent of what a person sees in the first few minutes forms a person's judgment (Mitchell, 1998). With that in mind, the intern should remember that he/she is no longer a college student, when baseball caps worn backward and logo T-shirts were the norm. At all times, the intern should dress appropriately for the workplace. should maintain good grooming habits (regarding hair, nails, teeth, and so forth). and should maintain good posture.

Since the intern is essentially auditioning for a job during the internship, he/she should also demonstrate a strong work ethic. This includes completing all assignments in a timely manner and offering assistance in obtaining organizational goals. In addition, the intern should be sure to keep his/her promises to complete certain tasks.

Many organizations utilize small groups or teams to complete tasks and/or solve problems. Therefore, the intern should become a productive member of any organization's team when he/she is given the opportunity. This will allow the intern to strengthen skills such as communication, collaboration, and demonstrating respect for others—thus becoming an effective team member (Parks, Quarterman, & Thibault, 2007).

Be Aware of Pitfalls

Cuneen and Sidwell (2005) note several special circumstances with which interns may be confronted. These circumstances may involve unethical/unprofessional behaviors, sexual harassment, as well as other issues. The last thing a student intern needs is to become involved in some type of negative behavior in the workplace. Any situation that may involve such behavior should be reported immediately to the faculty supervisor.

Ethical concerns and unprofessional behaviors are two circumstances that may arise during the internship. For example, an intern may be asked to fabricate reports and/or worker hours. The intern may be asked to violate company policy by skipping steps required in completing certain tasks. Sexual harassment is another circumstance that may arise. The intern should not be subjected to a hostile environment where he/she is made to feel uncomfortable because of unjust comments regarding dress, appearance, or social life. In addition, an intern may be taken advantage of by work overload—i.e., by being asked to work beyond what would be considered normal overtime. Finally, the intern should report any illegal behaviors (e.g., stealing, drug use, and so forth) and/or unjust accusations to the faculty supervisor.

On the other hand, interns must be aware that they should not purposely become involved in any of the above-mentioned circumstances. They should also be aware that electronic messaging systems are often monitored by employees; consequently, they should refrain from sending or forwarding off-color or pornographic e-mails. Furthermore, they should refrain from making sexual innuendos around other employees. During work hours, they should also refrain from utilizing cell phones for personal calls and should resist the urge to indulge in text messaging. And in all instances, interns should respect the company culture.

Concluding the Internship Experience

Interns may develop a sense of uneasiness as they reach the final stages and/or the culmination of the internship. They should begin a reflection that puts the experience into perspective and that creates anticipation for the future endeavors of finding a job (Sweitzer & King, 1999). If possible, the intern should arrange for an exit interview and a final evaluation meeting with his/her supervisor to discuss job performance. During that interview and meeting, it would be appropriate for the intern to determine if the supervisor and the agency/company could be utilized as an employee reference. If so, the intern should attempt to procure a generic letter of recommendation for inclusion in his/her personal/professional files.

A student intern's college or university may or may not require the student intern to complete a final portfolio. However, a final portfolio is recommended because it allows the student intern to collect materials that were completed throughout college and during the internship. These materials may include supervisor evaluations, reports, work samples, and research papers. The completion of a final portfolio provides the student intern with a time to reflect on the internship and to determine the areas which were most interesting, as well as those areas which could be improved. Reflection may also include determining which courses may have best prepared him/her for the internship (Palomba & Banta, 1999). Additionally, the final portfolio might be used to demonstrate sport management-related competencies in future job interviews.

Summary

- Promoting and delivering sport events and managing sport facilities have continued for centuries. However, a professional preparation program with a domain-specific curriculum in sport management is a relatively new phenomenon.

- In an attempt to eliminate criticisms of colleges and universities using a slightly altered physical education curriculum to increase student enrollment, the NASPE/NASSM Joint Task Force on Sport Management Curriculum and Accreditation has developed a standards-based curriculum utilized for higher education program approval. Program accreditation policy is continuing at press time. The major component of the standards-based curriculum is the required completion of a 400-hour supervised internship.

- The internship has been identified as being the most critical element of a sport management program and as having the greatest impact on the likelihood of a student becoming gainfully employed (Gillentine & Crow, 2005). The sport management internship is an experience in which students attempt to connect theory learned in the classroom with actual practice while they are participating in a company's workforce.

- The Kolb's Experiential Learning Cycle (i.e., the learning-by-doing theory) helps students proceed through four stages—from actual experiences to reflection to the creation of generalizations and finally to active experimentation (Kolb, 1984). Field experiences, practicums, internships, and professional development experiences are all ways to enter the social process of learning.

- Several steps are involved in the internship process: locating an agency, developing a résumé and cover letter, participating in an interview, actively participating in the organization's job force, and ending the internship with an exit interview and the development of a portfolio.

- An intern should beware of pitfalls such as illegal or unethical behaviors, sexual harassment, and/or work overload that may occur during the internship. An intern should immediately report any occurrence of these circumstances to the college or university faculty supervisor.

References

By the numbers (2003) *Street & Smith's Sport Business Journal, 5* (36), 148–154.

Casella, D. A., & Brougham, C. E. (1995). Work works: Student jobs open front doors to careers. *Journal of Career Planning and Employment, 55* (4), 24–27, 54–55.

Commission on Sport Management Accreditation. (2007). *Accreditation Manual.* NASPE/NASSM Joint Task Force on Sport Management Curriculum and Accreditation. (Draft Copy).

Cuneen, J., & Sidwell, M. J. (1998, Winter). Evaluating and selecting sport management programs. *The Journal of College Admissions*, 6–13.

Cuneen, J., & Sidwell, M. J. (2005). *Sport management field experiences* (2nd ed.). Morgantown, WV: Fitness Information Technology.

Gordon, D. (2002). Tracking internship outcomes through comparative quantitative assessment. *Journal of Career Planning and Employment, 62* (2), 28–32.

Gillentine, A., & Crow, B. R. (2005). *Foundations of sport management.* Morgantown, WV: Fitness Information Technology.

Helyar, J. (2006, September 16). The business of sports (a special report). Failing effort: Are universities' sports-management programs a ticket to a great job? Not likely. *Wall Street Journal* (Eastern Edition), p. R5.

Herr, E. L., Cramer, S. H., & Niles, S. G. (2004). *Career guidance and counseling through the lifespan: Systematic approaches* (6th ed.). Boston: Pearson/Allyn & Bacon.

Hesser, G. (1990). *Experiential education as a liberating art.* Raleigh, NC: National Society for Experiential Education.

Hite J., & Bellizzi, J. (1986). Student expectations regarding collegiate internship programs in marketing. *Journal of Marketing Education, 8* (3), 41–49.

Johnson, D., Appenzeller, T., DeWaele, C., Dondanville, A., Gearhart, T., Merkle, L., & Mclaughlin, D. (2007). *Wingate University Sport Sciences Department handbook.* Charlotte, NC: Catawba Press.

Kolb, D. A. (1984). *Experiential education: Experiences as the source of learning and development.* Englewood Cliffs, NJ: Prentice-Hall.

Letter, G. (2007). From the approval process to accreditation: The road that several sport management programs traveled. *The Chronicle of Kinesiology and Physical Education in Higher Education, 18* (3), 14–16.

Masterlexis, L. P., Barr, C.A., & Hums, M.A. (2005). *Principles and practice of sport management* (2nd ed.). Sudbury, MA: Jones and Bartlett.

McCormick, D. W. (1993). Critical thinking, experiential learning and internships. *Journal of Sport Management, 17,* 260–262.

Miller, L. K., Stoldt, C. C., & Comfort, G. P. (2005). Careers in sport management. In S. J. Hoffman (Ed.), *Introduction to kinesiology: Studying physical activity.* Champaign, IL: Human Kinetics.

Mitchell, M. (1998). *The first five minutes: How to make a great first impression.* New York: John Wiley.

NASPE/NASSM Joint Task Force on Sport Management Curriculum and Accreditation. (1993). Standards for curriculum and voluntary accreditation of sport management education programs. *Journal of Sport Management, 7* (2), 159–170.

NASPE/NASSM Joint Task Force on Sport Management Curriculum and Accreditation. (2007). *Commission on sport management accreditation manual.* Reston, VA: Author.

Norman, D. (1992). *How to secure an internship in athletic training, fitness, leadership or sport management: Practicing professionals tell it like it is.* Reston, VA: American Alliance for Health, Physical Education, Recreation and Dance.

Palomba, C. A., & Banta, T. W. (1999). *Assessment essentials: Planning, implementing, and improving assessment in higher education.* San Francisco: Jossey-Bass.

Paranto, S. R., & Champagne, L. N. (1996, April). Perceptions of the business community regarding program effectiveness at a selected university. Paper presented at the annual meeting of the American Educational Research Association, New York, NY. (ERIC, ED 395 551), 30–33.

Parkhouse, B. L. (2001). *The management of sport; Its foundation and application* (3rd ed.). New York: McGraw-Hill Higher Education.

Parks, J. B., Quarterman, J., & Thibault, L. (2007). *Contemporary Sport Management* (3rd ed). Champaign, IL: Human Kinetics.

Sweitzer, H. F., & King, M. A. (1999). *The successful internship: Transformation and empowerment.* Pacific Grove, CA: Brooks/Cole.

Van Horn, C. E. (1995). *Enhancing the connection between higher education and the workplace: A survey of employers.* Denver: State Higher Education Executive Officers and the Education Commission of the States.

Chapter 5

Web-Based Sport Administration Education

Robert Taylor

The technological advances that paved the way for the information explosion of the past two decades have made higher education easily accessible and readily available to today's consumers. A negative stigma was attached to early online education programs because of an actual, or perceived, lack of quality. Most were deemed little more than expensive correspondence courses, yet many were financially successful because of an unwillingness on the part of other academic institutions to venture into an unproven market. The negative stigma has slowly begun to fade as more and more colleges and universities have begun to develop online educational programs. The increase in demand for such programs has led to competition among institutions, which, in turn, has resulted in an increase in the number of quality programs entering the market.

Why Study Online?

Web-based instruction has provided many advantages to the student. Students have access to faculty members virtually 24 hours a day, 7 days a week, via e-mail. Most faculty have a policy of returning a student's e-mail within 24 hours of receipt. In the cyber education market, customer satisfaction is of paramount importance. Faculty members know that if students are not satisfied with their matriculation experience, they can easily enroll in the program of another institution. There is also greater diversity among the online faculty of most Web-based programs because there are no geographical limitations on where faculty may reside. This allows programs to recruit faculty from all over the globe to enrich the learning experience for students by providing insight and information from various degrees of education and background.

The ability of instructors to update course content in real time is a huge advantage of Web-based instruction over traditional classroom instruction. Course content can be updated to reflect current happenings in the sport industry so that students may apply the most recent changes in industry theory to current projects and tasks in the practical setting. The availability of electronic textbooks also enables instructors to update course materials to reflect immediate changes in industry standards and practices. Electronic textbooks are extraordinarily advantageous since most traditional textbooks are obsolete by the time they are printed.

The potential for a global classroom is a factor that can rarely, if ever, be accomplished in the traditional classroom setting. The diverse backgrounds of global classroom members provide invaluable opportunities for information sharing that simply cannot be replicated in the overwhelming majority of traditional classrooms. This environment not only provides incredible learning experiences; it also allows students to create or expand their professional networks regionally, nationally, and internationally.

Participating in an online program can also reduce the costs associated with obtaining an education. There are usually no travel costs, since most students can log on in the comfort of their own homes. In addition, students can enroll in many online programs at lower costs than those charged by traditional programs because of the lower overhead associated with online delivery. This is also true for nonresident students, who are usually forced to pay out-of-state tuition if they do not reside in the state of the institution they attend. Most online institutions are willing to waive resident requirements because they recognize that in order to take full advantage of Web-based potential, they must compete globally, not just locally.

Finally, the flexibility associated with most online sport administration programs is one of the most important factors for students to consider when contemplating Web-based instruction — especially students who have commitments such as work and family and may not be able to arrange their schedules to attend traditional classes. For asynchronous programs, students are never required to coordinate their log-on activities with instructors or other classmates. Such flexibility allows students to complete assignments during the times most convenient for them, thereby enabling them to work around other commitments.

Requirements for Student Success

For most students, the online learning environment is much more demanding than the traditional classroom setting. Students must first possess adequate computer hardware with high-speed Internet access and must be proficient in the use of such equipment and its software applications.

Online success is also heavily dependent on writing skills. Students must be able to convey their thoughts through written language since many courses place heavy emphasis on journal assignments, written papers and projects, and threaded discussions. Unlike the traditional classroom, the cyber classroom contains no "wallflowers." Students who might not participate in verbal discussions in the traditional classroom cannot hide in their cyber classrooms and therefore must have highly proficient writing skills so that they can communicate their thoughts and ideas to classmates and instructors.

Selecting the sport administration program that best fits the needs of the student is probably the most important determinant of student success in online education. Just as programs offered in the traditional setting vary, not all online program offerings are the same. Therefore, it is very important that students conduct research to determine which program is best designed for them to achieve success.

What to Look for in an Online
Sport Administration Program

Several online sport administration programs have come and gone in the past few years, but those that have been able to reduce student attrition and increase student satisfaction have several characteristics in common.

The most frequently asked question of online program directors by potential students is: "Is the program 100 percent online?" Many online programs have residency requirements that require students to visit the physical campus from one to four times during their matriculation in the programs. Such requirements can become quite expensive and inconvenient, especially when a student could potentially travel across the country, or internationally for that matter. "One hundred percent online" means that the student never has to set foot on the campus of the college or university, unless he/she desires to attend the graduation ceremony.

Reduced completion times are also associated with successful online programs. Once again, students want to complete their matriculation in a timely manner since they have outside commitments that must be met. Condensed courses and summer courses are very popular with online sport administration students because many are working as coaches and administrators during the traditional academic year.

The personalization of course content is another factor that students should consider when choosing a Web-based sport administration program. Online faculty members are able to incorporate practical and written assignments that allow students to apply current industry theory in their current work settings. Students seem to take ownership of a classroom task or project if it is specifically relevant to their individual professional situations.

Highly qualified faculty members are also a determinant of success for online sport administration programs that have been able to endure. Program faculty should not only be properly educated and experienced in the field of sport administration; it should also be a collection of individuals with diverse backgrounds who can offer various ideas and perspectives to students. Faculty members should also be easily accessible to students and provide adequate feedback in a timely manner. Online students want immediate feedback, and online instructors must understand this need and be able to meet the unique demands of their students.

The vast majority of Web-based sport administration programs are graduate programs—primarily because of the reduced amount of completion time for such programs when compared with undergraduate programs and because of the logistics associated with operating online undergraduate programs for relatively large numbers of students. Although far fewer undergraduate online sport administration programs are currently available, a recent increase in demand is ensuring that more and more undergraduate programs will be appearing in the market very soon.

Finally, successful online programs have committed immense resources for providing customer and technical support for students. Many institutions have created separate online divisions to deal specifically with the online student population. Students can e-mail or telephone service representatives who are specially trained to help them navigate through the cyber-educational experience with as little discomfort as possible. Twenty-four-hour technical support is also a characteristic associated with successful online programs. Many students have other commitments throughout the traditional workday during which most traditional college and university offices are open. These students require that someone be available to assist them with technical difficulties when they are attempting to complete course work late at night or on weekends.

As is the case with all other consumer products and services, the market dictates which online programs will survive. The brief history of the Web-based education market indicates that the successful sport administration online programs to date have possessed many or all of the above-mentioned characteristics.

The California University of Pennsylvania Model

The California University of Pennsylvania Master of Science in Sport Management Studies online program is in its third year of operation. In the past year, the program has seen an unprecedented 42 percent increase in student enrollment.

In order to meet the needs of working sport industry professionals who are seeking to increase their knowledge of sport management while obtaining a high level of professional growth, the Master of Science in Sport Management Studies online program was created and implemented within the California University of Pennsylvania Department of Health Science and Sport Studies in collaboration with the CalU Global Online Network.

The program emphasizes preparing students for positions of management and leadership within the sport industry. Indeed, the program recognizes the need for developing the student's capacity to solve many problems arising from ever-changing economic difficulties, political and regulatory conditions, and marketing strategies. Students study and discuss real-life scenarios to ensure their competency in today's competitive sport industry.

Students enrolled in the online program are primarily full-time working adults who are highly motivated and self-disciplined in seeking completion of a graduate degree. Distance learning via the Web is an exciting opportunity that offers the student the flexibility to take classes and earn a graduate degree without leaving his or her home or job.

Students have the option of completing the Sport Management Track, the Facility and Event Management Track, or the Intercollegiate Athletic Administration Track. Program length consists of 13 consecutive months, with new cohorts of students starting their programs in January and July. Approximately 30 students per cohort learn and communicate online and regularly function as a group of interactive peers. This virtual community creates a lively, dynamic educational experience that enriches the collaborative skills essential for success in the sport industry.

The curricular content is well positioned to be presented via the Internet. Sport Management theory and principles are presented with streaming video, narrated PowerPoint presentations, and online forums. Threaded discussion groups, chat rooms, and e-mail allow the cohorts to communicate and interact, adding unique insight into the discussion.

The Master of Science in Sport Management Studies online program curriculum has been designed to align with NASPE/NASSM standards, with the expectation of applying for program approval in the near future.

Within the past year, California University of Pennsylvania has also implemented a Sport Management undergraduate online degree program. This undergraduate degree offering is 100 percent online and allows students to transfer general education credits into the program or to take the full program (120 credits, including general education courses) in a fully Web-based course format.

There is no need for the undergraduate to ever set foot on California's campus since the program is designed for busy people, including working health and fitness professionals, military personnel, and so forth. The program will prepare students to work in fitness and wellness settings, including gyms, fitness clubs, and spas, as well as in corporate fitness, strength coaching, high school and collegiate athletics, and many other fitness/health/wellness areas.

Part 2

Program Management

Sport managers and administrators will have a greater degree of success in the emerging sport industry if they understand how to manage costs, generate revenue and account for money spent.

Nancy L. Lough

Chapter 6

Sports Medicine Services

Jerald Hawkins

Introduction

Of the various services provided by a sports organization to its clientele, none is more important than medical care. Whether such care takes the form of first aid, as with an injured or ill spectator, or complete injury care and rehabilitation, as with the competitive athlete, it is the responsibility of every organization to provide quality medical care for spectators and participants. The purpose of this chapter is to identify the methods which may be utilized in providing such medical care. Because of the diversity of medical care needs of nonparticipants (spectators, employees, and so forth) and active participants, it is necessary to consider two distinct aspects of medical care services: 1) first aid and emergency care and 2) sports injury management.

First Aid and Emergency Care

The primary component of an organization's medical care system is first aid care in the event of sudden illness or injury to one of its clients or employees. *First aid* is generally defined as that process by which nonmedical personnel perform simple care procedures designed to alleviate the immediate threat of further injury. In the case of life-threatening injury or illness, this definition may be extended to include life-saving procedures such as rescue breathing or cardiopulmonary resuscitation.

To adequately provide such services, careful planning and the development and utilization of available resources must be accomplished in the specific areas of training existing personnel to render first aid services, of providing first aid supplies which are easily accessible, and of establishing a system of emergency medical care.

Every employee in the sport-related organization should be certified in both first aid and cardiopulmonary resuscitation (CPR). This two-fold requirement is especially important for those whose daily responsibilities include direct contact with spectators and/or participants. First aid and/or CPR instruction is available in most communities through the American Red Cross, the American Heart Association, and other voluntary health agencies. It is often possible to schedule group instruction for an entire staff, thus making it possible for certification to be obtained with minimal inconvenience to the employees. With the skills acquired through first aid and CPR instruction, all staff members will be prepared to render first aid and emergency care whenever and wherever the need arises.

Most first aid and emergency medical care procedures require some form of specialized supplies. The nature of such supplies may range from cotton-tipped applicators for cleaning superficial wounds to inflatable air or vacuum-splints for use in immobilizing suspected fractures and dislocations. In order for first aid supplies to be used effectively, they must be stored in a location which allows easy access. The most efficient method of providing first aid supplies in a sport-related facility is to assemble several "first aid kits" and place them in a variety of locations throughout the facility. The number and specific locations of such kits will depend upon the size of the facility and the types of programs it supports. A list of the recommended contents of a first aid kit for recreational sports facilities is found below.

Contents of a First Aid Kit for a Recreational Sports Facility

Adhesive compresses (Band-Aids) — Assorted sizes
Alcohol (70%) — one bottle per kit
Antiseptic solution (Merthiolate, Betadine, and so forth) — one bottle per kit
Athletic-type adhesive tape-assorted widths
Burn ointment — one or more tubes per kit
Cotton-tipped applicators
Elastic wraps (Ace bandages) — Assorted widths
Emergency contact card — one per kit
Eye pads (sterile) — Several per kit
Gauze pads (sterile) — Assorted sizes
Gauze rolls — Assorted widths
Hydrogen peroxide-one bottle per kit
Insect sting kit — one per kit
Manual detailing current first aid procedures
Petroleum jelly — one tube per kit
Scissors (bandage or tape style) — one pair per kit
Soap (liquid or aerosol)

Other supplies which should be stored in a central location easily accessible to all employees include the following:

Blankets (preferably wool) — two or more
Splints (inflatable or vacuum air style, or padded wood) — Assorted lengths
Triangular bandages — one dozen or more

The third basic aspect of an effective first aid and emergency care program is developing and implementing a formal, policy-based approach to first aid and emergency medical care. When a participant or spectator is injured or becomes ill, it is important that he or she receive care that is promptly and correctly administered. To accomplish this, it is necessary that each employee not only be trained in first aid procedures but also be assigned a specific role to be performed in the event of an injury or illness in his or her work area. For example, ushers or pages in a spectator sport facility should be trained in basic first aid prior to being placed on the job. With this training complete, each usher or page should be assigned a specific duty within the emergency care program. These role assignments should include the following: someone (or, better, two people) to administer primary first aid care; someone to maintain order and decorum among the other spectators or participants who are in the immediate area; and someone to summon assistance either from on-site medical personnel or from a nearby medical facility or ambulance service. While this approach may appear somewhat simplistic and even unnecessary, the delivery of first aid to an injured spectator is too often hampered by the confusion of the moment.

To adequately prepare for effective emergency medical care, the manager of a sport-related facility must establish a positive working relationship with those agencies that will be expected to provide support services in the event of a medical emergency. In most communities, these will include the local law enforcement agency, emergency medical services, area hospital(s), and one or more physicians who may be contacted in time of need. The manager should meet with representatives of each of these support agencies to exchange information with respect to the specific role that each will play in the event of a medical emergency. At this time, the agency representative should be given the opportunity to identify the "normal procedures" of the agency, while the facility manager should provide information regarding the program's first aid and emergency care protocol. On the basis of this exchange of information, an agreement should be established that will govern the relationship between the facility and the support agency with respect to the specific role of each during a medical emergency. Although the specific nature of this agreement will vary according to the needs and capabilities of both parties, one basic policy should be established. During any spectator event (game, concert, and so forth), emergency medical personnel should be on-site to facilitate the immediate handling of any medical emergency. It is also recommended that a physician be present at all events, although this may not always be possible.

A simple, yet very important, step in providing effective emergency care involves placing "emergency contact cards" in all first aid kits and beside all business telephones. An "emergency contact card" is simply a small index card which contains telephone numbers needed in a time of medical emergency.

In communities where a single emergency code number has been established (e.g., 911), the "emergency contact card" may be simplified to contain only the emergency number and the names and numbers of physicians who may be contacted.

EMERGENCY CONTACT CARD

Ambulance: Triad Ambulance Service 555-1234
                 Metro EMS Service 555-5678

Physician: Dr. John Smith   (O) 555-1357
                               (H) 555-2468

                  or

                 Dr. Mary Brown (O) 555-1470
                               (H) 555-0369

Hospital: County General 555-1111

It is virtually impossible to eliminate the risk of sudden illness or injury to spectators and participants. However, it is possible to maximize the quality of emergency care provided through careful planning and the development of a systematic emergency care plan based on the following recommendations:

1. Require all employees, especially those who work directly with program clientele, to be trained and certified in first aid and cardiopulmonary resuscitation (CPR).
2. Assemble and maintain a complete inventory of first aid and emergency medical supplies, and make these supplies easily accessible to all employees.
3. Establish an "in-house" system for providing first aid and emergency medical care to program clientele and employees, and thoroughly orient all employees with respect to this system and the specific role that each employee is expected to play.
4. Schedule and conduct emergency care drills during which all employees are provided the opportunity to practice specific emergency care procedures.
5. Develop, in cooperation with local medical support agencies and personnel, a systematic plan for emergency care that meets the specific needs of the facility and its programs.

In addition to a standard system of first aid and emergency medical care, an organization must develop a plan for providing emergency medical care during events at which large crowds will be present. Because of the unique and complex nature of such emergency medical preparedness, this concept will be discussed in detail in a separate chapter.

Sport Injury Management

While participation in sports has been widely recognized as a privilege, it also involves some basic rights on the part of the participant. These fundamental rights may include quality health and medical care. Therefore, organizations such as schools, colleges, and professional and amateur sports teams are expected to provide medical and health care services for their athletes.

Until recently, the responsibility of a school or college to provide adequate medical and health care for its athletes was essentially viewed as a moral or ethical issue. However, the issue of medical and health care for the school or college athlete is now finding its way into the American court room, as evidenced by the case *Gillespie v. Southern Utah State College*, 669 P.2d 861 (Utah, 1983). In this case, a college basketball player brought suit against a college, its basketball coach, and its athletic trainer as the result of an injury he had received while playing college basketball and subsequent complications resulting in the loss of a foot. The athlete claimed that the severe injury complications were a direct result of inadequate sports medicine care, but the jury found that the athlete "was 100% negligent and such negligence was the proximate cause of his injuries." This case is merely one example of the increasing frequency of sports medicine litigation, and though no definitive legal precedent has yet been established, it is apparent that schools and colleges do have some legal obligation to their athletes with respect to the availability of quality medical and health care.

Regardless of an organization's legal responsibility to its athletes, there also exists a moral and ethical obligation to provide for the health and well-being of those who represent a school, college, or organization on the athletic field. This obligation involves not only the availability of qualified, on-site medical and health care personnel but also the provision of adequate health care facilities, quality supervision and instruction, and playing conditions that promote safe participation. In short, all sports participants should be afforded the opportunity to take part in the activities of their choice with the knowledge that everything possible has been done to assure that their participation will be safe as well as enjoyable and that in the event of an injury, they will receive immediate and effective care.

Recognition of the responsibility to provide adequate medical and health care is only the first step toward making such services available. Too often, this aspect of the total program is viewed as a "frill," or luxury. Therefore, there may be little or no planning with respect to such critical issues as the identification and utilization of qualified personnel, formal program organization, and the design and utilization of adequate medical and health care facilities.

Personnel — "The Team Approach"

It has often been said that "everybody's business is nobody's business." Unfortunately, this statement accurately describes the manner in which many organizations approach the issue of providing qualified medical and health care personnel within the total sport program. The high school or college coach may be required not only to perform his coaching duties but also to care for the injuries sustained by his or her (and frequently other) athletes. Quite often, the responsibility for injury care is shared by the entire coaching staff, and the issue suddenly becomes "everybody's business." In situations where personnel organization is allowed to develop according to the dictates of day-to-day needs, there is likely to be a serious lack of quality medical and health care for the participants. Even in those programs in which there is a "team physician" or "school physician" available, the absence of qualified on-site personnel (e.g., a certified athletic trainer) and the lack of a formal organizational plan for the delivery of medical and health care services will usually result in less-than-optimal medical and health care.

Medical and health care for sport participants may be most effectively rendered when there is a "team" of qualified professionals functioning cooperatively with the health and well-being of the participants as their common goal. While the specific composition of the "sports medicine team" may vary according to the unique needs of the organization and its programs, three persons are considered essential if effective sports medicine services are to be delivered: an administrative coordinator (athletic director, sports medicine coordinator, and so forth), a qualified on-site athletic trainer, and a program physician.

The administrative coordinator of a sports injury management program is basically responsible for such administrative functions as program planning and supervision, budget development and implementation, and personnel management. This role may be assumed by any one of a variety of people, depending upon the size and nature of the organization. In the small school or college setting, the administrative duties may be effectively handled by either the chief athletic administrator (usually the athletic director) or the head athletic trainer. In the larger, more diverse program, it may be desirable to place administrative responsibilities in the hands of a "sports medicine coordinator," thus relieving the chief athletic administrator and head athletic trainer of these duties. It is recommended that such a coordinator function within the purview of the chief athletic administrator and possess expertise in the areas of program administration and athletic training.

Every sports injury management program should have at least one qualified athletic trainer. This person is generally assigned the title of "Head Athletic Trainer" and assumes the primary responsibility for on-site program direction, including primary injury care and rehabilitation, day-to-day administrative details, and the training and supervision of student assistants. Although not essential, it is strongly recommended (and in most states required) that the head athletic trainer be certified by the National Athletic Trainers Association Board of Certification (NATA-BOC), since such certification is considered the standard of professional recognition in the field of athletic training. Criteria for certification may be obtained by contacting the National Athletic Trainers Association, Dallas, Texas.

The third member of the "sports medicine team" is the program physician. The "team doctor," as this person is often called, functions cooperatively with the administrative coordinator and head athletic trainer to provide such primary medical services as performing preseason medical examinations, providing consultation and recommendations relative to extended injury care and rehabilitation, providing primary medical treatment for injured athletes, and attending home athletic contests for the purpose of offering on-site injury care and supervision. Needless to say, the program physician must possess an interest in sports medicine and the desire to work, often without compensation, with injured athletes. It would obviously be desirable for the program physician to be a specialist in an area related to sports (e.g., orthopedics). However, the most essential qualifications for a program physician are a sincere interest and a desire to be a member of the "sports medicine team."

The program physician is the only member of the "sports medicine team" who is often not an employee of the school or organization. Therefore, locating and recruiting an appropriate program physician often proves difficult. The most common method of locating a potential program physician is to identify those physicians who already have some form of relationship with the organization. The relationship may be geographic (i.e., a physician who lives and practices in the local community), professional (i.e., a physician who is a school or organization board member), or personal (i.e., a physician with friend or family ties to the school or organization).

Once appropriate candidates have been identified, securing the services of a physician for the sports medicine program will often depend upon the compensatory nature of the position and the duties which the physician will be expected to perform. The issue of compensation for the services of a program physician may be resolved in one of three basic ways. If the organization's budget will allow, the physician may receive monetary compensation for services rendered, usually in the form of a retainer in an amount agreed upon by all parties and specified in a contract. If financial remuneration is not possible, many states will allow institutions to provide a physician with a "gift-in-kind" statement, which may be used by the physician as verification of charitable contribution in the form of donated services to the institution. If neither of these forms of compensation are appropriate, the program physician will simply serve as a "volunteer" member of the sports medicine team.

The duties or expectations of a program physician will vary, depending upon the unique needs of each program. However, the program physician is generally expected to provide the following services:

1. Compile and maintain a medical history of each program participant.
2. Conduct preparticipation physician examinations.
3. Attend all games or contests and as many practices as feasible.
4. Supervise and provide instruction to sports medicine personnel.
5. Be available to see injured program participants during regular office hours and provide treatment or referral as deemed appropriate.
6. Be "on call" for the emergency care of injured program participants at times other than office hours.
7. Make decisions relative to the return to action of injured program participants.
8. Work closely with the other members of the "sports medicine team" in establishing policy and coordinating program activities.

When a program physician has been secured, it is imperative that the physician's relationship with the program be spelled out in an agreement which specifically describes the physician's duties and the form of compensation (if any) which the physician will receive. A sample agreement appears as Appendix 1 at the end of this chapter.

As programs and needs expand, it may prove desirable to add additional members to the basic "sports medicine team." With the recommendation of the program physician, medical specialists (e.g., orthopedists, dentists, ophthalmologists, and so forth) may be included in the "sports medicine team," thus enhancing the specific services which may be provided.

Organization

All successful sports medicine programs share one common characteristic: they are well organized. Unfortunately, effective organization is not something that "just happens" but is the result of diligent planning and a commitment to excellence.

Several factors influence organizational success. Three factors which are critical, yet often overlooked, are as follows: the development and utilization of a formal organizational model; the establishment of policies within which the program will function; and the implementation of a system of record keeping that will facilitate and document communication among the members of the "sports medicine team," players, coaches, and others with whom formal communication is carried on.

A formal organizational model, or chart, delineates the relative relationship among the various persons within the sports medicine program. The specific pattern or organization will depend upon the precise needs of the organization itself. A "Sample Organizational Model" for a small college is presented as Appendix 2 at the end of this chapter.

Without a formal organizational plan, the sports medicine program will not function as effectively as desired. At best, it will become a group of individuals, each performing the duties that he or she deems appropriate, inevitably resulting in a duplication of some services and a complete absence of others.

As with any organization, the sports medicine program should function according to preestablished policies. Such policies should be developed as the result of cooperative planning by the "sports medicine team" and should reflect the specific functional needs of the program. Policies should be written and implemented with respect to standard injury care and physician referral procedures, the transportation of injured athletes to and from hospitals and other medical facilities, the operation of the training room, the processing of insurance claims and other records, and the specific responsibilities of staff members. These policies should be compiled and placed in a policy manual or handbook and should be made available to every person involved in the program.

Record Keeping

One of the most vital concepts in program organization is that of record keeping and its influence on organizational communication. Communication is often classified as "formal," the exchange of important information or ideas that requires written documentation, and "informal," the exchange of less important information that requires no written documentation. Most of the communication within the sports medicine program is sufficiently important to be considered "formal" in nature, yet too often it is carried out verbally. For example, an athlete or student athletic trainer carries verbal messages from the head athletic trainer to a physician or coach, often resulting in misunderstanding. If left unresolved, such misunderstanding may jeopardize the relationship that is essential among administrators, athletic trainers, physicians, players, and coaches. Effective record keeping will help alleviate many of the problems that may result from poor organizational communication.

Record forms are highly personalized communication vehicles. Therefore, it is necessary to design forms which reflect the unique needs of each program. Some typical forms are described below, but it should be noted that these are presented merely for the purpose of illustration. It should be further noted that in today's athletic training programs, record keeping may be largely computerized. However, this does not eliminate the need for written records as data lost during computer "crashes" are often irretrievable.

An essential instrument is the injury report form (see Appendix 3 at the end of this chapter). The purpose of the injury report form is to maximize the exchange of information among all of the parties involved in the injury management process. While a form of this type may be printed as a single sheet of paper, it is highly recommended that it be a multicopy (carbon or carbonless) instrument so that each person in the injury management process may retain a copy of the form for future reference. For example, if the form is prepared in four parts, it may be used in the following manner. After completing and signing the top portion of the form, the athlete would be given the top three copies to take with him or her to the attending physician. The bottom copy would be retained in the athletic training room as verification that the form had been sent with the athlete to the physician. The physician would then be asked to complete the lower portion of the form on the basis of his or her evaluation of the injury and to retain the bottom copy for his records. The athlete would then return the two remaining copies of the form to the athletic training room, where one would be filed and the other included with any insurance claim which might be submitted.

Some of the features of this specific form that enhance its effectiveness are the multiple-copy nature of the form, which provides written verification for all principal parties; the athlete's signature, verifying the circumstances under which the injury occurred and the immediate care provided; and the physician's written evaluation and recommendation relative to the severity of the injury, the appropriate rehabilitation, and the postinjury return to activity. This information may then be shared with the appropriate coach.

Since communication between the sports medicine program and the members of the coaching staff is critical to the success of both programs, the final form presented here is one designed specifically to facilitate athletic trainer-coach communication. The injury care recommendation form may be used to provide a written record for the coach, the sports medicine staff, and the athlete's injury file concerning any injury which will require the athlete to discontinue or alter his or her normal practice or usual routine. Constructed as a three-part form approximately the size of a small index card, this form contains information relative to the precise nature of the injury in question, the recommended procedures for caring for that injury, and the athlete's status relative to return to activity. (See Appendix 4 at the end of this chapter.) When the form has been completed and signed by the head athletic trainer, the bottom copy is given directly to the appropriate coach, providing him or her with a concise, written statement that answers three important questions: What is the injury? How will it be cared for? When and under what conditions can the athlete return to play? The second copy of the form may be posted in the athletic training room as a written guide for staff members in caring for the injury. The original copy of the form may be placed in the athlete's injury file for future reference. A form of this nature not only enhances communication between members of the sports medicine staff and members of the coaching staff but also provides written documentation of staff and/or physician recommendation should future questions arise.

Although effective record keeping requires a significant amount of time and effort, the benefits of improved program communication are well worth the time and effort invested. However, to reap these benefits, the "sports medicine team" must analyze the needs of the program and design and utilize record-keeping systems which will best meet those needs.

Facilities

To a great extent, the quality of medical and health care that an organization may provide its athletes is determined by the quality of facilities utilized for this purpose. As with previous factors which have been discussed, the specific size and type of injury care facilities will depend upon the nature and scope of the programs they are expected to serve. It is not the purpose of this chapter to present a detailed discussion of facility and equipment specifications, since such information is readily available in several sports medicine texts. However, it should be emphasized that all facility planning should include the direct input of all members of the "sports medicine team."

Summary/Conclusion

The manager of a sport-related organization, whether it be a spectator entertainment facility, a community recreation center, or a high school or college athletic department, assumes the direct responsibility for the health and well-being of his clientele. Therefore, every effort should be made to develop and maintain a program of medical services that will ensure the health and well-being of those he serves.

Appendix 1

Physician's Agreement

STATE OF _____.

CITY/COUNTY OF _____.

THIS AGREEMENT made and entered into the ____ day of ____, 2002, by and between ____, a college having its principal place of business in _____ (hereinafter referred to as "College"), and Dr. _____, a citizen and resident of _____ (hereinafter referred to as "Physician").

WITNESSETH:

WHEREAS, College is desirous of obtaining the services of Physician in connection with its _____ program, and

WHEREAS, Physician is skilled in the practice of orthopedic medicine (or other specialty) and is willing to assist College with its orthopedic (or other medical) problems in its _____ program,

NOW, THEREFORE, in consideration of the covenants and promises contained herein, the parties hereto agree as follows:

1. College hereby retains and Physician agrees to be retained by College as College's orthopedic (or general medical) consultant in College's _____ program for the school year 20__-__.

2. Physician will act as a consultant with the College's coaches, athletic trainers, athletes, and other personnel with regard to orthopedic (or other) medical problems incurred by athletes in the College's _____ program. Physician's consulting services shall include the attendance of all of College's games, a schedule of which is attached hereto and incorporated herein by reference, and shall also attend all scrimmages as scheduled from time to time by College, notice of which shall be given to Physician not less than 48 hours prior to such scrimmage. Physician shall also attend all/none of College's other practice sessions, excluding scrimmages, during the term of this agreement.

3. Physician shall make recommendations to the coaching staff, athletic trainers, and other personnel as to the handling of all orthopedic (or other medical) matters with regard to the athletes in College's _____ program. Such recommendations shall include prescribing treatment for injuries and other orthopedic (or medical) problems, and recommendations for surgical and other hospital procedures when necessary. All physician charges for such surgery and other hospital procedures are not covered under the terms of this agreement.

4. As compensation for all consulting services rendered hereunder, College agrees to pay to Physician the sum of $_____, to be paid upon the execution of this agreement.

5. It is understood and agreed that Physician is an independent contractor with regard to all consulting services to be rendered hereunder, and is not acting as College's agent, employee, or servant. [Optional: It is also understood that Physician is not an insurer of results in any medical treatment rendered under the terms of this agreement.]

6. This agreement is to be construed under and governed by the laws of the State of ___,

IN WITNESS WHEREOF, the parties hereto have executed this agreement in duplicate originals on the day and year first above written.

_____ College

By: _____

Dr. _____

By: _____

Appendix 2

Sample Organizational Model

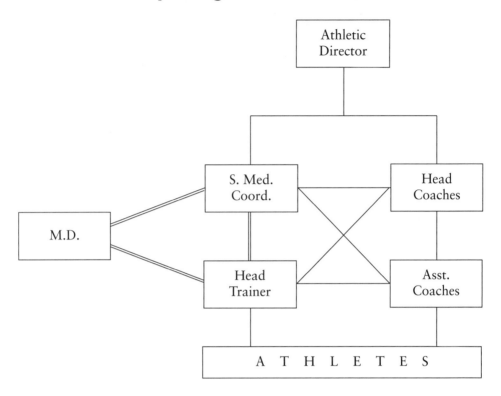

Appendix 3

Injury Report

INJURY REPORT FROM ATHLETIC TRAINER TO PHYSICIAN

Name: Sport: School:

Date of Report: Date of Injury:

Person Completing Report:

         (Athletic Trainer)   (Title)   (Phone)

Body Part Injured:

Mechanism of Injury (How? What Happened?):

Physical Findings:
Tentative Diagnosis:
Immediate Care:
Comments:

Follow Up: ☐ Physician Visit And/Or X-Rays Recommended

                   ☐ Physician Visit Not Recommended

_____   _____

(Athlete's Signature)   (Trainer's Signature)

INJURY REPORT FROM PHYSICIAN TO ATHLETIC TRAINER

Name: Sport: School:

Diagnosis:
Treatment/Rehabilitation Program:

Copy of Specific Program Enclosed: Yes   No

Estimated Time Loss:

Follow Up: ☐ Must see me/another physician prior to return to practice and/or competition.

                   ☐ May be checked by athletic trainer in lieu of visit to a physician.

                   ☐ May return to practice and/or competition upon successful *completion* of the treatment/rehabilitation program specified above.

                   ☐ May return to practice and/or competition immediately with the following modifications:

Comments:

_____   _____   _____

(Physician's Signature)   (Date)   (Phone)

Note: Keep pink copy for your records and return all other copies with the athlete.

Appendix 4

Injury Care Recommendation

INJURY CARE RECOMMENDATION

Name: Sport:

Date: Injury:

Recommended care:

☐ May continue regular activity
☐ Should modify activity as follows:

☐ Must see me prior to return to activity:
☐ Other:

_____
(Doctor's signature)

Chapter 7

Motorsport Management

Travis Teague

Motorsports is about speed. From a student's perspective, it is also about opportunity. Motorsport has become a global industry, supporting thousands of jobs throughout the nation and the world. Along with this thriving sport comes the need for competent employees capable of managing such diverse and ever-changing organizations. This truth is evident with the new academic programs that are beginning to spring up not only in the United States but also in Europe. These programs are designed to provide students with the skills necessary to manage the specific venues within the racing industry. The responsibilities of the manager in motorsports are as diverse as the different venues that exist within this global sport.

Facility Management

In the United States, 17 of the 20 highest-attended sporting events are National Association for Stock Car Auto Racing (NASCAR) events, with over 100,000 spectators present at each of the Nextel Cup races over a ten month season. (National Association for Stock Car Auto Racing, 2005). It is the responsibility of the motorsport manager to ensure that each facility is safe and clean and that, in many cases, it incorporates a large number of amenities for event guests and participants. Safety is the primary concern. Since all forms of motorsports involve speeding vehicles, the potential for injury is ever present—both for racers and crew members, as well as for spectators. It is the job of the facility manager to make sure that all steps have been taken to provide the safest environment possible. The responsibilities involve such tasks as managing the parking lots and campgrounds associated with the event the grandstands, concourses, garage, and pit areas. Successful operations within this realm of responsibility depend on proper planning and pre-event preparation, as well as organizing a qualified staff of both paid and volunteer workers. From ensuring that the consumer has a pleasant experience to managing the employees needed for these events, the motorsport manager's responsibilities are varied and enormous. The effective manager not only ensures that these facilities function on "game day"; he or she also ensures that these facilities are used to generate additional revenue. Leasing the facilities for car shows, concerts, driving schools, or private corporate functions are all important to the long-term success and survival of the organization.

Risk Management

The motorsport manager also has the critical role of developing and implementing a proper risk management plan to ensure that both participants and spectators are able to function in the safest environment possible. This plan includes not only issues related to driver safety, such as installing impact-reducing walls and instituting rules and policies related to driver and pit crew safety, but also issues of providing safe facilities for the spectators. The manager must stay current on the latest safety advances for facilities such as catch fences around the track and must institute and enforce policies related to crowd management and spectator behavior before, during, and after the event. Failure to implement and enforce proper policies and procedures in any of these areas can result in litigation against the facility and/or organization.

Corporate Sponsorship

It is important to realize that motorsports is *big business*. Numerous Fortune 500 companies are involved within the industry. NASCAR claims to have 75 million adult fans (National Association for Stock Car Auto Racing, 2005)—fans with unusual loyalty when it comes to their favorite drivers and teams, as well as extreme loyalty to the products that the teams and drivers represent. It is imperative that the motorsport manager be skilled in developing and nurturing corporate relationships that will lead to the sustained growth and success of the organization. Corporate sponsors are looking for ROI, or "Return on Investment."! The motorsport manager who has developed and maintained positive relationships and who can effectively communicate the benefits of becoming a sponsor within the sport will have a distinct advantage. Companies are not only looking for ways to reach the consuming public; they are also regarding motorsport as a good sponsorship route for establishing business-to-business relationships.

The business of attracting and maintaining sponsorship dollars is not only for "big-time" racing. It is also vital that the hundreds of smaller racing venues and teams across the industry acquire sponsorships. Companies are constantly looking for ways to generate more business and to keep their best customers loyal. Motorsport venues have proven to be highly successful in providing hospitality and product platforms for demonstration to the general public and already loyal customers. Motorsport managers must seek to provide these hospitality environments for corporate sponsors. The demand for extravagant seating for sponsors is growing within the sport. Tracks such as Las Vegas Motor Speedway and Daytona International Speedway have spent millions of dollars to enhance the spectator experience, while also luring potential sponsors into the sport. Such enhancement is especially evident within the infield areas of these tracks. Motorsport has long been known for providing opportunities for fans to have close interaction with the drivers. New concepts, such as the Neon Garage in Las Vegas, are enabling fans to view the teams working on the cars, to take pictures, and even to get autographs from their favorite drivers or crew chiefs—all through overhead views or glass windows. The primary reason for these unique modifications has been simply to enhance the customers' experiences. The motorsport manager is responsible not only for supervising these facilities but also for generating new ideas that will continue to move the sport forward and ensure success for the organization.

Motorsport Marketing

Sport is a unique phenomenon within society; marketing sport is a unique proposition as well. Motorsport consumers tend to be very loyal. This loyalty equates into a distinct advantage for the manager. A typical motorsport fan wants to feel a direct connection to the driver and team. Fans will wear the team's apparel, buy the sponsor's products, and travel great distances to be at one of the events. A wise motorsport marketer will understand this relationship and look for ways to enhance this loyalty at the venue and within the organization's communications with consumers. It is also important that consumer research be shared with potential corporate sponsors who consider entering the sport for business purposes. A wise motorsport marketer should remember that the sponsor is looking for return on investment.

Technical Knowledge

Another aspect of the industry important for the motorsport manager is the technical side of the sport. Many colleges and universities across the nation provide students with this sort of knowledge. These students are seeking jobs such as racing engineers or members of pit crews. However, it is also important that the manager have at least a basic knowledge of the issues and terminology involved with this aspect of the sport. The primary reason for this requirement is simple: In order to be able to sell or market a product, a thorough knowledge of the product is critical. Terms such as *camber*, *downforce*, and *engine dynamometer* may seem foreign, but some exposure to such terminology could assist the motorsport manager when discussing such topics with potential sponsors or competitors within the sport. A prudent student seeking management-related employment within the motorsport industry should stay abreast of some of these technical issues. Since the sport is so diverse in its venues, it is also important that motorsport management students expand their knowledge beyond their primary form of racing. For example, if the focus is primarily NASCAR, it is also important for the manager to be aware of the other forms of racing, such as Formula One or Motorcross. This awareness will enable the manager to make better-informed decisions.

Job Possibilities within Motorsport

Although the Nextel Cup Series is the showcase of NASCAR, many more opportunities are available for sport management students interested in motorsport careers. A review of the annual reports of two of the predominant motorsport corporations, Speedway Motorsports, Inc. (SMI) and International Speedway Corporation (ISC) reveals many other career opportunities for the motorsport management professional. For example, SMI owns and operates many different venues that accommodate a variety of racing series, including the Indy Racing League, the National Hot Rod Association, the Champ Car World Series, the International Race of Champions, the American LeMans Series, the World of Outlaws, the American Motorcycle Association, and Monster Trucks (Speedway Motorsports, Inc., 2004). In order for these ventures to be successful, there must be qualified personnel in place, applying sound management principles to daily operations.

One study indicates that the motorsport industry generated 24,406 jobs in 2003 for the state economy of North Carolina alone (Connaughton, Madsen,

Gandar, Arthur, & Krapl, 2004). A study entitled *Motorsports Industry in the Indianapolis Region* estimates that approximately 400 motorsport-related companies in the Indianapolis region were employing up to 8,800 individuals with an average wage of $48,359 (Klacik, D., & Cook, T., 2004). "Because motorsports does not neatly fit into a single code that enables analysts to easily measure the number of motorsports-related firms, employees, and wages, little is known about the total economic value of the industry in Indiana beyond the value of major racing events" (Klacik, D., & Cook, T., 2004, p. 4). It appears that a similar statement could be made regarding other regions of the country as well. Since the number of jobs is increasing within the motorsport industry, there is a need for specific academic programming to meet this growing number. This need is especially evident in specific regions of the United States, as well as in certain international marketplaces. What types of management-related jobs are available? In a recent study of motorsport facility Web sites (i.e., race tracks) across the United States, Teague, Hedrick, and Brown (2006) revealed that there were 163 different management-related job titles. These job titles were placed into one of nine *Categories of Management-Related Motorsport Jobs* (see Figure 1). These categories present many opportunities for students interested in careers within the motorsport industry. Positions ranging from those in facility operations and event management to those in technological support, such as the position of Web site manager, all represent entry-level options to the well-prepared student.

The primary sectors for employment seem to be race tracks; governing associations and sanctioning bodies such as NASCAR, the Indy Racing League (IRL), and the Federation Internationale de l'Automobile (FIA); race teams; and motorsport marketing firms. Finally, it is important for students to remember that the motorsport business is a global entity. The many forms of racing all present potential opportunities for the future motorsport management professional. The demand for qualified employees is growing in all sectors of the industry. These include not only NASCAR but several open-wheel venues, motorcycles, personal watercraft and boats, as well as off-road and monster-truck venues.

Regarding the business of motorsport, the responsibilities are great, but so are the opportunities. Students with formal training within the sport, a committed work ethic, and a desire for success have very few limits within this fast-paced environment. The industry is primed for young professionals willing to work hard to enhance this global enterprise.

Figure 1

**Categories of Management-Related Motorsport
Jobs and Reported Frequencies**

Management Category	Number of Different Job Titles	Three Most Common Job Titles by Management Category
Upper Level Administration	14	General Manager (35) President (25) Owner (16)
General Administration	16	Director/Manager of Operations (19) Office Manager (15) Director of Administration (3)
Advertising, Promotions and Public Relations	17	Director/Manager of Public Relations (17) Promoter (17) Communications Director/Coordinator (10)
Event Operations	32	Race Director (11) Event Coordinator/Manager/ Administrator/Director (10) Concessions Manager/Coordinator (7)
Facility Operations	30	Track/Speedway Manager/Coordinator/ Director (14) Facilities Manager/Director/Supervisor (12) Director/Coordinator of Safety (12)
Financial Management	13	Accounting Manager/Coordinator/ Director (13) Controller (6) Business Manager/Administrator (4)
Marketing & Sales Management	22	Director/Coordinator/Manager/ Administrator of Marketing and Sales (36) Vice President of Sales/Marketing (12) Corporate Sales Manager/Executive/ Coordinator (10)
Ticket Operations	11	Ticket Office Manager/Supervisor/ Coordinator/Director (32) Credentials Coordinator/Manager (6) Ticket Sales Consultant/Representative (4)
Technological Support Management	8	Webmaster (17) Web Coordinator/Designer/Editor (3)

References

Connaughton, J., Madsen, R., Gandar, J., Arthur, J., & Krapl, A. (2004). *The economic impacts of the motorsports industry on the North Carolina economy.* Charlotte: University of North Carolina at Charlotte, Belk College of Business Administration.

Klacik, D., & Cook, T. (2004). *Motorsports industry in the Indianapolis region.* Indianapolis: Purdue University Indianapolis, School of Public and Environmental Affairs: Center for Urban Policy and the Environment.

National Association for Stock Car Auto Racing (2005). *Fan Guide.* Daytona Beach, FL: Author.

National Association for Stock Car Auto Racing (2005). *Powering Brands.* Daytona Beach, FL: Author.

Speedway Motorsports, Inc. (2004). More ways to win. (Annual Report). Retrieved October 12, 2005, from http://library.corporateir.net/library/99/997/99758/items/145245/TRK_AR2004.pdf.

Teague, T., Hedrick, D., & Brown, A. (2006). *An examination of management-related job titles in motorsport venues.* Unpublished paper.

Chapter 8

Financial Management of Sport

Nancy L. Lough

Introduction

Sport at every level appears to be financially healthy. Indications of fiscal viability are evident in the escalation of broadcast rights fees for sport properties, professional player contract increases, and reports that more young people are participating in interscholastic sport than ever before. However, as each of these indicators increase, the need for a deep understanding and skillful approach to managing the money needed to produce quality sport offerings also increases. The growing number of sport properties being developed, along with the amount of resources available through sponsorship and media rights, suggests that securing funding for sport should be easier than ever before. Yet, with higher stakes available, the competition for athletic talent, spectators, and financial support grows more and more fierce. Therefore, sport managers who will be successful in the emerging sport industry are those with an understanding of fiscal responsibility and solid preparation in financial management.

Economic Reality

While professional sport continues to grow and expand, the economic reality in the 1990's was that most major league teams were losing money. According to Howard (1999), net income had declined steadily for all leagues, with the average net earning just 3% in 1996–97. The National Football League's profits fell 30% in 1996–97, while 78% of Major League Baseball teams and 75% of National Hockey League teams finished in the red that same year. By far, Major League Baseball had experienced the most severe decline, with average losses between $200 and $300 million annually since 1993. For the Cleveland Indians, the answer to securing a more stable financial position was filing with the Securities Exchange Commission an offer of $73.6 million in public stock for sale. This was an unprecedented move in Major League Baseball, yet a true indicator of the challenges possible during difficult economic times, even for big-time professional sport.

The new millennium has proven to be a profitable one for the U.S. sport industry. Reports indicated that the sport industry accounted for around $50 billion in revenue in the United States in 2007, which was an increase from just below $35 billion in 2001. Globally, total revenues were projected to be nearly $100 billion in 2007, as compared to $70 billion as recently as 2001. Every major league has experienced growth due to media contracts, new sponsorship deals and unprecedented ticket prices.

On the college level, the recent trend has been the move by smaller colleges and universities to the National Collegiate Athletic Association's Division I classification, once thought to be reserved for large universities. With potential revenue-sharing returns from conference representation in national tournaments and the potential for media attention, universities such as Portland State University have taken on the challenge of rising to Division I status. The move has required increasing the number of scholarships offered, boosting coaches salaries, and improving facilities. Still, university officials say they have begun to experience the benefits of media attention typically reserved for Division I programs. Evidence of increases was seen in the donations to athletics that rose from $120,000 in 1994–95 to $1.1 million in 1998–99. Football ticket sales increased by $120,000 from the previous year, and corporate sponsorships jumped from 190 to 490 (Di-Martino and Cohen, 1999). Figures such as these cause most intercollegiate athletic administrators to agree that the move up may well be the best strategy for financial viability.

However, the stakes are high to truly compete with the top NCAA Division I programs. In 2008, the single largest athletic program reported a budget of $109 million for 36 varsity teams and a total of 330 employees. Only a few programs can compete with Ohio State University when it comes to revenue generation, despite the growing number of programs that aspire to compete with OSU and others on the athletic field.

On the interscholastic level, athletics experienced continued growth in the number of participants, reaching three million in 2007. On both the intercollegiate and interscholastic levels, the most significant increases in participation numbers have been evident among girls and women. With one of every three girls in high school participating in sport, the need for increased funding has led coaches and administrators to become more aware of potential revenue-generating opportunities. Corporate sponsorship of state high school championships has influenced school districts, leagues, and even individual teams to seek sponsorships for support of athletic competitions and facilities. From the standpoint of interest, high school sport remains healthy and vital. However, when the amount of money needed to fund athletic programs is considered in accordance with decreasing budget allocations for public schools, the financial viability of high school sport becomes a concern.

Establishing the present financial climate for these three levels of sport may be the best approach to generating the interest and concern a future sport manager will need in order to understand the importance of finance to the administration of sport programs. While the managers in the examples given above undoubtedly have an awareness of financial principles, the escalating debt and the failure to secure a strong position suggest that future sport managers may need to be better prepared. Therefore, the objective of this chapter is to initiate an awareness of the basic financial principles that need to be understood by every sport manager. To initiate an understanding of the financial management of sport, we should begin with consideration of costs.

Table 1

Sport	Uniforms	Equipment	Supplies	Transportation	Officials
Athletic Trainers		$ 800	$ 76,800		
Baseball	$ 15,400	$ 2,200	$ 38,400	$ 31,000	$ 29,800
Basketball	$ 46,200	$ 4,400	$ 49,000	$ 72,600	$ 70,800
Football	$ 80,000	$34,000	$ 95,600	$ 70,200	$ 49,400
Golf			$ 17,600	$ 5,600	
Track	$ 33,200	$ 9,000	$ 52,200	$ 36,400	
Soccer	$ 39,800	$ 1,100	$ 52,600	$ 63,400	$ 35,200
Softball	$ 6,000	$ 950	$ 45,200	$ 31,200	$ 26,400
Swimming	$ 8,000	$ 3,600	$ 1,400	$ 11,400	
Tennis	$ 11,000		$ 14,400	$ 4,200	$ 1,200
Volleyball	$ 15,800	$ 3,200	$ 18,000	$ 30,800	$ 26,800
Wrestling	$ 17,400	$ 600	$ 23,200	$ 23,200	$ 24,200
Cross Country	$ 16,400	$ 1,000	$ 11,200	$ 24,200	
Subtotal	$289,200	$60,850	$495,600	$404,200	$263,800

Cost of Operations

Interscholastic. In the public school realm, athletic teams and coaches have found financial resources to be diminishing each year. The lack of financial support has most often resulted in special athletic fees for students who want to compete. For students who are multisport athletes, the fee structure may require them to pay substantial amounts of money for each sport season. Unfortunately, some high schools that require athletic fees have effectively eliminated potential talent simply because multisport student athletes do not have the resources necessary to play. To address this problem, many innovative programs have secured funding through community businesses investing in sponsorship and through significant fund-raising endeavors. Situations in which a coach simply manages the team and competition without needing to find some means of securing funding are growing increasingly rare.

The typical categories of costs that an interscholastic athletic director will need to consider are contained in Table 1. While actual costs will vary on the basis of the number of sports offered, the number of competitions, distances traveled, and state-regulated considerations such as those involving officials, each of the following categories represents a significant allocation of the overall budget: uniforms, equipment, equipment maintenance, supplies, transportation, meals/motels, laundry, coaching clinics and officials.

Intercollegiate sport. In 1989, the average NCAA Division I institution allocated $1.68 million for athletic scholarships. By 1995, the average had increased to $2.68 million for the typical allotment of 210 scholarships. For a major Division I program like the University of Alabama, $6 million was required by the year 2000 just for athletic scholarships (Howard and Crompton, 2004). In 2008 a typical Division IA program such as the University of Connecticut's supported as

Table 2

Traditional Revenue Sources		Nontraditional Revenue Sources	
Gate receipts	$ 8,200,000	Licensing	$1,100,000
Concessions	$ 2,300,000	Sponsorships	$1,800,000
State funding	$ 2,985,000	Sky boxes	$1,500,000
Booster club	$10,300,000	Team fund-raising	$100,000
Student fees	$ 2,460,000	Special events	$300,000
Media rights	$ 1,495,000	Subtotal	$4,800,000
Conference returns	$ 870,000		
NCAA allotments	$1,730,000		
Subtotal	$30,340,000	Total Revenues	$35,140,000

many as 650 athletes with a budget totaling $55 million (SBJ, 2008). Yet scholarships are a relatively small portion of the overall budget. Salaries for coaches, administrators, and support personnel require a significant portion of the budget, in addition to travel expenses, equipment costs, marketing, academic support services, facility maintenance, athletic training, and additional complementary services. As these categories demonstrate, the cost considerations for intercollegiate athletics are considerably more complex than those for the typical interscholastic athletic program.

To gain a perspective of the typical revenue a NCAA Division I institution can generate to pay for the growing costs associated with competing at the Division I level, review Table 2.

In the example provided, the Division IA athletic program counts on traditional revenue sources to generate just over $35 million. Nontraditional revenue sources generated a significant percentage of the total revenues, with approximately $5 million from licensing royalties, sponsorships, sky boxes, team fund-raisers, and special events. Yet close to $6 million comes directly from institutional support, state support and student fees. Gate receipts, concessions, booster clubs, media rights, conference returns, and NCAA allotments comprise the remaining revenue.

Professional sport. The worth of the professional sport industry was estimated to be around $350 billion in 1998, with half of that amount considered to be direct spending on spectator and participatory sport. Recent reports indicate that the U.S. sport industry represents the fourth largest growth industry in this country while also being designated as the 11th fastest growing industry globally (SBJ, 2008). With reports predicting continued growth well into the 21st century, it may be difficult to accept that many traditional revenue sources have stagnated while the costs for operating sport programs have increased. In professional sport, the escalating salaries of players have continued to drive an emphasis on development of new and innovative revenue streams. Naming rights attributed to new sport shrines are now a standard in the professional sport industry to eliminate a portion of the debt service created when a new sport facility is built. Even fans have been required to go beyond accepting increasing ticket prices and now find that personal seat licenses (PSLs) are required. This fee merely establishes the fan's right to purchase season tickets.

Ironically, more money is being spent on sport than ever before. Yet, with new sport properties being developed, competition for the existing resources has also become more fierce than ever before. Still, the amount of resources invested in revenue generation or fund acquisition is based primarily on the type and structure of the organization. Each of the three organizational types discussed previously have unique structures that involve differing levels of complexity. As a reflection of the relatively simple structure of a typical interscholastic athletic program, there may be only one primary athletic director with no specialized assistants in the areas of marketing, promotion, and fund-raising. Coaches often find that their responsibilities extend beyond the field of competition and into the community for promotion and fund-raising for their programs. Without question, coaches of high-profile sports at major universities have added responsibilities that are intimately linked to promotion and fund-raising. However, there are full time administrators in charge of marketing, media relations, and fund-raising that simply utilize the coach's influence to enhance the efforts for the entire athletic program. As intercollegiate athletics have grown in sophistication and complexity, the personnel needed have increasingly reflected the composition of a professional sport organization. With media rights fees increasing to levels that rival those in professional sport, the difference between the two types of organizations may seem to be diminishing. However, the overall goals of these two entities vary significantly, with professional sport being run as a business designed to be profitable. Intercollegiate athletics, on the other hand, is still part of an educational structure that is often considered successful as long as it can generate enough revenue to operate in the black and avoid falling into debt.

Generation of Funding

Sources of income. Public school budgets are based on income received from state and local taxes. Private schools utilize student tuition and other resources to fund athletic programs. In each case, booster clubs or athletic support groups can provide substantial subsidization for specific teams or programs. In one example, the $12,500 budget allotted to a local high school baseball program is only a small portion (25%), compared with the $50,000 in funding generated by the booster club. While not all sport teams can rely on significant contributions from athletic support groups, athletic directors can be instrumental in developing external resources that can be split among all athletic teams. As an example, profits generated from the sale of popcorn during lunch at a local high school have added up to $15,000 annually for the athletic program. In situations where tax support is no longer sufficient to sustain the athletic programs, innovative approaches to revenue generation, such as the above, can be the key.

In intercollegiate athletics, the institutional budget determines the amount of money the athletic department will receive. The state legislature allocates the funding for most public institutions. In certain circumstances, the legislature may even consider funding special projects that require major capital outlay, such as building additions to the university's football stadium or basketball arena. However, the determination of the funding most athletic departments receive is based on the overall institutional budget. Additionally, the amount allocated by the student government to support athletics through student fees can vary widely. Even what seems to be a small portion of the overall tuition and fees for students may add up to significant contributions for athletic departments that maintain healthy relationships with the student government. In the intercollegiate example from Table 2 above, approximately $2.46 million in student fees goes directly to the athletic department and contributes significantly to the overall revenue. While this is a relatively small percentage, finding another revenue stream to account for this percentage would be challenging.

Revenue Streams

To begin to understand this phenomenon, some specific concepts and terms need to be defined. The terms *revenue* and *profit* are often discussed as if they are interchangeable. While the goal of generating revenue is typically to generate a profit, each term has a unique definition. *Revenue* is the gross income returned by an investment—which points to the reality that it takes money to make money, even in sport. *Profit* is a valuable return on an investment realized as a gain. While revenue may appear to be profit, the situation often facing organizations in sport is that the money invested may not be fully returned. Revenues are reported separately, since money comes in over time, which often gives the appearance that large amounts of revenue must in fact be profit. But only when all the expenses have been balanced with all the revenue generated can a true profit be determined.

Typically, the media report the revenue generated by a sport team and therefore establish an image that sport has more than enough financial support. For example, bowl game revenues can amount to millions of dollars, causing spectators and fans to believe that athletic departments are providing sufficient support for all teams and programs. Yet few understand the expense of operating the non-revenue-generating sports or the revenue sharing mandated by many athletic conferences and by the NCAA. Athletic administrators understand the likelihood that a program in the same conference as a winning team will stand to gain a share of the bowl game or championship revenue. That many programs expect, and often figure into their budgets, this shared revenue points to the artificial cushion that can easily disappear and create a glaring debt.

Traditional revenue streams. Sport organizations must create revenue streams and produce cash for operations. In the case of intercollegiate athletics and professional sport, large amounts of money need to be generated each year just to sustain operations at the current level. Two categories often utilized when considering revenue streams are traditional and nontraditional. Traditional revenue streams are the sources most often counted on year after year to provide significant contributions to the overall allocation of funds. Examples included in the traditional category are ticket sales/gate receipts, concessions, licensing royalties, parking, and broadcasting or media rights. In the nontraditional category, examples may include corporate sponsorships, PSLs, naming rights, endowments and other fund-raising activities, and marketing innovations.

In the area of traditional revenue, ticket sales generate a significant amount of income for most sport programs. Increasingly, the value associated with the opportunity to experience women's sporting events and competitions previously offered for free has gained recognition. While spectators and fans are not yet willing to pay the same ticket price for intercollegiate football and men's basketball games, they are willing to buy tickets (and, in many cases, season tickets) to women's basketball, volleyball, and soccer games. However, setting the price for a ticket is no simple task. A sport manager should not become too ambitious. When setting the price for a ticket, there are several considerations to make. In addition to the price printed on the ticket, spectators have time, travel, and additional costs, such as those for concessions, parking, and merchandise. The actual price of the ticket is typically one-third of the actual cost paid to experience an event. Factors such as time spent waiting to park, waiting in concessions lines, and waiting for restroom access can cause some fans to reconsider their willingness to pay. For these reasons, the sport manager and facility manager need to work together to insure a valuable and worthwhile experience for the spectators.

When increasing the price of a ticket, there is a certain threshold that should be considered relative to the fan's willingness to pay. For example, increasing the price of a ticket from $5.00 to $10.00 may not, at first, seem like a big increase. Yet, in reality, the price was increased by 100%. In a situation where the price is extremely low, the backlash from fans is likely to be minimal. However, if a $50.00 ticket is increased to $100.00 (again, a 100% increase) from one season to the next, one can expect the fans to complain. For this reason, many sport managers believe it is better to increase the ticket price by a small percentage each season rather than making a big increase in one season and thus risking spectator dissatisfaction. Yet increasing a ticket price every year may eventually result in frustration among long-time fans. Thus, a decision to maintain a price for several seasons may be necessary. The most important consideration needs to lie with the faithful fans and insuring that they are not being turned away by high ticket prices or other peripheral costs.

Season ticket sales are beneficial to the financial management process because the money is paid up front and can be figured into the budget. To accommodate those fans who want to be season-ticket holders but who cannot afford the price of an entire season or do not have the time available, miniplans have been developed. A wide variety of these unique "season-ticket" plans exist, all with the idea that securing money for upcoming games prior to the season benefits the overall financial status of the organization.

Concessions, merchandising, and parking were traditionally thought of as minimal contributors to overall revenue generation. However, recent innovations at new sport facilities have included the addition of restaurants and microbreweries on the stadium or ball park concourse, as well as premium parking associated with specific ticket packages. Concessions can add such a large contribution to revenue generation that many organizations are reconsidering the decision to contract out the concession services. Yet, with more products desired by spectators and with service considered a premium, the contracting of a professional concessionaire can prove vital to revenue generation while alleviating additional concerns during events.

Nontraditional revenue streams. In many sports, broadcast and media rights are traditional sources of revenue. However, with the unprecedented deals made lately in both collegiate and professional sport, the evolution of this revenue stream is far from complete. For example, broadcast rights for the NCAA men's basketball tournament known as "March Madness" were recently purchased by CBS for $6 billion over 11 years. Major League Baseball was only able to squeeze $815 million out of ESPN in a deal that lasted from 2000 through 2005 (Lombardo, 2000). Yet these media-rights deals involve far more than the traditional broadcasting of competitions. With Internet rights added to the mix, innovations in the utilization of the sport property can be expected to unfold in new and creative ways.

Corporate sponsorship has been a growing revenue stream for many sport properties and programs. Many believe that sport could not exist today without the revenue generated from corporate support through sponsorships and advertising. Additionally, developing a licensing program has become a requirement for any sport property that has a need to *protect*, *promote*, and *profit* from its name and image. These three P's of licensing have become increasingly important as sponsors and advertisers have found value in associating their name and image with that of a sport property. For intercollegiate athletic programs, the royalties received from the sale of licensed merchandise and memorabilia can provide a significant revenue stream. However, there is no comparison between college sport and professional sport regarding licensing revenue. For the NBA, the 1998–99 season was a low point, with only $1 billion in worldwide retail sales. By 2003, the NBA sold $3 billion in licensed product along with Major League Baseball. The same year the NFL sold $3.2 billion in licensed merchandise.

Additional innovations in revenue generation have included the evolution of private seat licenses (PSLs), sky boxes/loges, facility naming rights, and Internet rights. In the area of fund-raising, more universities are looking toward the establishment of major endowments that will provide interest on a yearly basis that can be utilized by the athletic department without depleting the source of income. Stanford University has been a leader in the securing of endowments, with the long-term goal of providing full scholarship allotments for all sports through interest generated by endowments.

While these large dollar figures are far from the reach of the typical interscholastic athletic program, the trickle-down effect of revenue generation strategies should be acknowledged. Sponsorship acquisition has become increasingly common in high school sport. Media rights are rare, yet radio and television coverage of high school sport has increased. Still, the biggest revenue generation tool for interscholastic programs is the implementation of sound fund-raising strategies. Before embarking on any fund-raising effort, some key components should be considered. The time involvement necessary is an important component that is often overlooked. Some activities that appear to be quite simple may, in fact, require a large time commitment by a number of people.

Questions that should be asked before beginning a fund raising effort:

What are the goals of the fund raiser?
Who benefits?
Who is involved, and how?
How much organization is required, and by whom?
How many people are needed to be effective?
Is this an activity that can be repeated as an annual event, or is it a one-time effort?
What is the level of difficulty for those involved?
How much money will need to be invested?
What is the likelihood of a return on that investment?

Understanding the current economic climate for sport and becoming aware of the methods utilized to generate funding are two extremely important aspects of financial management. Yet much more knowledge is needed to understand the operation of a sport program or property. The next section will address the tools a sport manager needs to understand in order to successfully meet the challenges that lie ahead.

Accounting Applications to Sport Management

Two critical aspects of financial management that sport managers need to understand are accounting procedures and the budgeting process. Accounting records provide most of the information needed to develop the budget. When these methods are understood and utilized appropriately, accounting methods can protect an administrator or coach from misuse of funds or carelessness.

The six objectives of accounting:

1. Provide data specific to each program for future planning.
2. Determine the method for authorization of expenditures.
3. Develop standardized contracts, purchase orders, and other forms as needed.
4. Develop a standard system for authorizing payments and monitoring received goods or services.
5. Provide a method for handling special funds not managed by the central administrative office.
6. Provide the necessary information for an audit.

Three financial statements utilized in the accounting process need to be understood by sport managers. They include the *balance sheet*, the *income statement*, and the *cash flow analysis*. Each of these tools assists the sport manager with financial aspects of the sport business and is crucial to planning for success.

The *balance sheet* shows the financial condition of the business and has four primary uses:

1. Illustrates change in business over time.
2. Shows growth or decline in various phases of business.
3. Demonstrates the ability to pay debts.
4. Shows financial position through ratios.

Four important terms to know in order to understand the balance sheet include *assets*, *liabilities*, *equity*, and *depreciation*. Assets are simply what the business owns. The three primary assets listed on a balance sheet are (1) current assets, (2) long-term investments, and (3) fixed assets. Cash on hand, or any asset that could be converted to cash within 12 months, would be considered a current asset. Any investment, such as a CD with a maturity date beyond 12 months, would be considered a long-term investment. Fixed assets include items such as real estate (land or buildings), furniture, equipment, automobiles, and other items a business owns. Assets can depreciate or diminish in value over time. This concept is of importance to sport managers because depreciation can be calculated over time and become tax-deductible.

The balance sheet shows the balance of assets held compared to liabilities and the owner's equity. Assets are listed on the left side of the sheet, while liabilities are listed on the right. Liabilities are considered the amount of money a business

Table 3

Assets			Liabilities	
Cash on hand	$10,000		Accounts Payable	$14,000
Cash in bank	$100,000		Notes Payable	$45,000
Accounts receivable	$35,000		Mortgage payments	$72,000
Inventories	$15,000		Accrued salaries	$35,000
Prepaid insurance	$36,000		Accrued taxes	$18,000
Prepaid advertising	$12,000		Shareholder equity	$1,319,000
Fixed assets—facility	$1,350,000			
Less: Reserve for facility depreciation	$125,000	$1,225,000		
Fixed assets—equipment	$90,000			
Less: Reserve for equipment depreciation	$20,000	$70,000		
Total assets	$1,503,000		Total Liabilities	$1,503,000

owes to other parties. Current liabilities are debts that must be paid within 1 year, while long-term liabilities include larger loans that do not need to be paid immediately. Both current and long-term liabilities are added together to determine the total owed as liabilities. In addition to liabilities, the right side of the balance sheet lists the owner's equity. *Equity* is defined as the amount of money invested by owners, whether partners or individuals. Earned income is then added to the investment and withdrawals made by the owner are subtracted to determine the total owner's equity. In the case of the Cleveland Indians, and other publicly held properties, equity includes the stockholder's purchased shares of stock. Total equity is then added to total liabilities. The balance sheet should then show that the combined values equal, or balance with, the total assets calculated in the left column (see Table 3).

A balance sheet posting expenditures should be regularly updated and maintained by the sport manager so that those affected by the budget know the current balance.

The *income statement* shows profit or loss in the business operations. The income statement is a crucial analysis tool for determining success of a business. By comparing the cost of running a business with the sales generated, the income statement provides indication of profit or loss. The items included will depend on the type of business. To read an income statement, start at the top of the form with "gross profit" and then proceed down to the last line, where "net income" is found. Key components listed on the income statement include "revenue," "operating expenses," "net income" and a "percentage column." *Gross sales* are listed under the revenue heading and are defined as the total amount of revenue (excluding sales tax) that is generated. Revenue sources discussed previously, such as traditional and nontraditional streams, are listed here. Further down the income statement, the *operating expenses* will include all other expenses a business accrues during day-to-day operations. Examples may include salaries, insurance, advertising or marketing, utilities, and rent or loan payments. *Net income* is listed at the bottom of the income statement and can be defined as the amount of money remaining after all expenses have been paid. When a net loss has occurred over the year, the amount of loss will be shown in parentheses. Last, the *percentage column* on the right shows what percentage of net sales has been spent in each area of the business. This is a very useful management tool because it allows a manager to quickly assess which percentage(s) may be too high compared to the percentage(s) on previous statements. Changes in the percentage column may assist a manager in making decisions that could lead to a better utilization of resources.

The *cash flow analysis* serves a separate purpose from the previous two records discussed. The balance sheet shows the manager the business's financial condition, and the income statement shows the profit or loss, while the cash flow analysis documents the "cash in" and "cash out"—typically on a monthly basis. By showing the cash sales and disbursement (expense) records, the cash flow analysis gives the manager the ability to assess the financial situation over time.

PUMA AG Rudolf Dassler Sport

Top of Form

91292   A   income

Annual Income Statement

Bottom of Form

View: Annual	Dec 06	Dec 05	Dec 04
Revenue	3,125.7	2,105.1	2,087.3
Cost of Goods Sold	–	–	1,004.4
Gross Profit	–	–	1,082.9
Gross Profit Margin	–	–	51.9%
SG&A Expense	–	–	644.8
Depreciation & Amortization	–	–	26.3
Operating Income	–	–	497.9
Operating Margin	–	–	23.9%
Nonoperating Income	–	–	7.8
Nonoperating Expenses	–	–	0.0
Income Before Taxes	–	–	505.6
Income Taxes	–	–	152.4
Net Income After Taxes	–	–	353.3
Continuing Operations	–	–	353.3
Discontinued Operations	–	–	0.0
Total Operations	–	–	353.3
Total Net Income	347.2	338.5	351.0
Net Profit Margin	11.1%	16.1%	16.8%
Diluted EPS from Total Net Income ($)	–	–	–
Dividends per Share			

Sport is seasonal and thus affects inflows and outflows differently. *Cash flow* can be defined as reported net income plus amounts charged off for depreciation, depletion, amortization, and extraordinary charges to reserves that are bookkeeping deductions and not paid out in actual dollars (Regan, 1991, p. 369).

Comparing periodic records may provide patterns of cash flow that indicate a need to make adjustments at specific points in time or to provide some time for strategic planning. These accounting practices vary according to the form of business ownership. However, the three financial statements discussed serve three important purposes and should be utilized together. While a much more in-depth knowledge is needed to be successful in financial management, the awareness of these primary accounting procedures will allow sport managers to be prepared for the challenges ahead.

The Budgeting Process

A *budget* is a management plan for the revenue and the expenses of an organization for a period of time, usually one year. The two most important skills a sport manager must have relative to budgets are (1) the ability to prepare and justify the annual budget and (2) the ability to control the expenses and disbursements once the budget has been approved.

According to Barber (1991), budgeting provides several advantages. Seven specific advantages include the following:

1. It substitutes a plan for "chance" in fiscal operations, and it prepares for additional staff or maintenance work that needs to be done with resources available.
2. It prevents overbudgeting or padding because it requires review of the entire operation in terms of funds available and revenue needs.
3. It promotes the standardization and simplification of the operation, and it establishes priorities and objectives while eliminating inefficient operations.
4. It provides guidelines for all staff to follow, insuring more consistency.
5. It provides factual data for evaluation by governing bodies regarding the operation's efficiency.
6. It allows contributors such as the taxpaying public to see where revenues come from and where expenditures are spent.
7. It acts as an instrument for fiscal control.

Fundamental principles should be followed when constructing a budget. Budgets are made out annually and have individual characteristics based on the type of organization or business. Preparation of a new budget begins when the previous budget has been accepted. While top administrators at educational institutions are responsible for the overall budget, an athletic director or department head should be involved in the budget preparation process for her/his program—just as coaches or physical educators need to be involved in the preparation of the budget for their specific programs. This bottom-up approach provides more quality information for making budget decisions. It also increases the satisfaction of the staff because their thinking was incorporated into the decisions that will directly affect their work. Budgets should be planned well in advance of the fiscal period during which they will be used. The fiscal year for most educational institutions is July 1 to June 30, but any 12-month period may be used, depending on government regulation and local policy.

The 10 primary steps in constructing a budget:

1. Examining the organization's present mission, objectives, and goals in relationship to the previous year's budget
2. Collecting the necessary information relative to the needs, strengths, and resources of the organization
3. Soliciting input from others with expertise in the collection and evaluation of information needed
4. Reviewing the data collected and analyzing it in terms of what was done previously, what is required presently, and what the future may hold immediately
5. Preparing the budget document in accordance with the stipulations and requirements established by the organization or governing body
6. Checking to insure the document is accurate, feasible, and realistic
7. Submitting a "rough draft" for critical analysis by an expert or colleague prior to making the formal presentation to the board or administration
8. Preparing for anticipated questions prior to the presentation
9. Implementing the approved budget (once changes have been made as needed) with the knowledge that flexibility may be necessary as time progresses and events transpire
10. Auditing the budget following the conclusion of the budget year to assist the sport manager in gaining proficiency and competence as a fiscal manager

The decision on the type of budget to use is usually based on the sophistication of the program that will be utilizing the information. However, in educational settings, the type of budget is often mandated by the educational institution or organization. For this reason, a sport manager or administrator should be familiar with different budgeting procedures and should be prepared to use the strengths of each when involved in the budgeting process.

Types of Budgets

Line-item budget. The term *line* refers to the listing of each item as a line in the budget. This approach is one of the most simple budgeting approaches to use and understand. It can be constructed in a reasonable amount of time because the specific expenditure items that form this type of budget are based on information from previous years' budgets together with anticipated changes such as escalating costs, new programs, or enrollment shifts. For these reasons, this approach is one of the most commonly used for physical education or athletic programs.

Program budget. The program budget separates an organization by units. For this reason, it can be easily adapted to fit an athletic department or sport organization. The three components of a program budget include (1) overall organizational goals, (2) program-specific goals, and (3) unique features of the program. A program budget is then followed by a line-item budget for support. With each sport preparing a separate budget along with a narrative description of the sport's goals and the features of its program deemed most important, the athletic director can compare various budget requests and make decisions based on a more in-depth understanding.

Planning-Programming-Budgeting-Evaluation System (PPBES). The purpose of the PPBES is to focus on the end product of the service provided rather than the actual cost. Additionally, providing a rationale for each of the competing units within a department can be accomplished since the PPBES provides a narrative picture of expenditures rather than simply listing the amount of money spent.

Planning requires careful consideration of goals and objectives.
Programming means that programs are developed to reach the established goals.
Budgeting refers to the allocation of resources to accomplish the goals of the programs.
Evaluation is the final step, which requires assessment of the results.

Following evaluation, further planning generates the start of the next budgetary cycle. This system provides the administrator with a means of objectively evaluating programs and determining where resources should be allocated.

Zero-based budgeting. The basic premise behind this approach is that the organization begins each year with no money. A budget is then prepared by justifying each expenditure as if it is a new expense. The purpose of a zero-based budget is to control overbudgeting and waste. Each budget request is carefully considered in relationship to the overall organization. This approach has been considered a radical departure from the traditional methods described previously.

Capital budget. Long-range budget items and capital expenses are covered in a capital budget. Typically, major purchases such as new facilities and equipment that are not found in operating budgets (reflecting only one year) are found in a capital budget. Capital expenditures are those which involve a significant amount of money. A narrative explanation and/or justification should be provided for each expense.

Summary/Conclusion

In the present economic environment, an understanding of basic financial principles is paramount. Sport managers and administrators will have a greater degree of success in the emerging sport industry if they understand how to manage costs, generate revenue, and account for money spent.

Terms to review:

Assets: what a business owns
Liabilities: a business's debts; how much a business owes to other parties
Equity: amount of money invested by owners
Depreciation: a decrease in value of an asset as it gets older
Percentage column: a useful management tool that shows what percentage of the net sales is being spent in specific areas of the business
Revenue: the gross income returned by an investment
Profit: a valuable return on an investment realized as a gain

References

Barber, E. (1991). Accounting and budgeting. In B. L. Parkhouse (Ed.), *The management of sport: Its formulation and application*, pp. 343–362. St. Louis: C. V. Mosby.

DiMartino, Christina, & Cohen, Andrew (1999, November). Movin' on up. *Athletic Business*, 43–52.

Howard, Dennis R. (1999). The changing fanscape for big-league sports: Implications for sport managers. *Journal of Sport Management, 13*, 78–91.

Howard, Dennis R., & Crompton, John L. (1995). *Financing sport*. Morgantown, WV: Fitness Information Technology, Inc.

Lombardo, John. (2000). Houston goes on PSL spree. *Sports Business Journal, 37* (2), 6.

Regan, Tom H. (1991). Financing sport. In B. L. Parkhouse (Ed.), *The management of sport: Its formulation and application*, pp. 363–373. St. Louis: C. V. Mosby.

Stier, William F., Jr. (1999) *Managing Sport, Fitness, and Recreation Programs: Concepts and practices*. Boston: Allyn and Bacon.

Street & Smith's SportBusiness Journal (2004). By the numbers 2004, 6(36), 10–14, 84, 127.

Why sports? (1998, August 10–17). *The Nation, 3*, 21.

Part 3

Marketing Management

To give away money is an easy matter and in every man's power ... but to decide whom to give it, and for what purpose and how, is neither an easy matter nor in every man's power. Hence it is that such excellence is rare, praiseworthy, and noble.

Aristotle

Chapter 9

Corporate Sponsorship of Sport

Nancy L. Lough

Sponsorship Defined

Sport offers many unique attributes that are attractive to any business that seeks association with a winner or an effective addition to their communications mix. *Sponsorship* has been defined as "the acquisition of rights to affiliate or directly associate with a product or event for the purpose of deriving benefits related to that affiliation or association" (Mullin, Hardy, & Sutton, 2007). As a unique element capable of cutting through the clutter present in traditional advertising and promotional approaches, sport sponsorship has grown dramatically from the mid-1980s to the present.

Sponsors use their relationship with a sport property to attain established marketing objectives. Typically, a sponsorship agreement will be utilized by both the corporate partner and the sport property to contribute to the overall marketing mix. Product, price, place, and promotion comprise the four primary elements of the marketing mix. Manipulation of these four elements, to meet the target market's needs in an ever-changing environment, is the job of the sport marketer. By implementing a sport sponsorship agreement, a sport marketer can integrate components of all four elements to effectively meet the established marketing objectives.

The average person is exposed to more than 5,000 selling messages each day. Thus, separation and retention of information is difficult for most consumers. By utilizing sponsorship as an alternative channel for communication, many companies have found that they can achieve new levels of exposure. Additionally, sport sponsorships are often positioned at a lower cost than traditional advertising media. Costs for television and print ads have consistently been on the rise with no apparent change on the horizon. For example, a 30-second television advertisement during the NFL's 1998 Super Bowl cost $1.3 million. This was more than triple the cost 10 years previously. In 2000, the same 30-second slot averaged $2.2 million, then climbed to $2.6 million by 2007. Projections for 2009 have estimated a further increase to $3 million for 30 seconds due to the unequalled ratings and global interest this mega-event creates. Such figures indicate the extreme desire of many companies to associate their products or brands with a "winning" sport property. The Super Bowl represents the two top teams in the United States competing for the title of World Champions. It also represents the largest single-event television audience—not only in the United States but also internationally. For sponsors involved with this sport property, the association translates to brand equity through enhanced image and spectators' intent to purchase, resulting in product sales.

On the opposite side of the equation, sport managers and marketers have come to rely so heavily on the monetary support provided through the sponsorship medium that many believe sport as we know it today could not exist without corporate sponsorship. How pervasive has sponsorship become in sport? At present, the relationships between companies seeking the sport affiliation and sport properties willing to sell those opportunities extend beyond professional and intercollegiate sport to interscholastic and youth sport teams, organizations, events, and facilities.

As just one example, the New Mexico Activities Association (NMAA), the governing body for high school sport in New Mexico, signed a State Farm Insurance Agency in 2000 to the association's first recognized sponsorship deal. The State Farm agency benefited by being the exclusive sponsor of the most recognized and one of the most influential sport organizations in the state. Potential exposure to consumers extended beyond high school student athletes and included their parents, grandparents, and extended family members (many of whom may sufficiently value the association of State Farm with high school athletics to consider the insurance company in future insurance decisions). The benefits for the NMAA included receiving money for organizing and implementing championship events, while also establishing the value for its affiliation with additional sponsorships. By 2007, the organization listed eighteen corporate partners representing business interests that varied from insurance to construction companies to restaurants.

Sponsorship Growth in the United States

The 1984 Olympic Games in Los Angeles have been recognized as the catalyst for modern corporate involvement in sport. Before the 1984 Olympic Games, host cities lost money, and many incurred debt that lasted for decades beyond completion of their last Olympic competition. To prevent such an occurrence to the city of Los Angeles, Peter Ueberroth, president of the Los Angeles Olympic Organizing Committee (LAOOC), initiated a corporately subsidized Olympics. The number of sponsors was limited to 30 to avoid clutter and provide product exclusivity. This limitation allowed Ueberroth to develop corporate partnerships, suggesting that both parties would achieve benefits by working as partners to create desirable results.

Following the enormous success of the 1984 Olympic Games, corporate sport sponsorship began to flourish. By 1990, a 15% growth rate was predicted for each subsequent year. In terms of millions of dollars, this was a staggering prediction. Yet by 1997, the figure had increased to $5.9 billion spent by North American companies. The growth has yet to see any significant slowing, since the $6.8 billion figure for 1998 revealed a 15% increase over the previous year. Sponsorship spending was expected to grow at a faster rate in 2007 than it had in 2006 and to continue on an upward trend. For example, North American companies were projected to increase spending by 11.7% in 2008, reaching $14.93 billion according to the IEG Sponsorship Report's 22nd annual industry forecast. Global spending on sport sponsorship has also risen dramatically to the unprecedented level of $37.7 billion expected in 2008, an 11.9% increase over the 2007 mark of $33.7 billion.

As more companies become interested in sport sponsorship and as more sport managers seek sponsorship dollars, sport properties previously nonexistent or overlooked have become increasingly attractive to cut through the clutter of more traditional sport sponsorships. For example, in 1992 sport sponsorship for women's sport was at the unprecedented level of $285 million in the United States. By 1997, that figure had more than doubled to $600 million. Before 1997, most sponsorship money spent on women's sport was allocated to golf (LPGA), tennis (WTA), and figure skating (Lough, 1996). However, following the 1996 Olympic Games, which effectively served as the catalyst for women's sport sponsorship, new women's sport properties such as the Women's National Basketball Association (WNBA) secured corporate support through sponsorship that established the sport property as viable and valuable. By 2001 the total sponsorship revenue reported for women's sport passed the $1 billion mark and was expected to continue to grow at a similar rate.

Yet, sport sponsorship is often considered to include considerable risk for the corporate sponsor, since certain elements of sport can not be controlled. For the organizers and event promoters of the 1999 Women's World Cup Soccer Tournament in the United States, securing sponsorship was not easy. For the sponsors who jumped on the World Cup Soccer bandwagon when the U.S. men's team played host in 1994, the elimination of the U.S. team translated to a poor return on their investment. However, the success of the U.S. women's team in 1999 became a tide of emotion that was transformed into enormous financial success for event organizers and sponsors. In the case of the Women's World Cup, the risk that some corporations were not willing to take turned into valuable benefits for those who were willing to commit. Similarly, in the new millennium, sponsors have found an expanded media platform for sponsorship activation through partnerships with innovative sport properties such as the LPGA. As one of the few sports that have experienced double-digit television growth in the United States since 2005, prices have increased substantially. Tournament title sponsors were charged as much as $100,000 for a three-year contract, compared with their previous rates of $15,000. The rationale for a seven-fold increase in fees was based on the new commissioner's justification that value had increased substantially, along with service and exposure.

Why Corporations Buy into Sport

Three of the most significant reasons that corporations buy into sport have already been discussed. First, the cost of advertising will undoubtedly continue to escalate, along with the number of companies competing for consumer dollars. Additionally, the number of media outlets will make the competition even more fierce as Internet use becomes increasingly sophisticated and mainstream. Second, the use of sport sponsorship as a component of the marketing strategy that can help a company cut through the clutter and media "noise" will only enhance the third rationale—that strong brand *equity* can be achieved through association with a winning sport property.

One important attribute somewhat unique to sport is the element of emotion. When the home team wins, the fans feel that they are winners; as a result, they often enjoy celebrating "their" victory. Sport fans and sport consumers have strong emotional ties to teams, athletes, and specific sport properties or events. Corporate sponsors seek emotional ties with consumers that will translate to brand loyalty. As a prime example, consider the National Association of Stock Car Racing (NASCAR). Spectators for these auto races not only buy rickets to attend the events; they also buy merchandise with sponsors' logos prominently displayed to support both the driver and the sponsors who support the driver. Fans acknowledge that without corporate sponsorship, their sport could not exist. Many fans even admit to changing brands if sponsorship changes for their favorite driver. The strength of this association is unlike any other. In this example, sponsors can count on a degree of brand loyalty simply by maintaining sponsorship of a specific driver.

Yet, sophisticated sponsorship decision makers consider many aspects before committing to a specific sport sponsorship. Identification of a market segment that the corporate sponsor needs to reach provides a significant selling point. Target market demographics of sport consumers suggest a viable avenue for corporate sponsors to communicate with specific groups that are most likely to purchase their products. As an example, the WNBA focuses on a family demographic inclusive of kids, parents, and grandparents. While in typical demographic terms, this focus is actually a combination of several specific segments, the family approach has appealed to ticket buyers as well as national corporate sponsors and local businesses. By providing a wholesome, fun, exciting sport experience in an exceptional arena, the WNBA has been able to provide access to an audience which sponsors such as Discover Card are willing to pay to reach. For those who sell a wide variety of products to service a family demographic, the sponsorship fit with the WNBA has proven to be successful. On a more grass-roots level in WNBA cities, fans can get player autographs by visiting local sponsors' stores on scheduled appearance days. The WNBA players effectively drive traffic into and through the local sponsors' stores where fans will be exposed to the many products that are attractive to this target market.

Sponsors' Rationale

Sport properties and events can offer opportunities that extend beyond simple advertising and that reach consumers at the point of experience. This attribute is one of the many aspects corporate sponsors seek in relationships with sport. Extensive research has been conducted to determine the objectives sponsors most often utilize when making sponsorship decisions. Objectives as identified in research are provided in the revised sport sponsorship proposal evaluation model (Irwin & Sutton, 2004). The objectives most often utilized in decisions to enter a sport sponsorship agreement include the following:

To achieve sales objectives.
To generate media benefits.
To secure entitlement or naming rights.
To increase public awareness of the company, the product, or both.
To alter or reinforce public perception of the company.
To identify the company with a particular market segment.
To involve the company in the community.

To build good will among decision makers.

To create an advantage over competitors through association or exclusivity.

To gain unique opportunities in terms of hospitality and entertainment.

As an illustration of how many of these objectives can be achieved simultaneously for companies involved in a specific sport sponsorship, consider the case of the ESPN X Games. Sponsorship of this unique sport event created by ESPN allows companies such as Mountain Dew, Jeep, New Balance, Taco Bell, and Shick to reach the specific demographic group of teens and "millenials." Through guaranteed quality exposure on multiple media outlets, including ABC, ESPN, ESPN2 and EXPN.com, the sponsors' message and image will be communicated to the target market they are seeking to reach. Image enhancement for these companies will be achieved through association with the ESPN property that has been the leader in showcasing extreme and alternative sport competition in both winter and summer venues. The association includes on-site exposure through use of a jumbo-tron screen that continuously provides coverage of the ongoing event along with repeated play of sponsors' advertising spots for the several thousand spectators milling on the event site. Additionally, the interactive village allows sponsors the opportunity to meet potential consumers (spectators) face-to-face for product trial and demonstrations. Products are also provided to many of the people involved in running, staging, and producing the event through "schwag." Typically, a sponsorship package inclusive of all that has been described would be sufficient. Yet additional aspects X Games sponsors find appealing include the hospitality provided for sponsors and the opportunities for trade networking with other corporate representatives that include companies such as Disney and ESPN. Today, the primary objectives for business-to-business marketing include opportunities such as 1) entertaining clients and prospects, 2) demonstrating products and services, 3) providing incentives for the sales force and distributors, 4) accessing cosponsors for networking and sales, 5) selling products and services to rights holders, and 6) raising the company profile.

Win-Win Strategies

The creation of symbiotic relationships—ones that are mutually beneficial to each of the separate entities—often provides the best strategy for establishing long-term, successful sponsorships. In the case of intercollegiate athletics, establishing win-win sponsorship relationships with community businesses often proves to be the best source of consistent revenue. In 1991, "70% of NCAA Division I athletic programs lost money, continuing a trend in place for several years" (Associated Press, 1). More recently, Funk (2005) reported that the average deficit for schools in most NCAA divisions continued to grow despite increasing revenue generation. With accountability more closely scrutinized as the collegiate sport environment begins to more closely resemble professional sport, reports of revenue generation to offset other financial challenges have grown increasingly important. New initiatives have evolved to address the growing costs for remaining competitive in intercollegiate athletics. The most significant avenue for many athletic programs to generate new revenue has become enhanced involvement with corporate sponsorship programs. Although NCAA Division I football and basketball typically generate more revenue each year, the two sports also continue to demand a bigger share of the overall athletic budget to continue to remain competitive. Thus, to sustain current programs, more financial resources are required each year. With this significant need for revenue, athletic administrators have increasingly hired sport marketing personnel to develop revenue streams such as corporate sponsorships. "The college demographic is one with which all national corporations wish to have involvement" (Milverstedt, 1989). A successful relationship between college sport and corporate sponsors can be established with athletics serving as the vehicle. Corporations are seeking a means for communication with the college-age target market because it comprises one of the largest groups of potential consumers and should soon have significant purchase decisions to make. Developing brand preference at this impressionable age is highly valued, as evidenced by the growing list of corporate sponsors for the NCAA, college sport conferences, and specific university-affiliated athletic programs. Similarly, in recent years the addition of mobile marketing via the Internet has dramatically widened the media-based communication efforts that drive sponsorship value.

Recognizing the value in a sport property that sponsorship is being sought for begins with the sport organizers. In the case of intercollegiate sport, the NCAA has led the way by establishing value in the Division I men's basketball championship tournament known as March Madness. The most recent media deal signed by CBS and the NCAA established the overall value of the men's national championship basketball tournament at $6 billion. For corporate partners associated with the NCAA, this figure translates to considerable value added to their established relationship. Thus, the sport organization benefits by selling the media rights to the highest bidder, while the NCAA sponsors benefit by being associated with a property that has increased in value exponentially in recent years. Yet the "wins" in this situation also include benefits for the fans of men's intercollegiate basketball since sponsors and event organizers have teamed together to provide a high quality, easily accessible, televised event. This exposure also allows corporate messages to be communicated to a wider audience. Associations that provide benefits such as these rarely experience difficulty in renewing sponsorship deals simply because the "wins" are measurable.

Creating a Match

All of the examples provided previously were outcomes of what was once a sponsorship proposal. Initially, the concept was merely an idea that was then translated into a working document. To take these ideas and actually develop a successful sport sponsorship plan, several key steps need to be accomplished.

Identifying Potential Sponsors

First, one should consider specific business relations of one's own institution or organization. There may already exist some natural relationships that would be strengthened or enhanced through a sponsorship agreement. Additionally, businesses that do business with one's institution or corporation often have a vested interest in its success. Considering a sponsorship agreement with a business that is already a supplier can be readily altered to include more benefits for both parties. Another consideration involves examining the business interests represented among the participants, parents, or other individuals closely associated with the organization. A parent that owns or manages a business may find a sponsorship option as a very attractive means of further supporting the team or sport opportunity. Good inside contacts can be very beneficial when initiating sponsorship interest. Even if a contact within a business is not known, one should make sure to do the necessary research to determine a) who is the correct person to approach, b) who will in fact make the decision, and c) what is the best time and method for reaching these individuals.

Sponsors' Needs

One of the most pervasive problems in sport marketing has traditionally been the myopic focus that sport tends to create. When securing sponsorship, the problem is manifested by the failure to consider what the sponsors need in a sport relationship. Typically, the focus is the benefits of the sport. While sport is often a unique opportunity with elements that are not easily attained in alternative options, those seeking to develop sponsorship relationships must also consider what the business which becomes involved in sponsorship needs to achieve. Wilkinson (1988) was one of the first to classify corporate objectives into various categories. Overall categories often include sales objectives, image objectives, awareness objectives, and employee motivation. The objectives discussed previously can easily be placed into one of these categories. When sales objectives are sought by a sponsor, aspects that they desire may include increasing the sales levels of certain brands or getting people to sample a product. Floor traffic, meaning the number of people who come into the store, and product-sponsorship-related displays are also common elements of sales objectives. Ultimately, these objectives have proven to be the most often sought. Research has revealed that a return on investment is the key for most sport sponsors (Lough & Irwin, 2001). To achieve this desired objective, a number of tactics have been employed. Event-themed coupons can be made available in the sponsor's place of business, or event tickets can be redeemed as coupons at the sponsor's stores. At certain events, product sampling can be provided through special displays on the event site. Coupon-related tactics have been utilized effectively in intercollegiate sport sponsorship. In one example involving a Midwestern NCAA Division I university, points scored at a winning football game translated into a percent discount at a sponsor's business if the game ticket was brought in on the following Monday. At a separate university, basketball tickets were printed with a sponsor's coupon on the reverse side to be redeemed as entry into a contest awarding a shopping spree to winners at the conclusion of the season. In each example, sponsors achieved the objective of driving traffic into their store via the sport-sponsor relationship.

Image objectives can be enhanced through sport sponsorship when a logical link is made between the sport property and business sponsor. Community-related businesses such as banks or financial institutions often utilize the image of a university association such as a basketball team or tournament to communicate their image as "supporting our community." Companies also seek to alter their image via sport sponsorship. By becoming linked to a specific sport property or event, the image associated may be assimilated by the sponsoring company. Mountain Dew has gained significant presence as a brand because of their image as an "extreme" beverage that has been furthered through their decade-long sponsorship of the ESPN X Games.

Awareness objectives are often abused by sport marketers. For years, signage at an event or on a T-shirt was enough to secure financial backing from sponsors. Yet as more companies have become involved, the sophistication of meeting sponsors' needs has increased. Awareness of a brand is most often crucial when that brand is being introduced or altered. Consumers now have exposure to so many forms of advertising that awareness alone will not often suffice. Combining the opportunity for awareness with additional objectives may prove to be a more effective strategy for meeting sponsors' needs. For example, extended media coverage that includes saturation of the market through television, print, and the Internet would be viewed as more valuable than simply providing signage at the venue. Providing exposure for the sponsor through multiple outlets can be one of the advantages of sport sponsorship. The cost to sponsors for newsprint publicity is free when the event is covered by the media, making it difficult for those selling advertising to compete, given the high fees for advertising in the same publication.

Employee motivation as an objective of sport sponsorship can be achieved by providing opportunities for employees that may not have existed or may have been too expensive for individuals. Tickets to events are often provided to sponsors who then can reward employees by dispersing the tickets for specific reasons. A sport organizer can enhance this objective by creating a special "meet and greet" the athletes and/or coaches after the game or during a pre-game meal. The cost to enhance this experience for sponsors is minimal to sport organizers, but the experience may prove quite valuable for employee motivation and sponsor satisfaction.

Criteria for Sponsorship Evaluation

Considering how businesses can best evaluate their sport-sponsorship agreement is a key element to securing successful sponsorship deals. Companies often have an established list of requirements for becoming involved in sport sponsorship. The abilities of management, the sport organization's status and reputation, along with the sanctioning body, are often key factors in sponsorship decisions (Stotlar, 1993). Corporations want to be associated only with high-quality organizations run by competent and stable management. The number of events and the geographic representation also need to be considered. Securing a sponsor that has no presence in the primary market(s) will not provide positive feedback during evaluation, unless the sponsor is primarily seeking awareness and has an additional plan for gaining a presence in that market. Securing sponsorship will undoubtedly be more difficult for first-time events or for organizers that do not have an established history or developed reputation. In these circumstances, gaining the support of a sanctioning organization, such as a National Governing Body or similar established club, can assist in insuring potential sponsors that the event will be run well and managed efficiently.

Recognizing Why Sponsors Drop Out

Considering all the time and effort that must go into securing a sponsorship agreement, it would seem that sport organizers would be concerned with keeping sponsors once they have been secured. Yet one of the primary reasons that sponsors drop out or fail to renew a sponsorship agreement is the lack of attention and service paid during the agreement. Feedback should be provided to allow the sponsors to determine whether their investment is paying off or may need to be altered. However, when no feedback is provided, the conclusion realized most often by sponsors is that the relationship is not worth the investment. Commonly cited reasons for dropping out include lack of service, decreased market value of the event as determined by reduced attendance or a drop in television ratings, and a change in corporate direction.

Providing attendance figures, crowd demographics, and copies of newspaper clippings of the event can be simple means for giving feedback to sponsors. Interpreting these elements relative to established corporate objectives is the type of service necessary for a sport organization to retain a sponsor in this highly competitive environment. Yet too often sport organizers fail to simply provide feedback. Communicating with the sponsor throughout the agreement is crucial to continued success. Taking proactive measures to prevent a perceived decrease in value or ineffective strategy can go much further than being reactive when change may be too late. The value that corporate sponsors involved in both general sport sponsorship and women's sport sponsorship place on key objectives may assist in the formulation of new strategies to better meet sponsors' needs (Lough and Irwin, 2001).

Another common rationale for dropping out of a sponsorship agreement is a change in corporate direction. In many instances, this rationale is simply a reflection of a dissatisfied sponsor. However, in certain circumstances, the fit between the new image the company is seeking and the established image of the sport event or property is too distant to be remedied. The best strategy for sport marketers in this circumstance is to maintain positive relations with the business, in case the corporate direction changes some time in the future. The most effective approach to take in preventing a sponsor from dropping out is to work the relationship to meet the sponsor's criteria, to provide service and data to justify the sponsor's continuation, and to help the sponsor establish the measures for a successful sport sponsorship.

Summary/Conclusion

Developing a successful sport sponsorship plan requires attention to five primary areas: (1) the description of the sponsorship, (2) the plan objectives, (3) the plan components, (4) the budget, and (5) evaluation/relationship management. The initial document developed to create interest and motivation for potential clients to review the entire proposal is the executive summary. In this short, often single-page document, the major points of interest are clearly provided for the potential sponsor. Once interest is created, the proposal should illustrate objectives that sponsors can achieve by becoming associated with the sport opportunity. The section that presents plan components should establish the unique opportunities available through various levels of sponsorship. Typically, the top level, or most expensive, opportunity will include aspects such as categorical exclusivity and rights to the use of specific marks protected by and belonging to the sport property. The fourth section outlines the investment required to achieve specific levels of sponsorship. The concluding section provides the evaluation measures that will be implemented and the feedback that can be anticipated to maintain a strong working relationship between the sport property and the sponsor.

Creating successful sport sponsorship relationships requires skill, creativity, and attention to detail. If all of the above areas are researched prior to engaging a corporate client and if a professional document that includes these components is presented, the likelihood for achieving success will be greatly enhanced. Securing sponsorship for sport properties and/or events is a crucial element in today's competitive sport landscape. By incorporating the ideas discussed, one's organization or institution will be capable of competing for and establishing successful sport-sponsorship agreements.

References

Ensor, R. J. (1987, September). The corporate view of sports sponsorship. *Athletic Business,* 40–43.

Funk, D. (2005). 2002–03 NCAA revenues and expenses of Divisions I and II intercollegiate athletics program report. Indianapolis: National Collegiate Athletic Association.

Irwin, D. (1993, May). In search of sponsors. *Athletic Management,* 11–16.

Irwin, R. L., & Sutton, W. A. (2004). A model for screening sponsorship opportunities. In *Sport promotions and sales management, human kinetics.* Champaign, IL: Author.

Lough, N., & Irwin, R. (2001). A comparative analysis of sponsorship objectives for women's sport and traditional sport sponsorship. *Sport Marketing Quarterly, 10* (4), 16–27.

Lough, N. (2005). Sponsorship and sales in the sport industry. In A. Gillentine & B. Crow (Eds.), *Foundations of sport management* (pp. 99–108). Morgantown, WV: Fitness Information Technology.

Lough, N. L. (1996). Factors affecting corporate sponsorship of women's sport. *Sport Marketing Quarterly, 5* (2), 11–18.

Milverstedt, F. (1989, March). Colleges courting corporate sponsors. *Athletic Business,* 25–26.

Mullin, B., Hardy, S. & Sutton, W. (2005). *Sport marketing* (2nd ed.) Champaign, IL: Human Kinetics.

Stotlar, D. K. (1993). *Successful sport marketing.* Dubuque, IA: Brown & Benchmark.

Wilkinson, D. C. (1988). *Event management and marketing institute.* Willowdale, ON: Sport Marketing Institute.

Chapter 10

Why Sponsorships?[*]

Tim Lynde

Reasons Why Companies Sign Sponsorship Deals

Most companies sign sponsorship deals to achieve specific business objectives. Sponsorships are too expensive, and corporations face much greater scrutiny in terms of financial accountability than in years past, not to have the investment tied to measurable business objectives.

That being said, below are some of the reasons that companies sign sponsorship deals:

• Companies like to sponsor their "hometown" teams or events (or feel an obligation to do so to be labeled as good corporate citizens).

  This can be witnessed by reviewing the sponsor line-up of the Atlanta Braves. The following Atlanta-based companies all sponsor the hometown team — Coca-Cola, The Home Depot, Georgia-Pacific and Delta.

• A top executive is a fan of a certain sport, team or athlete, and makes the decision for the company to sponsor.

  Many fans are extremely passionate about the teams, players and events they support. Fans come in all ages, backgrounds and income levels. When a fan is also an executive at a major corporation, he or she can have the influence to determine sponsorship decisions. Many sponsorship decisions are still made in this manner.

• The event or team is based in a market, state, region or country into which the sponsoring company is moving or expanding.

  Qwest Communications signed a naming rights deal for the Seattle Seahawks' new stadium, Qwest Field. At the time, Qwest was new to the Seattle-area and wanted consumers to have a top-of-mind awareness of the company (*Seattle Times*, 6/3/04).
  A slight twist to the example above would be a company signing a sponsorship in an area where they already have a small customer base that they want to grow. An example of this would be Tennessee-based First Horizon National Bank which signed on as a sponsor of the club area at Philips

---

[*] Reprinted with permission from *Sponsorships 101, An Insider's Guide to Sponsorships in Corporate America*. Lynde & Associates, Mableton, Georgia 2007.

Arena in Atlanta after Bank of America didn't renew its partnership. First Horizon was looking to expand in areas where they had a good collection of mortgage customers and Atlanta was one of those markets. Philips Arena was attractive to the bank due to its year-round events and also the demographics of the clientele attending the club area during events (*Atlanta Business Chronicle*, 11/17/06).

• The employees of the company are fans of the sport or team.

Several NASCAR sponsors have entered the sport because their employees and associates have requested it of upper management. For example, The Home Depot got involved in the sport of NASCAR because associates told Home Depot co-founders Bernie Marcus and Arthur Blank during store walks that they really wanted a Home Depot race team to generate a greater sense of pride and togetherness within the company.

• The sponsoring company uses tickets and hospitality to entertain key customers or employees.

At the 2006 Winter Olympic Games in Torino, Italy, first-time worldwide Olympic partner, General Electric, entertained 2,000 guests. For a company that focuses on business-to-business as much as business-to-consumer, this time together with their current and prospective clients was invaluable (*Around the Rings*, 2/16/06).

• The property's media is an effective way to reach the company's target audience.

Companies can purchase media for a sporting event without purchasing the marketing rights to become an official sponsor of the event. Properties are looking for an overall spend level from corporations. In some cases, a large media buy can lessen the dollars needed for the sponsorship rights fee. Either way, the purchase of media and sponsorship rights can be an effective way to reach the company's target audience.

• The company buys a sponsorship to keep its competition from purchasing it.

Although this would not be the recommended approach for determining which sponsorships a company should purchase, some companies do make defensive buys to keep their competition out. If the sponsor doesn't also have plans to leverage its investment to drive the company's business, this type of sponsorship could be a longterm mistake.

• The demographics of the company's customers match the avid supporters of the property.

In early 2006, Ford ended its PGA Tour and Senior Players Championships event title sponsorships to refocus on the brand's true identity—"strength and progress." As part of this effort, Ford became title sponsor of the Professional Bullrider Association's 30-city "Built Ford Tough" Series Tour. As Ford realized, golf may not have been the best fit for the company since its sales are dominated by its pick-up truck line (*Detroit Free Press*, 3/13/06).

• The sponsoring company would like to do business with current sponsors of the property.

> In addition to utilizing the assets of the property, some sponsors use the property to develop relationships and create business via other sponsors of the property. This could happen in many different categories, but especially in those that have products focused on businesses (office supplies, overnight delivery service, telecommunications, computers, CPG's, etc.). Realizing this could be a way to generate business for its many partners which could then help in future renewal discussions, NASCAR recently created the "NASCAR B-to-B Council" to help its official sponsors and partners identify business opportunities within the NASCAR sponsor family. (Business-to-business, or B-to-B, occurs when companies generate business from other corporations. Examples include companies using products such as gasoline, computer equipment, overnight delivery service, etc. in their normal course of business.) (IEG Sponsorship Report, 7/26/06).

• The sponsoring company would like to be considered in the same "class" as the property's
other sponsors.

> This usually happens when a new company or brand signs a sponsorship with a proven property that has a well-established sponsor family. In 2005, DHL launched its brand in the U.S., and one of its first steps was signing sponsorship deals with Major League Baseball and the United States Olympic Committee.

• The sponsor is expanding its reach to a new demographic and partners with a property that can deliver the desired target audience.

> All sponsorship decisions should be linked to a target audience. This is a little different in that the sponsor is hoping to raise credibility with a new target audience by using the property. As more and more American companies hope to capitalize on the increasing number of Hispanics in the U.S., properties that can deliver that audience (soccer, boxing, baseball, etc.) will be well positioned to capitalize on the growth.

• A company signs a sponsorship to more closely link its brand with a new fan base.

> Foreign-born players have become an increasingly larger part of the American sports scene, especially in the NBA and Major League Baseball. Japanese stars such as Hideki Matsui of the Yankees and Ichiro Suzuki of the Mariners have been very successful in attracting Japanese fans to those teams. This influx of new fans has created a market for companies interested in marketing to this nationality.
> The Boston Red Sox recently signed top Japanese pitchers Daisuke Matsuzaka and Hideki Okajima. Capitalizing on the interest many Japanese have for these players, the Red Sox entered into a partnership with Japan-based Funai Electric Company that includes several key sponsorship elements. Funai will receive a billboard behind the outfield wall at the Red Sox Spring Training facility as well as the tent in which the two pitchers will con-

duct interviews with the Japanese media. A backdrop bearing the Funai name will be used at all Red Sox games (home and away) during the 2007 MLB season (*Boston Herald*, 2/15/07).

• The company signs a sponsorship to provide differentiation and awareness for its brand.

Austrian energy drink maker, Red Bull, purchased naming rights to two soccer teams in the last two years. In 2005, it bought SV Austria Salzburg and changed the name to Red Bull Salzburg. Then, in 2006, Red Bull bought Major League Soccer's NY/NJ Metrostars and changed the name to the New York Red Bulls. It's no coincidence that Red Bull chose the largest city in the U.S. for the naming rights opportunity.

• A company signs a sponsorship deal with a property because the property will guarantee the company business in return.

The National Thoroughbred Racing Association (NTRA) is comprised of member race tracks and horse owners, all of whom are purchasers of specific products in their daily operations. The association has developed a "group purchasing program" in which its members have agreed to purchase sponsor products. In exchange for this guaranteed business, the sponsor must agree to a media and marketing spend with the property. Through this approach, the NTRA has attracted several high-profile brands including Dodge, UPS and John Deere.

Primary Objectives for Sponsorship Decisions

The above list could go on and on. However, when you look more closely, many of the points above can be grouped into a few primary reasons, or objectives, for the partnerships:

• Brand-building
• Driving the company's business
• Motivating and exciting the company's employees
• Supporting a hometown or regional property

Let's look at each one in a little more detail.

Brand-Building

At the most basic level, corporate America enters into sports sponsorships to tap into the passion that fans have for their favorite team, athlete, sport or event. The challenge is to utilize the brand equity of the property to achieve the company's business objectives.

One common business objective for companies involved in sponsorships is to enhance the sponsoring company's brand due to its affiliation with a well-known and respected property. The hope is that the positive feelings fans have for their favorite property will be transferred to the sponsoring brand. In these instances, a company sponsors a property that has a better developed, entirely different or similar image or brand.

For example, after the International Olympic Committee (IOC) awarded the 1996 Olympic Games to Atlanta, GA, the Atlanta Committee for the Olympic Games, led by Chief Executive Billy Payne, began its search for sponsors to help fund the tremendous expense of organizing and managing all aspects of the international sporting event. As the committee began its search, they came into contact with two primarily "Southern" companies who were considering expansion to other regions of the U.S. outside the Southeast. NationsBank (now Bank of America), based in Charlotte, NC, and The Home Depot, based in Atlanta, were two of the first $40 million sponsors of the Atlanta Olympic Games.

Both companies made deals for similar reasons. They were both in the midst of national expansions and wanted to enhance their profiles throughout the entire United States. What better way to do that than sponsor the U.S. Olympic Team and the 1996 Olympic Games? In addition, they also wanted to be held in the same regard as the other companies who were Olympic sponsors—Coca-Cola, IBM, Delta, McDonald's, etc. Being mentioned in the same breath as these blue-chip companies does wonders for an up-and-comer's image. Obviously, all of the growth and success that both companies have realized in the last decade isn't based on their sponsorships of the Atlanta Olympic Games, but the games undoubtedly impacted their growth.

When a corporation gets involved for brand reasons, this could take on several forms:

- Enhance C A company sponsors a property that has a well-developed image or brand. (examples above)
- Alter C A company with a certain image (not necessarily a negative one) partners with a property, or athlete, to appeal to a different consumer segment. One example of a company using sports and an athlete to alter the perception of its brand was General Motors' Buick brand signing an endorsement deal with PGA Tour professional Tiger Woods. Buick had traditionally targeted older men, and the company was interested in contemporizing its brand and making it more relevant with younger consumers. Tiger was in his mid-20s at the time and was already one of the most recognizable athletes in the world with a broad appeal to young consumers.
- Maintain C A company sponsors a property that would be considered an image and brand "peer." This usually happens when top-tier brands join together with top-tier properties (Anheuser-Busch and Major League Baseball, Visa and NFL, etc.). Companies such as Anheuser-Busch and Visa are leaders in their respective business categories and sponsorship deals with top properties help them maintain their leadership positions.

Driving the Company's Business

Another main reason that companies sign sponsorship deals is to utilize the relationship and the tangible assets received in the deal to drive the company's business. Depending on the business of the sponsor, this can take on many different forms. Let's explore a couple of ways below.

One way is to utilize the sponsorship assets, most notably the premier tickets that are received, to influence key customers. These tickets can be used as a prize for purchasing a product (spend $100 and you are entered to win Super Bowl tickets, etc.) or as a reward for business provided (take a key customer to the Super Bowl for business received to date or to influence future business). The first example is referred to as B-to-C (Business-to-Consumer) and the second example is known as B-to-B (Business-to-Business). In most cases, business generated via B-to-B is larger than business generated from individual consumers.

Another way to drive business is by partnering with a property that can utilize your company's products or services, or provide ways for your company to demonstrate products or services through the property. For example, an airline sponsor of a property should expect that all of the property's employees will use the airline when traveling for business. Also, the property should work within its sphere of influence to direct other business to the airline. The situation is the same for a credit card sponsor of the property. All of the property's employees should utilize the card when making business-related purchases. In addition, the property should direct all of its stakeholders (fans, teams, owners, etc.) to utilize the card as well.

One of the reasons cited earlier in this section for companies to get involved with sponsorships is that their consumers or associates are avid fans or supporters of the property. Because that passion exists, the assets gained in the sponsorship (use of logos, tickets, player appearances, etc.) can be used to influence customers or associates, which, in effect, will hopefully drive business.

Motivating and Exciting the Company's Employees

Another primary reason that companies sign sponsorship deals with properties is to utilize the assets from the deal to motivate or excite the company's employees. Similar to how assets are used to influence consumer behavior, the same holds true for company employees. Many companies create incentive programs to motivate their own associates. Sponsorships and their many assets can be used to add excitement to the programs. A program designed to improve customer service is more exciting if it is themed with NASCAR, NFL or another property's graphics and prizes.

Many sponsors keep their own employees at the top of the list when developing activation plans. Whether its providing special ticket purchase offers or even having the company's NASCAR driver or another athlete sign autographs at the company headquarters, there are many things that can be done to motivate or excite associates.

NASCAR is a great example of this. By purchasing a race team, a company gains tremendous advertising and awareness during the television broadcast of races, but it also provides the company and all its employees a "rallying cry" each race weekend from February to November. This gives the company a unifying bond and something for which they collectively cheer throughout the year.

One program that helps motivate and excite its employees is The Home Depot's Olympic Job Opportunities Program (OJOP), in conjunction with its U.S. Olympic Team sponsorship. This program provides Olympic hopefuls a part-time job with full-time pay and flexible work hours to allow for the necessary training and competition schedules. It's obviously a fantastic program for the athletes who are a part of it, but it also provides fellow co-workers the opportunity to work with, get to know and cheer for Olympic athletes as they pursue Olympic gold.

Supporting a Hometown or Regional Property

Most companies take tremendous pride in their hometowns and want consumers to recognize them as good corporate citizens. No major company wants their main competitors to sponsor a popular team or event in their hometown. Beer companies (Anheuser-Busch, Miller Brewing Company, Coors Brewing Company, etc.) are all very active in sports sponsorships. Imagine if you went to either a St. Louis Cardinals baseball game (in the hometown of Anheuser-Busch) and saw a huge Miller Lite sign in the outfield and could only purchase Miller products at concession stands, or, if you attended an event in Miller's hometown of Milwaukee, WI, and saw a Budweiser sign and could only purchase Budweiser products at Milwaukee Brewers baseball games. If you look closely at those specific markets, you'll see the hometown company not only sponsored the local MLB team, but also took a major leadership position via naming rights of the team's stadium (the Brewers stadium is named "Miller Park" and the Cardinals new stadium is called "Busch Stadium").

A company's support of local teams and events in its hometown should never be underestimated. There is a tremendous amount of pride, along with local pressure, at stake in those decisions.

Hopefully the rationales and specific examples of why companies get involved in sports sponsorships make some sense and you feel like you have a better grasp on why these decisions are made.

The purpose of this lesson was to provide a better understanding of why corporate America gets involved in sports sponsorships. You've learned that there are many different factors that can influence or determine what properties, if any, a company sponsors.

Key Takeaways

- Most companies sign sponsorship deals to achieve specific business objectives.
- Although there are many different reasons corporate America gets involved in sponsorships, most of them fall within one of the four reasons below:
    - Brand-building C Can involve enhancing, altering or maintaining the perception of a brand.
    - Driving the company's business C Typically refers to sales via consumers (B-to-C) or businesses (B-to-B).
    - Motivating and exciting the company's employees C Utilize the sponsorship assets to make employees feel better about their company and provide incentives for jobs well-done.
    - Supporting a hometown or regional property C Companies have pride in their hometowns and don't want their competitors to establish presences in "their" home markets.

Chapter 11

How to Choose a Sponsorship*

Tim Lynde

This chapter will focus on how to choose the best sponsorship for a particular company. There are two steps in this selection process:

- Internal—Understand the sponsoring company or brand
- External—Understand the sponsorship market and the options that exist

One of the biggest mistakes a sponsorship marketer can make is not taking sufficient time to learn the company's business. Until you have a solid understanding of the company, you won't be effective in identifying the right sponsorship for the company or activating a sponsorship to meet objectives and drive business. If done correctly, sponsorships should be used to address specific company needs or business objectives. Sponsorship activation involves utilizing the equity and assets from the property to drive the company's business. Unless you know the company's objectives, you're not using sponsorships for the right reasons.

There are many different ways in which a company can reach consumers, including those listed in the chart below. The list is not all-encompassing; it provides an idea of how companies target consumers. Utilizing the 360-Degree Marketing Approach, the goal is to surround consumers with key company messages in many different forms and mediums. It's important to note that sponsorship is just one element in a company's overall marketing mix. In most cases, none of the elements will work entirely on their own. Consumers are affected by and behave differently to various marketing tactics. It takes a well-rounded approach to successfully reach consumers.

Key Areas of the Company to Understand

Listed below are key areas about the company of which you'll need to have a sound understanding before you should ever pursue any sponsorships:

- Overall company objectives and marketing objectives
- Products and brands
- Seasonality
- Target audience
- Brand awareness

---

* Reprinted with permission from *Sponsorships 101, An Insider's Guide to Sponsorships in Corporate America*. Lynde & Associates, Mableton, Georgia 2007.

- Brand attributes
- Geography of business
- Employees and associates
- Key challenges
- Sponsorship history
- Executive interests
- Approval process

There are many things you should know within each of the categories above. This lesson will go through each in greater detail.

Before reading any further, select a company and attempt to answer each of the questions on the next few pages with your selected company in mind. Some questions you won't be able to answer, but thinking through each question will help you understand what is important to know.

Company: _____

Overall Company Objectives and Marketing Objectives

- What are the specific sales goals for your product(s)?
- Is the company looking to bolster its customer database? If so, how many names are you looking to add?
- What are the top three to five overall objectives for the company this year?
- What are the top three to five marketing objectives for the company this year?
- Is your company interested in increasing shelf space at your key retail accounts?
- Is your company interested in increasing the number of customer test drives?

Overall company objectives should drive sponsorship objectives. If these aren't aligned, a sponsorship's value to the company will most likely be questioned.

Product and Brand

- Does your company manufacture one product or many?
- If your company is a retailer, how many products/brands are sold in your stores?
- Are there new products/brands that will be introduced soon?

What products or brands will be aligned with the sponsorship? In some cases, there will be several products that can be used with the sponsorship. Beverage companies like Coca-Cola and Pepsi-Cola often negotiate exclusive sponsorship relationships that allow them to use any of their portfolio of brands in the sponsorship. Therefore, it's the responsibility of the sponsorship marketer to work with the appropriate brand teams and senior management to determine which brand(s) make the most sense for the property and the demographics the property delivers.

For years, brewing company Anheuser-Busch has aligned its Busch brand with NASCAR's second-tier racing series (Busch Series), while Budweiser (MLB) and Bud Light (NHL) have been targeted at other properties. Anheuser Busch's Michelob brand is positioned as more of a premium brand and, therefore, was positioned with the PGA Tour due to the higher demographics of the property. In 2005, Pepsi, for the first time used its NFL sponsorship to push its Diet Pepsi brand rather than the flagship Pepsi brand. Diet cola sales continue to increase among men, and Pepsi felt the sponsorship would be an avenue to further bolster that brand's image among the NFL's male-driven fan base.

If there's a constant in corporate America, it's that priorities often change without much notice. This was the case with Pepsi's NFL deal. The lead brand at the beginning of the sponsorship was Pepsi, but it later changed to Diet Pepsi. By negotiating the ability to use all of a company's many brands, sponsors will have the option to be flexible when business priorities change. In addition to current brands and products, it's also important that you know if any new products are in development by the company. It's much easier to negotiate prior to the deal being signed than it is to go back after the deal has been completed when the company's priorities or focus may have changed.

Seasonality

- When is the key season for your business?
- Is there a time of year when the majority of your sales are made?
- Is your business fairly consistent year-round?
- If you have a business with multiple brands, when are the top sales seasons for each?
- Is there a specific time of year when the company needs an increased focus on sales?

Let's look at these in a little more detail from the standpoints of three different types of business:

- Manufacturers—Is there a specific time of year during which you sell the most product? For example, a majority of isotonic beverages (Gatorade, PowerAde, etc.) are sold during the summer months when people tend to be more active. Therefore, the obvious objective for any of these companies would be to increase business during the key summer season. On the other hand, sales could be down significantly during the other times of year and the brand might be interested in adding increased focus during these times. As a sponsorship marketer, knowing the focus and priorities for each brand is essential.

- Retailers—As with manufacturers, most retailers have good sales numbers during the holiday gift-giving time of year. Retailers selling school items or kids clothes usually do well in the back-to-school timeframe in late summer. But are there other times of year when specific retailers need a sales boost? How do flower companies drive sales outside of the major holidays—Valentine's Day, Mother's Day, etc.?

- Service Providers—Gyms and health clubs usually experience a membership boost at the start of each year as the "New Year's resolutionists" and others attempt to get in better shape for the coming year. Are there other times of year when they should be pushing either new memberships or renewals? How about insurance companies, credit card companies, cable/satellite systems or banks? When are the best times of year for their business?

For each of the following companies, when do you think is the key sales season?

Campbell's Soup   _____
Dunkin' Donuts   _____
Papa John's   _____
John Deere   _____
Breyer's Ice Cream   _____
Miller Lite   _____
Nestle Hot Chocolate _____
Exxon Mobil   _____
Coppertone   _____

Target Audience

- Who is the company's primary consumer?
- Gender
- Age
- Ethnicity
- Education
- Income
- Geography
- Who is the company's secondary consumer?
- Gender
- Age
- Ethnicity
- Education
- Income
- Geography

It is essential to know who is buying a company's products, shopping at its stores, eating in its restaurants or using the company's services. Regardless of the company's line of business, one can never know enough about its customers. Research should be conducted to learn as much as possible about why the target audience selects your brand vs. the competition, or vice-versa. Most major U.S. corporations have extensive research and market intelligence groups that can provide this information about key customers as well as other pertinent information. Once a target market is known, it can now be matched with sponsorships and media that deliver that particular audience.

Brand Awareness

- What percentage of the population knows about your company/brand/ product?

- What percentage of your primary target group knows about your company/brand/product?

How aware of your company, product(s) or service(s) are consumers? Similar to target audiences, most companies conduct detailed consumer research to glean this information. A sponsorship decision and related assets in the sponsorship package could be very different for a company that is well-known versus one that is new to the marketplace.

If your company is hoping to improve its brand awareness, would you rather have a sign behind home plate or four season tickets? Why? For a product to sell, consumers must be aware that it exists. Many top companies have very high brand awareness scores (90% or more of the population are aware of them). Examples include such notables as Anheuser-Busch, The Coca-Cola Company, The Home Depot and Visa. While the parent company (such as those listed above) may have top awareness among consumers, some of the brands/products/services within the companies' portfolios do not have that same high level of awareness.

Newer brands such as Budweiser Select and Coca-Cola Zero need greater awareness to be successful. Sponsorship assets such as signage, sampling opportunities and media could be converted to these brands, if and only if, the demographic of the property's fans and attendees is the right fit for the brands. For example, with Coke's NCAA sponsorship, Coca-Cola Zero (a male-focused brand) could be featured within and around the Frozen Four (the college hockey championship which offers a male-dominated audience). Conversely, driving brand awareness for Coca-Cola Zero doesn't make as much sense around the Women's College World Series, which skews heavily female for both attendees and television viewers.

Brand Attributes

- What do people think of when they hear the name of your company or brand?
- When the name of a company or product is mentioned, what are the first words that come to mind?
- What images are conjured up?
- What are the key ideals of your company?

In most cases, the answers to these questions are known as brand attributes for that particular company or product. For example, when someone mentions the iPod you might hear some of the following terms—edgy, trendy, cool, high-tech, etc. These are brand attributes for the iPod. Similarly, when someone mentions the NBA, you might hear some of the following—hip-hop, urban, global, fast-paced, entertaining, etc. These are brand attributes for the NBA.

What are the first words that come to mind when you hear the following?

McDonald's

1. _____
2. _____
3. _____

Sony

1. _____
2. _____
3. _____

BMW

1. _____
2. _____
3. _____

It's important for a brand to have certain characteristics that are recognizable by consumers and help differentiate the brand from its competitors. If not, the brand is in danger of becoming a commodity. It's possible that consumers' perception of a brand is not consistent with what the company would like it to be. If that is the case, the company must either change the product itself or the marketing mix and advertising messages to transform consumers' image of the product or brand.

When selecting a sponsorship, it can be important to select a sponsor that has similar brand attributes to your company or brand. However, if you're interested in transforming the image of the brand, partnering with a property that has the image for which you're looking, rather than the current image of the brand, is a good first step in the transformation of the brand. The earlier example regarding Buick's partnership with Tiger Woods is a perfect example of a brand hoping to take on the attributes of a property, or in this case, an endorser.

Geography of Business

- Worldwide
- U.S.A. only
- U.S.A. — regional
- U.S.A. — single state
- U.S.A. — single market

Does your business cover the entire U.S. or just one region or city? Are your products sold internationally? In most cases, companies hope to continually expand the reach of their products or services. As part of that growth and expansion, marketing and advertising will accompany the product into new areas. Sponsorship could be part of that marketing mix to reach a certain demographic that is passionate about a sport, event, team or other property.

Employees and Associates

- How many employees and associates does your company have?
- Are all the employees based in the same building or are there several offices around the country or world?
- Do the employees have the same role (sales) or are there many different aspects and departments within the company?
- Generally speaking, are the employees content with their jobs or does a morale problem exist within the company?

Many companies get involved with sponsorships or utilize sponsorships to motivate and reward their employees. Depending on the importance of this to a company, it will need to know what interests the employees or associates of the company. If the interests lie within the sporting world, sponsorships can be an effective way to solve the problem.

Key Challenges

- What are some of the challenges facing the company?
- Does your company have image issues due to scandal or other negative press?
- Is the company having difficulty retaining employees?
- Are the company's sales down due to a changing marketplace?

Depending on a company's challenges, it's possible that sponsorships can be used to help solve the problems. Sponsorships can be used to help build and enhance a brand, drive sales and even motivate employees.

Sponsorship History

- Does your company currently have any sponsorships? If so, how were they chosen?
- Are the sponsorships being measured against a set of objectives? Are the objectives being met? Why or why not?
- If your company has sponsored a property in the past but has since dropped the sponsorship, why did that happen?

It's important to know what properties, if any, have been sponsored in the past, if they were successful and how people felt about them. Knowing this information will help you avoid mistakes made by the company in the past, as well as garner valuable information from successful sponsorship programs.

Executive Interests

- What are the interests of the Chief Executive Officer (CEO), Chief Marketing Officer (CMO) or other influential executives within the company?
- What are the interests of the Board of Directors?

Companies sometimes sponsor a property because an influential executive has a personal interest in that sport, team or event. Knowing this information can help steer your attention in the right direction. These situations can be very delicate and must be handled with care. If an executive is leaning in a direction you feel is wrong for the company, you will need to determine how comfortable you are voicing your alternate opinion. Depending on the personalities involved, such a move could be harmful to your career at that particular company, or the person may respect your willingness to speak up.

Approval Process (Internal)

- Who will ultimately approve any new sponsorship(s) within your company? Does one person make the decision or is it a group decision?
- If it's made by one person, what are his or her "hot buttons" or interests?
- How long does the process typically take?

Depending on the company, obtaining full approval on a complex sponsorship can take a great deal of time, especially if a large number of people need to weigh-in on the decision. If it's not obvious who must approve the new deal, do yourself a favor and figure it out early in the process.

Select any company you like and complete the "Business Snapshot" below. Feel free to use the internet, textbooks, annual reports or any other means to find the information.

Company:
Key brand(s) and Product(s):
Key Sales Season(s) for the brand(s):
Target Audience(s):
Brand Awareness Level:
Number of Employees:
Location:
Top Retail Accounts (if applicable):
Strategic Priorities and Objectives:

The goal of this section was to show you there is much to learn about a company BEFORE you can begin to make smart, informed decisions regarding sponsorships and marketing activation plans. You may be accustomed to reading books or manuals that provide answers rather than merely asking questions similar to those provided in this section. It was done this way for a reason. You need to be well-versed in asking the types of questions necessary to understand a company or business. Once you are able to do that, then you can begin to determine which sponsorship(s) might make sense for the company. It's essential that the importance of this step isn't underestimated. If it is, you won't know pertinent information about the sponsoring company and your chances for sponsorship success are greatly diminished.

Keys to Remember

1. One of the biggest mistakes a sponsorship marketer can make is not taking sufficient time to learn the company's business. Until you have a solid understanding of your company's business, including key products and services, there is no way you can effectively market them utilizing sponsorship relationships as the conduit.

2. Sponsorship is one element within a company's total scope of marketing activity.

3. Sponsorships must align with the company's overall marketing goals. In many cases, sponsorships are tactics for a much broader objective (drive sales, increase brand awareness, etc.).

4. The following key areas about a company or brand should be fully understood prior to a review of sponsorship opportunities:

- Overall company objectives and marketing objectives
- Product(s) and brand(s)
- Seasonality
- Target audience(s)
- Brand awareness

- Brand attributes
- Geography of business
- Employees and Associates
- Key challenges
- Sponsorship history
- Executive interests
- Approval process

Chapter 12

Athletic Fund-Raising

Charlie Patterson

The extraction of money from individual, corporate and foundation pockets for any cause is an art as well as a science. It requires diplomacy as well as logistics, tactics as well as strategy, pressure as well as persuasion, organization as well as planning, knowledge as well as determination.

—Unknown

Background

Charitable giving has been uniquely American since the very beginning of our country. As a matter of fact, America's first known fund-raiser was Benjamin Franklin, who spent a great deal of his time convincing friends and colleagues to give generously to causes not supported by the new government. Educational institutions were first allowed to receive federal tax-deductible contributions in 1917.

World War II

While alumni associations were started in the late 19th and early 20th centuries with dues, fund-raising as a science really hit its stride during and after World War II, as Americans gave generously to causes affected both directly and indirectly by the war. Those causes included War Bonds, United Ways, YMCAs, YWCAs, colleges and universities, churches, the American Red Cross, Boys and Girls Clubs, and many other organizations seeking private gift support. Those nonprofits sought support in a systematic and organized way during the 1940s and into the 1950s.

To get a better feel for the history of fund-raising and some of the basic principles which are still valid today, one should read what is considered to be the bible of fund-raising books, *Designs for Fundraising*, by Harold J. Seymour, published by McGraw-Hill in 1966. Almost half a century later, most of the thoughts and ideas expressed by Seymour in his book are still used today in successful fund-raising activities, including athletics.

There were athletic fund-raising efforts prior to WWII, but those efforts did not really begin to flourish until after the war. They were more common in Big Ten schools, the Ivy League, and in the South. Clemson's program was the granddaddy of them all, established in 1934 and named IPTAY, with its letters standing for "I PAY TEN A YEAR." The booster club was started with 1,000 donors giving $10 each to provide $10,000 to support the Clemson athletic program. In 2007, total gift support to IPTAY was over $15 million.

1950s–1970s

College and university fund-raising became much more significant during the 1950s and the 1970s with the development of alumni associations and capital campaigns to build facilities and with the growth of endowment programs through bequest giving. The Council for Advancement and Support of Education (CASE) was founded as a result of a 1974 merger between the American Alumni Council (founded in 1913) and the American College Public Relations Association (founded in 1917). As those programs developed, so, too, did athletic fund-raising through the booster club programs and many other forms of athletic "revenue production."

During this period of time, athletic fund-raising was considered to be anything that produced revenue, whether an alumnus or alumna made a gift or bought football season tickets or paid for advertising. Just as today, the rising cost of athletics in schools and colleges meant finding revenue from any source possible. Usually, the administration of the school or college prohibited the various departments, including athletics, from soliciting alumni or alumnae who were being courted and solicited for general support of the school or college. Therefore, athletic directors became extremely creative in finding ways to "produce revenue."

1980s–Today

Not until the early 1980s did schools and colleges become more sophisticated in athletic fund-raising (the art of seeking private gift support), and to some degree, that sophistication was brought on by the Internal Revenue Service and its efforts to clearly identify the difference between a charitable gift to a nonprofit cause versus a payment to receive something in return, i.e., game tickets and advertising.

At this point, the booster clubs were becoming much more sophisticated in annual gift solicitations and were beginning to attract professional development officers, just as had been the case in the schools and colleges through alumni/alumnae relations, capital campaigns, and so forth.

In 1993, the National Association of Athletic Development Directors (NAADD) was established and soon thereafter formed a partnership with the National Association of Collegiate Directors of Athletics (NACDA). The two groups hold their annual workshop and convention in conjunction with each other.

Today, many institutions with large athletic development fund-raising staffs mirror the advancement (development) staffs of the schools and colleges themselves. As a result, many opportunities exist for cooperation between athletics and the general administration of the institutions.

Basic Principles

The Three-Legged Stool Concept

A good fund-raising program can be illustrated by a three-legged stool, with each of the legs important in order for the stool (or the athletic fund-raising program) to stand firmly in place.

Leg one is Annual Gift support.

This leg represents gifts made on an annual basis to support the ongoing athletic program. Usually these gifts are in the form of various cash amounts, with gift clubs representing different levels of giving. For example, at Wake Forest University, the Deacon Club, which supports annual scholarships for student athletes, has several thousand members, each giving from $125 a year to $50,000 a year. There are nine levels of membership in the Deacon Club, with each receiving different degrees of benefits and privileges, which are valued and must be subtracted from the amount of the gift for charitable-gift income-tax deduction purposes.

Similar programs exist in most schools, colleges, and universities across the country, with various levels of giving and benefits for the donor.

Obviously, in the 21st Century, Clemson's IPTAY is no longer $10 a year as it was when it was first started in 1934.

So one leg of the three-legged stool is the annual fund to provide funding for scholarships and the general operations of the athletic program.

Leg two is Capital Campaign support.

Unlike the annual fund program, capital campaigns occur at various times in the life of a school or college and are an addition to the annual fund. Donors are asked to contribute to the institution in order to build facilities and to provide special programming needs over and above the general operating budget of the athletic department. Capital campaigns usually seek three-to-five year pledges from donors. Athletic capital campaigns today are conducted like school and college capital campaigns, and in many instances, they are even a part of the general school, college, or university capital campaign. Donors are asked to make capital gifts other than cash gifts (as they usually do with their annual support); thus many campaign gifts are made in the form of appreciated stock, real estate, and so forth. There can be many tax advantages to a donor who makes a capital gift. Once again, the Internal Revenue Service watches such giving very closely because of the perks and benefits available through athletic programs; usually a portion of the gift must be deducted from the total gift for income-tax deduction purposes.

Leg three is Planned Giving support.

Planned gifts include gifts made through wills, life insurance, trusts, and other life-income gift arrangements, and they are generally considered a more complicated type of gift than the gift one gives to the annual fund by simply writing a check or using a credit card. Often, planned gifts involve a donor's attorney, trust officer, or other financial advisor. In most cases, planned gifts consist of those that will come to the school or college at some future date rather than immediately.

How planned gifts are counted at institutions varies a great deal, like the benefits and perks that might be made available to the donor through the athletic department.

The athletic program of a school or college should sit firmly on the seat of the three-legged stool. If one leg of the stool is not set firmly "on the floor," the athletic fund-raising program is obviously not in place.

And just what is this small three-legged stool known as? For those who have been involved in farm work, it was simply called the "milking stool"—a term very appropriate to athletic fund-raising.

The Five "*I's*" of the Fund-Raising Process

Through the years, over and over again, using the five *Is* has been the soundest process for all fund-raising activities, whether for athletics, schools, colleges, universities, or other nonprofits. Using the five *Is* is indeed the most effective way to have a successful fund-raising program.

1. Identification

Identifying who prospective donors are, knowing something about them, and establishing reasons why they should be supporting a particular program are clearly a first step. Those who are identified are usually alumni/alumnae of the institution, both past and present parents of students, former athletes, community leaders, corporations, foundations, and so forth.

2. Information

Once the prospective donors have been identified, they are provided *information* about a particular cause. That information may come via direct mailing explaining the school's or college's needs at a special event and letting prospective donors know of needs for student athlete scholarships or for operating budgets for travel, meals, equipment, facility maintenance—or maybe for new facilities, endowments, and so forth.

In essence, prospective donors are provided information through the presentation of the case for support of the particular cause—a presentation which should be clear, concise, and compelling. The case for support should be as expansive and as important as possible. For example, the case should be made not only for the need of a student athlete for a scholarship to play a sport for an institution but also for the importance of a student athlete's education and of the influence that he or she can have after graduation, whether it is obtaining a job or continuing to play a sport professionally and influencing young people. Once the information has been presented, prospective donors, hopefully, will become more aware and concerned about a program—an awareness and a concern which leads to the third *I*.

3. Interest

After their interest has been obtained, prospective donors will want to know more about a program. They will actively pursue more information and will naturally evolve to the fourth *I*.

4. Involvement

Prospective donors can become involved in a fund-raising program in a number of ways, such as volunteers or as participants who come to games and special events, thus becoming closer to an athletic program and understanding its needs as well as its impact not only on the young people involved in the program but also on those who enjoy athletics.

5. Investment

The fifth *I* in the fund-raising process is investment. Once the prospective donors have been identified and have been informed of the successes, plans, and needs, and once their interest has been obtained and they have become involved in the program, then their investment and their willingness to make a gift to help with the program activities will follow.

All too often, athletic fund-raising programs go from the first *I* of identifying a prospect to the fifth *I* of asking for the gift without going through the three middle *I*'s, which are the most important aspects of the best athletic fund-raising program.

And once a donor makes a gift, the five-*I* process starts all over, thus leading to larger annual and capital campaign gifts — and perhaps an ultimate planned gift.

Those involved in athletic fund-raising have a wonderful opportunity to inform and to obtain the interest and the involvement of prospective donors because of the unique aspects of athletics in special events and in games played year round.

Methods of Solicitation

1. Direct Mail (Hard or Electronic)

Direct mail is obviously directed toward the masses of people and the large numbers of prospective donors who may be on a school's list of prospects. It is clearly the least expensive way to solicit gifts. Today, more and more nonprofits are using the electronic method of gift solicitation over the traditional postal direct mail method. Direct mail is the most impersonal method of solicitation and also the least effective, but it certainly gives an athletic program the opportunity to reach large numbers of prospective donors.

2. Telephone

"Phonathons" are gatherings or events where volunteers, such as alumni/alumnae, students, and student athletes, telephone former athletes, alumni, parents, and current and past or prospective donors to the athletic program. A phone solicitation can occur as a special event with a group of callers in the same room creating excitement in an atmosphere that can be heard over the phone — with a goal for a night, bell ringing and generally having a good time. A "phonathon" clearly a way to get alumni, student athletes, and other volunteers involved in the fund-raising activities. Phone solicitations are more costly than direct mail but are a bit more personal because there is at least a voice conversation with the prospective donor.

3. Person-to-Person

The third method is person-to-person, face-to-face. Obviously, this reaches a smaller number of people than either direct mail or telephone, but it does give a solicitor a chance to explain the needs of a program in a personal way and has the greatest amount of return as far as gifts are concerned. Larger gifts certainly need to be solicited in a more personal manner than through direct mail or telephone. Personal solicitation of major gift prospects should be conducted by the athletic director, coaches, and sometimes even the president or head of the school and a key volunteer, such as a member of the board of directors or a trustee.

When asking a prospective donor for a gift, basically the three methods above are the main vehicles for solicitation.

People Giving to People and Relationship Giving

Veteran fund-raisers constantly talk about relationships and the importance to a successful program of building a relationship with a prospective major gift donor. People do, indeed, give to people. Much of the success of a fund-raiser has to do with who actually makes the request or who has gotten a prospective donor involved in a program and what the prospects' relationships are with the fund-raising staff, the coaching staff, and the athletic department staff. Positive relationships are probably the most important aspect of athletic fundraising.

Also, it is important to note that over the course of many years, anywhere from 83% to 90% of all gift dollars given to nonprofit causes in the United States have not come from expertly managed corporations or foundations required to give a certain percentage of their assets away each year, but from individuals.

According to the 2007 issue of *Giving USA*, the 52nd Annual Report on Philanthropy, over $295 billion was given to nonprofit causes in America in the 2006 calendar year. Of that amount, almost 84% came from individuals, either through outright gifts or bequests (planned gifts.) So where should athletic fund-raising for the pure gift dollars concentrate its efforts? Clearly on individual donors.

Also, according to the same issue of *Giving USA*, 13.9%, or $41 billion, of all charitable giving in America in 2006 went to educational institutions — an amount which has increased 5.9% per year over the past ten years. Clearly, a significant amount of that $41 billion went to athletic programs.

Volunteers

Use of volunteers in athletic fund-raising is extremely important for a number of reasons. Volunteers are the essence of the fourth *I*, Involvement, and through their involvement, volunteers become some of the most significant donors (investors) to programs. In addition, volunteers augment the limited number of staff that a school or college might have, and they extend the athletic department contacts to potential donors who are involved with athletic activities. Volunteers should be treated with tender loving care and nurtured in a very special way.

At the same time, educating volunteers on what they can and cannot do is extremely important because the more zealous volunteers should not become so active in a program that they accidentally, or even purposely, violate NCAA rules. While volunteerism is important for success, it needs to be treated with a great deal of integrity. Institutional control of all aspects of an athletic program — fund-raising included — must be maintained.

Donor Recognition

Major gift donors should have the honor to name buildings, other athletic facilities, rooms, programs, endowment funds, and even lockers. Donor recognition is one of the most important elements in a successful fund-raising program. As the saying goes, "A plaque, plaque here, a plaque, plaque there, everywhere a plaque, plaque." Also, it is important to recognize donors through gift announcements and annual publication of an honor roll of donors.

While most people will say they have no desire to have their name highlighted and recognized, there is still that human need for recognition and for being a part of something successful. A good fund-raising program should have outlined and approved by boards the dollar value for major gifts in order to name various facilities and endowments.

Just what is a major gift? The amount will vary from institution to institution. At one school, a major gift may be $1,000, and at another, it may be $25,000, and at still another, it may be $50,000. Each institution determines its major gift amount on the basis of its past and future private gift support and needs.

Professional sports, and even college and universities, have reached the point of "selling" the naming rights of facilities for a short period of time. For example, the CP3 Corporation Football Stadium may be "sold" by a team or a school. That type of naming right is not considered a charitable gift but an advertising expense of a corporation and usually lasts for a specified period of time, after which the professional sports team or school might change the name of the stadium. But when someone makes a charitable gift for naming rights, usually the name lasts for the life of the facility or the endowment fund or the program that is established with the name.

Again, one should remember that there are different forms of athletic "revenue." Some are gifts and some are business deals, and the two should not be confused.

Professional Consulting

Professional consultants can be of great help to an athletic fund-raising program, just as consultants have been extremely helpful to major college and university programs and other nonprofit fund-raising programs through the years.

1. Internal Audit

An *internal audit* is an unbiased study to determine whether or not a program has the qualified professional staff as well as the number of staff in order to have a successful fund-raising program. In addition, the professional consultant evaluates budget, donor lists, goals, and so forth. The audit will confirm if a school or college is prepared to move the athletic fund-raising program to the next level. An internal audit is almost essential before launching any kind of a major fund-raising activity.

2. Feasibility Study

This study goes far beyond the internal aspect of preparation for a fund-raising activity and includes interviews with current and prospective donors, past and present key leaders, and current and prospective volunteers.

The feasibility study will determine if goals and objectives are realistic and marketable and if the case for support is compelling. Are the prospective donors ready for a major gift campaign? Is the athletic development staff ready for a major gift campaign? Are there enough capable volunteers necessary to conduct a successful campaign effort?

The study can help determine realistic goals and objectives as well as requirements necessary to meet those goals. A feasibility study is the first, and perhaps most important, step in a successful capital campaign. No capital campaign should be started without an unbiased, totally independent feasibility study.

3. Ongoing Consulting

Usually this area of professional consulting is performed during a visit to the athletic development office one or two days a month to discuss the progress of the fund-raising program, or perhaps to change direction in some areas, and to generally evaluate efforts and provide the athletic development office with an ongoing road map for the annual fund, a capital campaign, or a planned giving program. Some institutions describe ongoing consulting as having the fund-raising "personal trainer work out" with the development program on a regular basis.

In all three of these consulting areas, costs will vary but the cost is money well spent to make absolutely certain that the athletic development office is preparing and following a game plan and, in a sense, making sure there is a coach making the development team stick to the things that need to be done in order to win the fund-raising game.

Planning

One should never start any fund-raising activity without substantial planning. That planning process can include an evaluation of gift potential and an evaluation of volunteers, budgets for printing, travel, technology needs, and so forth for the various activities needed for a successful program—direct mail, marketing, staff size, training of staff, and all the different ingredients that go into putting together an effective fund-raising program for an athletic department.

Marketing versus Development (Fund-Raising)

As mentioned earlier, both marketing and fund-raising are revenue producers, and both are very important to successful athletic programs. The difference between marketing and development is income (revenue) versus private gift support.

Usually marketing income includes ticket sales, sponsorships, advertising, concessions, and merchandising. All of the above, indeed, provide income for operating an effective athletic program, but they should never be confused with the fund-raising activities involving gifts. Gifts are clearly defined by the Internal Revenue Service, and donors who make gifts to athletic fund-raising should not be guaranteed benefits from their gifts.

A gift to an athletic program is, indeed, a gift with no strings attached and thus qualifies the donor for an income tax charitable-contribution deduction. The tax laws are quite clear on this matter. Every athletic program should do everything in its power to try to keep gift support totally separate from the marketing income.

For many years athletics depended on many of these income-producing activities to support their programs; therefore there has been some confusion between marketing (income) and the fund-raising gift support for athletic programs. The Internal Revenue Service is a constant watchdog over the differences between income and gift support for athletic programs, and therefore the warning must be presented to all programs to clearly define the differences between income and gift support.

Uniquely Athletic

One should remember the five *I*s and the three middle *I*s that are so important to a successful athletic fund-raising program. Those three *I*s, Information, Interest, and Involvement, are critical to success. Athletics has a unique opportunity involving those three *I*s of the development process.

1. Game Tickets

Game tickets have value, whether for a championship or a regular season game. Tickets to athletic events are in great demand and thus athletic departments have the use of tickets in cultivating and building relationships with donors and potential donors.

2. Seat Location

While tickets are extremely important to athletic donors, the location of those seats is even more important. Thus, athletics has the opportunity to make sure that top donors have the best seats for athletic events and the opportunity to invite special donors and prospective donors as guests of the athletic department in special seat locations.

Many institutions have begun to use what is called a "point system," which ranks donors on the basis of points awarded to their various giving levels to annual funds, to capital campaigns, and to bequests and future planned gifts. In addition, number of years or consecutive years of giving can earn points. Points are then totaled, and donors receive the right to "buy" a certain number of game tickets, seat locations, and other perks on the basis of their points, which also are used to rank the donors in their booster club programs.

3. Travel

Athletic teams travel all over the country for games; therefore, donors and potential donors have the opportunity to travel, either in a group such as a booster club or, in some cases, with the team to games that might occur in exciting locations around the country or even around the world.

4. Hero Association

Athletes themselves are considered heroes in our society, as are coaches of various teams, and it is rewarding to major gift donors and potential donors to have the opportunity to get to know the coaches and the athletes. In this regard, each institution must be very careful in making certain that it does not violate NCAA rules.

5. Special Events

The games themselves provide special-event opportunities for pregame or postgame meals and activities or for monthly booster club luncheons, at which time a coach or student athlete has the opportunity to speak to the donors and potential donors so that they might learn more about the athletic program.

6. Exposure

Visibility at games and other special events related to athletic programs is very important to the ego of individuals, and the exposure companies receive by being involved in athletic programs is considered "good business."

7. Postseason Tournaments/Bowls

All the various activities in postseason tournaments/bowls are unique opportunities for athletic departments to cultivate, thank, and involve donors and potential donors.

8. Entertainment

All of the above provides donors with great entertainment opportunities — not only for themselves but also for their families, friends, clients, and their business prospects.

Future

The future of athletic fund-raising is indeed bright as school and college athletic programs have built in all the positive and exciting ingredients of the three middle *I*s of a successful fund-raising process. Continued professional development and growth, along with the entertainment aspect of sports, will make athletic fund-raising an appealing and attractive career objective for future generations to pursue.

And competition from existing and new nonprofits for the private "gift" dollar will grow, and more and more educated, trained, and experienced professionals will be needed for programs to succeed in the years ahead.

As Aristotle put it:

To give away money is an easy matter and in every man's power ... but to decide to whom to give it, and how much, and when, and for what purpose and how, is neither an easy matter nor in every man's power. Hence it is that such excellence is rare, praiseworthy and noble.

The best athletic fund-raising programs today and in the future must be established to seek the "rare, praiseworthy and noble."

Chapter 13

Funding of Interscholastic Sports

Tom Appenzeller

Interscholastic sports have a long history and have been a vital element of the comprehensive public high school model that developed in the 1920s. The Public School Athletic League relied an outside funding, and that reliance has continued over the years. Football in Ohio, Pennsylvania, and Texas, and basketball in Indiana and Kentucky are examples of how a particular sport has served to bind a local community. Two movies, *Friday Night Lights*, about a Texas football team, and *Hoosiers*, a story about life and basketball in rural Indiana, serve to demonstrate the importance of high school sports in some communities. Massillon, Ohio, a depressed steel mill town of 30,000 citizens, is a football town. Massillon's Washington High School has a football booster club of 2,700 members, a lighted, 20,000-seat stadium, a 109-page *Official Football Media Guide*, and it employs a statistician, a trainer, a football information director, a head coach, and 10 assistant coaches (Rader, 2004).

Today, however, many school districts all across the country are struggling to fund extracurricular activities, especially sport. There are a number of reasons why school boards and superintendents find themselves in such a financial crunch. Until the 1970s, high school sport was still the holy trinity of football, basketball, and baseball, with an occasional track team, wrestling team, tennis team, or golf team thrown in for young men. In 1972, the United States Congress passed federal legislation, called Title IX, which mandated the addition of team sports for women in institutions receiving federal funds. Title IX created a need for more interscholastic teams, coaches, uniforms, officials, facilities, equipment, and travel budgets, without providing additional funds. By the mid 1980s, not only were school districts expected to provide sport opportunities for females but the male Echo Boomers (children of the Baby Boomers) began to expect and demand more diverse sport opportunities. Schools began to add sports such as soccer, swimming, cross country, and lacrosse to the traditional sports in order to meet the demands of a new student population. High schools have gone from offering four or five athletic teams until it is not uncommon today for a school to offer over 30 interscholastic squads. These nonrevenue, or Olympic, sports for men and women have created a financial drain on high school athletic departments. As a result, all across America, school boards, administrators, and parents are struggling to save and to fund high school sports. Never before have so many students competed in so many sports, but these sports cost money.

There are three ways to save high school sports: raise taxes, charge user fees, and utilize booster clubs and fund-raising. The first option is not very popular, since the average citizen believes that he or she is already overtaxed. Increasing taxes, even for the basic necessities of education, has become a difficult sell in communities all over America. It is hard to raise taxes today for buildings and books, much less sports, which are considered a luxury and not a necessity. Politicians understand that the quickest way to be thrown out of office is to raise taxes. In Oregon's ranch country, two facts have remained constant over the years in local communities: there is a love of high school football and a disdain for new taxes (Silverman, 2003). According to Silverman, Associated Press writer, some people see taxes as the only way to save extracurricular activities, while opponents believe that any new taxes should help fund academics, not athletics (Silverman, 2003). New taxes, or raising taxes, in today's climate will probably not happen, so let us examine some other alternatives.

One alternative to funding interscholastic sport is to charge students who want to play a fee to cover the expense. A pay-to-play plan has been implemented in school districts all across the country. In Massachusetts, school districts have begun charging fees for all extracurricular activities — and even for riding the bus. For students who do not ride the bus and drive to school, there is a parking fee. According to an article in the *Patriot Ledger*, Bob Jones of Canton paid $120.00 so that his daughter could ride the bus, but when the fee reached $180.00, he asked her to walk to school. Braintree approved a $280.00 fee for busing, sports, and clubs, while Randolph High students pay $300.00 to play sports (Gerdeman, 2004). In Howell, Massachusetts, Superintendent of Schools David Hawkins has proposed a plan to save sports, but to do so would require participants to pay $360.00 per sport (Holland, 2004). At Oakmont Regional High School in Ashburnham, Massachusetts, pay-to-play fees were $800.00 for football and $500.00 for track. In 2002, the local voters turned down an increase in property taxes that could have reduced the need for extracurricular fees. According to local officials, sport participation has dropped 35% since the district started charging fees (Staples, 2003). Students at Pasco High School in Tampa, Florida, pay $60.00 to play football and $50.00 to play basketball and other sports such as track (Staples, 2003). Fieldcrest High in Minonk, Illinois, charges its student athletes $150.00 per sport, and there is a $200.00 activity fee for all students (Dennis, 2004). In Arkansas, according to Melissa Nelson of the Associated Press, "some wonder if fielding football teams at Arkansas' smaller schools makes much sense when the state is struggling to find money to strengthen a public school system that the State Supreme Court has declared unconstitutionally deficient." Mike Huckabee, the governor of Arkansas in 2003, accused local communities of being more interested in sport than education (Nelson, 2003).

The concern with pay-to-play funding is that students from lower socioeconomic levels will be eliminated from extracurricular activities. Pay-to-play funding impacts the student populations that can least afford the fees and that, without sports, are at risk of dropping out of the educational process. Right or wrong, sports keep children in school, and even Dr. Phil admitted on one of his audio tapes that the only reason he finished high school was to play sports. Administrators worry that more affluent communities will continue to have good programs and that the less affluent communities will suffer a competitive disadvantage. The playing field will tilt to the rich.

The alternative to student fees for extracurricular activities is to simply eliminate some sports. In Milwaukee, Wisconsin, boy's and girl's cross country, boy's and girl's tennis, boy's golf, and freshman basketball are at risk of being eliminated (Roquemore, 2004). Under one proposal, certain sports that would be eliminated from the high schools would be shifted to the Milwaukee Recreations Department, according to Superintendent William Andrekopoulos (Roquemore, 2004).

School districts all across America have already eliminated middle school, freshman, and junior varsity teams. The cost of the federal mandate, "No Child Left Behind," has driven some districts to cut sports and other extracurricular activities. In 2004, Winthrop School System, north of Boston, eliminated all school sports and cut 17 teaching positions after the town rejected a 4-million-dollar tax increase (Gerdemon, 2004). At West Contra Costa Schools in California, sports were saved in 2004 by the passage of a parcel tax and by private donations (DeFao, 2004). The additional funds prevented the school district from becoming the first in the state to eliminate high school athletics (DeFao, 2004). Even though sports were saved for the time being, the funding was half of what it had been in 2002 (DeFao, 2004).

Reduce funding, pay to play, or eliminate teams—administrators are scrambling nationwide to find the money to save interscholastic sports.

Booster Clubs

One way that school sports teams have been saved has been through the efforts of booster clubs. Booster clubs are voluntary organizations usually made up of parents and alumni/alumnae who raise money to support various extracurricular activities. Luther Gulick used prominent businessmen to fund and support the New York City Public School Athletic League, and that tradition continues today in 2008. Not all booster clubs are equal: some have better leadership than others, while some have a tradition of support that goes back decades. At Grimsley High School in Greensboro, North Carolina, the Athletic Booster Club helps fund 36 teams on the varsity and junior varsity level. The club raises money through annual projects such as a golf tournament, membership dues, sale of clothing, program ads, concession stands, raffles, and special events (Brown, 2003). Grimsley High School is over 100 years old and has a very large and loyal alumni/alumnae base to draw upon. The money raised by the booster club is earmarked for the maintenance of the athletic fields, for renting buses for travel, and for purchasing equipment not budgeted by the school (Brown, 2003). The Aiken All-Sports Booster Club in Aiken, South Carolina, raises about $60,000.00 a year, and according to Mark Crawford, "if it was not for the booster club we could not have half the sports we have" (Ethridge, 2004). In Birmingham, Alabama, the Hoover High School Booster Club raises over $300,000.00 every year for the athletic program (Kraft, 2005). Booster clubs all across America hold raffles, auctions, celebrity nights, bake sales, car washes, and dinners, and operate concession stands, sell season tickets, offer preferred parking, host golf tournaments, sell advertisements, solicit sponsors, and perform various other activities.

However, there are several issues when using booster clubs to financially support extracurricular activities, especially sports. Some booster clubs, or members of booster clubs, believe that financial contributions mean control of the hiring and firing of school employees. Financial support creates an expectation that influence will follow the money, and some clubs use their contributions to push their own personal agendas. In September 2004, the booster club's president and a few key members went to the principal of West Montgomery High School in rural Troy, North Carolina, and demanded that the head football coach be replaced four games into the season (Houston, 2004). The principal gave in to the demands of the booster club, and the first football coach fired in 2004 was not Ron Zook or Ty Willingham but a double A coach in rural North Carolina.

Another issue with booster clubs is financial accountability. Every year we read accounts of booster clubs where funds have come up missing. Booster clubs at Hillside High School in Durham, North Carolina, at George Jenkins High School in Lakeland, Florida, and at Polama Valley High School in California have all been audited recently and have been found to have irregularities in their bookkeeping. The audit of the Hillside Booster Club found that the club checking account was used to buy beer, cigarettes, and blue jeans and that concession revenue might be missing (Petrocelli, 2003). Whenever money is coming into any organization, particularly one with volunteers who change over time, issues of financial management will arise. Financial control of the funds moving in and going out can create a headache for administrators who are responsible for but who have limited control over the volunteer organizations.

Another concern with relying on booster clubs to fund extracurricular activities is that the rich get richer. Not all booster clubs are equal, and schools with wealthy clubs have definite advantages over schools from poor areas. Coaches always talk about playing on a level field, yet wealthy booster clubs create an unfair advantage. The wealthy clubs are able to entice more qualified coaches to the school, to send more athletes to camps, or to purchase better uniforms and equipment. If the booster club happens to have an extremely rich benefactor, the competitive balance may be altered even more.

The last issue with booster clubs and financial support is a legal one called Title IX. How does Title IX apply to booster club spending? At Douglas County High School in Colorado, when the football team needed new helmets and new uniforms, the Quarterback Club was there to fund the purchase of helmets (Sanchez, 2003). The 30-member Quarterback Club raises up to $65,000.00 a year, but recently it has been told by school officials to back off. Superintendent Jim Christenson is worried that female sports teams will not be able to match their male counterparts, thus creating an issue of gender equity (Sanchez, 2003). The superintendent's concern is also related to a Title IX lawsuit from another district in Colorado. Tony Bruno, softball coach at Northglenn High School in Adams 12 School District, filed a suit against the United States Department of Education, Office of Civil Rights. Bruno claimed in his suit that the school's booster club favored the men's teams. One of the issues was money given to light the baseball field. According to federal law, booster money is equivalent to regular taxpayer dollars and therefore should support male and female teams equally (Sanchez, 2003). School districts in New Mexico and Washington have lost Title IX suits involving booster clubs, and according to Deborah Blake, associate professor at the University of Pittsburgh School of Law, "if boosters are putting tons of money into men's sports, then they are putting the district in jeopardy" (Sanchez, 2003). Recently, the United States Supreme Court, in a 5–4 decision, came down on the side of a fired coach who had filed a Title IX suit against his school. The case involved Roderick Jackson, who claimed he had been removed from coaching after having complained that his girl's team was not receiving equal funding and equal access to facilities and equipment (Richey, 2004). Booster clubs can be good or a necessary evil, but they are not the best method of funding high school sports.

Personal Experience in Fund-Raising: Pitfalls and Profits

There are two rules to remember about coaching and working on the middle school, high school, junior college, and small college level. The first rule is that there is never enough money to go around, and when the budgets are cut, athletics is usually the quickest to feel the ax. The second rule is that a coach and teacher will have to raise money for the team, the athletic department, the school, or even the community. Over the last 30 years, I have seen or done it all in fundraising—from chocolate bars to Thunderbirds and everything in between. I have sold barbeque, spaghetti, hot dogs, chicken, popcorn, peanuts, doughnuts, steaks, T-shirts, calendars, pictures, banners, game programs, bird seed, vegetable and flower seeds, light bulbs, cakes, magazines, bumper stickers, decals, game balls, and video tapes, just to name a few. I have operated concession stands and drink machines, and I have been in a dunking booth, have had a pie in the face, have sponsored sock hops, and have ridden a donkey. I have also sold raffle tickets for cars, trucks, motorcycles, shotguns, dinners, golf vacations, clothes, sporting good equipment, and numerous miscellaneous items. I have also asked people for money to buy weight equipment and uniforms, to send athletes to camp, and to send teams to postseason competition. If I have not done it all, I have at least seen it all—from the Harlem Globetrotters to the King and His Court to the ACC and Carolina All-Stars to championship wrestling and blue grass, gospel, and rock and roll concerts.

Magazine, Fruit, and Sock Hops

Unfortunately, fund-raising has become a very important part of every athletic department. During my first year in coaching, I was initiated into the world of fund-raising in a very big way. When I was at a high school from 1973 to 1975, the county did not provide funds for coaching supplements, the principal's secretary, or athletic equipment. Our coaching supplements came out of gate receipts and the football and basketball concession stands, while the secretary's salary was paid out of the money from several soft drink machines located on campus. The principal sold ice cream and snacks at break to pay for office supplies for the faculty and staff. In addition, students sold magazines, flower seeds, and Florida citrus fruit, and each class was expected to have a fund-raising project to help pay for the junior and senior prom.

It seemed as if every week there were car washes, doughnut sales, a raffle for a shotgun, television, or some auto part. In the summer, the coaching staff would sponsor several slow-pitch softball tournaments for men, women, and churches, and with registration fees and the concession stand revenue, the coaching staff was able to buy extra athletic equipment. The athletic director and his wife also operated a concession stand all summer for the recreation and church leagues that played their regular season games on the softball field. The athletic director also went by Wake Forest University and Guilford College on a regular basis, and any equipment they were going to discard ended up at our school. After every home football game and Friday night basketball game, the coaching staff would sponsor a sock hop. The coaches would clean the gym, hire some students with an eight-track tape player, make all the students take off their shoes, and let the dancing begin. Admission fee was two dollars, and the guys would stand around talking about their cars while the girls would be dancing with each other. I had never seen a sock hop or girls dancing with each other before, but we made some money and the students had a good time. In 1984, I went to a high school in Staunton, Virginia, and I found that the sock hop after the game was still alive and well, and a part of the local culture.

Inmates versus the Guards

The easiest money for my school's athletic department was made at my first job when the faculty (i.e., the coaches) played the senior students in basketball. The contest would be played during the second period, and students had to pay $1.00 to be able to attend the game, which was held in the gym. Now what high school student would *not* pay to get out of class to watch a senior try to hurt one of the coaches? The school had 825 students in four grades, and it would usually make over $700 for the game. Over the years, I played in 12 student-versus-faculty basketball games and have a 12–0 record. I never lost to the students, and only a few games were even close. I still remember that first game, getting to school early in the morning and warming up for over an hour. The coaches won the game, I scored 26 points, and we raised $720. Our coaches even played the middle school booster club one night to help raise money, and we almost lost that game. The middle school had brought in a ringer, Van Williford, a former North Carolina State University All-American, and he had 28 points at halftime, and there were three near fights. Fortunately, Williford left at halftime, a couple of the middle school's better players were injured trying to crash the boards, and we pulled out a hard-fought victory in the second half. This was the only time I remember playing the faculty-student game during the school day, and eventually the State of North Carolina ruled that those types of activities took students away from instruction and had to be eliminated. Faculty-student games were a good way to make money while they lasted.

Barnstorming Tours

Several high schools also held faculty-student basketball games to raise money, and the faculty always won. However, we also played either the ACC All-Stars or the Carolina All-Stars, and the faculty never won those games. The ACC All-Stars were a group of senior basketball players who, after the ACC tournament and the NCAA tournament, would barnstorm across the state, playing in local rural gyms. The All-Stars would usually take 70% off the top of all tickets sold, and a minimum of $1,000 in adavance ticket sales would be required for them to show up. In the 1970s, a chance to see an ACC senior in person would pack most local gyms, and the booster club would be able to keep all the money made in the concession stand. In 1978, we played the Carolina All-Stars who, because UNC had so many seniors and because they were the most popular players, formed their own barnstorming tour independent of the ACC All-Stars.

One year we played against Walter Davis, UNC All-American and soon-to-be NBA player. The final score was something like 126–62, but the highlight of the game occurred when our math teacher went one-on-one with Walter Davis. Lewis Miller, the math teacher, was a young guy, just out of college, and he was a good basketball player. In the third quarter, Lewis drove to the baseline, pump-faked five times, and then went up for the shot. Not only did Walter Davis block the shot, but he knocked the ball into the cheap seats. Some of the ACC and Carolina All-Stars were nice guys, but most were just looking to pick up some quick cash and hit the road. One year we were going to play the ACC All-Stars with Rod Griffin, a Wake Forest All-American, but on game day the booking agent called to say that Griffin would be at the game but would not play, so the principal cancelled the game. The principal felt that the students would be paying to see Griffin play and that it would be less than honest if he just sat and signed autographs.

Those all-star games and the student-faculty games were always fun, even if they sometimes were a little too hotly contested. The basketball games were a good and inexpensive way to raise money and also to allow the students to see teachers in a different environment. However, just as in the old Burt Reynolds movie, *The Longest Yard*, it was important that the guards beat the inmates—to maintain control and the status quo.

Pie in the Face

I had the two worst fund-raising experiences and my best fund-raising success at the same high school. One winter we had a basketball player get very sick and almost die. The local hospital was unable to treat the young man successfully, so he was transported to Duke University Medical Center, where his life was saved but at a tremendous financial expense. To help the family, the principal decided to raise money by having a few select faculty members brought out to midcourt in the gym and letting the students bid for the opportunity to put a whipped-cream pie in the face of their favorite or infamous teacher. Naturally, I was one of the few select teachers to be given such a high honor. My bid was one of the highest because there were several former and current students who wanted the opportunity to hit me in the face with a pie. In the end, two young ladies pooled their resources and bid $52 to hit yours truly in the face with a cream pie. I did not enjoy the experience at all.

Buckin' Betty

During the mid-1970s in North Carolina, an organization toured the state putting on donkey basketball games. Buckeye Donkey Basketball, Inc. had trained donkeys, and it was the major league of fund-raising organizations. Buckeye Donkey Basketball was very professional, with well-trained donkeys and handlers. After the pie-in-the-face auction, the principal decided that a donkey basketball game would be an outstanding idea. We had an open date on a Friday night late in the basketball season, so the game was scheduled. We could not afford Buckeye Donkey Basketball, Inc., but we were able to locate Colonel Corbett and his Demon Donkey Basketball with Buckin' Betty. If Buckeye Donkey Basketball was major league, then Colonel Corbett was single A or rookie league. On Friday afternoon before the game, Colonel Corbett arrived at school with eight of the mangiest, ugliest donkeys that I had ever seen. Then the Colonel staked the donkeys out on the front lawn and even took Buckin' Betty down the halls to let all the students see the animal. Thirty years before, when my father had been a high school teacher and coach, he had the opportunity to ride a donkey in a basketball game, and I grew up hearing about his fateful ride and the injury and pain it caused. I had no desire whatsoever to ride one of Colonel Corbett's donkeys in the gym, and I explained my concern to the athletic director, who was sympathetic to my fears. Now the athletic director wanted to ride, and he had a great time that night. In fact, he was as excited as he had been on the first day of football practice in August. The athletic director told me not to worry—that he would take care of everything.

That night we had one of the largest crowds in school history; the gym was packed. Not only did we have donkey basketball but we also sold everything we could possibly sell in the lobby: cakes, pies, cookies, popcorn, soft drinks, hot dogs, barbeque, T-shirts, bumper stickers, pennants—you name it, we sold it. We had a raffle for a shotgun and even had some casino tables set up in the cafeteria. I was told to stay at the table where the cakes were being sold, and to stay out of sight and out of the gym. Everything was going well until just before halftime when a student came running to my table and told me the principal wanted me in the gym to ride. I politely told the student that I was selling cakes and could not leave my table.

At halftime, Colonel Corbett brought out Mrs. Colonel and had her lay down on the gym floor, and he put a watermelon on her stomach and cut it in half with a sword. The crowd loved the sword-and-watermelon trick and in a few minutes, another student came to my table and stated in no uncertain terms that the principal said that I should come inside the gym now or not come to work Monday. Reluctantly, I walked into the standing-room-only packed gym to a chaotic scene out of Dante's *Inferno*. It looked as if there were donkeys everywhere, with teachers, coaches, and students hanging on for dear life. The principal saw me, and he pointed to a riderless donkey standing alone by the baseline. It was a big donkey, and Colonel Corbett helped me get on her back. The donkey started slowly walking toward the home bleachers. The butterflies in my stomach were making malted milk shakes as I rode my steed uneasily across the hardwood. I stayed on the donkey exactly as long as she wanted me to—10–12 seconds, as it turned out. Just as we approached the sideline, all of the sudden and without warning, I had the unnatural sensation of flying backwards through the air like a feather tossed in a tornado. The donkey had dropped her head and then in the same instant had bucked me off her back with a swift and powerful move. I was flying effortlessly through the air until the gym floor brought an abrupt end to my flight of fantasy. The flight was not too bad, but the landing on the hardwood floor knocked me unconscious, and the basketball coach came over to see if I was alive. The coach leaned down and shook me; I opened my eyes, rolled over on my stomach, got up on my hands and knees, and crawled off the court into the locker room and never came out the rest of the evening.

After a few minutes, I was joined by our assistant principal, who had also been an unwilling participant in the festivities. The assistant principal was from

Roanoke Rapids, North Carolina, and he loved to play golf. For three years, he had been trying to get a tee time scheduled at the famous Pinehurst Number Two golf course. Finally, after three years of trying, he had a tee time scheduled for the legendary golf course, and it just so happened to be the Saturday morning after the donkey basketball game. The assistant principal told the principal that he would work that evening but that he did not want to ride. The principal informed him that he would be riding. Not long after my unfortunate encounter with the gym floor, the assistant principal was thrown off a donkey and landed on his right wrist. The basketball coach put an ice pack on his wrist, and together the assistant principal and I sat in the varsity locker room reflecting on how unfair life was and how mean the principal was for making us ride in a charity basketball game. The pain increased for the assistant principal, and later that night he had to go to the emergency room and had a cast put on his broken right wrist. He never made it to the tee time at Pinehurst Number Two. Whoever said charity is painless never rode a donkey in a basketball game.

The Last Ticket

I found the best fund-raising project in 30 years in rural Stanley County, North Carolina. One Friday night in 1977, I was scouting the South Stanley Rebels, and as I entered the stadium, I saw a brand new car and a sign that read: "To Be Given Away." When I got to the press box, I asked one of the administrators how much the tickets were for the car raffle. He told me $50, and I almost fell out of my seat. All the raffle tickets I had seen before were either $1 or $5, and you could buy as many tickets as you wanted. But $50 a ticket seemed steep. However, the administrator explained that only 300 tickets would be sold and that every ticket would be drawn out and the last ticket drawn would win the car.

The next Monday, I told the athletic director and head football coach about the raffle, and he liked the idea. The athletic director was tired of nickeling and diming everybody in the community with bake sales and car washes and saw the raffle as a once-a-year, one-and-only fund-raising campaign. We decided to try the car raffle in the spring, and the athletic director went to the local Ford dealership to see what a new Thunderbird would cost. For the mathematically challenged, 300 tickets at $50 per ticket equals $15,000, which was a good amount of money in 1977. We were able to get the Thunderbird for $6,000 and change, so we stood to clear about $9,000 for one event. We were able to get a local restaurant to underwrite the cost of printing the 300 numbered tickets, and the restaurant also printed 100 posters to place around the community.

A big part of the raffle was a steak dinner with all ticket holders invited. After the meal, every ticket would be drawn out and placed on a big board. The first ticket drawn would win a prize, and then every 30th ticket drawn would win a prize valued at $100 or more. The excitement would be to see who were the last five and then three and two left in the contest, and also to give other people an opportunity to buy a ticket from one of the remaining individuals if they wanted to sell. The prizes were all donated, and we had gift certificates for food, golf, clothes, and travel, and the first ticket drawn would win a free weekend at Pinehurst. The dinner was held on a Saturday night in the school cafeteria, and the Jaycees donated the steaks and cooked the meal. We had a 50/50 raffle on the side where, for $5, a person could bet on which ticket number would be drawn for the car. We sold 200 numbers for $1,000 and split the pot with the person who picked the number closest to the one that won the car. We made $500 on the side raffle and used that money to help pay the CPA we had hired from Raleigh to conduct the drawing. His job was to draw out every ticket and post it on the big board, because we wanted a neutral person drawing out and posting the tickets. The critical factor of the evening was that all 300 tickets had to be accounted for and drawn out.

The first booster club raffle was a fun and enjoyable evening; the food was good, and it was exciting waiting for the tickets to be drawn out to see who would win the Thunderbird. I made it to the final 20, and when we got to the final three, we had them stand up and gave them a chance to sell their tickets if they wanted to. None of the three chose to sell, and in the end, the brother-in-law of a teacher won the car, and everyone went home happy. The next year, a teacher from a rival high school won the Thunderbird. The car raffle was a very successful fund-raising campaign for years.

In 1984, when I arrived at the high school in Virginia as the athletic director, the president of the booster club told me the club was in debt. I told him about the car raffle, and the booster club decided to try it. Once again, it was very successful. In 1984, we gave away a new Pontiac Sunbird, and the booster club was able to clear over $7,000. The winner of the raffle was a retired school board member and one of the most loved and respected members of the community. We could not have selected a better person to have won the car. Everyone enjoyed the steak dinner and the excitement of the drawing, and the booster club was happily out of debt.

Warning: Can Be a Crime

One important word of warning about fund-raising and money in general is to be careful. Money will get a coach, teacher, principal, president, or superintendent fired more quickly than almost anything else. All too often I have seen people get in trouble because they could not account for funds, and even honest mistakes can be very costly professionally. When we did the car raffle, we always hired a CPA from outside to draw the tickets and to be impartial; we did not want any hint of scandal or impropriety. People expect honesty and accountability when dealing with school funds, whether the people are taxpayers or individual contributors. When I was an athletic director and assistant principal, I could sign checks, but early on, I was told never to sign a check that had been written out to me. Doing so would not seem appropriate at the bank, and people talk in small-town and big-city America.

I also learned that checks are safer than cash because cash can get misplaced, lost, or stolen, and it is difficult to recover. During my first year, I was collecting magazine money in home room, left the money locked in the filing cabinet, and went to lunch. Somebody walked in and stole the money while I was in the cafeteria, and the principal was very upset. The principal could have made me pay the money back, but he did not, and I never left money in a classroom again. There should also be receipts written for any cash or checks collected, since all money has to be accounted for.

Another lesson I learned the hard way early in my career was the pitfalls of ordering equipment for athletes without having the money first. One year I ordered shoes for the basketball players, Converse All-Stars, and the players were going to pay me when the shoes came in. Most of the players paid, some forgot to pay, and one quit the team. I ended up having to pay the difference out of my own pocket. I was young and struggling financially, but since I had ordered the shoes, I had to pay off the bill. I was also burned on some T-shirts one year. After that experience, I never ordered any equipment for an athlete or a team. I did not want the hassle of collecting money and of being responsible for the quality of the merchandise. Every year I see coaches ordering T-shirts, shoes, sweat pants, or warm ups, and every year I see those same coaches paying out of their own pockets when the items do not sell or students do not pay for them. Sears and Wal-Mart understand cost, profit, and marketing and can make money, but for me, the less money I have to handle, the better.

Cow Patty Bingo

It is a fact of life that teachers, coaches, and administrators have to raise money, and there are people in the profession who excel in this enterprise. The athletic director and head football coach at Lancaster High School in Lancaster, South Carolina, was one of the best. Every year at Lancaster, the administration and the athletic department held cow patty bingo, golf tournaments, yard sales, auctions, and dinners and also created banners. And they raised a great deal of money. What I learned at junior college as executive director of the booster club is that people do not mind being asked for money if the request is handled in a professional manner. The secret of asking for money is knowing how much to ask for, when to ask for it, and what is expected in return. I still believe that people would rather write one large check than write numerous small checks every time they are asked for money. In addition, all donated money comes with strings attached. The person may want a parking space, extra tickets, VIP treatment, recognition, or a thank-you note. Indeed, as my grandmother always said, "Money never comes free." The secret in a community is to know the pretenders from the real big-money people. The pretenders talk the talk, but when the time comes for requesting donations, talk is all they do. The people with big money seldom reveal their financial resources in public, but when push comes to shove, they can help.

Priming the Pump

When I first started as the head football coach, our weight room was in bad shape, and the principal suggested that I talk with a former alumnus whose family owned a local hosiery mill. I went to the mill and met the alumnus and talked to him about what we needed to improve our strength-training program. The alumnus had played football at the school, had his own personal gym equipment at his house, and worked out on a regular basis. A few days later, the alumnus came to school to look at our weight room, to watch an after-school work-out session, and to talk with some of the football players. A week later, the alumnus came back to school and told me to get what I needed and that he would pay for it. The next day, I asked the principal how much money we were talking about, and he just said to let my conscience be my guide. I was to get what I needed, but not to go overboard. I ordered several thousand dollars worth of equipment, but the amount was reasonable, and the alumnus paid for everything and was very satisfied with the program. The equipment he provided allowed us to develop an outstanding strength program.

If you do not ask, you cannot receive. But it is important to develop a relationship before asking for money. The first time I went to see the alumnus, I never asked for or even talked about money or equipment. In eastern North Carolina, in the old days before indoor plumbing, if someone wanted a drink of water, he or she had to prime the pump first and then work that handle like crazy.

Raising big money is the same: someone has to prime the pump, establish a relationship, get to know the person, and then work that relationship until the money flows. The deeper the well, the colder the water, and the deeper the pockets, the more money is available. But deep water and deep pockets take much more time and work. When the water and the money come in, however, boy is it sweet.

Knowing How Much

Another key to fund-raising is not to err on the low or cheap side. Never ask for $1,000 when the donor is able to give $10,000. When I was at a junior college, I learned that lesson the hard way because certain people were off limits to the athletic department. The president did not want the booster club to ask someone to give $1,000 when he was trying to get a major donation of $100,000 or more. It is not a good situation when the president asks a donor for a significant contribution and the donor says he or she has already given $500 to the booster club. Needless to say, I heard very quickly whenever the president was turned down and the reason given was the donor had all ready contributed to the athletic department. The sad reality of higher education today is that college presidents have to spend all their time and efforts on fund-raising and trying to bring in millions of dollars every year. Unfortunately, the same is becoming true for athletic directors and coaches, who have to spend more and more time raising money to provide the necessities of a first-class program. Some people call fund-raising begging, while others see the fund-raiser as a salesperson; nevertheless, fund-raising is part of coaching and leadership on every level of amateur sport.

Remember that it is easier to sell the product if someone believes in the product, believes in the institution, and believes in the positive benefits of athletics. However, always be honest and make sure that all money is accounted for. Keep accurate records, always give a receipt, and never spend money that is not yours without written permission. Whether it is funds from the concession stands, drink machines, or raffle tickets, make sure every penny is properly handled. Make sure there is a paper trail.

Conclusion

In the late 1970s and early 1980s, California, with Proposition 13, and Massachusetts, with Proposition 2½, initiated what many believed to be a trend in taxpayer revolts. The cry went up in California and Massachusetts that public education as we knew it was over. Dr. Harold VanderZwaag, Professor of Sport Management at the University of Massachusetts, predicted that the tax revolts would cause high school sports in America to become obsolete. Dr. VanderZwaag argued that the private sector could operate sport programs more effectively and economically than the school districts. Volunteer coaches and nonprofit organizations such as the YMCA, the YWCA, and Boys Clubs, along with city and county recreation departments, could operate youth sport programs better and more cheaply than the public schools. Sport for young Americans could follow the European model and move out of the educational setting. It has been 25 years since Dr. VanderZwaag made his prediction about high school sport, but old traditions die hard. As we prepare for a new wave of tax revolts and not enough funds for basic education, maybe it is time to reexamine the role of sport in the school setting. Today, with Title IX and the Olympic sports, it is becoming more and more difficult to locate adequate funding. The Echo Boomers are almost finished with their educational pursuits, and the Baby Boomers are becoming concerned more about Social Security, retirement, and extended-care facilities. Will the Baby Boomers be willing to support more and higher taxes for schools their children no longer attend? Today, with soccer, tennis, baseball, cheerleading, gymnastics, volleyball, softball, and AAU basketball, we have a pay-to-play system already in place. It is not uncommon today for students to play on an interscholastic team while at the same time participating on select, travel, and elite squads in the same sport during the same season. Now college coaches do not even recruit players from high school teams but spend all their time and efforts scouting these travel teams that play year round. Today's parent has no problem with paying money to send a child to camp, to join a travel team, or even to hire a coach for private lessons. Do high schools today need to duplicate sport and extracurricular activities that are taking place in the private sector? With an aging population and severe limits on educational funding, what can we do to provide the greatest good for the most children? We know that children today can obtain their sport experience outside the school house door, and it may be time to turn over control of sport to other agencies that can provide the opportunities for play with less funds. At some point, we may return to the classical approach of education championed by Charles W. Eliot, of Harvard, and Robert Hutchins, of the University of Chicago. When the Baby Boomers use the power of their numbers and vote to no longer fund the comprehensive model of education, sport as we know it will have to change.

References

Allen, Karie. "Athletic Boosters." *Press Enterprise*. Riverside, California. September 21, 2004.

Bence, Steve. "A Chance for Prep Sports Supporters To Come Together." *The Oregonian*. February 9, 2004.

Biesecker, Michael. "Audit Shows Booster Club Irregularities." *The News and Observer*. Raleigh, North Carolina. August 2, 2003.

Braig, Kevin. "A Game Plan to Conserve the Interscholastic Athletic Environment After Lebron James." *Marquette Sports Law Review*. Spring 2004. 14 MARQ Sports L. Rev. 343.

Brimmer, Adam Van. "Rah-Rah Revenue." *Savannah Morning News*. Savannah, Georgia. August 17, 2003.

Brown, Jennifer Atkins. "Parents Team Up to Help Grimsley Sports Teams." *Greensboro News and Record*. Greensboro, North Carolina. September 28, 2003.

Communities for Equity V. Michigan High School Athletic Association. 26 F. Supp. 2nd. 1001 (1998).

Defao, Janine. "Back to School with a Sigh of Relief." *San Francisco Chronicle*. San Francisco, California. September 10, 2004.

Dennis, Jan. "Budget Woes Land Sports, After School Programs on Chopping Block." *Associated Press State and Local Wire*. April 5, 2004.

Donovan, Marie. "Tyngsboro Schools Centralize Athletic Fund Raising." *Lowell Sun*. Lowell, Massachusetts. September 24, 2003.

Dunn, Andrew. "Audit of School's Accounts Reveals Numerous Errors." *The Ledger*. Lakeland, Florida. May 22, 2004.

Ethridge, Karen. "Booster Clubs Come to Aid of Cash-strapped School." *The Augusta Chronicle*. Augusta, Georgia. September 10, 2004.

Gerdeman, Dina. "Schools Fees Squeezing Parents." *The Patriot Ledger*. Quincy, Massachusetts. February 28, 2004.

Hanson, Eric. "Schools May Ok Ads to Fatten Funds." *Star Tribune*. Minneapolis, Minnesota. November 24, 2004.

Holland, Adam. "High School Sports Are Spared in Tyngsboro." *Lowell Sun*. Lowell, Massachusetts. July 14, 2004.

Houston, James. "West Coach Resigns." *Montgomery Herald*. Troy, North Carolina. September 16, 2004.

Jacobson, Gary. "High School Football in Texas is Big Business." *Dallas Morning News*. Dallas, Texas. September 3, 2004.

Kraft, Scott. "Bigtime Boosters." *American Football Monthly*. March 2005.

McAllister, Kristin. "High School Athletes Have Dig Deep To Go Deep." *Dayton Daily News*. Dayton, Ohio. March 29, 2004.

Morrison, Bill. "School Funding Reform Needed." *Tri Valley Herald*. Pleasanton, California. January 30, 2004.

Nelson, Melissa. "Small Schools Struggle to Field Teams." *Associated Press State And Local Wire*. August 15, 2003.

Oleson, Ellie. "Providing Quite a Boost." *Worcester Telegram and Gazette*. Worcester, Massachusetts. June 14, 2004.

Parrott, Jeff. "John Glenn Plan Draws Opposition." *South Bend Tribune*. South Bend, Indiana. April 23, 2004.

Petrocelli, Michael. "Hillside Boosters Money Trail Thin." *The Herald-Sun*. Durham, North Carolina. August 2, 2003.

Rader, Benjamin. *American Sport*. Prentice Hall. Saddle River, New Jersey. 2004.

Radtke, John. "Private Funding A Public Issue." *Chicago Daily Herald*. Chicago, Illinois. September 19, 2003.

Richey, Warren. "A Test of How Far Title IX Protections Reach." *Christian Science Monitor*. November 30, 2004.

Roquemore, Bobbi. "MPS Budget Crisis Puts Sports At Risk." *Milwaukee Journal Sentinel*. Milwaukee, Wisconsin. February 27, 2004.

Sanchez, Robert. "Holding Back Boosters." *Rocky Mountain News*. Denver, Colorado. November 10, 2003.

Schomberg, John. "Equity V. Autonomy." *New York University School Of Law*. New York, New York. 1998.

Silverman, Julia. "Oregon to Decide on Tax Hike For Activities." *Associated Press Online*. September 14, 2003.

Staples, Andy. "Lights Out for School Athletics?" *The Tampa Tribune*. Tampa, Florida. October 5, 2003.

Swanson, Richard. *History of Sport and Physical Education in the United States*. 4th Edition. Brown and Benchmark. Madison, Wisconsin. 1995.

Chapter 14

Marketing Events and Services for Spectators

Frank Russo

Introduction

Sport managers are accountable for achieving a set of desired objectives and results, whatever type of facility they operate. Whether they report to a city council, a university board of regents, a corporate board of directors, or any other form of hierarchy, their professional well-being depends upon their ability to satisfy the expectations of superiors.

In most cases, however, striving to accomplish the primary objectives of the sport manager's facility is not necessarily compatible with the ever-increasing pressure to balance the budget. To come as close as possible to these objectives requires considerable marketing expertise. The facility manager must know how to market a variety of services to tenants and the public in a manner which produces maximum profit and results in an ever-increasing level of repeat business. This chapter is designed to help the sport manager better understand the marketing aspects of various in-house services, such as scheduling, advertising, box office, concessions, merchandising (e.g., sale of programs, novelties, T-shirts, and so forth), parking, and television.

Importance of the Event Calendar

Most sport managers are encouraged to book a well-rounded schedule of events geared to satisfy the desires of the market. Since rental income is such a major portion of annual operating revenue, this is an extremely important process—especially considering the tremendous level of competition for quality arena events.

If the facility has a sports franchise, its home game dates will form the skeleton of the annual schedule. Basketball and hockey teams, for example, usually hold their dates at least one year in advance. Also serving as part of the skeleton will be major family show attractions (e.g., circuses and ice shows). Once these dates are confirmed, the process of booking "fillers" or "one-nighters" begins in earnest.

Fundamentals of Booking Events

To book a successful schedule of events, a good first impression must be made on tenants and the ticket-buying public. The facility should be clean, well maintained, well lit, and environmentally comfortable. The staff should be friendly, courteous, and professional in the delivery of box office, parking, concession, merchandising, and other services.

Another factor that plays an important role in securing events for the facility is the level of confidence others have in the quality of services. In order to trust an outside agency, there is a responsibility to be familiar with the local media (i.e., radio and print media as well as television) so that the ads placed for an event are most likely to reach potential ticket buyers rather than those who might be marginally interested in the event, or not interested at all.

If there is an in-house agency an advantage is gained in that the facility can either keep the normal 15% ad-placement commission as a revenue source or use it to purchase additional advertising for the same show.

It is possible to increase the advertising schedule for an event on a noncash basis if the attraction and manager are willing to allow a radio station (or, less commonly, a newspaper or TV station) to be the show's official media sponsor. For example, a concert artist whose music is in popular demand by a radio station's listening audience would make that station eager to become associated with the show. In return for some complimentary tickets which the station can give away through various contests as well as for the opportunity to have one of its disc jockeys as the show's emcee, the station is likely to provide two or three times the value of the complimentary tickets in additional advertising and promotional spots, which are designed not only to increase ticket sales for the show but also to increase listenership for the radio station.

The sport manager should never allow a media sponsorship to be construed as a sponsorship exclusive. The sport manager should offer the media sponsor a promotional exclusive but clearly retain the right to advertise anywhere else it is appropriate to do so. Other radio stations and newspapers and, very rarely, television will accept tickets as noncash trade for advertising.

In addition, media sponsorship should not preclude an overall show sponsorship deal. For example, the sport manager might offer a member of the corporate community an opportunity to become involved as the official show sponsor. The executive director of the Hartford Civic Center secured the sponsorship of the Heublein Corporation for a Christmas concert that featured Tony Bennett and the Hartford Symphony Pops Orchestra. These two attractions, either alone or together, would not normally fill a 16,000-seat arena. The funding of $15,000 provided by the sponsor was used to offset the show's advertising and promotional costs and offered Heublein the following returns:

1. Total name identification on all advertising as well as on the tickets, posters, display cards, and on the Civic Center's own message center and outdoor marquee.
2. Fifty complimentary seats at cabaret tables on the arena floor.
3. A $2.00 group discount for all Heublein employees.
4. A cocktail party with Tony Bennett backstage after the event.
5. A Heublein banner in the arena, as well as a program distributed to all patrons and tent cards on each table (Heublein paid for these items separately).
6. A rebate to Heublein of $1.00 per ticket sold, which Heublein, in turn, gave as a tax-deductible donation to the Bushnell Park (restoration)

Foundation. Because of this no-risk fund-raising opportunity, Foundation volunteers helped the show by working hard to sell tickets.

This sponsorship technique and variations on it may make an event possible that might not otherwise be economically feasible.

Another aspect of advertising is that which involves making potential tenants aware of the sport manager's facility. The sport manager should make every effort to budget funds each year for advertisements in various publications such as *Amusement Business, Variety Magazine, Aud-Arena, Billboard Magazine, and Performance Magazine*. These national publications are read by people who make decisions to rent facilities such as the sport manager's for their events.

The sport manager should budget funds each year to advertise the schedule of events in local newspapers in a format which people can clip out and retain on a month-to-month basis. Many facilities also publish a monthly in-house newsletter, which is used as a direct-mail piece as well as a handout at the arena, the box office, and other high-traffic locations.

If unable to maintain an in-house agency, it is advisable to interview and select a local agency to serve the facility and any tenant that needs such help. To some managers, ad agencies represent 85% confusion at a charge of 15%. Therefore, if an outside ad agency is engaged, the agency's performance must be constantly monitored in order that more than simple ad placement is accomplished. The agency should advise the facility manager and the tenants of the most appropriate advertising media plan for a given event, and it should have a good sense of promotion and public relations.

Depending on policy, advertising can be sold in a variety of media throughout the facility. The possibilities include a scoreboard system, concourse display cases, Zamboni (ice resurfacing machine), in-house publications, message centers, outdoor marquees, upcoming event display cases, ticket envelopes, ticket backs, and concession product containers (e.g., soda cups, beer cups, popcorn boxes, napkins). There are a number of potential advertisers for these items within the corporate community. Concession-product vendors are willing to advertise their names and products on concession containers. This willingness, coupled with discount sale promotions, will increase food and beverage sales for the facility as well as for its vendors.

Box Office

Booking outstanding events does not guarantee high-volume ticket sales. The key to selling tickets is good information and easy access for the ticket-buying public.

Two basic elements of an event are the performers and the audience. The mission of the box office is to facilitate the selection of audiences. This task is accomplished by providing tickets to patrons. As a result of the service, audience and performer are brought together, with the dollars generated from the sale of tickets held by the box office until the distribution of monies among those responsible for providing services (performer, promoter, agent, sponsor, and facility) is determined. The box office operation also serves a public relations function since its personnel frequently provide the only contact between patron and facility.

A considerable amount of planning and preparation is required before the box office opens for business. The primary product of the box office is the ticket. Selection of the type of tickets and the method by which they will be sold require careful study. A number of factors must be considered, including the physical characteristics of the facility, its seating plans, and the type of ticket system, pricing structure, and sales incentive plans utilized.

Reserved seating is the preferred method. It assures a customer a specific seat location at the time the ticket is purchased, well in advance of the event. This method will encourage early reservations and sales and the convenience of having seats together for couples or groups.

More and more facilities are introducing computerized ticket systems as a substitute for the traditional hard-ticket approach. Using computerized tickets improves service to the public by providing a number of remote ticket outlets throughout the market area, usually in popular retail outlets. These outlets increase customer awareness of the facility and bring people from greater distances than normal to see events.

Many facilities have further expanded service to the public with the addition of a telephone credit card service whereby customers simply call a special box office number and charge tickets to MasterCard, VISA, and occasionally American Express. This service brings the box office into people's homes. With a "chargeline" system, it is essential that each transaction be validated. The sport manager should allow adequate time to process the order, pull the tickets, and either mail them or leave them in the "will call" window so they can be picked up prior to show time. Such a service, if properly advertised and managed, can account for 20% or more of the sport manager's annual gross box office sales. The sport manager should consider imposing a service charge per order. This charge is not part of the box office settlement with the tenant and can produce a substantial amount of net revenue each year for the facility.

The group sales department generates volume purchases by making advance tickets available at discounted prices. It is very important that all group tickets be paid for in advance since groups tend to reserve more tickets than they are able to sell and may try to return them at the last minute. This tendency may result not only in a significant drop in the number of tickets sold but also in "large holes" in arena seating. These consequences can be avoided if arrangements include either advance payment or the return of tickets in time to permit resale. Group sales account for as much as 30% of the total ticket sales for a multiperformance family show.

The box office also produces substantial revenue for the facility. Generation of monies above those shared by facility and promoter is accomplished by the following:

1. Charging on a "cost plus" basis for season-ticketing services.
2. Charging a flat fee or a percentage of gross ticket sales (whichever is greater) for each event. It is not uncommon for facilities to charge a minimum of approximately $500 to $1,000 or 3% to 4% of gross ticket sales. Normally included in this fee are the salaries for box office sales staff and the charges for ticket printing, for the group sales campaign, for staffing, for telephone service, and for credit card service.
3. Imposing a per-order service charge for all credit card purchases.
4. Reimbursement from tenants for direct printing and mailing costs for group sales material.

5. Charging a special handling fee for all mail orders. This fee is totally retained by the facility and is not part of the financial settlement with the tenant.

The amount of success realized by the box office operation is directly related to the degree that it is visible and convenient to the ticket-buying public. Box office personnel must be well trained, courteous, friendly, knowledgeable, and interested in the special needs and desires of the ticket-buying public.

Concessions

Don Meyers, manager of the Memorial Coliseum in Ft. Wayne, Indiana, spoke effectively of the significance of the concession operations when he offered: "A well-operated concession department is more often than not the determining factor in the financial success of an auditorium or an arena. Rarely is an auditorium successful without a sound concession operation. It is an accepted fact that good food and drink go hand in hand with recreation and sports." Over a decade later, Don Jewell, author of *Public Assembly Facilities: Planning and Management*, made a similar observation:

The importance of good concessions operation to the average arena or stadium cannot be overemphasized. The role of the concessions department drops proportionately with the size of the facility to the point that it may be of only slight concern in many performing art centers. Rarely is an arena, auditorium or stadium financially successful without an efficient concession operation. If the public decides that its entertainment and recreational needs are being properly served, it will return time and time again. The total experience, however, must be consistently satisfactory. Percentages vary, but all arenas report concessions revenue as an important and vital part of total volume.

The Hartford Civic Center is an example of the revenue potential from concessions. Concession revenue amounted to $2,130,000, or 36% of its operating revenue.

A fundamental matter facing all event managers is how concessions should be handled. The basic choices are in-house operation or leasing the operation to a private contractor.

In-house operations offer the following advantages:

1. Management has complete control of concessions. This permits immediate response to needs that arise.
2. Management controls pricing. A fair market price can be maintained, thereby avoiding customer complaints of "rip-off" or "price gouging."
3. The quality of the product can be controlled.
4. There is greater potential for generating revenue.

The Hartford Civic Center realized a net profit that was at least 15% greater than the return that any concessionaire was able to guarantee.

Concessionaires stress the following advantages of a lease arrangement:

1. Volume purchasing enables the vendor to provide quality products at reduced prices.

2. Sales will be expanded beyond anything that could be generated with an in-house system. The concessionaire can return to the facility more revenue than would be possible with an in-house operation because of its supervisory experience, efficiency, expertise, and capacity.
3. Capital outlays for equipment are avoided.
4. Management, staff, purchasing, maintenance, inventory, storage, and vendor relations are eliminated.

Before making a decision regarding arrangements for concessions, information must be gathered. A survey of facilities of comparable size and profile is essential. The analysis should include such categories as profitability, purchasing and product costs, personnel and labor costs, the ability to maximize sales, accounting and controls, facility management's involvement, and right of approval and capital investment. Other sources of information are the national headquarters of both the International Association of Auditorium Managers and the National Association of Concessionaires. Arranging for concessions will be one of the most important deals ever negotiated for the facility.

Information gathering is also a must if physical design problems are to be avoided. Major shortcomings are as follows:

1. Not enough concession stands to serve the number of seats
2. Inadequate kitchen location and space
3. No installation of floor drains in kitchen and stand areas
4. No provision for a commissary for hawking (vending) operations
5. Service elevators on the opposite side of the building from storage areas
6. No provision for exhaust (which causes a severe limitation in ability to present an attractive menu, especially with fried foods)
7. Loading docks and storerooms on different floors than needed
8. Inadequate ventilation
9. Insufficient energy and water availability
10. Lack of wide concourse areas to facilitate traffic flow

Geoff Older, formerly with the Volume Services Division of the Interstate United Corporation of Chicago, stated: "You can have stands that are functionally perfect, but located in an improper position." Invariably, architects give more attention to toilets, which are so often located where the concessions stands should be. Bert Pailey, also of the Volume Services Division, states: "Toilets do not generate revenue and people have a way of finding them. Those prime locations should be for concession stands."

Don Jewell, in *Public Assembly Facilities Planning and Management* points out that to be effective, stands should be conveniently located to all seats. The patron should be able to reach the nearest stand in 40 to 60 seconds. Stands should be well organized, with clear indications of where the patrons should line up for service. Equipment, food, and cash registers should be conveniently located so that items can be quickly served by a single person in each selling station. This arrangement will help minimize confusion and interference among the stand workers and will also expedite one-stop service to patrons.

Concession stands should also be bright, colorful, well lit, and decorated with attractive pictures of the food and beverage being served. Menu boards should be installed clearly, indicating the products and prices. The ability to generate the aroma of food such as popcorn into the concourse will also stimulate concession sales.

In 1982, the National Association of Concessionaires (NAC), in conjunction with Coca-Cola USA and Cornell University, published a study for NAC members entitled, "Creating and Handling Buying Fever," which discusses the basic elements of a successful concession operations marketing plan, such as the menu, realizing profit potential, merchandising, promotions, and cutting service delay time.

The study acknowledges that concession revenue often determines whether the facility operates on a profit or a loss. A profit can only be accomplished with the right products and the right packaging at the right prices, provided the location is easily accessible. In order to be successful, a concession stand must influence the customer to purchase on impulse. The NAC study states: "[H]uman beings experience the world through five senses: sight, smell, touch, taste, and sound. A sensation that has a positive effect on any one or a combination of the senses creates a favorable response in a person's mind. It's when that response is translated into action that the sale is made. The impulse purchase."

The smell of a hot dog cooking on a grill is often all it takes to trigger a purchase. Attractive photographs of a soft drink or popcorn will also influence a patron to buy something before finding a seat. To create *buying fever* the snack bar has to be an "attention grabber." The more senses positively affected, the better.

One of the first items noticed by a potential customer is the menu. An impulse can be destroyed if it is overcome by resistance to high prices. The pricing structure should be reasonable for the products being offered. Brand name products are easily recognized by customers, thereby eliminating questions about the quality of the merchandise. The menu should include items that require minimal preparation time and have a low average unit cost. This requirement will cut labor expenses and increase profitability while permitting reasonable prices. It is advisable for the facility manager to sample the products being offered and periodically conduct a comparative price check with competing facilities.

The NAC report stressed the value of cleanliness and employee training. People are turned off by employees that look dirty or by concession stands that look unclean and poorly maintained.

In 1981, concession sales surpassed $3.5 billion in the United States. Stan Briggs, in another NAC report entitled "Concession Employee Training," published in INSITE '82, points out that the industry needs a manual which can be a real working tool and a blueprint for training employees and managing successful concession operations. Employee training is a critical aspect of a successful concession operation. Briggs maintains that management has a responsibility to train its employees. The industry is heavily dependent on young people who are starting their first jobs, thus increasing the importance of a training program. Employee training is also a key ingredient in merchandising concession products. The concession manager should train employees to sell suggestively. For example, one out of three customers orders a soft drink in a small size. Suggestive selling is a proven technique for increasing that trade. The concession manger should have his or her employees take the initiative by *asking* if customers want a large size. The employee must act to convince the customer that all items are reasonably priced and that buying larger sizes actually results in saving money. The menu board is the main vehicle for communicating values to the customers.

Promotions and marketing are also key elements of a successful concession operation. The Hartford Civic Center introduced these elements as factors in the bid criteria for the purchase of certain resale items. For example, in the award of the hot dog contract, the successful bidder was Grote & Weigel, which not only had the quality product but also committed up to $40,000 in advertising. The basic theme of its campaign was that Grote & Weigel franks were the official franks of the Whalers (Hartford's Home NHL Hockey Franchise) sold at the Hartford Civic Center. This theme had a significant impact on sales. Grote & Weigel and other suppliers enhanced the appearance of menu boards and product displays. They also purchased advertising space on the scoreboard and in concourse display cases.

In general, today's suppliers are in a position and are often very eager to offer the facilities promotional devices, ideas, and other information to move their products. In this manner, they actually become partners in the concession operation. They will provide promotional ideas, devices, and, especially with a new product, colorful promotional posters and displays which can be extremely helpful in catching the customer's eye.

The key points of the NAC's "Buying Fever Check List" are listed as follows:

1. Review merchandising and menu boards for clarity. Communicate and make it easier to order.
2. Cut down on inquiry time through effective menu board layout.
3. Use combinations of menu items to reduce the number of customer decisions.
4. Keep your equipment in good repair. Perform preventative maintenance checks regularly.
5. Locate equipment and supplies for soft drinks and popcorn adjacent to the dispensers.
6. Place the menu board so that it is easily visible to all customers.
7. Ensure that employees check supplies during slack time and that additional supplies are easily accessible.
8. Make lettering on the menu boards large enough so that it is easily readable for all customers. List all brands of soft drinks carried in their logo script and all the names of sizes and prices for all items.
9. Provide containers or boxes for customers to carry large orders.
10. If you do not have a cash register, place an adding machine or table of prices for popular combinations for the employees to use.
11. Design your stand with promotions in mind. Build in space to handle premiums such as plastic cups and posters.

Many facilities do not capitalize on another highly profitable aspect of the concession operation—having "vendors" or "hawkers" take food and beverages to the people in the seating area who are reluctant to get up and risk missing part of the event. Another contribution made by "vendors" or "hawkers" is that they relieve the pressures placed upon permanent concession stands during intermission, when customers literally swarm the concession facilities

Merchandising

The term *merchandising* means the process of selling programs, novelties, T-shirts, and other event-related souvenirs. This business has changed dramatically in the last two years, as T-shirts, jerseys, and painter's caps commemorating each rock act's tour have become the fashion among concertgoers. Bands and acts, beginning with Billy Joel on July 11, 1980, are now routinely obtaining injunctions and seizure orders from federal courts to protect trade rights to their names, pictures, and symbols. These rights were being exploited by unauthorized bootleggers at great loss to both the artists and the facilities in which they performed.

Because of the huge potential for the artist, there is tremendous pressure on facility managers to both maximize sales and reduce the percentage rates they charge to the performers. Many managers are accused of charging exorbitant merchandising fees by representatives of the various attractions and supporting franchises. Herbie Herbert, manager of the rock act Journey, and Dale Morris, manager of the country-and-western band Alabama, are perhaps the most vocal crusaders against such high charges by facilities.

Merchandising seminars have proven to be the hottest topics on the agenda of various meetings and conferences of the International Association of Auditorium Managers. The rock act Journey, for example, in its 200 concerts in less than two years, will gross an estimated $20 million in T-shirts and novelty sales. This is big business, and Journey and most other acts are looking more closely at percentages charged by facilities, which usually average 355 to 40% of gross sales. While facility managers and rock artist representatives are battling one another over percentage rates, they unite to combat bootleggers. Bootleggers have a tremendous impact on merchandising sales for both the artist and the facility. The Hartford Civic Center coped with the problem in the following manner. On August 2, 1982, attorneys obtained from the United States District Court in Hartford a permanent injunction and an order of seizure permitting the restraining of the sale of counterfeit T-shirts, posters, and other unauthorized merchandise at musical events at the Hartford Civic Center. The order, which was issued by the U.S. District Court Judge José A. Cabranes, was only the third such order ever issued in the United States. The other two were issued in Philadelphia and Cincinnati; however, the injunction in Hartford set a precedent since it imposed no geographical or time limitations.

The Hartford Civic Center was very active in obtaining temporary orders for most of its concerts prior to obtaining the permanent one. Concerts for which injunctions were obtained normally achieved merchandise sales of $3.31 per capita, while others achieved only $1.08 per capita. In addition, since 1980, three major rock shows at the Hartford Civic Center brought in average sales of $6.60 per capita. These shows included The Rolling Stones ($8.90 per capita), AC/DC ($5.63 per capita), and Rush ($5.11 per capita).

Prior to obtaining the permanent injunction, judges in Connecticut were issuing orders allowing the seizure of bootleg items sold at the Civic Center rock shows on a case-by-case basis. The new orders eliminated the need to go to court before each show, thus saving a minimum of $2,300 per show in attorney's fees alone, which had been deducted off the top before the Civic Center split merchandising with the artist.

Because of the Hartford Civic Center's aggressive stand in obtaining the permanent injunction and because the permanent injunction resulted in significantly increased sales, there was less pressure to reduce the facility's standard commission of 35% to 40%. Everyone made more money in this relatively unique approach to the merchandising wars.

Most facilities use an outside merchandising contractor rather than an in-house staff. The contractor is paid a percentage of gross sales—usually between 10%

and 15% — and in turn provides and pays all sales staff, consigns over and inventories the merchandise from the artist, and provides a full accounting of sales to both the artist and the facility. It is not uncommon for such contractors to invest up to $25,000 for attractive and permanent merchandise display stands in key areas in the facility's concourse.

Rock acts, as well as family attractions and sporting franchises, are looking more and more to merchandise revenue to balance their budgets. It is vital that the facility managers create and maintain an environment where merchandising can be maximized with a minimum of friction between the facility, its tenants, and the merchandising contractor. The net effect is substantially increased revenue.

Parking

Parking is always a problem, but if handled properly, it can also be a very lucrative source of revenue. Virtually all persons who attend an event arrive by car, but they do not necessarily have to park in the facility's lot. Parking operations in most cases, therefore, cannot be taken for granted. Careful attention must be given to creating an easy traffic flow so cars can enter and exit quickly. The lot must be well paved, well lit, and secured, and management should have a graphic system that makes it easy for people to find their cars at the conclusion of events. An adequate number of cashiers and attendants will improve operations.

Additional parking revenue (at least $1.00 per space) can also be achieved by offering preferred or special parking for customers willing to pay the price to park closer to the building.

In many respects, parking is a very difficult operation to manage. Having good employees with qualities of honesty and trust is much easier when the facility manager has tight financial controls. John Root, manager of the San Francisco Cow Palace, presented a paper entitled "Parking — New Sources Of Revenue" to the 1980 National Conference of the International Association of Auditorium Managers. He shared the results of a survey conducted by the Cow Palace regarding different controls in effect at other facilities. They included the following:

1. Sensors or loops buried in each entrance line.
2. A single pass lane.
3. A cashier or checker watching the sellers and authorizing passes.
4. Spot checks on sellers.
5. Different colored tickets for different events, days, or hours.
6. Cash registers.
7. TV monitors.
8. Clean graphics and signs indicating special entrances.

The parking operation is second only to the box office in terms of direct contact between facility and patron. A well-designed and well-managed parking operation will ease crowd tension and allow for sufficient time for patrons to buy a snack and still get to their seats on time — and in a good frame of mind. There is no question that the ease of access and parking is a major factor in increased public acceptance and attendance at events.

Televising Events

Dante Cork Vickers and Jim Millet wrote an interesting article entitled "Cable TV—A New Day Dawns for Facility Managers," which appeared in the April 1983 issue of *Auditorium News*. The authors offer: "[P]ay television may one day lead to crowdless games played before a cameraman and technicians. Not only will there be no fans paying for tickets, there will be no fans to park, to eat refreshments or to buy [programs] or souvenirs."

More and more events, especially sporting events, are being televised either on cable, pay, and/or network television. It is still too early to properly assess the impact that televising home games will have on actual attendance levels; however, there is a clear danger that if tenants are allowed relatively unrestricted ability to televise home games, some facilities may turn into little more than large broadcast studios.

Some in the industry, such as Joe Cohen of the Madison Square Garden's Cable Network, see cable television as an opportunity. This, of course, stems, in part at least, from the fact that the owners of the Madison Square Garden Cable Network also own Madison Square Garden, as well as its two prime tenants, the New York Knickerbockers and the New York Rangers. In such cases, televising events can be controlled so that when the teams are playing poorly and attendance is down, revenue levels can be maintained by televising the product, whereas when the teams are playing well and there is a strong demand for tickets, television can be restricted.

Most facilities are not in such a powerful position. The owner of the facility and the owner of the sporting franchise become adversaries on the issue of whether or not to allow televising of a home game. One possible compromise is to negotiate a "make-whole" clause in the agreement with the franchise, whereby the franchise agrees to reimburse the facility for any drop in attendance at televised home games. For example, assume that the Hartford Whalers played non-televised home games against the Minnesota North Stars in the 1982 and 1983 seasons and the average paid attendance was 9,000 per game. The Whalers were then offered a lucrative contract by a local television station to televise the 1984 game against Minnesota. The Hartford Civic Center granted permission, and the game drew only 8,000 paid attendees. By virtue of the "make-whole" agreement, the Whalers would be responsible for paying the Civic Center for lost rent and concession revenue on the basis of the following formula:

1. The average ticket price for the Whaler's 1982 and 1983 games was $9.50. This amount ($9.50) times the difference between the average attendance for 1982 and 1983 and the actual attendance for 1984 (i.e., 1,000) produced a revenue shortfall of $9,500 for the 1984 game, a shortfall which, it is assumed, was due to this game's having been televised. The $9,500 shortfall in ticket sales times the Civic Center's rental charge (13%) equals $1,235 in "make-whole" rent payments to the Hartford Civic Center.

2. The Hartford Civic Center's actual concession sales for the 1982 and 1983 Whaler games averaged $2.50 per capita. Both the Whalers and the Civic Center agreed that the Civic Center achieved a 55% net profit on its concession operations. By virtue of the make-whole agreement, the $2.50 per-capita figure would be multiplied by the difference in at-

tendance (1,000), which would equal $2,500. This figure would then be multiplied by the 55% net-profit factor (so that the Whalers would not have to reimburse the Civic Center for overhead, staffing, and product costs not actually incurred), thus requiring the Whalers to pay the Civic Center $1,375 in lost concession revenue.

The total formula would result in a reimbursement penalty to the Civic Center of $2,610. There are a number of variations to this formula, but the basic intent is to ensure that the facility does not suffer lost revenue as a result of a franchise's desire to televise one or more home games. With such a "make-whole" provision, it becomes less risky for a facility to allow its franchise to televise home games. And there may be certain intangible benefits derived by the facility and the franchise. For example, seeing a team play well and sensing the excitement in the arena may encourage more people to buy tickets and see the action live.

Once the facility and the franchise are properly protected, it then becomes time to look more positively at the opportunities that television offers. For example, while tenants have the right to televise their product, they do not necessarily have the right to provide the "hookup" for the station (or stations) that has been granted the broadcast rights. The actual hookup contractor should be investigated. Contractors should be charged with installing permanent cabling/wiring in the facility to make hookups more efficient and economical. They should also be responsible for providing complete state-of-the-art television, AM/FM radio, and closed-circuit television equipment (including uplink capacity), as well as the personnel and technicians required for the operation and maintenance of this equipment.

The television hookup contractor must also be able to clearly demonstrate the ability to reduce the cost of originating television transmissions from the facility while at the same time providing the facility with the greatest possible financial return. Without any investment or risk, a net of $500 to $1,000 per hookup can be realized.

Knowing downside risks and having the spirit of cooperation with tenants, the television industry can result in considerable benefit to the facility. There is no question that television will become an ever-more dominant factor in the presentation of live events. Television revenue is too lucrative to pass up, and many franchises need it just to break even. While facility managers should not stand in the way of such progress, they should first protect their own interests. *They should be a partner—not a victim.*

Summary/Conclusion

The facility is, in the final analysis, a sales and marketing organization. Management's primary responsibility is to satisfy the tenants who rent the facility and the customers who attend the events.

A strong sales and marketing capacity is critical to success. Once an event is confirmed, there is a limited amount of time to conduct the promotion, marketing, and advertising campaigns, and to sell the tickets and actually produce the event. How the entire package of services and functions discussed in this chapter (i.e., scheduling, advertising, box office, concessions, merchandising, parking, and television) is handled will determine the immediate and long-range success of the facility. The facility manager should not forget to be ever-conscious about providing a well-run, clean, and safe environment. This will add to the enjoyment of those attending the events, and patrons in a good frame of mind will be more likely to purchase food, beverages, and merchandising and to return to other events at the facility. The sport manager should take time to review the organization, inside and out, from a sales and marketing point of view. In fact, this should be a continuous process because management should never take tenants or the public for granted.

Part 4

Media Management

Public relations in sport management is not a luxury — it is a necessity.

Jeaneane Williams

Chapter 15

Public Relations in Amateur Sports: New Efforts in a Changing Business World

Debra Korb

We all realize that the world is changing around us. Depending on where you live, however, will determine how willing and how fast the business world fosters change and, in turn, how willing and how fast change is accepted. Metropolitan regions tend to embrace change more readily. After all, change is what has helped them to industrialize, grow, reinvent, and grow again. In rural areas, the same formula for change is recognizable in the fields, through crop rotation, but other aspects of the rural business community often do not seem to accept progress as quickly as metropolitan regions.

Similarly, a large divide exists between corporate sports marketing/public relations and amateur, or nonprofit, sports organizations. A good starting point for exploring is the budget: the multimillion dollar salaries and the team licensing/product endorsements.

Working on a Shoestring Budget

Whether the sports organization is a community Babe Ruth league, a collegiate soccer team, or even a large and fancy steeplechase race, creative networking and media exposure is imperative. Obtaining sponsorship dollars can be a challenge. Large companies often limit requests to once a year so they can budget appropriately, and smaller businesses, while more flexible in *when* they can spend, have small budgets. The more unique and targeted you are in demonstrating how your event will reach an audience, the more likely you are to secure funding. Be creative in finding ways to provide exposure, perks, and publicity to a potential sponsor.

Example: A huge spring horse event, although aimed at the well-heeled crowd, did not have a television advertising budget. The organizers of the event teamed up with a local car dealer and an event sponsor with a TV budget, and created a win-win campaign. The ads ran for a period of time during several time slots and offered two free passes for admission to the event with every test drive of a GMC vehicle. To sweeten the deal, all test-drive participants were eligible for a drawing to win an upgrade to the next best seating level at the event.

Networking

The business community has been in the "networking business" for a long time. While the majority of groups have a mission to serve the community for a special cause, they nonetheless hold breakfast meetings, lunch meetings, after-hour receptions, or dinner meetings that provide an opportunity to exchange business cards and encourage introductions: the perfect venue for industrious "deal-makers."

- Business Community. Join or encourage your staff to join your community's Chamber of Commerce, Rotary, Lions, and Kiwanis. Of course, you will meet people, but remember that such community organizations look for speakers *every week*. Tell your story and enlist support. Depending on your program, you may gain support from area YMCAs and local hospitals, as well as from community health services agencies.
- Tag-team with a viable business partner and make a joint presentation. People are busy and will appreciate your saving them time by connecting the dots for them.
- State and Local Government /Schools (kids are very influential)/Parks & Recreation: All public entities offer a way to get involved. *Join boards, run for office* (even though probably 92% of you are not cut out for that), or *rally support* for someone who shares similar thoughts and ideas and who can make intelligent compromises. Involve children, and it is a win-win outcome. Offer learning opportunities for them. They are not only impressionable and make good apprentices; they are also fabulous ambassadors and are able to draw enthusiasm and support from parents.
- Retail Business. In the "olden days," bars or restaurants would sponsor neighborhood softball teams. Modern times call for more health-conscious measures, and sponsors such as General Nutrition Centers (GNCs) and Subway Restaurants. Get *their names* on ball caps, team jerseys, ballpark banners, and so forth. The win-win here is that many chain restaurants look for local memorabilia to decorate their restaurants and to embrace the local community; thus, such chain restaurants are logical places to approach for sponsorships and relationship marketing.
- Sports-Related Attractions. Sports museums, sporting goods stores, and sport amusement locations may offer good cross-promotional opportunities.
- No matter how much money you spend, no matter how many clever outlets *you think* you have covered, you will hear the sinking words, "Oh, if only I had known." Submit press releases, offer to write a feature column, and send news bits for community calendars to newspapers, local TV stations, trade publications, professional associations, and trade organizations; in addition, join blogs.

Example: A regional Babe Ruth tournament was started by a group of baseball dads. They applied for and secured the privilege to host two tournaments in a county just south of the border of a major, up-and-coming Southern, cosmopolitan city. With eight hotel/motel properties in its jurisdiction, with no novel attractions, and with only chain restaurants to offer, the group called upon the local chamber of commerce for help. The chairman of the board of the chamber of commerce sent letters to the city Manager and the county Manager, outlining the economic impact the visiting teams and their coaches and traveling families and fans would have over a six-day stay. (Many claim that it takes eight or nine times for a message to sink in, so the more people you can gather to tell your tale, the better off you will be.) This letter of endorsement requesting sponsorship opened doors since it came from a respected member of the business community.

Finding the Workforce and the Funding

Engage the help from students at a local high school, community college, or university. Enlist the help from retirees who belong to a senior center. Church youth groups and neighborhood sports associations are always looking for volunteers, so they should be willing to swap favors. Hopefully, they will bring other family members or friends.

Fund-Raising

Fund-raising runs the gamut from selling candy bars and wrapping paper to cow-chip bingo. (Cow-chip bingo involved dropping sacks of flour on a football field converted to a bingo card and was a real crowd pleaser.)

Example: A company that set up and ran regional triathlons was looking for volunteers. It offered to pay a nominal fee per volunteer and a bonus for hitting a certain number per group. Two nonprofit sports groups organized volunteer teams and were able to have fun working at a sports event while raising funds to help support their own sports endeavors.

It's Always About the Brand!

Partnering and cross-promotion make financial sense, but the important rule to follow is to partner only with companies who place the same value on quality and customer service equal to or exceeding that of your company. Brand recognition is earned over time, and you do not want to lose respect in the market by being associated with a company whose brand is less respected.

Example: Bundling and copromoting extended brand products in similar products channels can be an effective form of promotion. Buy a set of Ping clubs and receive a box of Pro V-1 golf balls. Get a ball cap with the purchase of a golf shirt.

Advertising Placement

Advertising placement will be dictated by where your audience is located. Plug in to a variety of organizations at regional, state, and local levels.

- Division of Tourism and Sports Development
- Sports Councils
- Sports Publications
- Local Media
- Community Newsletters: Schools, Churches, Homeowner Associations

Measuring Results

The age-old challenge of figuring out the effectiveness of your marketing strategy/ad campaign continues. Although you might not realize immediate sales results, there is a reason to stay in front of an audience. (Remember that it is always about the brand.) If your name is not circulating, someone else's is, and will become "top of mind."

Example: Here is a clever tracking method employed by Clemson University fans. Clemson fans have a tradition of taking $2 bills when they travel to an away game, especially a bowl game. The tradition started in 1977 when Clemson had been playing the Georgia Tech Yellow Jackets several years in a row. Georgia Tech was not a member of the Atlantic Coast Conference at the time, but the rivalry was still a great one because of the short two-hour drive between Atlanta and Clemson.

Prior to the 1977 football season, the Georgia Tech administration decided that it did not want to play Clemson anymore. George Bennett, director of IPTAY, and other Clemson fans wanted to show Atlanta businesses the kind of economic impact which Clemson fans have.

To prove their point, for the 1977 Georgia Tech game, Clemson fans took all their spending money in the form of $2 bills. Atlanta businesses were flooded with these $2 bills, and they all knew they had come from the Clemson faithful (some bills had a tiger paw stamped on them). Because merchants did not have a slot for the $2 bill in their registers, having stacks of these bills in the registers really made an impact.

The local media gave this phenomenon plenty of press time, and every Clemson fan supported the idea. Later that year, when Clemson traveled to Jacksonville, Florida, for the Gator Bowl, all the Clemson fans took $2 bills to spend on everything. Since then, Clemson fans have been traveling with the $2 bills to all away games and bowls.

More Evolution

And then, just when you think you've mastered the art of marketing a sport, a half-dozen new competitive sports arrive on the scene: wakeboarding, kiteboarding, skateboarding, and. most recently, text messaging!

Chapter 16

The Spinning World of Media Relations

John Horshok

Once upon a time, the shortest distance between two lines of communication was up close and personal.

Now the mission and the journey are a menu of breaking news, gimmicks, and mass information transit.

The Internet has provided a field of dreams for media and public relations folks, yet sometimes it may gurgle up the process and remove the good old-fashioned touch of one-on-one relationship building.

Quite frankly, it can be perceived as a runaway bread truck with solid opinions not even close to being on the same page.

A One-Dimensional System

Joe Klein has been the general manager of three major league baseball teams (the Cleveland Indians, the Detroit Tigers, and the Texas Rangers).

"When I was at Texas we had a one dimensional communication system—the telephone," Klein recalls. "We basically worked our deals and information from 9 to 5—that was it—and you worked directly on your relationships with your beat and column writers because you saw them just about every day."

Now, as executive director of the highly successful Atlantic League, Klein has "new challenges to make deals and propel communication," he says.

This past summer, Klein had to handle the nationally publicized bat-swinging incident of former major league player José Offerman. who made headlines and TV while playing in the Atlantic League. Klein has also had John Rocker and other "distractions" that brought the Atlantic League unique publicity.

"Sometimes it's true ... there are times when there isn't really bad publicity when it calls attention to the league."

"Let's see ... Internet, cell phone, fax, blogs, teleconferences ... it seems like you are never off the job these days. I don't know how we did it in the old days," he pointedly added. "The information gets out so fast it cannot be packaged any-more."

"I Don't Use the Internet"

Linda Pereira is Director of Player Relations for the San Francisco Giants' San Jose affiliate. She has been with the same team for 41 years. She started performing tasks for the team as a kid in sixth grade and continued doing so during and after attending San Jose State University.

"I don't use the Internet for business," she says bluntly.

"I want to talk with people. I like to talk with people. I don't want to become like so many people who hide behind caller ID and voice mail," she asserts. "Yes, I am old-fashioned," she admits, "but it is just too easy to have voice mail and get away from talking to people in this business. I won't do that."

"I'm Not a Computer Geek"

It is tough to find many sports broadcasting professionals like Johnny Holliday. Holliday has covered many sports teams in his career during and after being a nationally known DJ. He has been the "Voice of Maryland" for 29 years and has been with ABC Sports for 28 years. In addition, he currently conducts a pregame Washington Nationals show with Ray Knight and Don Baylor.

"I'm not a computer geek," he declares.

"I am tired of being sent to Web sites for information. I miss the old days when one-on-one communication was of value in this business," he said. "I have been doing this a long time and I recently went to an ACC campus twice — once for basketball and once for football — and never met or saw the Sports Information Director of either trip," he complained. "That is wrong — all media relations people should step back and see how and why the job was created. When I get calls I always try and help the other person do their job."

"When you travel town to town you rely on the information people to tell you about injuries, trends, milestones or possible records to be broken, etc.," he indicated. "This is really bad when people hide behind the Internet and lump everyone together to sort out what they need. The Sports Information people used to be your personal touch and your eyes and ears to help you provide the best coverage ... it's just not there in many, many situations these days," he said.

He really rails when he is sent to a Web site. It's a real sticking point with him and his busy schedule. "I really miss the days when personal touches built relationships if not friendships," he concludes. "I know the difference in the process quality now and the process quality then."

He quickly added that some teams have kept up quality standards and offered the University of North Carolina as one of the best.

Steve Kirchner runs the UNC Tar heel media operation.

Steve worked at age 10 for the Bristol, Connecticut, minor league (Red Sox) affiliate. He fell in love with being the quarterback of sports information. He agrees in part with Holliday.

Media Has Changed the Process

"The Internet has become a crutch," Kirchner says. "It can be so easy and so impersonal but it can reach sooooo many people by just hitting a button. We all use it but I recognize that more is not better."

"It is an unfiltered way to communicate and we know that everyone doesn't care about 20 pages on field hockey ... but players, parents, boosters, recruits and sponsors do," he offers. "I know you cannot meaningfully talk directly to people on a Web site." The truth is, of course, is that there really isn't enough time to fairly represent each sport on an up-close and personal basis, and that truth does bother Kirchner.

"I think the evolution of the Internet is mostly positive but what has changed is the focus of the press who have made PR people guarded," Kirchner explained. "Media has changed from what happened to why things happen. The salaries, off-the-field troubles, anything relative to money or controversy has caused adversarial relationships between team representatives and the press."

Catch-22 Just Got Tougher

"And," Kirchner continued, "it is telling that at the University level upper management has made very little effort to to get any 'closer' in their relationships with the media."

"We used to be a service area ... we really could impact season ticket sales, recruiting, awards and coverage but now we are on call at all times in this job because of the instantaneous nature of the news." Kirchner paused to make a prediction: "I don't see things changing with the fascination of the press with sensational stories that sometimes just make upper management cringe when they are not getting hammered."

Tricky Dick Started This Mess

Blame it all on Richard Nixon.

Ike Pappas was *the* guy standing beside Lee Harvey Oswald when Jack Ruby shot him. Pappas has done it all in journalism and has even appeared in movies. He worked in legendary times and in company with CBS TV and Walter Cronkite.

"We thought we were a part of the strong fabric of America," he reflects. "As corny as it sounds we wanted to get the news first but, more importantly, we wanted to get it right." Pappas recalls that it was standard for CBS News Director Cronkite to call him and others minutes before they went live nationally to question a story and ask for verification of sources and quotations. "If Walter was not satisfied he would either kill the story or push it back in the broadcast."

Pappas offers, "You don't seem to have to prove anything anymore because the 24 hour cable news cycle has created huge pressure to produce news even when there is no news. The same stories run ad nauseum over and over and over again and people think because they run over and over that they are important. The cable networks simply must produce a huge supply of news to fill 24 straight hours and stories that aren't really big news get huge play through the process of repetition."

Oh yeah, the Nixon part.

The Spin Zone: Pre-Bill O'Reilly

"The White House started the spin business," Pappas contends. "The Nixon administration started it all when Nixon sent Vice President Spiro Agnew to Des Moines one day [Pappas covered the speech] and Agnew launched into his attack on the press calling them "Nattering Nebobs of Negativism."

Pappas called back to CBS from Des Moines, charging: "This guy [Agnew] wants to take on everybody."

The press *was* unfavorable to the Nixon administration on many fronts, including Vietnam and Watergate and, well ... you know the rest.

"If you didn't agree with the White House you were branded a 'liberal' and it is still happening today. 'Liberal' is a bad word. The powers that be want you to believe that no one is impartial anymore," Pappas asserts. "It is a running gun battle between the White House and the press."

To Blog or Not to Blog ... That Is the ... What?

One key area that irritates Pappas is the explosion of blogs.

"The blogs allow millions of opinions ... anyone can have one." The inference is clear that blogs combined with the mass-produced opinions of cable TV analysts should not be confused with traditional and quality journalism.

Pappas weighs in fairly often on "the overall scope of work." "There are good journalists out there but they must do it the way the network does it today. Eye witness accounts are not the fashion—front office advertising made the news big money."

"We had pride in following the 'highest standards' in journalism at the time," Pappas added, with a tinge of pride in his voice.

The Twilight and No Spin Zone

Despite the climate unfurled by Nixon and Agnew, there was a day before the Internet, cell phones, and the like when the White House created another initiative to get the attention of the world. According to Robert Jones, it was the classic No Spin Zone.

It was simple. President Jimmy Carter decided that because the Soviet Union had invaded Afghanistan—a UN member country—the United States must pull out of the 1980 Moscow Summer Olympic Games.

Carter decided to announce his decision at the 1980 Lake Placid Winter Olympic Games. But he canceled his scheduled appearance in Lake Placid and sent attorney and White House Counsel Lloyd Cutler to frame the remarks with Robert O. Jones, who worked in concert with the United States Olympic Committee (USOC). Cutler summoned Jones to Lake Placid from an assignment in the Sahara Desert. Jones said, "I arrived late and had to sleep on a couch at the 'Presidential House' designated for President Carter. ... Vice President Walter Mondale was there but it was Cutller who told me I had to go tell Juan Samarach [head of the IOC] that the United States was not coming to the Moscow Games that summer." "Samarach was staying at the old Lake Placid Hotel and it had protruding pipes and was a little frayed and the only place to sit was with him on his bed," Jones remembers. "He reminded me that in real life he was the ambassador to the Soviet Union [for Spain] and told me this was going to be difficult because if it was handled wrong he would be replaced as the head of the IOC with an Eastern Bloc official likely to be appointed."

"He offered me a glass of whiskey—we didn't have any ice—and he was a little guy with his legs dangling off the bed while we discussed how to break the news to the press."

"Samarach handled the press conference as well as he could and he was right about staying in power," Jones added.

"He was politically supportive of the West but neither he or I even thought about gathering any support from the press before the press conference."

A Classic "No Spin" Approach

What was the fallout for Bob Jones?

"The USOC members blamed it on me . . .'a shoot the messenger thing,'" Jones remembers.

Bad news, good news?

"After VP Mondale and Cutler fled back to the White House I got full use of the 'Presidential House' for the rest of the Olympics," Jones laughed.

"Carter's decision had explosive consequences and was huge world news but I can't see how we could have handled it any other way. . . . I certainly don't think modern technology could have helped that process," Jones offered.

Just a Little Bit Outside

Randall Swearingen wrote the most recent book on baseball legend Mickey Mantle.

The book is titled *A Great Teammate — The Legend Of Mickey Mantle.*

"The Internet was a savior for me," Swearingen maintained."It provides accurate research . . . it is vital."

Here's a famous story.

It's Mantle's last season, and 31-game winner Denny McLain is on the mound for the Detroit Tigers, working with a 6–0 lead in late-season game. Several books, including two by Mantle, recount McLain calling star catcher Bill Freehan to the mound.

The fix is "inside."

McLain tells Freehan to tell Mantle that he's "not going to work on him." Mantle takes the first grooved medium fastball in disbelief. He steps outside. McLain and Freehand smile crooked grins. Mantle holds his bat out to indicate where he wants the next pitch. McLain obliges, and Mantle slams the ball into the right field stands for a home run and runs around the bases with his classic "head down" trademark as the Detroit fans applaud loud and long to emotionally pay the Yankee legend honor and respect for his awesome career.

The story has been reported verbatim for years by writers, fans, and former players. But Swearingen points out one single flaw in the story.

The catcher was backup Jim Price. Freehan was in the dugout applauding.

"The problem is," Swearingen says, that with writing about anything that happened in the past, "memories are not perfect."

"The Internet can find press coverage of articles written the next day about nearly every event," Swearingen remarked. "It is really hard to collect accurate information even with a first hand account."

Sports stories are especially vulnerable, since retired athletes' careers seem to get better and better every year as memories fade and the facts get embellished or changed or invented.

Swearingen is a huge apostle of the legend of Mickey Mantle and owns one of the biggest collections of Mantle memorabilia that exist. He leans it occasionally, and even Major League teams have used it to draw fan interest. He has a substantial sports library and currently serves on the board of a baseball-related charity in Houston. He is a pure baseball fan.

"Sports stories aren't hard to track down," he contends. "They're hard to get right."

Swearingen reeled off story after story that turned out to be ... well, just a little bit outside of the ... facts.

One day Mantle launched a rocket in old Griffith Stadium in Washington, D.C., off a guy named Chuck Stobbs. The ball was measured down the block at 565 feet. The fun part of the story was always hearing about Billy Martin (Martin told it countless times himself) trying to crack Mantle up as he headed to third in his humble, head-down trot. Martin was acting as if he were going to tag up, and Mantle almost passed him to run out the home run until third base coach Frank Crosetti screamed at Mantle to stop and Martin to move. Great story. I heard it myself from both Mantle and Martin. Hilarious stuff. I still tell that story several times at golf-outing dinners and parties. Hilarious. If I close my eyes, I can see them hanging on each other and laughing like crazy right now.

"It didn't happen," Swearingen said.

"I checked the next day coverage and box scores and Yogi Berra was on first base and Martin was in the dugout," he recounts, with genuine disappointment.

That story has been circulated and retold by radio, TV, books, and writers to millions of sports fans.

To Yankee fans, this new information is worse than the Grinch who stole Christmas.

Swearingen has more "story change orders" like these two. Lots more. I have heard them all personally ... just not this new way with real facts. It makes me want to check the next-day coverage of Noah's Ark.

Swearingen sighs, "The Internet gives you finger-ready facts and research that jumps in your lap in just seconds.... You cannot operate without it in the writing or research business."

"Memories are not perfect," he repeats. "Stories and facts change as memories fade."

The Internet. Swearingen and writers everywhere wouldn't have it any other way. It serves and protects. It propels new businesses at the speed of light. It is good for research and reality.

It is bad, however, for legendary yarns.

He Said/She Said ... Some Final Words

This evolution of spin and media relations is firmly in the middle of a significant growth spurt without boundaries.

Page Crawford, who anchors the NBC Webcast in Raleigh, says bluntly, "Newspapers and television and radio stations are almost completely obsolete at this point."

Those times that "are a changing" — Get this ...

"News organizations of every sort are becoming multi-media providers for every platform. They have to in order to survive," Crawford says flatly.

"A webcast is a great way to get the news to a generation that is used to getting what they want, when they want it. *Now*!" Crawford explains.

That, of course, is news to some generations.

The final word?

Page's husband is Jake Fehling.

Fehling came up the traditional way in sports and, in fact, was a college intern to Steve Kirchner, who gets the highest possible rating from Johnny Holliday, who basically thinks the whole new direction … well … stinks.

"I was trained by some great professionals like Kirchner, Mike Moran of the USOC and John Blundell [Media Director of Major League Baseball] … it is not just learning, it is learning the right way," he contends. Fehling is currently the Director of Media & Public Relations for USA Baseball.

"I agree with both sides here—a personal relationship versus an electronic one—but in the end I know that it's not my e-mail signature that is going to get remembered—it's my handshake."

Different strokes, different folks.

Where is it going?

I dunno, where's Waldo?

"They are changing the world."

I have now worked in one fashion or another in the world of sports for nearly 40 years.

The opinions expressed in this chapter are like a bunch of different patterns that make up one big quilt. Sports is like that. Putting square pegs into round holes is a constant exercise like trying to blend the many personalities of individuals into a team. The formula is a moving target. So is the sports industry. Let's see, night games at Wrigley, steroids, player scandal after player scandal. Yup, things are changing.

I have met many famous people and, yes, sports legends, during my tour of duty.

One of my personal favorites (including Mickey Mantle) is Eunice Kennedy Shriver, a real-life angel who has changed everything from laws to lives in the world of intellectually challenged individuals. Yes, that's right. We do not say mentally retarded any longer. That has also changed.

Eunice Kennedy Shriver started the Special Olympics program. I think she is one of the most effective persons in our country.

In the mid-1970s I was hired away from an international sports program I was directing in connection with the U.S. State Department by Coca-Cola USA. The term *sports marketing* was not used back then. That, too, has changed. I was hired to expose all of the Coca-Cola bottlers in the United States to the Special Olympics program. These were/are the same bottlers used to running blond beach boys and bunnies in all of their mainstream advetising. I was charged with convincing them to host and promote persons with noticeable physical and mentally retarded features. I thought my task would take a week or two.

It took eight years.

Mrs. Shriver spent one whole sunny afternoon in 1975 at a Special Olympics soccer clinic in New Jersey, challenging me as a former sportswriter to help her design strategy to get Special Olympics and Special Olympians on the sports pages and not buried with token coverage in the other sections of newspapers. Special Olympics was only about seven years old. There were enormous growing pains. Change happened every day.

We were sitting in the stands watching Kyle Rote, Jr., run a clinic with about 100 Special Olympians.

"They are changing the world," Mrs. Shriver maintained. "It is not enough that our athletes finally get access to facilities and activities like everyone else—the real challenge is for us to get our athletes in the sports pages like every other athlete. They *are* athletes!" she declared, with more than a little passion. "They are achieving things that people never thought they could achieve. They are fantastic! They must be recognized just like every other athlete … this is a valuable part of the change we are making … we must involve them in the mainstream of sports, society and life itself!"

I visited with Mrs. Shriver at her house several times this past year for several different events and reasons, and we had a chance to talk about that talk we'd had over 30 years ago. Mrs. Shriver is 86 these days. She has not lost her passion or her energy.

She remembered our conversation from so many years ago. She picked back up on it as if it had happened five minutes ago.

"Oh, it's been grand," she reflected on all the changes in the international program that now serves 2.5 million intellectually challenged individuals in 165 countries—almost as if she personally had nothing to do with it.

"We get so much wonderful press around the world with the television [the International Games have been on network TV since 1979] and such—but we still must work hard to get these athletes in the sports pages. It is simply something we must do," she said determinedly. I smiled. She has done so much. She needs more.

Eunice Kennedy Shriver's efforts have changed the world.

She insists on change. She has made it happen.

She has been fierce and tireless. She is changing things right now as you read this.

One way to get comfortable with change is to create it.

If You Pick the Fruit, Feed the Roots

If there is a point to this exercise, it is that all of the points above are valid. They expose feelings about the evolution of the Internet. Both sides need to examine their options.

I recently met a man who calls himself "Radha," short for N. Radhakrishnan Pr.D., P.E., Vice-Chancellor for Research and Economic Development for North Carolina Agricultural and Technical State University.

Radha is from India. He is very smart, and his business card is very full.

Radha was lamenting the challenge to graduate quality engineers—an endangered species in the United States these days—while finding the money from fund-raising to sustain, develop, and advance his mission statement.

Radha put it simply:

"If you pick the fruit, feed the roots."

So there you have it.

The Internet was created by a person. Not vice versa.

If this was that Paul Newman/*Cool Hand Luke* movie, we could say, "What we have here is a failure to communicate."

Change is good.

But don't forget that change is a people business.

The Internet didn't get you your job. It won't take you to lunch to advance your efforts. It isn't much fun sitting next to it at a sporting event. Business is personal. Very personal. You will really remember the hands you shake.

You can look it up on the Internet.

Chapter 17

Fire the Coach.com

Tom Appenzeller

It was widely reported several years ago that the day after Ron Zook was named the new head football coach at the University of Florida, a Web site appeared named "FireRonZook.com." In the words of an old Bob Dylan song, yes, the times they are a-changing. Faster than a speeding Dale Earnhart, Jr., more powerful than a Shaquille O'Neal pick, able to leap tall buildings better than Michael Jordan, able to spread information, rumor, and gossip quicker than Oprah, the Internet is changing the way fans follow their favorite teams.

The sports manager of today has to understand not only public relations but the new technology of the Internet.

Sport fans now have access to blogs, chat rooms, message boards, MySpace, and YouTube, as well as numerous Web sites. A recent Google search of high school football turned up 22,800,000 sites in just 12 seconds. The Internet is changing the face of public relations for all athletic organizations. It was the Internet that helped bring down Don Imus, and it was YouTube that showed America a coach attacking a player in a Pop Warner football game.

Brevard College is a small liberal arts college of 600 students located in western North Carolina. The NCAA Division II school reinstated intercollegiate football in the fall of 2006 after a 50-year absence. When the athletic director fired the head football coach in the spring of 2007, message boards, blogs, and chat rooms blasted him for his decision. It is one thing for a local newspaper to carry the story, and another for the story to be circulated all over the world via the Web. What effect the message boards, blogs, and chat rooms will have on football recruiting at Brevard is yet to be determined, but the school took a public relations hit on the Internet.

Former Head Basketball Coach Matt Doherty at the University of North Carolina discovered the power of the Internet firsthand. Doherty made a private, off-hand remark about the Duke cheerleaders before a game in Cameron Indoor Stadium. The comment was overhead and recorded by a fan sitting near the bench and was all over the Internet before halftime. Needless to say, the Internet flack did not help Doherty solidify his position as the head men's basketball coach at UNC and was very damaging to his career in Chapel Hill.

The University of Oklahoma football team recently had to forfeit eight wins from the 2005 season because three players had accepted improper payments from the Big Red Sports and Imports car dealership. The Sooners' 8–4 record became 0–4, and Head Coach Bob Stoops' career record dropped from 86–19 to 78–19. The alleged tip that started the investigation came from a Texas A&M alumni blog, where it was reported that some big, well-known Oklahoma players were getting paid by the car dealership but without having done any work.

In North Carolina, former State House Speaker Jim Black, once one of the most powerful men in Tar Heel politics, was sentenced to five years in prison and fined $50,000 for illegally taking cash from chiropractors. Joe Sinsheimer, who once ran a Web site calling for Black's resignation, is credited with bringing down the veteran lawmaker. Sinsheimer was honored by the North Carolina Press Association with the annual Lassiter Award that goes to a nonjournalist who furthers the cause of the First Amendment. A basketball coach, a football team, and a politician are just three examples of the impact the Internet is having on American society.

Today's sport administrators must be able to handle and access the Internet as well as the local media. One of the pioneers in sports public relations is Kathleen Hessert, the president and CEO of Sports Media Challenge. In 1988, Hessert, an award-winning television anchor personality, used her experience and expertise to begin counseling colleges as well as professional and Olympic athletics. The former talk show host became a media and speech coach for big-name coaches, athletes, and organizations all across the country. In 1991, Sports Media Challenge added Issue Management, Crisis Planning, and Crisis Intervention for their clients. According to Hessert, "For today's athlete and coach, winning is no longer enough."

Traditionally, major Division I universities and professional clubs have had to deal only with the mainstream media. The positions of sports information director and public relations director were created years ago to facilitate the relationship between the sport organization and the media. That structure worked well for years, but now the Internet has given fans a whole new way to be involved with their team. Sports radio talk shows came along and allowed a few fans to vent their joy or frustration, but again, the audience was limited to a local or regional area. Now the fan has unlimited access 24 hours a day to every rumor, piece of gossip, or conspiracy theory ever imagined.

The Internet is like the tabloid *National Enquirer* on steroids, and it is not just about the celebrities anymore. Web sites, blogs, message boards, and chat rooms have been established that focus on small colleges, high schools, and even youth sports. Just consult with any number of high schools and colleges who found embarrassing hazing incidents playing on YouTube over the last year.

Kathleen Hessert, of Sports Media Challenge, believes that athletic organizations need to monitor the Internet—the good and the bad. It is critical to have a handle on what might be called the "fan buzz." Since the Internet is going to be there, the athletic administrator needs to uncover and use the information. The Sports Media Challenge gives eight reasons why coaches should listen to and track online fan word of mouth:

1. It is a proactive public-relations tool for the athletic department.
2. It is an effective tool for crisis management.
3. It manages a reputation by protecting and enhancing it.
4. It efficiently and comprehensively tracks recruits online.
5. It identifies compliance violations early.
6. It identifies and enlists "influencers" and advocates.
7. It allows fans to trust other fans first and then spread their opinions.
8. It allows for the growth of fan power and passion online.

Chapter 18

Duke Lacrosse: A Case Study on Internet Buzz[*]

Sports Media Challenge

Charlotte, NC—The Duke lacrosse story provides an abject lesson for any sport organization or its sponsors on the power and influence of the Internet. Every team or program wants to maintain a high and positive profile with fans, and every sponsor wants to be sure it is enhancing its brand by associating with the team.

When players on the Duke lacrosse team were charged with sexual assault, the university responded through the traditional media, sending spokespeople and even the university president to issue statements for the local, national, and even international media.

But while the casual fan might have been satisfied when the traditional media relayed Duke's prepared comments, the bloggers and chatters who make up the growing universe of Fan Generated Media(tm) were just getting started.

Nowadays, few subjects outside of politics generate as much online activity and "buzz" as sport. Indeed, the most dedicated and passionate fans are increasingly gravitating toward the chat rooms, message boards, and other online channels that make up the Fan Generated Media (FGM). These fans are analogous to a political organization's "base"—the audience segment whose ongoing dedication is most critical to its long-term stability and success. That is why sport organizations and sponsors, like their political peers, must pay attention to the FGM—because of its capacity to drive the discussion into the mainstream.

"The Internet provides a rich source of emotional reaction to events, and an important outlet for dedicated fans—a program or team's 'base' audience—and other critical constituencies to express those opinions," said Kathleen Hessert, President of Sports Media Challenge (SMC), a Charlotte, N.C.-based company specializing in reputation management for major sport organizations.

"That combination of emotion, opinion, and expression has tremendous power to affect the brand reputation of any sport organization. These word-of-mouth FGM opinions, and the organization's responses, can build excitement around sport brands, but can also cripple them.

"Collegiate Athletic Departments, pro teams, leagues, and corporate sponsors need to understand what fans, critics, and competitors are saying online—and to manage that discussion effectively."

---

[*] Reprinted with permission from Kathleen Hessert of Sport Media Challenge in an interview with Tom Appenzeller. Charlotte, NC 2007

The Duke case shaped up as a powerful example of the kind of crisis that can generate significant online word of mouth from fans and critics—and the potential to impact a national sport brand.

Starting in mid-March, shortly after the news broke, and for the next three weeks, Sports Media Challenge culled and analyzed content from sport-related, feminist, ethnic, academic, social networking, and other Internet outlets. The results were presented in a Dashboard Report that provided cogent, actionable real-time analysis.

Hessert believes this real-time analysis could have helped Duke respond to people who were confused or unconvinced by reporting in the traditional media.

When the rape allegations were made, the public quickly jumped to the support of one side or another, even though facts were being revealed slowly, contradictorily, or not at all. With each new day, Internet "buzz" continued to grow, even when traditional media reported nothing new.

At first the FGM showed little patience or sympathy for the student-athletes implicated in the alleged crime. The university was chastised for tolerating behavior that was "boorish" at best and for allowing a climate that reeked of "entitlement" for student-athletes (and, in some people's opinions, for the advantaged Duke community as a whole).

After seemingly exculpatory DNA results were released by the defense attorneys, the FGM skewed more neutral. But any positive response was muted by expert commentary that no DNA results "didn't mean no crime" and by news that the district attorney had vowed to continue prosecuting the case.

Throughout, a portion of the FGM was supportive, while another contingent was very aggressively expressing its disgust over what fans and other online commentators were describing as "elitist," "racist," and allegedly "criminal" behavior.

Critically, these intense opinions were being expressed not only about the individual players but also about the Duke lacrosse team, the athletic department, and the university itself.

"Understanding the ongoing reaction from these fans and special interests can provide invaluable insight that could have been part of the university's crisis management and communication," stated Hessert.

"Despite what ultimately became aggressive outreach by Duke, the volume of public buzz mushroomed, and public emotions went through the roof."

Hessert noted that online activity spilled beyond the base and into other niche audiences, touching so many sensitivities and differences that the university could not get a true sense of the way the crisis was resonating with the public.

Weeks into the crisis, the most highly trafficked blogs and message forums included lacrosse, political, feminist, Duke, ACC, and proactive justice sites, to name only a few. Fans were devouring the scandal. Lacrosse forums had 40 times more views than posts, showing that fans who did not care to share their opinions were still intensely interested—and were turning to the FGM for information and comment that must have influenced their own opinions about Duke.

One political blog, which averages 18,191 unique visits per day, closed comments to new posts because of high volume. A Web site established claiming to be a "watchdog, information hub, and activism vehicle to ensure the women receive the justice they deserve" averaged 1,500 unique visits per day.

"It's no secret that society is segmenting itself into different niches," Hessert said. "And the most passionate and intense fans and consumers often identify themselves into one or more of these 'niche' audience segments, especially when a hotly charged issue like this one arises."

Hessert said sport institutions—and their sponsors—have to listen to these online discussions to understand the scope and intensity of feelings in the various communities of interest.

"These online discussions are more genuine than focus groups because they are uncontrolled, so they offer important insights we can't get from focus groups," Hessert said.

"We can only understand the real magnitude of an issue when we aggregate and analyze *all* of the niche discussions.

"Once we understand the different viewpoints, we can help tailor appropriate communication strategies in response."

Perhaps the most obvious example came when Duke's president described the situation as "a teaching moment." He was clearly unaware of the strong critique in the FGM (particularly on feminist and local Durham blogs) of Duke's "lackadaisical ignorance" and "elitism," and the intense discussion of the school's perceived role in perpetuating racial, class ("town and gown"), and gender divides in the university area.

Had Duke understood the intensity and scope of the online discussions, the school could have responded more quickly, more vigorously, and more accurately. That could have helped the university control the wildfire spread of damaging comments.

Part 5

Facility and Event Management

When the unforeseeable does occur you may still be held accountable, no matter how unfair. Accordingly, you better work on your seer imitation.

Dave Maraghy

Chapter 19

Crowd Management

Kenny Morgan

Effective crowd management has always been and will always be the most important aspect of any successful sporting event, concert, or trade show. Without experienced management and an adequate number of properly trained staff, event organizers can guarantee themselves major problems—sometimes before the doors even open. Crowd managers have no control over the outcome of a game or the quality of a concert, but they can control the ease, peace of mind, and safety of everyone moving throughout the venue.

In management, regardless of the field, everything begins with a structured plan that is properly communicated and executed through a defined chain of command. Event managers must have at least four plans for any event: ingress, run of show, egress, and emergency plan. These plans are usually formulated by a team consisting of venue managers, event managers, and local public safety officials, with the ultimate goal being the safety and well-being of everyone involved, including the participants, spectators, and employees.

The first aspect of crowd management is ingress, or the process of people entering the venue. Economically, this is a critical part of any show because it sets the stage for the remainder of the event. If ingress is managed poorly, patrons will have difficulty entering the venue. causing them to wait an excessive amount of time or miss part of the show. The likelihood of return business will suffer greatly, not to mention the prospect of patrons being in foul moods and looking to complain when they enter the facility.

Expected attendance and crowd behavior are two main determining factors on how ingress is managed. On the basis of expected attendance, event managers must decide on how many entrances to utilize and how many event staff to schedule. For a series of regular events, such as NFL football games, every public entrance is normally used to accommodate the large crowds and returning fan base. With events such as these, managers can follow a recognizable routine because ingress generally occurs in the same manner with each event. In no way am I suggesting complacency, because no two ingresses are ever the same. I am simply implying that a manager has a good expectation of attendance and crowd characteristics for recurring events. There are many factors, however, that can cause this routine to quickly deviate from normal. For example, if an event manager does not have an adequate number of staff, he or she must make important staffing decisions in a short amount of time because the doors will open and the show or game will go on. Changes in crowd behavior also affect ingress. A night football game, for example, will drastically change the crowd behavior to a more rowdy level because fans have more time to intoxicate themselves. Rivalry games, inclement weather, and fan giveaways, among other factors, can all influence attendance and crowd characteristics, thereby influencing ingress.

For other special events, such as concerts or seminars, ticket sales are tracked through the box office to determine expected attendance. These events change on a night-to-night basis and can have crowds ranging from several hundred to tens of thousands, depending on venue size. Some events will not presale many tickets but have a large walk-up crowd buying tickets on the day of the show. Event managers prepare for such events by researching attendance figures for the same show in similar markets or looking at attendance numbers for the same event in past years.

As these events change on a nightly basis, so do the crowds attending them. As one can imagine, the crowd attending a concert of the Gaither Gospel Singers will be quite different from those attending a concert of the Red Hot Chili Peppers. Similarly, the crowd at Sesame Street Live would be much different from those at the George Carlin comedy show. All of these shows could have the same attendance, but the crowd characteristics would be quite different. Because these shows are so different, managers must prepare for them in different ways. For example, shows with rowdier crowds often require metal detecting at ingress. Metal detecting requires the scheduling of more staff to operate the wands or walk through detectors.

For any event, large or small, managers should have all the entry gates set up prior to patron arrival. Any set up done after patron arrival creates unnecessary safety hazards to both employees and guests. Most facilities utilize metal bike racks for temporary security boundaries and ingress chutes for arriving patrons. The purpose of these chutes is to create single-file lines of people that can be easily managed. Having a single-file line allows event staff to properly screen each individual. Single-file controlled lines also govern the number of people entering the venue, allowing for an orderly flow to the ticket-taking area and into the facility proper. Screening should always consist of a visual inspection but can also include a bag check, metal detection, a pat down, or any combination of these. The event staff working ingress should be trained on how to properly execute these procedures. In some areas, state or local laws may govern how these procedures are implemented.

Once most of the patrons have arrived and are inside the building, crowd managers must then move into the run-of-show plan. Ideally, this is a self sustaining plan in that the guests primarily stay in their seats and watch the game or show until it is over or until they have decided to leave. However, depending on the event and related crowd behavior, it is sometimes necessary to take corrective action, or even eject guests who are disrupting the event. Every venue should have a code of conduct that guests are to follow. These rules are generally the same from venue to venue and cover behaviors such as intoxication, fighting, possessing prohibited items, and smoking, among others. When ejecting a patron, it is vitally important to document as much information as possible concerning the incident. This will aid in the defense of the event manager, his or her company, and his or her building in the event legal action is pursued.

Once an event is completed, it is time for the patrons to exit the venue; this plan is often referred to as "egress." The plan is usually the quickest and easiest one to execute. It is often as simple as making sure the exits are open and clear. It is a good idea to have some event staff standing next to trash cans, encouraging patrons to finish or throw away any remaining alcohol. Once most of the patrons have exited the building, some staff may be needed to politely inform any remaining guests that it is time to exit. After most concerts, the stage crew and the floor crew immediately begin dismantling the stage and removing chairs from the floor. This procedure can quickly become a safety hazard if guests are still remaining in these areas.

Once the bowl of the arena or stadium is free of remaining guests, a sweep of the concourses should be conducted, beginning from the upper levels and continuing to the lower levels. During the sweep, event staff should check all restrooms, smoking areas, and any other areas out of plain view from the concourse. Conducting a thorough postevent sweep ensures the building management that the facility is empty and safe and can be locked.

Upon the conclusion of an event, it is recommended that a brief meeting be held to discuss particulars of the event. The meeting should include as many representatives from the different venue departments as possible. Issues covered in the meeting should involve procedures and plans that could be improved in future shows. Ejections and any other issue involving paperwork should be discussed, making sure that all necessary steps were taken to protect interested parties in any liability case. Having a postevent meeting creates additional opportunities for beneficial communication among various managers at a given facility. The more communication there is among building managers, the better the building will be.

Before any venue can be opened to the public, its managers must formulate an emergency operations plan. The purpose of such a plan is to minimize the risk of personal injury to venue patrons and employees by avoiding panic and confusion. When carried out by trained professionals, a thorough and structured emergency operations plan can save lives. The plan cannot address every possible emergency, but it should include steps to be taken in most emergencies, including natural disasters, bomb threats, fires, power failures, inclement weather, and mass-casualty incidents. The most important aspect of managing an emergency is preventing panic and confusion among patrons and employees.

As with any operations plan, an emergency plan should have a clear and defined chain of command, beginning with the facility director at the top and descending from that position to the remaining venue managers. If a state of emergency is declared, the director must then determine the scope of the situation and decide to implement either a partial or total evacuation. On the basis of this decision, crowd managers would then position the staff to assist patrons in exiting through predetermined evacuation routes. Once the area or venue has been safely evacuated, the staff must then either evacuate themselves or keep the area clear until emergency responders have arrived.

Within the last twenty years, the sport and entertainment industry has experienced unparalleled growth and popularity. Currently, stadiums with billion-dollar budgets are being built — with amenities that were unimaginable until the recent past. And with each passing year, more stadiums and arenas are being built not only to exceed the expectations of their tenants but also to cater to potential patrons in the hope of profiting from their entertainment dollars. Competition for this dollar is fierce, with the many options Americans can choose from to entertain themselves. And the price people are paying for those choices is only getting higher. As a result, it is incumbent upon facility directors and crowd managers to recruit, hire, and train the best staff they possibly can. Since the newness of any venue can quickly fade, a knowledgeable and friendly staff can easily separate one venue from the next. Similarly, not every town has a new venue that people can get excited over. Therefore, it is up to the staff to create a warm and inviting atmosphere for their customers and keep them returning to the venue. In today's market, the entertainment consumer has high expectations for the money he or she spends on tickets. Crowd managers cannot control the outcome of games or the quality of a concert, but they can provide a trained staff focused on customer service and knowledgeable of the facility and building operation plans.

Chapter 20

Event Management: Tools of the Trade

Frank Russo

Introduction

There is a phenomenon that causes managers of public-event facilities to recognize the importance and specialized nature of the role of the event manager. Each event must be managed; if not, it will assuredly mismanage itself. In the past, the event manager simply coordinated activities before, during, and after an event to ensure that equipment, physical setups, and personnel were provided to meet all contractual requirements. Now, however, the event manager must become involved in many, if not all, of the following important tasks:

1. Scheduling and directing event, admission, and crowd-control staff, including ushers, ticket takers, security guards, private-duty policemen, firemen, and emergency medical service personnel.
2. Ensuring that tenants understand and comply with house policies and rules and regulations.
3. Making tenants fully aware of all that is involved in staging an event in the facility to avoid surprises, hidden costs, and arguments. This task is usually best handled at a production meeting with the tenant.
4. Developing, implementing, and monitoring emergency operations and evacuation procedures.
5. Ensuring compliance by all tenants of federal, state, and local fire, building, and life safety codes.

During an event, many things occur simultaneously that must be coordinated and managed. The box office, which is often the only contact many patrons have with a facility, is open and in full operation. The concessions department sells food, beverage, and merchandise. Security concerns itself with admission and crowd control and the ushering of people quickly and safely to their seats. The facility crew puts the final touches on the event setup and keeps all public areas free of debris, trash, and obstructions. The engineering department makes sure that the Heating, Ventilation, and Air Conditioning (HVAC) system is working properly so that everyone is comfortable, monitors the life-safety systems, and responds to such mundane tasks as repairing a plugged toilet or leaking faucet. Meanwhile, stagehands and other technical crew members are tending to a variety of details necessary to successfully stage the event.

Since the coordination and the management of a facility are complex, a clearly established liaison between the tenant, the public, and the building management is critical. This responsibility often falls on the event manager.

The event manager is responsible for the protection of the performers as well as the physical plant and, most important, the well-being of the attending public. The rest of this chapter will provide practical information for developing a comprehensive plan that will cover all these areas of responsibility. Emphasis will be placed on how to manage events rather than constantly reacting to one crisis after another.

Radio Communication: A Critical Tool of the Trade

A key to successful event management is a properly functioning radio communications system, since total and instant communication, in certain situations, may mean the difference between life and death.

If a radio system is not available, it is advisable to contact a local police, fire, or civil preparedness department for guidance.

In an operational radio system, there are basic radio usage rules that should be followed:

1. Radios and pagers should be used for business purposes only.
2. Since the number of radios and pagers being used by various personnel places limitations on air time, transmissions should be concise, and any unnecessary conversation should not be tolerated.
3. Because Federal Communications Commission (FCC) regulations govern all language on the air, use of profane and/or obscene language and derogatory remarks should be strictly forbidden.
4. Because they are very costly to replace or repair, radios should be placed in holsters and not carried by hand. Microphones connected to the radio make this easy and very convenient. Also, earphones make it possible to hear even during a loud concert.
5. A code system to communicate critical information should be developed, and all security personnel should be required to memorize and use it. Such a code system should be developed for the following types of situations:
   Fire (specify location)
   Bomb Threat (discussed in more detail later in this chapter under "Security and Emergency Procedures Manual")
   Medical Emergency (specify location)
   Engineering Emergency (specify kind of emergency as well as location)
   Elevator Emergency
   Telephoning Fire Department
   Telephoning Police Department (specify need—i.e., police or ambulance)
   Accident (specify location)
   Disturbance and/or Breach of Peace (specify location)
   Assistance Needed (specify location)
   Return to Headquarters

Telephoning Headquarters or Other (specify)
Trying to Locate (usually a person)
Assignment to a Certain Area or Check of a Certain Area
Discovery of Something of a Suspicious Nature (specify location)
Standing By for an Announcement (emergency pending)
Resuming Normal Activity
Signing on the Air
Signing off the Air (give location)
Testing Radio Equipment
Break

Architectural and Physical Considerations

Thomas Minter, currently the manager of the Lexington Kentucky Civic Center, stated to the International Association of Auditorium Managers that "security begins on the drawing board." He observed that many problems can be avoided by proper design and planning of public facilities. This observation is supported by Don Jewell in *Public Assembly Facilities: Planning and Management* (New York: John Wiley and Sons, 1978), when he states that "safety begins with good architectural planning." Jewell correctly points out that while such considerations are well covered by governmental building and fire codes, to some extent management's need to guard the entrances and exists to restricted or ticketed areas may be in conflict with rapid evacuation in emergency circumstances. Careful planning by the architect in cooperation with the management team and state and local fire officials as well as the facility's insurance representative (risk manager) will do much to prevent serious operational and public safety problems. But the process does not end here.

Because management is morally—and legally—responsible for public safety, ensuring it is an ongoing process which requires constant inspections of the physical plant to make sure that all hazards and potential hazards are eliminated before the public arrives.

Another architectural/physical consideration is Thomas Minter's recommendation that a facility be zoned into "activity areas" as follows:

1. The "public area" is the zone where the public may move about freely and have access to all public facilities, concession areas, first aid services, restrooms, drinking fountains, facilities for the disabled, and public telephones. These public accommodations should be available without requiring access by the public into other zones within the facility. They must also be provided in sufficient number in order to discourage public demand to exit and return through admission areas.

2. The "performance area" includes backstage and dressing facilities. These facilities require separation from the audience and service areas as much as possible. Such physical separation greatly enhances the ability to provide privacy and security for the performers or athletes. The use of backstage passes for those persons necessary or desired in the back of the house is mandatory if effective control is to be maintained.

3. The "service area" includes workshops, custodial and concessions supply rooms, the shipping and receiving entrance, utility rooms, and

equipment storage areas. The service area can most effectively be secured when performer and public access is restricted. Employee theft can best be reduced and general order and inventory control maintained if this area is further restricted only to those persons actively employed by the facility.

4. "Support personnel areas" include police and security offices and the first aid station. These areas should be adjacent to public areas but should have access to the entrance at the back of the house in order that those persons who serve the public may enter and leave without public surveillance and that those persons who require medical attention or police detention can be removed from the facility.

Admission and Building Access Control

Only persons who have purchased a ticket or have been given authorized passes should gain entry to the facility.

Admissions control actually begins in the box office with the ticket itself Tickets must be clearly printed on a type of safety stock to prevent counterfeiting. The ticket must allow the staff to quickly check the event's date and performance time, as well as the section, row, and seat number(s). Admissions-control personnel should be trained to spot strange-looking tickets. Tickets should obviously be printed by a reputable and bonded ticketing company that ships them with the audited manifest directly to the box office to be counted, racked, and distributed under direct control. Of course, an alternative to process is computerized ticketing, which may offer even greater control.

Most admission-type events fall into two basic categories: "general admission," which permits a person to sit in any available seat on a first-come-first-served basis, and "reserved seating," which provides patrons with a specific seating location.

It is advisable to open the doors to the facility approximately one hour and fifteen minutes before the scheduled starting time. This will allow patrons adequate time to find their seating location, go to the restroom, purchase a snack, socialize, and get settled before the event begins.

The event manager should constantly monitor the size and mood of a crowd in the lobby and outside the facility before the doors are opened. In addition, he or she should have an adequate number of ticket takers and turnstiles to allow the crowd to enter in a quick and orderly fashion. Before opening the doors, however, the event manager should conduct a radio check to ensure that the performers and the house staff are ready for the public. The ticket takers should be supported by a supervisor, a "customer relations representative" to handle problems, and an adequate number of security guards and policemen to handle trouble and/or to supervise a search-and-seizure operation. The duties and responsibilities of the admission control staff are discussed in more detail later in this chapter.

There should be a system for admitting people to the facility who do not have tickets. Many facilities use a photo ID system, which provides one of the best means of identifying persons with legitimate business. Employees, show personnel, and service contractors do not have an inherent right to be at an event. A system of IRs and backstage passes designed to restrict entry is absolutely critical to building security and safety.

Crowd Management

In any crowd situation, a risk to public safety is inherent and cannot be totally eliminated. While no facility can anticipate all the situations which might lead to disorder, cooperation between the facility management staff and promoters, agents, performers, admissions control staff, and security, police, fire, and government officials will do a great deal to minimize risks.

Crowd management requires *always* being prepared for the worst. The worst happened at Cincinnati's Riverfront Coliseum on December 3, 1979. Thousands of patrons were awaiting admission to a concert to be played by the Who, a very popular rock group. General admission with festival seating had been established for the event. The anxious crowd (which was held outside the building until just before the concert was to begin) mistook the sounds of musicians warming up as the opening of the concert and rushed the door. Eleven people died, and eleven more were injured. The situation was not riotous or out of control, and the deaths were senseless. But this incident, more than any other in recent memory, graphically shows the need for advance planning, precautions, and sensitivity to people who buy tickets for events. Regardless of the size of the crowd, proper management is essential to minimizing, and hopefully preventing, unsafe situations. The tragedy promoted a careful study by the City of Cincinnati. Recommendations presented in *The Report of the Task Force on Crowd Control and Safety* are given below.

1. There should be clearly defined and published house policies which should be followed for each event. The facility management staff should be clearly in charge and ensure compliance with all laws, house rules and regulations, health standards, and common sense practices.
2. Carefully evaluate the effects of the sale of alcohol. If necessary, place a security person, or preferably a uniformed policeman, at the sales outlet.
3. Clearly define the chain of command and the duties and responsibilities for the event manager, as well as all policemen, security guards, ushers and usherettes, ticket takers, and first-aid personnel. Be sure they are constantly trained on how to properly react in an emergency situation.
4. Encourage patrons to report dangerous and threatening situations.
5. Avoid general admission ticketing and seating if at all possible.
6. Carefully plan the sale of tickets, especially when the demand will greatly exceed the supply. Develop a fair and equitable distribution system. Control your lines. Treat the crowds well and courteously. Do not allow line cutting. A wristband ID system works well here. And if necessary to ensure fairness, establish a maximum number of tickets each customer may purchase. And if it appears that some people in line will not reach the box office before the event is sold out, let them know as soon as possible and do not allow any more people to stand in line.
7. Conduct search and seizure to confiscate bottles, cans, and other items which may be used to injure others.
8. Establish legal attendance capacities for each event setup, and obtain the written approval of the fire marshal and building inspector. Also, desig-

nate handicap-wheelchair locations in a manner least likely to cause them to serve as obstructions in case of an emergency evacuation.

9. Pay close attention to the architectural plans and designs of your facility. Do not allow illegal and dangerous obstructions. Be careful where you place your turnstiles. Make sure your graphics system works to your advantage and to the crowd's advantage by helping them get to their seats and other conveniences and exits as quickly and safely as possible.

10. Develop an emergency evacuation plan.

Some other comments and observations by the Cincinnati Task Force are worth noting here.

1. A clean, well-maintained building and a hassle-free atmosphere will do much to reduce crowd tension.

2. Be in control of the stage and the attraction. Do not allow the attraction to overly or dangerously excite a crowd.

3. Before and after an event and during intermission, play soft, soothing music.

4. Do not turn the lights off completely. Allow at least three foot-candles of light to illuminate aisles and emergency exits.

5. Keep people without floor tickets off the floor.

6. Keep aisles clear.

7. Make sure the public address system works and that its volume and clarity are adequate.

The International Association of Auditorium Managers (IAAM) established the IAAM Foundation. The first major project to be undertaken by the Foundation will be a crowd management study. The project is an outgrowth of years of behind-the-scenes planning and research on the part of Dr. Robert Sigholtz, the Foundation's first chairman, and Dr. Irving Goldaber, an internationally known sociologist, specializing in the study of social violence.

The first phase of the project calls for a comprehensive review of crowd control literature, supplemented by the combined field experience of facility managers within the IAAM.

Goldaber recently stated:

Crowd management encompasses all that is undertaken by professional personnel in the public assembly field to facilitate the comfort and safety and lawful nature of crowd gatherings so that those in attendance may have satisfying experiences. Crowd management activity occurs in both the inner administrative office and the outer public parking lot. It focuses, for example, on aspects of executive decision-making, managerial expertise, supervisory responsibility, public relations, patron services, traffic regulations and safety and security. It includes among its concerns such matters as architecture and interior design, food and other items either provided or vended to those present, and the sociological capability to read "the mood of the crowd." An effective crowd management approach begins with the first blueprint for the event or assemblage and ends when the last patron has vacated the area. For this reason, crowd management deals with planning, preparing, conducting and taking remedial action. It is the sum of all that is undertaken to obviate the need for crowd control action involving forcible restraint.

Crowd Violence

A growing problem in facilities throughout the United States is that of crowd or spectator violence, especially at rock concerts which attract large numbers of young people. Often a metamorphosis occurs when certain fans go through the turnstiles. They virtually abandon the constraints normally placed upon them by society and feel totally free to act in an uninhibited manner, including the physical destruction of property, physical threats, and other antisocial behavior.

Contributing factors to crowd violence, according to Goldaber, involve a number of low-level sources of tension, including close and involuntary contact with strangers, abnormal physical discomfort, and competition for space, goods, services, and information. These sources of tension tend to frustrate fans and make them more irritable and belligerent than they are when they are alone or in smaller groups. Crowds also provide a degree of anonymity which encourages troublemakers to act more irresponsibly than they might in situations where they can easily be identified and punished.

Everything possible should be done to make the facility hassle free and comfortable. Large public assembly facilities—sport facilities in particular—when compared with those offered to other crowds, are often somewhat inefficiently designed, uncomfortable, and unattractive. As a result, the fast and easy flow of such basic emotions as elation, anger, panic, and vengeance are contagious within a crowd and may create so-called mass hysteria. Moreover, sporting events regularly draw the largest crowds of any public event.

People lose control when they identify so fully with an athlete or a team that they begin feeling physically aggressive. Crowds at sporting events regularly respond by cheering, booing, hissing, stamping their feet, waving their fists, screaming, and threatening and yelling at officials.

One problem in particular offers facilities a serious dilemma. Because competition for events is becoming greater and facilities are forced to offer overly competitive rent deals, the facilities must exploit their concessions and other ancillary sources of income in order to make a profit. The sale of alcoholic beverages unquestionably contributes to fan violence and crowd disorders. Yet beer, wine, and cocktails are perhaps the most profitable items a facility sells. The facility manager must therefore exercise close and constant care in monitoring alcoholic beverages sales and must be prepared to call them to a halt when necessary—even if doing so means giving up an extremely lucrative source of revenue.

Another problem which complicates an event manager's ability to manage a crowd is violence on the part of professional athletes. Richard B. Horrow, the author of *Sports Violence: The Interaction Between Private Law-Making and The Criminal Law* (Washington: Carrollton Press, Inc., 1980) emphasizes the alarming trend toward excessive violence in all professional sport. The well-known comedian Rodney Dangerfield once quipped that he "went to a fight the other night and saw a hockey game break out." As athletes become more competitive and as the pressures to succeed become stronger, the possibility of violent conduct during a game increases, which causes a spontaneous reaction with the crowd. Athletes are taught to be aggressive and to be tough because one of the skills of sport is violence. The fans expect and demand violence, and the players themselves accept the fact that many less-talented players must be more violent to compensate for their inferior talent.

If violence erupts on the playing surface, the security team should be prepared to respond. For instance, it should be watching the crowd and not the event. It should be polite but firm with any troublemakers who, if uncooperative, must be ejected.

One way to effectively manage a crowd and contain violence is for the event manager to conduct an advanced assessment of the anticipated audience. This will help the manager decide on the necessary level of security staffing. The event manager must bear in mind that security requirements are not the same for all events. Each event has its own particular personality and should be considered separately from all others. The event manager should obtain as much advance information as possible about the audience and the performers and then plan and be prepared. Good sources of information are counterparts at other facilities where the event was already held. They can describe the nature of the crowd and how it reacted during the event. The box office is also a good source of such information, since it has already had contact with part of the crowd during the ticket-buying process. The local police department should also check with its counterpart in other cities to determine what type of criminal activities and disorders occurred.

Security and Emergency Procedures Manual

There is no substitute for well-trained security staff. The most basic training tool for security personnel is a manual covering as many pertinent topics as possible in plain and simple language. The event manager should use the manual to welcome and orient the security personnel. The manager should emphasize that the personnel are to provide professional service on behalf of the facility. The manual provides security personnel with guidelines and helps them be alert and safety conscious.

The manual should contain a clear outline of the chain of command in the facility. Moreover, it should provide security officers with guidelines such as the following:

1. Know how to handle any abnormal situation which you may encounter, and know how or where to get help if required.
2. Be alert at all times while on duty. Always watch for activities, conditions, or hazards which could result in injury or damage to persons or property.
3. Have an attitude that reflects proper human and public relations.
4. Be helpful. When fans arrive at an event, they are usually confused. The location is unfamiliar, and they are often late and do not know where to go or what to do.
5. Be courteous but firm at all times.
6. Fully obey and execute all orders given by superiors.
7. Take pride in your duties and maintain a keen interest in your job. Such pride and interest will become apparent in the manner in which you perform your duties and will be recognized by all who come in contact with you.
8. Act without haste or undue emotion. Do not argue with visitors, fellow employees, or supervisors. Present a calm and friendly bearing.
9. Remember that courtesy earns respect, that knowledge gets results, that patience receives cooperation, that service increases good will, and that the total application of these qualities gets the job done well.

However, written procedures are meaningless if they are not read, understood, and carried out by security personnel. Such service will be exemplified on their part by their use of tact, friendliness, and courtesy while they maintain a professional attitude in the performance of their duties. In addition, the event manager should let them know that they are important members of the professional crowd management team.

Besides these general guidelines, the manual should list and explain the specific duties and responsibilities of each job.

Usher Supervisor

The usher supervisor should supervise, not usher. As a result, he or she will be free to respond to problem areas. Each event should have an appropriate number of usher supervisors assigned according to the total number of ushers being used and the anticipated size of the crowd. An usher supervisor should be alert for any problems or unusual difficulties encountered by any usher under his or her supervision and should offer assistance and advice if needed.

Usher

An usher, on the other hand, is primarily responsible for making certain that the patron is assisted to the correct seat. In addition, an usher should perform the following duties:

1. Greet each patron properly.
2. Check each ticket for event, date, performance time, as well as section, row, and seat.
3. Offer clear directions to seating locations and service accommodations.
4. Act on customer complaints and, if necessary, refer complaints to the usher supervisor.
5. Keep aisles clear at all times.
6. Ask patrons to surrender any bottles or cans in their possession and, if necessary, refer unwilling patrons to the usher supervisor or a law enforcement officer.
7. Try to anticipate problems and act on them before they become serious.
8. Enforce house policies such as "no smoking."
9. Use a flashlight to assist patrons to their seats when the lights are down.
10. Be sensitive to the needs of mobility-impaired people such as senior citizens and handicapped persons.

Event Security Officer

The event security officer is a key figure in the safety of each facility. He or she is a figure representing authority and safety to the various patrons and visitors of the facility. His or her professionalism and courteous attitude will make the patrons feel that they are in good hands. With an officer's presence alone, potential troublesome situations may be avoided. Specifically, the security officer is responsible for the following duties:

1. Reporting on time and ready to work.

2. Wearing the proper and complete uniform.
3. Following instructions by reading and memorizing post orders.
4. Remaining at an assigned post until relieved.
5. Exhibiting proper courtesy at all times.
6. Refraining from eating, drinking, and smoking while on duty.
7. Being alert to minors possessing alcoholic beverages.

Another key element of the manual is the section on emergency procedures. For this portion of the manual, the event manager should solicit the input and written approval of the state and local fire marshal, the police and civil-preparedness departments, and his or her contractual medical and ambulance services.

The most common form of emergency is the bomb threat. The manual should therefore explain the role of employees in dealing with the threat, as well as the overall emergency evacuation procedure. Employees should be instructed to cover assigned areas carefully when they are asked to make a search, and they should be instructed to note any unusual package or item. If one is found, they should be instructed not to touch it but to notify the supervisor immediately.

If the facility must be evacuated, event security officers should follow very carefully any instructions given. They should always remain calm and in command of their area, avoiding the use of any panic-producing statements such as "bomb," "fire," or "explosion." Many lives may depend on their calm and efficient actions.

Many facilities use the Phase Coding System which was designed as a safe method of conveying to event personnel the type of problem, its location, and the action to be taken without alarming any members of the general public who happen to overhear radio transmissions, telephone conversations, or person-to-person communication. The purpose of this system is to prevent the greatest of all threats — panic.

The Phase Coding System is an escalating and compartmentalized plan used to help prevent another great threat — overreaction — while simultaneously informing all necessary personnel of the type, location, and current status of the problem.

Phase 1A indicates smoke, water, a small crowd disturbance, or an equipment or lighting failure. Descriptive information should be provided about the location, size, seriousness, and nature of the problem. Security personnel should clear the immediate area until the problem has been brought under control.

Phase 1B indicates that a bomb threat has been received and that all staff should immediately conduct a search for an explosive device. Notification should be given when the search is completed.

Phase 2A indicates a serious fire, flood, crowd disturbance, equipment failure, or other problem. Security personnel should be posted at the location of the problem and should control access to the area.

Phase 2B indicates that a suspicious package or device has been located. The fire department and police bomb squad should be dispatched to investigate and to decide whether or not a full or limited evacuation is necessary. Ambulances should be called for standby.

Phase 3A indicates the need for an orderly evacuation because of a failure of the regular power system. Such a failure will most likely result in the cancellation of the performance. An appropriate prerecorded message should be activated over the public address system, and ambulances should be called for standby.

Phase 3B indicates the need for an immediate emergency evacuation. Appropriate alarms must be sounded and prerecorded messages activated. Ambulances should be called for standby, and the security/usher staff should begin to calmly but firmly evacuate patrons. Security personnel should also be sure that no patrons reenter the building, regardless of the reason.

The facility manager must take great care to clearly establish the chain of command in case of an emergency evacuation. It must be clearly understood who has the right and responsibility to call for an evacuation. In most cities, this responsibility is that of the ranking on-site member of the police bomb squad.

A way to ensure that proper procedures will be followed is to have a telephone bomb report form. If any member of the house or security staff takes a call during an event, this form, or one very similar to it, should be used, and as much pertinent information as possible should be recorded and immediately conveyed to the event manager or police department.

A person who actually puts a bomb in a building wants to be caught or wants the bomb found before it goes off. If possible, the telephone operator should keep the person talking because he or she may disclose the location of the bomb. Having the phone operator trained by the police bomb squad would be very helpful.

Preparation for emergency evacuation is absolutely critical. Drills should be conducted on a regular basis. A standardized routine should be developed for each type of event. Once the routine has been set, it should be typed and posted in strategic locations such as the office, the security room, the usher's locker room, backstage, lunch rooms, and refreshment stands. The facility and its patrons are always vulnerable. The best defense is a plan carefully evolved to fit the facility and the organization. Being able to evacuate a facility in an emergency with a minimum of injury or loss of life is one of the greatest challenges and responsibilities of the facility manager.

Search and Seizure

The issue of search and seizure is a complex but important aspect of security and crowd management. Most facility managers believe the procedure is necessary in order to keep people from bringing beverage containers and weapons into facilities. But each facility manager must be very cognizant of the requirements of the Fourth Amendment of the United States Constitution.

Normally, the event manager, in conjunction with the facility manager and the chief of police, decides if a particular event (usually a rock concert) will draw a crowd of unruly patrons, many of whom will likely be in possession of bottles, cans, and other containers, as well as assorted weapons and drugs. In such an instance, the facility's own security force and ticket takers must be supplemented by additional personnel to prevent these items from being brought into the facility. This relieves tension and protects people from being injured by objects used as missiles. But the facility manager should be sure to obtain sound legal advice from the facility's attorney before he or she establishes any procedures for search and seizure.

The September 1982 issue of *Auditorium News* (the official monthly publication of the International Association of Auditorium Managers) contained a very interesting article by Jerome O. Campane, a special agent of the FBI Academy, entitled "Amendment IV, the Fourth Amendment at a Rock Concert." The article provides an enlightening update of the issue and offers some guidance on how to conduct a legal search-and-seizure operation. Campane indicates that the courts agree that civic authorities are entitled to take certain steps to prevent injury to the public and to provide protection for those who attend events by prohibiting the introduction of contraband and dangerous items. However, this cannot be done in a manner which violates a person's rights under the Fourth Amendment, which states: "The right of the people to be secure in their persons, houses, papers, and effects, against unreasonable searches and seizures, shall not be violated, and no Warrants shall issue, but upon probable cause, supported by oath or affirmation, and particularly describing the place to be searched, and the persons or things to be seized." Therefore, the facility manager should have an attorney provide him or her with written search-and-seizure guidelines—and perhaps even occasional on-site supervision.

Campane offers some practical advice on how a facility manager can cope with the problem. For example, a notice on tickets and signs at the entrances to the facility will give the impression of voluntary consent. The availability of checkrooms for the deposit and safekeeping of large packages will also help, as will the elimination of festival seating, which will prevent the rush through the turnstiles as doors first open, thus giving the security personnel a better opportunity to observe the patrons. When items are seized or arrests made, mass-media publicity of the seizures or arrests may help convince patrons not to bring prohibited items to future events. Campane states that, above all, any procedure should be uniformly applied. It should not be employed only at rock concerts and only against teenagers. The facility manager should carefully document any incidents of violence and unruly behavior and apply the same screening procedure to all events where such incidents are likely to occur. These procedures are obviously not all inclusive, and again, the facility manager is urged to meet with an attorney for specific guidelines regarding search-and-seizure procedures.

Summary/Conclusion

This chapter has provided the facility manager with a considerable amount of practical information that can be directly applied to his or her own operation. Because the business of facility management is exciting and because it is therefore easy to get caught up in the "glamour" of the events hosted, it is sometimes possible for the facility manager to lose sight of the most important responsibility: protecting the lives of patrons. By preparing for the worst, the facility manager will make each event a professionally managed, safe, and enjoyable experience for the public and the performers. This, more than any other factor, will enhance such a manager's reputation and assure the success of a facility.

Chapter 21

Event Management: A Practical Approach

David R. Maraghy

Introduction

Since the early 1980s. when I began my involvement with the Greater Greensboro Open, one of the oldest stops on the PGA TOUR, I have reveled in the process of marketing, promoting, and operating all kinds of events—from golf tournaments to polo matches to rock concerts, and even a softball world series. It is very satisfying to sit back after such efforts and reflect on all the many pieces which came together to make the event successful.

A sure sign of the individual who thrives on the frenetic pace and chaos which are usually at the center of any event is the pure enjoyment the individual has received, as he or she proceeds from one problem to the next and finds solutions, knowing that while things are unsettled, the spectators, participants, and guests at the function think all is well. Now that self-deception is really fun!

If you have ever been involved in the process of marketing, promoting, and operating any kind of event, you can identify with the above feelings. While you may not thrive on the feeling of being in a kind of "war," you may also realize that controlled commotion is inherent to every activity which brings together large numbers of people in one place.

With experience and planning, you should be able to minimize greatly the risks involved with staging an event. Much of the planning process involves identifying risk areas and then formulating the right questions related to such risks. Another key to success is to reduce the potential for surprises and the attendant risks which follow.

In this chapter, the term *risk* is sometimes interpreted broadly to cover not only physical injury and potential litigation but also financial loss. In fact, risk can even mean failure in terms of not fulfilling the expectations of the spectators and/or participants—maybe even the simple fact they did not have fun. Therefore, the event was not successful, money was probably lost, and the event will not be supported in the future.

The purpose of this chapter is to provide some practical advice on avoiding risks. The actual solutions for each challenge you face will vary, depending on the particular event and the nature of the risks. Therefore, this chapter emphasizes developing the ability to ask the proper questions as opposed to providing any general panacea.

The patient lying exposed on the surgical table never wants to hear the attending physician utter the word "oops." Hopefully, this chapter will aid you in avoiding the use of that same dreaded word in caring for your "patient"—the event.

Planning and Organization

There is an old adage: "Plan your work, and work your plan." The crucial element in striving to reduce risks associated with operating an event is careful planning.

In the proper planning of an event, there is no substitute for experience. Therefore, when facing your first few projects, do not be shy about seeking assistance, knowledge, and advice from experienced sources. If live mentors are not available or experienced individuals are too competitive to lend assistance, then do your research. A trip to the library will reveal articles on planning almost anything: a golf outing, a conference, a marathon, or a car rally.

As you gain experience in this area, you will find that your expertise transcends any one specific field. While the particulars of marketing the event will change on the basis of the demographics of the target audience, the logistics will be very similar. I find this rule to run true in my dealings with successful event managers of all different sports and activities.

Accordingly, the Organizational Chart provided below was developed through the years primarily in designing and implementing golf events. Nevertheless, it has also been used quite successfully to plan and operate many other events by gearing the questions raised toward that particular sport or activity.

Your concept of planning needs to move beyond thinking in terms of simply following any outline or chart. Instead, sit alone with a pencil and large sheet of paper, a computer, or whatever creative tools you find comfortable and run through all aspects of the event—from the very first stages to the desired conclusion.

For me, this process results in an outline containing many sections and subsections. Also key to this process of analysis is a narrative or editorial comments on those sections where necessary. This exercise also results in a backup checklist added to the Organizational Chart used to structure and plan the event.

The narrative and comments are such a crucial ingredient in my recipe for success because they reveal the *"what ifs."* Again, careful planning like this helps to eliminate risks. More often, events fail, people are injured, or money is lost because the promoter did not anticipate well the risks inherent to the activity or event.

Organizational Chart

Through experience, as well as trial and error, you will develop the form of chart which works best for you as a planning and operational tool. In the meantime, this section will offer you some general considerations. The suggestions will be geared toward the issue of avoiding, or at least reducing, risks of injury/liability or financial failure.

In planning any event, my organizational structure takes the form of a schematic skeleton. This chart usually contains ten major sections with an average of ten subsections or subheadings of more specific areas of responsibility.

The subsections will vary according to the kind of activity, but the ten primary sections seem to cross over very effectively. Therefore, those ten sections are enumerated below, while only those subheadings pertinent to risk issues are discussed. You will note that some key considerations such as crowd control, security, and transportation actually extend beyond just one section and will be addressed in several sections.

Sales: Ticket Sales

Plan for the procedures related to sales of tickets at the event site. How will you monitor sales and enforce spectators' purchasing? Provide necessary security for locations with cash.

In terms of crowd control and possible risk of injury, formulate a well-conceived plan for sales, thereby avoiding long lines and frustrated spectators. Walk through the actual processes of selling the ticket, picking up the ticket, providing adequate staffing, using cash versus credit-card services, and ingress and egress through narrow entrance areas. Uniformed officers in the area provide a calming effect on customers waiting in line, thereby deterring pushing and possible jostling or injury of others.

Do you need to allow for bilingual or multilingual ticket sellers to speed the process and render it more effective? Similarly, will your ticket sellers need to convert money? If so, find bright people and provide them with the necessary conversion tables, charts, calculators, and so forth.

Large signs that are clear, simple, and easy to read can also quicken the sale process. Prices of tickets, available seating, and the cost of goods or concessions can all be grasped, and the appropriate money can be made ready while customers wait in line. Again, consider whether the signs should be printed in several languages and whether prices should be available in more than one currency.

Do you need to allow for an area for "will call," where spectators can pick up tickets left for them or purchased in advance? Where will such an area be best located to avoid confusion and the clogging of lines for ticket sales?

Similarly, do you anticipate a large number of individuals with special status for discounted prices or perhaps for free admission: military, students, seniors? If so, the process will be smoother if you provide special lines to accommodate such individuals.

Services for Sponsors

Most subheadings here address the area of promotions and hospitality functions for large dollar sponsors as opposed to any real risk issues. When considering financial risks, however, you should take care of these folks.

Actually, in caring for your sponsors, you will face many vital areas of event management, but they are all addressed elsewhere in this chapter. Such issues are transportation (will there be valet parking?), planning and maintaining a safe hospitality area (seating, special tents, and so forth), security and credentials, and crowd control.

Contestant Services: Special Consideration of Accommodations, Security, and Transportation

What special arrangements need to be made for your contestants, performers, artists, players, or drivers? Consider not only issues of comfort but also issues of safety.

If you are dealing with a bona fide superstar, do you need to find very secure, private accommodations? Will you reserve an entire floor of the hotel? How much of an issue is security at each stage of the event? Do you need to assign security guards to the individual 24 hours a day?

Is transportation an issue? Do you need to provide for reception at the airport? How many cars, vans, or limousines are necessary? Think through every transportation need—air and ground—from the beginning to the end of the event.

How will the contestants get to and from the event? Is a special traffic lane necessary? What about getting to and from a stage, field, track, or course?

What security will be required during the actual performance, race, match, concert, or tournament?

With the disturbing increase of terrorism and other senseless acts, such as the victimization of Monica Seles, one of tennis' brightest stars, where is the event business headed in terms of liability? How much planning and security will be sufficient, both in terms of protecting the contestant and protecting you from financial ruin through legal actions by an injured performer? You will have to balance carefully your risk of exposure to liability for injury to a contestant versus the potentially prohibitive costs of obtaining necessary security and special expensive accommodations and modes of transportation.

Hospitality: Liquor Liability

Most subheadings here concern the entertaining of guests, sponsors, and VIPs. Nevertheless, for all social functions, you must again consider all the relevant questions posed in other sections in this chapter: access, ingress/egress, security, traffic flow, crowd control, and other questions concerning large numbers of people.

One additional key area of concern is the ever-growing body of law on liability for an event or function serving alcohol. I offer this caveat with a few examples of how others have attempted to prevent problems. Be aware of your very high exposure to potential liability when serving alcohol to someone who is then injured and/or injures others as a result of actions performed while under the influence, especially driving.

When hosting an event, seek legal consultation on the prevailing law in your jurisdiction. Sound advice on this subject will be worth every penny. Discover if case law or statute offers guidelines to be followed in such circumstances which may help insulate you from liability.

Some examples of preventive measures being employed at events are suggested below. *Nevertheless, nothing contained in this chapter is to be taken as a guarantee that such measures will relieve you of liability in such situations.*

Many stadiums now cease selling alcohol prior to the end of the game. This strategy provides two benefits: it shortens the amount of time spectators can drink, thereby hopefully reducing the number of intoxicated persons; and it lengthens the time between the last drink and when the spectator climbs behind the wheel of a car. You should certainly consider such a time-control device in your event.

Common at many functions is the stringent check of age identification for the purchase of alcohol. Attendant to that process is a means (such as hospital-type wrist bands) of identifying individuals legally permitted to consume alcohol throughout the event. Again, uniformed officers with power of arrest in the jurisdiction can be quite a deterrent, as well as very useful if a scene becomes disorderly.

Many events now offer free sodas or other nonalcoholic beverages for designated drivers.

Another strategy is to provide access to designated-driver services—whether hired by the function or paid for by the user. Some of these services have drivers who will actually follow an intoxicated person home in his or her car so it will be there in the morning when he or she wakes up.

Ready access to traditional cab service can also be effective.

Whatever route you choose, know that you are very vulnerable on this point.

Operations: Crowd Control

This area is naturally the heart of any event. Its subheadings, therefore, are many and varied, depending on the type of event. In my organizational chart, however, one subheading cries out for consideration regarding risks: crowd control. Some of the relevant questions have been posed above, and you should review them as they relate to this issue. A new, very pertinent consideration in avoiding liability, however, is where you place your spectators.

Incredibly, there is a body of law that hints a golf tournament might be held liable if a spectator is hit by a golf ball straying into the gallery area as marked by gallery ropes. Some courts have indicated that by placing gallery ropes behind which spectators must remain to observe golf action, the tournament has somehow implied that those areas are safe. Actually, I always thought the gallery ropes were intended to protect the players from the crazed fans.

More seriously, whatever happened to the legal theory of "assumption of risk"? That theory holds that whoever attends a golf tournament or a baseball game or a car race should be presumed to know that balls go out of play and cars run off the track. Therefore, the event should not be held liable providing it exercises reasonable efforts to allow for the safety of the spectator.

Be aware that this area of the law may not be working in your favor as much as it once did. Once again, therefore, consult legal counsel for the applicable law in your geographic area, your legal jurisdiction, and your particular event. Standards may well differ for a highly dangerous sport like auto racing as opposed to a professional badminton exhibition of India versus Korea.

What level of precautionary measures are sufficient? Should the netting behind home plate extend all the way down both the first and third foul lines to prevent injury from one of those wicked foul-line drives? How high should the protective glass be in a hockey rink? Is it reasonable to lower that glass on the sides of the rink but extend it to the ceiling behind both goals where errant shots fly? What areas for the viewers at an auto race are safe from flying debris, tires, and flames when a tragedy occurs?

Assess your event carefully; try to envision the worst thing that could happen no matter how remote or unlikely it may seem; and plan accordingly.

Site Management: Construction, Electrical, Maintenance, and Signage

This section involves several areas of potential risk: construction, electrical, maintenance, and signage. Legal analysis on the duties imposed on you by the first three items would constitute a voluminous treatise on the law of business invitee. Since this section lacks such space, it can only raise real warning flags for you in organizing your event.

You are inviting onto your business premises—be it arena, stadium, golf course, or race track—potential litigants in large numbers. Are you building or providing bleachers for them to sit on? Do not assume the competence of anyone erecting such structures or the soundness of any provided. Take reasonable, necessary steps to ensure the safety of fans using those seating areas.

Once everything is in place, you will bear the responsibility of maintaining the facilities and grounds in a safe manner. Your actual standard of care under the law may vary in different jurisdictions, but be aware of common hazards: water on the floor, holes on the golf course, loose steps, and dead tree limbs.

Are you providing power? If so, has the electrical work been performed competently? Are there exposed power lines? Is the proper current provided where necessary? Are the heaters in the corporate hospitality tents a fire hazard?

Signage is the final subsection to be considered for purposes of risk. Place warning signs in areas where errant golf balls, baseballs, flying cue balls, if applicable, may somehow come into contact with spectators. Jurisdictions vary on the efficacy of such signage in insulating the event from liability. Nevertheless, risk consultants strongly recommend such signage as a useful piece of evidence when you present your side of the case.

Provide information plainly, clearly, and often on what to do in case of emergency, lightning, or other dangerous inclement weather. What is the emergency procedure and where should the spectator go if a warning siren screams of approaching lightning?

Exit signs should be clearly marked.

If effective in your area, signs disclaiming any responsibility or liability whatsoever for anything should be displayed.

If you know of the existence of a dangerous condition you cannot rectify, then rope off the dangerous area and surround it with bold warning signs. If necessary, consider assigning security personnel to the area to prevent entry.

Concessions: Licenses, Taxes

Most of the risks here are financial.

Know the various licenses you may need, as well as the applicable taxes for sales of any kind. Regarding food and beverage, what are the county, state, and ABC licenses or permits required? What, if any, is the governing tax associated for such sales for which you will be accountable?

If merchandise is the issue (e.g., souvenirs and the ubiquitous event T-shirt), again, what licenses and taxes apply to it? Is there a legal way to avoid such taxes—such as nonprofit status, 501(c)(3) status under the Internal Revenue Code, the status of a charitable institution, the status of a church, another status?

If you are selling items on a consignment basis, know how stringent the accountability will be on you to return either the product or the equivalent in cash.

The bottom line here is to ensure you are not assessed a fine, a penalty, a tax, or other invoice you were not expecting.

Be aware of the freshness of food/beverage products where that is an issue. Are there any special requirements for preparation of certain foods? You could also be held liable if consumers at your event become ill through bad food.

Finance

If you undertake the sale of tickets on behalf of "someone else," be clear regarding your accountability at the end. Too often I have seen situations where someone felt that he or she was acting more as a favor to the promoter in helping to distribute tickets but at the end of the event, a dispute arose regarding an unreal expectation of strict accountability for such sales.

What measures should be taken to reduce your financial risk? Some events use scrip tickets instead of cash for the purchase of food and beverage. It is easier to control the sale of scrip. You need fewer people to handle the money. You also have an easier accounting system because a quick tally of tickets compared with cash reveals any discrepancies.

Do you have adequate security for people and areas handling large amounts of cash? Are the proper systems in place for dealing with credit card sales? How will you safely transport cash and make deposits? Who will do so?

Establish a sound system of controls for tickets, merchandise, and concessions products. What is your system for monitoring all spectators to ensure display of proper tickets or credentials and for enforcing sales to those individuals lacking such items?

Insurance is a vital issue failing under this section. Because of its importance, however, it is discussed separately below.

Support Services: Health and Safety, Communications, Traffic Control, Transportation, and Parking

Considering the litigious nature of society, the topic "Health and Safety" deserves special attention from you in your planning. You must guard against any failure to provide reasonably adequate medical care for your spectators and contestants. At every event site, you are certainly not expected to provide a fully-equipped medical unit equivalent to a transportable Mt. Sinai Hospital. You will, however, be expected to provide for some measure of medical care that is reasonable under the circumstances. Anticipate.

What you provide will be dictated by the distance from the nearest medical facility, the size of the crowd, the nature of the event, the demographics of the crowd, and the inherent danger in the event or of the site. One example: During an outdoor event in the summer in the South, one can expect sunburn and dehydration. Take steps to protect individuals against such conditions—for example, providing water stations and shade areas—and to provide treatment when they do occur. A second example: A surfing contest will add to the first example the need for expertise and personnel to provide rescue services in large seas and surf.

A third example: The medical problems to anticipate will differ greatly—by worlds, in fact—if you are hosting a croquet championship in Newport, Rhode Island, as opposed to being involved in a NASCAR event in South Hill, South Carolina.

While the examples are endless, you should allow for at least an acceptable level of on-site care: EMTs, volunteer doctors/nurses, transportation for such personnel, adequate supplies, and a satisfactory treatment area. The key here is to anticipate, do your research, and respond to the data appropriately.

The next subsection is an essential tool not only in preventing risk situations but simply for ensuring smooth operation: communications. Have a sufficient number of radios, walkie-talkies, cellular phones—whatever it takes to keep key personnel in contact with each other. You or your designate should be capable of communicating with and monitoring conversations of all necessary department heads. By monitoring, you can anticipate problems and defuse the situation. You also want the proper personnel to be able to react quickly to emergencies of any kind and magnitude: medical, parking, traffic, security, inventory control, even running out of ice in the title sponsor's hospitality tent.

In your advanced planning, be cognizant of potential traffic control and parking problems. Snarled traffic can mean lost revenue in tickets and concession sales. Moreover, are you allowing a hazardous situation which might result in injury? Has your lack of attention to detail in this area created a dangerous intersection somewhere? Because of your failure to plan for an orderly departure from crowded parking lots, are your spectators engaged in a spontaneous demolition derby?

Do you have adequate security to control traffic and provide safe parking areas? Is your signage directing traffic sufficiently clear and well placed?

The final pertinent issue is transportation. In nearly every event of any kind, transportation issues tend to be the most bothersome.

Shuttling large numbers of fans brings about images of long lines at shuttle stops, uncomfortable buses, and generally a miserably inconvenient experience.

Transporting a small number of VIPs—sponsors or celebrities—can also be a nightmare. Nothing will lose a key sponsor faster than when its CEO stands cooling his heels on some sidewalk waiting for his or her ride. My experience is that such little things cost you sponsorship dollars more often than major catastrophes. Therefore, spend plenty of time planning for these details.

A couple of hints should be very helpful to your planning in this area. Drive the routes to be taken to confirm actual time and distance. Be sure that all drivers know the directions well—and that they even practice driving the routes. Do not laugh. While it is incomprehensible to me, I have seen significant events where the hired drivers show up for work and have no idea of the location of elemental destinations: the airport, the host hotel, and even the site of the event. This sort of ignorance was a source of criticism during the 1996 Olympics in Atlanta.

Educate your drivers on rush hours to be reckoned with during the event. Discover reliable shortcuts and alternate routes.

Convey all this information to the drivers in writing. Provide simple maps. Provide accurate, detailed, written schedules to everyone. Place a cellular phone in each vehicle.

Realize, too, your tremendous potential liability in hiring drivers and providing transportation. Be a smart consumer. Is it ultimately cheaper and wiser to hire a transportation or destination company with large umbrella insurance coverage than to try to manage transportation yourself? Under the circumstances, can this step insulate you from disastrous risks?

If you insist on hiring drivers, be aware of a range of issues—from obtaining adequate insurance to screening drivers by checking motor vehicle records for DUIs or similar severe violations. Otherwise, you could be held grossly negligent in a legal action. Do your research on this issue in your venue and jurisdiction, and with your insurance advisor and legal consultant.

Advertising, Promotions, Media Relations

Unless you assault an esteemed member of the paparazzi for snapping a photo of you in a compromising position, your likelihood of risk for injury under this section is slight. Nevertheless, several angles are worth considering.

First, you may open yourself up to ridicule and some risk of financial liability if you are not careful with your advertising. While you may be desperate to promote your event and increase sales, do not declare that Michael Jordan will be coming when it is actually Vernon Jordan. As a rule, underpromise and overdeliver, and you will be a hero with your sponsors and spectators. By performing well under that guideline, you are assured of a long and successful event career.

Be careful around the press. I enjoy working with the media, and I have been fortunate to enjoy a good relationship with the media for any event or individual client I was promoting. Remember, nonetheless, that the media always have more power, ink, and videotape than you ever will, so do not go to war with them. Offhand remarks, or "off-the-record" comments made to members of the press you do not know can end up as headlines. Derogatory comments by you which are broadcast or published can result in your calling yourself by a new name: The Defendant.

Also, use the press to help you. The media may not always cooperate, but often they will aid you in disseminating information. Do not limit their assistance to trying to sell tickets. Use the press to help control traffic by providing a map and designating alternate routes to your event. Provide necessary information about parking, shuttles, and transportation.

Insurance

To paraphrase an old real estate formula for success: "There are three factors which will reduce your exposure from risks associated with organizing and operating an event: insurance, insurance, insurance." While it is preferable to prevent problems by all methods and considerations such as those contained in this chapter, I am an advocate of insurance. This is not the area in which to cut corners financially. Thus, the issue is important enough to justify using this brief section to offer a few general comments and principles.

Find a good insurance company specializing in the area of your event. Assess its track record in terms of providing service and any pertinent history of paying off on losses when necessary. A good insurance representative with experience in this field is a useful tool in your planning efforts to reduce your exposure. Find a representative who has handled similar event business.

Determine a sufficient amount of insurance coverage for your event. Do you need an umbrella coverage for liability of $1,000,000 or $5,000,000?

Moreover, establish a minimum requirement of insurance for any subcontractors who will work on your event. Require such proof of insurance before they are allowed on site. Be certain that you and your company are named as insured on the policy. Identify the other individuals and entities who also should be named as insured.

A good insurance group will serve as a clearinghouse for all certificates of insurance which must be collected from the various subcontractors for your event: caterers; transportation companies; maintenance services for the golf course, the arena, the stadium; parking services; contractors; electrical services; sanitation companies; and so forth.

Discussed above was the risk associated with hiring drivers. For a fee, an insurance company can check the motor vehicle records of your potential drivers to determine past serious violations.

Together with your legal counsel, your insurance representative can advise you on the dangerous area of liquor liability. The representative will want the certificates of insurance covering that risk from the caterer, the site, and any entity serving alcohol at your function.

Over the years, the experienced representative I use has been very helpful in creating a trusty checklist of risk factors for a particular event. Find an insurance advisor who can perform the same valuable service for you.

Be cognizant of the kinds of specialty insurance coverage which are available. Although such coverage is somewhat expensive, you should at least consider the viability of event cancellation insurance whenever you conduct an outdoor event. Determine exactly the conditions under which you can recover. In addition, determine what items you will recover: expenses only, lost profits?

Even narrower kinds of coverage are available. In golf, American Hole 'n One will insure prizes for rewarding a hole in one at your golf event. The standards will be very strict regarding the yardage required on the hole to be covered under the policy, the number of players participating, the permitted number of shots, the sequence of shots, the number of officials needed to observe and verify the hole in one, and whether or not professionals are eligible (this will increase the premium). Naturally, the premium amount will fluctuate, depending on the value of the prize.

We have been very successful in creating excitement about and promoting a major event with ancillary contests such as a "Hole in One" for significant cash amounts or a Mercedes or other prizes. An ancillary contest is also a good way to bring in sponsors who can gain exposure by taking title to the contest. Do not forget to build into the sponsorship package the cost of the premium.

I suspect you can find insurance—for a price—to cover almost any event you want to stage. Consider creative incentives when examining ways to add excitement to your event and thereby to market it more effectively. Is it financially feasible to offer a bonus for winning three races at your steeplechase race? In your series of monster truck races, the tension will be unbelievable if you provide a $1,000,000 bonus for winning two races in a row.

A client of yours may want to enhance the value of its title position in several events by offering a similar kind of bonus. For example, a company is the title sponsor of two or three tournaments on the golf or tennis tour. It wants to ensure the highest caliber of the field of participants. As your client, that company may call on you to devise some bonus program to encourage the stars to play all the titled events, with a big reward for winning two or more. You will want to be able to respond to that inquiry by seeking the consultation of your trusted agent in the field of specialty insurance.

Waivers

As mentioned above, there is a vast body of law on the issue of waivers. The advice here is simply to obtain the opinions of your legal counsel and insurance representative on the most effective form of waiver for your jurisdiction and event. Incorporate that waiver into your entry process. Be sure that every participant has signed such a waiver along with the entry form.

In addition, know the law in your area regarding the validity of such a waiver. What are the age requirements? Is every participant 18 years of age or older? Is parental consent necessary? If so, is such parental consent evident on the waiver?

Many events include a waiver of liability somewhere on the ticket purchased to gain entrance to the event. Again, how binding such a waiver is will depend on the law of the jurisdiction and on the circumstances. Nevertheless, it certainly cannot hurt to place that waiver on the ticket. Such a placement could be one more piece of useful evidence for your side in case the worst happens and you are dragged into our legal system.

Contingency Plans

A solid contingency plan can reduce the risk of physical injury and perhaps even save lives. It can also affect the other aspects of the term *risk* as explained in this chapter under the headings "Finance" and "Unforeseeable." Once your planning and organization have revealed a potential problem, then you must be creative and flexible enough to design the appropriate and effective contingency plan.

Anticipation

One of the best examples of the many benefits of a solid contingency plan involves the greatest fear of any outdoor event: dangerous inclement weather. For purposes of this example, we examine the most difficult outdoor activity to control, the golf tournament.

Golf tournaments are uniquely difficult because unlike an auto race, tennis match, concert, or ball game, many spectators are spread out over a vast area watching the athletic activity unfold over that same area. Neither your contestants nor the spectators are concentrated in any one place. Accordingly, all the usual problems associated with those other outdoor activities are magnified greatly.

In recent years, golf tournaments, especially at the professional level and at the knowledgeable level of the United States Golf Association, have become more sophisticated in protecting players and spectators. It was not long ago, however, that various professional players were injured when struck by lightning and a spectator was killed by lightning at a major golf tournament.

Naturally, the first defense against such disasters is advanced warning. Modern radar and related weather technology now supply very accurate and timely progress reports on approaching bad weather. Be sure to do your research and make the arrangements to take advantage of that technology. Use all such tools available to you.

Do not panic: you do not have to purchase expensive electronic wizardry to render your event headquarters an NASA station. Such services are available for a reasonable fee on a per-event basis, and they will provide you with up-to-the-minute reports on approaching weather during the event.

Now, suppose you have determined there is a problem of advancing dangerous weather conditions. "What next?" you might ask. In golf, a horn or a siren signals that play will stop because of lightning. Nevertheless, both players and spectators remain at risk out on the course. So you now carry out the evacuation plan you devised when you were planning the tournament.

First, the signal should be given in ample time for the spectators to seek shelter. Because of limited space in the clubhouse, tournaments have provided alternative safety areas out on the golf course—facilities equipped with lightning rods.

For considerations of both safety and comfort, the players and the caddies are quite often treated differently. At the Virginia State Open, large utility vehicles are parked on the golf course. When play is stopped because of lightning, the volunteers serving as gallery marshals or the scorers near those vehicles are designated to drive the players and caddies back to the clubhouse in them. Remember that this plan works *only if the vehicle keys are accessible to the designated drivers*. Nothing is quite so frustrating and scary as observing very irate players abusing a poor volunteer as he or she stands in the pouring rain outside a locked evacuation vehicle outlined against a backdrop of a dark gray sky streaked by lightning flashes.

Unforeseeable

Inherent in the term *unforeseeable* is the inability to guard against an unfavorable circumstance with any contingency plan because you cannot possibly predict its occurrence. Nevertheless, when the unforeseeable does occur, you may still be held accountable, no matter how unfair. Accordingly, you should work to enhance your innate ability as a seer—and thus prepare for "the highly unlikely."

As an example, I am very proud of a contingency plan developed for a wonderful golf experience, "Fantasy Golf Camp."

The Fantasy Golf concept is to allow amateurs to spend five nights and four days with PGA TOUR stars in a very close environment. Not only does the amateur receive daily instruction from the TOUR players and then play 18 holes of golf, but at night everyone gathers for drinks, dinner, and camaraderie. The experience far surpasses a one-day pro-am, where the amateur may hear barely a word from the pro for 18 holes.

Socializing with the pros after golf and intimate access to the TOUR players made the Fantasy Golf Camp really special. Add to that experience the venue of Las Vegas, and everyone involved had the unique opportunity to become friends.

As you can imagine, this event required significant financial underwriting for the hotels, the meals, and, most of all, the fees for the TOUR players. Imagine the investment it took to assemble the Fantasy Golf "staff" of true luminaries who attended—such as Tom Kite, John Daly, Curtis Strange, Davis Love, III, Lanny Wadkins, and Payne Stewart. Therefore, it was crucial to ensure that the participants had the fun they expected or else financial failure could have resulted to the organizer.

I go to such great lengths to describe the experience because this particular Camp took place in early November in Las Vegas. Everyone, especially the Las

Vegas contacts, assured me that the weather would be acceptable. We might need sweaters and windbreakers, I was told, but it never rains that time of year. Fair enough, I thought. It did not occur to me, however, to inquire about the likelihood of *snow*.

Yes, on the very first day of the Camp, with expectations soaring and grown men and women acting like children in the presence of the TOUR stars, it snowed. It was so cold I wanted to weep. But wait . . .

The day would be saved because of a contingency plan. I mentioned earlier I was so proud of this plan because we had ignored all the assurances of pleasant, if not balmy, weather. In fact, the day turned out to be the best possible kickoff for the Camp.

Many months prior to the Camp, arrangements were made with a local golf shop to have indoor golf practice equipment ready and on standby. A large ballroom was reserved at the host hotel for a practice facility. Within one hour of the first camper facing cold weather, we were set up inside with Tom Kite offering full swing instruction to campers hitting off a moveable practice tee into a net. Noted instructor Scott Davenport, of the famous Golf Digest Schools, was providing swing analysis with the aid of the latest technology. Other PGA TOUR stars were working one-on-one with campers on putting mats.

The biggest hit of the day was TOUR player Peter Persons organizing a chipping contest into nets. Peter was also collecting the bets while he cajoled the campers into competing, wagering, and verbally abusing each other. The campers were having a ball! Cocktails and food were plentiful, and the entire atmosphere reeked of camaraderie.

We finally had to drag people out of the practice facility in time for dinner. No one wanted to stop having fun. From that first makeshift day, many friendships were made, and a fantastic tone was set for the rest of the Camp.

Summary/Conclusion

Assess the potential problems applicable to your event, and formulate contingency plans accordingly. Be creative and flexible. Do not let yourself be bound by thinking in terms only of the usual or normal. While precedent and experience are very helpful, also take the time to envision those things "unforeseeable" to other, less successful event managers. Accumulate all the information you can from all sources on ways to organize and operate an event. Speak with experienced individuals. Assemble all the written materials available. Use that research to create your own organizational chart which you trust.

Make a solid attorney and insurance representative a standard part of your event team. Seek advice before the problem occurs. Preventive legal advice is much cheaper than bringing in attorneys to defend you later in litigation.

Part 6

Risk and Legal Management

No longer will risk management be viewed as a necessary evil rather it will be considered a management priority.

Sarah Young 2005

Chapter 22

Importance of Risk Management[*]

Herb Appenzeller

In the 1960s, tort liability was a key word in litigation involving sports, physical activities, and recreation. A few states that abrogated the doctrine of governmental immunity included California, Connecticut, New Jersey, and New York. These states permitted themselves to be sued for negligent conduct, while the remaining states used governmental immunity to protect themselves from lawsuits. The common law principle which protected school districts with immunity was used as a defense by school districts without regard to the circumstances of the case in question (Appenzeller, 1978).

Harry Rosenfield, an opponent of sovereign and governmental immunity, expressed his opposition to the immunity doctrine by protesting:

> The present rule in my judgment is completely inconsistent with all modern concepts of justice and social responsibility. It is unreasonable to require an injured person to bear a disproportionate part of the normal operating cost of activities undertaken by the entire community.

Rosenfield continued his dissent by pointing out:

> The whole community pays for the school building for light, heat, books, school contracts, etc. Why should the injured pupil or teacher pay out of his/her own pocket for an item that is an operating cost of the school budget—in fact, if not a law. If the school breaks a contract, it is liable in law. If it breaks someone's neck, it is not. I submit that this does not make sense. (Appenzeller, 1978).

Slowly but surely, public opinion prevailed and many states abrogated the doctrine of sovereign and governmental immunity, which led to an unprecedented increase in litigation against schools and their sport programs and personnel. From the 1960s to the present, huge damage awards continue to escalate. At the Society for the Study of Legal Aspects of Sport and Physical Activity (SSLASPA) Conferences, tort liability issues were presented. (SSLASPA is now the Sport and Recreation Law Association [SRLA], and at its conference in 2000, the majority of its 80 presentations involved risk management.) Sport risk management is a vital component of management. George Head and Stephen Horn II (1997) observe:

---

[*] Reprinted with permission from *Cheerleading and the Law: Risk Management Strategies*, Carolina Academic Press, Durham, NC 2008.

Risk management occupies an important place in the broad definition of management—that devoted to minimizing the adverse effects of accidental loss on the organization.

It is obvious that risk management is a new companion to sport law with its implications for business, the insurance industry, and the medical profession. Sport risk management, which encompasses sport, physical activities, and recreation, addresses accidental loss and financial loss. It is crucial not only to minimizing loss exposure but also to protecting participants and spectators from unforeseeable accidents and injuries and to protecting an organization from financial loss.

Importance of Risk Management

George Head and Stephen Horn II, pioneers in risk management, write: "Being able to apply the risk management process in both its decision-making and managerial dimensions is the most important skill any risk management professional can possess" (Head & Horn II, 1997). It has been said "that the most important task for sport administrators may be the most overlooked, legal management that implements risk management strategies" (Appenzeller, 2000).

Dr. Betty van der Smissen, a risk management authority, states:

It becomes imperative that managers and administrators as well as policy boards of entities offering leisure and educational services affirmatively and aggressively give attention to management of financial and programmatic risks to effectively reduce costs and enable desirable programs and services to be continued. (Appenzeller, 2000).

Ronald Baron, Director of the Center for Sport Law and Risk Management in Dallas, Texas, comments:

Risk management helps those who direct a sport program comply with their legal duties, provide safe programs, and enable sports personnel to defend themselves and their programs in the event of a lawsuit. (Appenzeller, 2000).

Dr. Betty van der Smissen, commenting on an effective risk management plan, writes:

[R]isk management is the systematic analysis of one's operation for potential risks or risk exposure and the setting forth a plan to reduce such exposures. (Appenzeller, 2000).

She further suggests:

A good risk management plan analyzes all potential risks that an organization faces and selects the optimal method to treat each. (Appenzeller, 2000).

She emphasizes that a risk management plan is more than a safety check list (Appenzeller, 2000).

Dr. Rob Ammon, a risk management expert, describes the importance of risk management as the ability to combine business interests with those of the sport industry. He believes that risk management may be viewed as the control of financial and personal injury losses from sudden, unforeseen, unusual accidents and intentional torts (Cotten & Wilde, 1997).

Ammon indicates that today's sport manager can utilize the risk management process to meet the litigious society he/she experiences. He says:

Sport managers have been exposed to a new society during the past 20 years in a society that has become enchanted with litigating and to which many professionals in the sports environment have fallen victim. Society will not tolerate inappropriate behavior and sport managers, especially those managing sports facilities must develop an awareness of the hazards for which they will be held accountable. An effective risk management plan will help to diminish the risks that confront today's sport manager. (Cotten & Wilde, 1997).

In *Athletic Liability: An Assessment Guide*, Burling and Gallagher (1992) write:

As athletic programs and activities proliferate on college campuses, so do the inevitable risks and accidents. Managing the risks associated with athletic activities must be a top priority for college and university administrators, as such programs are a source of extensive liability.

In addition, an article by United Educators' writers maintains that "not surprisingly, in recent years, the number of sport negligence lawsuits against coaches and schools has increased dramatically" (United Educators, 1991). The article concludes:

A comprehensive risk management program can help evidence that those in the care of the college or university have received necessary care and attention. Furthermore, a well structured management policy executed and enforced by a committee of senior administrators is the key to both preventing injuries and minimizing liability. (United Educators, 1991).

Risk Management: A Specialty of Management

Accidents with accompanying loss are a fact of life. "Activity in sport results in loss exposure, loss of property, income, life and health and liability to others. Losses may strike a venue, a business, a nonprofit or governmental organization providing a service. Risk management attempts to minimize the adverse effects of those losses" (Head & Horn II, 1997).

According to George Head and Stephen Horn II, risk management involves a two-fold process: a decision-making process and a management process.

Decision-Making Process.
1. Identifying the Problem.
2. Analyzing Loss Exposure.
3. Selecting Techniques.
4. Implementing Changes.
5. Monitoring Results.

Management Process.
1. Planning to Protect the Program.
2. Organizing the Personnel.

3. Leading the Personnel by Motivating Them to Carry Out Responsibilities.
4. Controlling and Evaluating Process.
   (Head & Horn II, 1997).

Furthermore, Head and Horn II maintain that applying risk management to a program is the "most important skill a management professional can possess." They stress the importance of applying the risk management process to any organization to manage exposure to accidental loss (Head & Horn II, 1997).

Dr. Annie Clement, a sport risk management authority, believes that risk management must be comprehensive. She points out that risk management consists of the identification of potential problems and the evaluation of identified risks "for probability, severity and magnitude to determine the amount of risk that exists" (Clement, 2004).

According to Clement, control is the third component in a successful risk management program. Clement believes that liability can be controlled in four ways. These include the following:

1. Accepting the Risk and Assuming Responsibility.
2. Retaining the Activity and Transferring the Risk Through Contracts and Insurance.
3. Altering the Activity to Reduce the Risk.
4. Eliminating the Risk.
   (Clement, 2004).

No one text can provide total information on risk management. Each program is unique and needs a risk management plan tailored for the organization's individual needs.

Sport Law Literature

The Society for the Study of Legal Aspects of Physical Activities (SSLASPA), now the Sport & Recreation Law Association (SRLA), published a list of sport and law texts in 1995. It believed that the publications were an attempt to meet the needs of teachers, coaches, and administrators who were being sued more frequently involving sport, recreation, and physical activities. In the 1970s, it listed five books: Herb Appenzeller's *From the Gym to the Jury* (1970), *Athletics and the Law* (1975), and *Physical Education and the Law* (1978); Lionel Sobel's *Professional Sports and the Law* (1977); and John Weistart and Cyn Lowell's *Law of Sports* (1979).

In the 1980s, when litigation in sport increased dramatically, 43 texts were published; in the 1990s, 38 additional texts were published in the field. From the 1970s through the 1990s, the number of authors increased from 4 to 117. In addition, in the 1990s, journals, manuals, periodicals, videos, and other material appeared on the SSLASPA's list.

In 2000, when risk management became widely accepted by legal scholars and practitioners, 80 presentations were made at the SSLASPA annual conference, and the majority of the presentations involved risk management.

Timothy Davis, Alfred Mathewson, and Kenneth Stropshire, editors of *Sports and the Law: A Modern Anthology* (1999), comment on the rise of scholarly work:

> What became apparent in our review of articles, books and other materials for inclusion in our anthology is the breadth and quality of contemporary

scholarship in the sports context. We attribute this in part to the growing number of quality sports and entertainment law journals that provide increased opportunities for publication.

We also noted, however, the proliferation of sports-related scholarship published in highly respected mainstream journals. Those phenomena suggest the multi-dimensional nature of sports-related scholarship and the significance of legal issues that arise in the sports context. (Davis, Mathewson & Stropshire, 1999).

It is apparent that publications on risk management will increase substantially in the 2000s as the number of risk management practitioners and scholars continues to rise.

Trends in Risk Management

Dr. Sarah Young, a risk management scholar in recreation, conducted a research study regarding the status of risk management and future trends through 2020. Young used the Delphi technique, "based upon the collective opinion of knowledgeable experts." A group of 69 experts arrived at a consensus of 11 key trends:

1. Liability issues will continue to manifest as problems requiring sound risk management plans.
2. Sport managers must continue to educate themselves in risk management in an attempt to provide safer programs.
3. Risk management will continue to be a key element in the design of recreational sport programs.
4. There will be an increase in the number of people with disabilities participating in recreational sport.
5. Professional preparation in liability and risk management will become more important for students pursuing careers in sport management.
6. Risk management planning will take on increased importance to recreational sport programs.
7. More recreational sport programs/agencies will develop comprehensive risk management plans.
8. There will be an increased demand for employee certification in specialized activity programs such as aerobics and aquatics.
9. Sport equipment manufacturers and recreational sport managers will continue to provide safer and more protective equipment so that individuals do not suffer as much risk of injury from potential defects in products.
10. There will be an increased willingness of participants to engage in litigation to resolve issues related to participation in recreational sport.
11. There will be an increased demand for the requirement that safety equipment be worn by recreational sport participants.
    (Appenzeller, 2004).

Defining Sport Risk Management

Defining *sport risk management* is not an easy task. Many risk management scholars and practitioners admit that its definition is complex and at times confusing. However, in a review of over ten definitions of risk management by scholars and practitioners, several factors are consistently mentioned. These include an attempt to identify loss control as it pertains to the minimizing of personal injuries to participants and spectators, avoiding litigation by creating a safe environment for both participants and spectators, preparing a risk management plan, developing sound risk management strategies, and preventing loss exposure and financial loss. Defining sport risk management emphasizes the need to identify and analyze potential problems, select procedures and policies to develop a sound process, monitor and evaluate the results of the risk management plan, and be ready to review and adjust the plan to meet the changing goals, objectives, and needs of the organization.

This author suggests the following as a potential definition of *sport risk management*:

> Sport risk management is a process that develops a comprehensive risk management plan designed to eliminate or minimize loss exposure for injuries to participants and spectators and to limit or avoid financial loss. Sport risk management strategies need constant reevaluation, compliance with legal duties, and the responsibility to create a safe environment.

References

Ammon, R. 2008 in *Cheerleading and the Law*, Durham, NC: Carolina Academic Press.

Appenzeller, H. 1978. *Physical Education and the Law*, Charlottesville, VA: The Michie Company.

Appenzeller, T. 2000. *Youth Sports and the Law*, Durham, NC: Carolina Academic Press.

Appenzeller, H. 2004. *Risk Management in Sport: Issues and Strategies*, Durham, NC: Carolina Academic Press.

Burling, P. and Gallagher, G. 1992. *Managing Athletic Liability: An Assessment Guide.* Chevy Chase, MD: United Educators Risk Retention Group, Inc.

Cotten, D. and Wilde, T. 1997. *Law for Recreation and Sport Managers.* Dubuque, IA: Kendall-Hunt.

Clement, A. 2004. *Law in Sports and Physical Activity*, 3rd Edition. Dania, FL: Sport and Law Press.

Davis, T., Mathewson, A. and Stropshire, K. 1999. *Sports and the Law: A Modern Anthology.* Durham, NC: Carolina Academic Press.

Head, G. and Horn, S. 1997. *Essentials in Risk Management*, 2nd Edition. Malvern, PA: Insurance Institute of America.

United Educators Insurance Risk Retention Group, Inc. 1991. *Managing Athletic Liability: An Assessment Guide:* Chevy Chase, MD: Institute for Liability Management.

van der Smissen, B. 1997 in Cotten, D. and Wilde, T.J. in *Sport for the Sport Manager*, chp. 23, p. 175. Dubuque, IA: Kendall-Hunt.

Chapter 23

Fitness Center Safety

David L. Harlowe

Introduction

Whether one is starting a new facility or updating an existing facility, this chapter is designed to help fitness center owners, managers, and support staff understand the risks inherent in the sport industry. Management must take a proactive approach when establishing its fitness center. A facility can be a simple, small town gym or a sophisticated training center for athletes. Regardless of the size or scope of the facility, certain risks must be recognized and addressed. While there are no set rules for the fitness industry, the American College of Sports Medicine (ACSM) has developed standards and guidelines for safety in fitness centers. Various guidelines of the ACSM will be addressed throughout this chapter.

Facility Layout

There is a growing variety of fitness centers out there today: sports-related facilities, circuit-training facilities, cycling studios, and so forth. Regardless of the type of facility, care must be taken in safely laying it out. Five main factors must be addressed:

1. Fitness Center Flooring (or Fitness Floor Types)
2. Equipment Positioning
3. Facility Lighting
4. Facility Environment
5. Facility Signs (or Facility Signage)

Fitness Floor Types

When setting up a fitness facility, one must consider what each area will be used for. There are at least four areas to any fitness facility, each with its own special needs. The first priority is always the safety of the people using the area. Choosing the right floor will help prolong equipment life and reduce the chance of injuries because of equipment failure. Below are the four main areas and the recommendations for the type of floor that should be used.

Free Weight Area

The floor in the free weight area will take the most abuse because dumbbells and weight plates will be in constant use. In theory, these pieces of equipment should be returned to their respective racks when not in use, but in reality they will be dropped on the floor too many times to count. To help reduce damage to this equipment and the floor in the area, rubber padding should be used. It is recommended that a permanent rubber floor be used throughout the area. The rubber floor should be at least ½" to ¾" in thickness and should meet OSHA and ADA minimum standards for traction. When permanent flooring is installed, it is very important that the edge of the floor be level in the transition from one area to another. At the very least, the edge of the floor should be beveled in order to reduce the chance of someone tripping when entering the area. Extra padding should be added in the dumbbell area since people tend to drop the dumbbells on the floor after use rather than returning them to the dumbbell rack.

Selectorized Equipment Area

When choosing the floor type for the selectorized machine area, one has more options. This type of equipment is heavy and stationary. The floor in this area could be made of rubber or wood or covered with carpet. If rubber flooring is used, it should be epoxy-bonded to the subfloor to form a nonporous, seamless surface. The floor should be secure so that gaps and bulges will not form from machine movement over time. An uneven floor presents a major trip hazard. If wood floors are used, rubber pads should be placed under the equipment's frame legs to provide shock absorption and protection to the floor, as well as to keep equipment from shifting from continuous use. Carpeted floors are the most common type of floor in this area. Carpeted floors should be checked periodically to make sure equipment has not shifted from use and formed raised seams that could make someone trip.

Cardiovascular Area

Typically, the floor in most cardio areas is carpeted. This type of floor is acceptable as long as the carpet is cleaned regularly to prevent bacteria and fungus buildup from sweat and dirt. The wood floors in the cardio area can be aesthetically pleasing, but they can become a problem if the floor becomes wet from sweat or spilled water. Equipment such as treadmills tends to move from its original position when people use the elevation option on wood floors. If a wood floor is in the cardio area, it is recommended that rubber pads be placed under the equipment.

Many fitness centers today are using elevated decks for the cardio area to create a more functional atmosphere for audiovisual purposes. An elevated deck can pose a danger if the flooring on it is a solid color or texture throughout the entire area. There must be a clear distinction between walkways and the deck. Steps leading up to the deck must contrast in color with the deck. This contrast will help prevent people from losing their bearings and stumbling or falling.

Group Exercise Area

In the group exercise room, various classes are conducted—ranging from aerobics to martial arts. It is therefore important that the floor be durable yet forgiving to the people using the room. A "forgiving floor" has proper shock absorption to help reduce the number of leg injuries to class participants. Most floor manufacturers use the DIN Floor Standards. DIN is an acronym for *Deutsches Institut für Normung*. The DIN Standards were developed in Germany and are recognized worldwide as the best method for evaluating sports floors. The standards were developed to ensure that aerobic athletes received the greatest degree of safety and performance from a flooring surface when participating in aerobic exercise.

DIN Floor Standards:

Shock	DIN Standard	Explanation
Absorption	53% Minimum	Insufficient shock absorption causes activity-related injuries to ankle and knee joints. Correct shock absorption reduces fatigue and significantly lowers the risk of injury.
Resilience	2.3 mm minimum	Inadequate energy return in a floor causes sore ankles and a surface too "hard" for safe, strenuous activity. Excessive energy return creates a trampoline effect and potential for injury.
Surface Friction	0.5 Minimum 0.7 Maximum	Rotating and pivoting motions create strain on joints without the proper friction coefficients to minimize stress. On a friction scale of .1 (ice) to .9 (fly paper), .5–.7 is the DIN Standard.
Impact Isolation	15% Maximum	Without proper impact isolation, participants' movements can interfere with each other, creating the possibility of injury.
Rolling Load	337.6 lbs	Proper foot stability is essential to reducing foot roll-over and other injuries to participants.

Equipment Positioning

The next important step in setting up a safe facility is to strategically set up the equipment. Overcrowding an area is one of the biggest risks that management can create. ACSM guideline 10.G14 is a good rule to follow when one sets up equipment in a fitness center:

The design and layout of a facility should provide at least 20 to 40 square feet for each piece of equipment. The exact amount of space to be occupied is determined by the size of each particular piece of equipment and the recommendations of the manufacturer. (Tharrett, Peterson, & American College of Sports Medicine, 1997)

Free Weight Area

The free weight area can be a complex area to lay out safely because of the various sizes of benches, machines, and accessories available. Much traffic is moving through this area at various times of the day, so it should be organized in a way that allows users plenty of room. The free weight area should be divided into sections, and special attention should be paid to the storage of the weight plates. A section should be designated for Olympic-style flat benches and incline benches. This section should have its own set of plates and plate trees for proper storage. Weight plate trees should be evenly placed throughout the free weight area to reduce traffic and to ensure proper storage of the plates. The weight horns should be clearly labeled with the poundage the tree is designed to hold. As a result, fewer 45-pound plates will end up on 25-pound weight horns and cause the weight tree to tip over.

There should be a designated dumbbell area within the free weight area. Olympic-style benches are not designed for dumbbell use, and improper use could lead to an injury. Adjustable benches should be placed in the area to provide a variety of settings so that dumbbell users will not attempt to use Olympic benches designed specifically for barbell use. These benches should be positioned with at least three feet of space between them to reduce the chance of a dumbbell striking another person while it is being used.

Selectorized Equipment Area

The equipment in this area will most likely be placed in a particular order to create a circuit. Regardless of equipment order, positioning of the equipment should be well planned. There should be at least two to three feet of unobstructed space between each piece of equipment in this area. The unobstructed area should include an allowance for any moving arms that could extend into traffic areas. A good way to test the range of the equipment is to have someone get on the equipment and move through its entire range of motion while someone else walks by. Such simple checks can greatly reduce the chance of injuries.

Cardiovascular Area

The cardiovascular section of the gym should be well planned because many risks are associated with the area and the equipment used in it. The incorrect placement of electrical cords is one of the most common risks found in the cardio section. Cardiovascular equipment that requires electricity to function must be placed near available outlets. New facilities have the advantage of installing outlets where they are needed. Existing facilities are sometimes victims of preexisting outlet placement. In any case, equipment must be positioned so that cords will not create an unnecessary trip hazard.

Another issue of concern in the cardio area is the placement of treadmills. The distance between treadmills is mainly a comfort issue in that most people do not want any type of interference from someone too close beside them. There should be at least one foot of space between treadmill units. A major concern with treadmills is the amount of space behind each unit. People have been, and will continue to be, ejected from running treadmills. The only way they can fall is backward, which creates a major safety concern. While the ACSM does not address this risk, several major treadmill manufacturers have recommended that there be at least three feet of unobstructed space behind each unit. There should not be any walls, windows, poles, or other pieces of equipment within three feet of the back of the treadmill.

Facility Lighting

Having a low level of light in a facility is a risk because floor edges, cables, and so forth can be concealed and become trip hazards.

ACSM guideline 10.G24 states:

The fitness floor should have an appropriate level of light. The level of illumination should be at least 50 foot-candles at the floor surface. (Tharrett, Peterson, & American College of Sports Medicine, 1997)

If an area has dark-colored carpet or black rubber flooring, the minimum of 50 foot-candles should be increased to the point that all traffic areas are clearly visible.

Facility Environment

A facility's environment is important for a number of reasons. First, a warm facility with poor air circulation could create condensation, which can cause rubber floors to become slippery and equipment to rust and ultimately malfunction. Second, elevated temperatures in a club can add to physical demands already placed on a person from normal exercise. As a result, a person could become overheated and possibly pass out, or worse. ACSM guideline 10.G23 recommends the following:

- Temperature: 68 to 72 degrees Fahrenheit.
- Humidity: 60 percent or less.
- Air Circulation: 8 to 12 exchanges per hour.
  (Tharrett, Peterson, & American College of Sports Medicine, 1997)

Facility Signage

Once the layout of the fitness center is addressed, signs must be strategically placed throughout the facility. Signs can play a variety of roles in a fitness center. There are warning signs, policy and procedure signs, directional signs, and so forth. We will concentrate on warning signs.

Warnings signs act as an additional staff member whose sole purpose is to constantly remind members and guests about facility rules and regulations. These rules and regulations are designed to create safety awareness and to reduce the number of incidents. The following guidelines should be followed when signs are used to warn members and guests about risks.

Signs should be professionally printed. Computer printouts and handwritten signs should be avoided. Concerning class schedules and other club announcements, professional signs will stand out from printouts.

Signs should be posted no higher than 4'–6' from the floor to ensure that they will be easily viewed.

Large print and borders should be used on a warning sign to make sure it stands out and grabs a person's attention.
Sign sizes will vary, depending on their location and the message they must convey. It is highly recommended that policy and procedure signs be at least 18" x 24" in size to ensure maximum visibility. Individual policy signs can vary in size and makeup. Decals can be used on mirrors to attract attention to rules.

Signs are important, but the facility should not be cluttered with so many of them that their significance is lost. Below are descriptions of two key signs that should be used in fitness centers and the areas where they should be placed.

Facility Rules

This sign should state a facility's policies regarding the use of equipment. At least one of these signs should be posted at the entrance of the facility, one in the selectorized equipment area, and one in the free weight area.

Spotter Sign

This sign should recommend the use of a spotter when one is using free weights. The sign should only *recommend* a spotter. If management *requires* one, it is responsible for providing one at all times. The sign should be posted conspicuously throughout the free weight area.

Numerous other types of signs can be placed in a fitness facility. For example, signs stating facility policies about theft can be placed in the locker rooms, and signs urging members to replace their weights when done can be placed in the free weight area. The ultimate goal of the signs is to help provide a safe, productive environment for people using the facility.

Overall Facility Safety

Now that we have addressed strategies for safely setting up a fitness facility, we can address specific safety issues.

Supervision Guidelines

Qualified supervision is very important in reducing the number of incidents in a fitness center. Staff members should be trained to walk periodically through all areas to see if anyone needs assistance. This assistance could involve spotting someone at the bench press or giving simple advice on using the correct technique. Supervision duties in a fitness facility consist of the following:

- Providing new members with orientations on equipment use.
- Setting up basic workouts for new members.
- Modifying workouts for existing members.
- Assisting members by adjusting equipment and/or acting as a spotter.
- Patrolling locker rooms and sauna areas.
- Daily maintenance of equipment (e.g., cleaning, lubrication, and so forth)
- Storing barbells and dumbbells left on the floor by members.

Management should require all personnel who deal with members on an instructional basis to undergo an orientation program that familiarizes them with all equipment and areas of the facility. Equipment orientation should cover every task from adjusting seats to operating equipment properly. It is highly recommended that all instructors be certified in exercise instruction before they create programs for members or instruct them in exercise techniques.

Supervision does not merely consist of watching members exercise. It also involves watching for trouble areas on equipment. Staff members should watch for torn upholstery, worn cables, broken plastic housing, and so forth. Staff members should utilize maintenance logs and schedules when carrying out these duties.

Free Weight Area

Several rules should always be observed in the free weight area. People performing barbell exercises should be required to use bar collars at all times. The use of bar collars will help reduce the number of incidents in which weight plates slide off the ends of the bars, potentially landing on another person or injuring the user. Spotters should be recommended for all exercise involving heavy loads. Such exercise can range from heavy bench press moves to heavy squats. Staff members should make sure that people do not lean weight plates against walls or equipment. This can cause a trip hazard in which someone could hurt his or her leg or foot. The dumbbell area comes with its own set of risks that can be reduced. Each rack on which dumbbells are stored should be appropriate for each style of dumbbell used. This will ensure that people's fingers and hands will not get pinched or smashed because of improper design. Staff members should periodically check the dumbbells for damage and loose parts. Members should be told not to drop the dumbbells after using them in order to avoid damaging them. This rule should be posted on a sign in the area.

Selectorized Equipment Area

Probably the biggest risk found in this area is the misuse of equipment. Proper orientation and instruction will help reduce that risk. However, there are still risks involved with selectorized equipment. The key risk components are padding, cables, and selector pins. It is important that the padding and upholstery covering the equipment be checked periodically for tears or missing pieces of pad that could expose a person's leg or arm to bare metal.

Staff members must make sure that the weight stack selector pins are the correct size. If a selector pin is too short for the weight stack in which it is being used, it could slip out during movement and lead to an injury. One danger in this area that often goes overlooked involves equipment with steel cables. For example, if the cable breaks on the lat pull-down machine, the user will be struck in the head or neck. Many of today's equipment manufacturer's have replaced the steel cable with a Kevlar belt. Routine maintenance is the key to identifying cut or frayed cables.

Cardiovascular Area Safety

The cardiovascular area is one of the most frequently used areas in a fitness facility. Treadmill usage alone has increased by 720 percent over the past ten years. The treadmill is a high-risk piece of equipment because if a person falls, he or she will first hit a running belt and then be thrown backward. Consequently, treadmill safety is very important. Earlier we discussed the importance of providing unobstructed space behind the treadmill. The next step in promoting treadmill safety is providing proper instruction on how to safely start and stop the treadmill. Instructions on properly operating the treadmill are usually found on the console of the unit. Additional operating instructions should be covered by staff members during orientation for new members.

All treadmills are equipped with an emergency stop button. Newer treadmills are equipped with an emergency stop cord in addition to the stop button. The emergency stop cord is becoming a hot topic in litigation involving ejection from treadmills. Most people do not want to use the emergency stop cord for a variety of reasons. However, management must highly recommend members' use of the stop cord while they are exercising. Some treadmill manufacturers have placed warnings on the console of the treadmill instructing the user to put on the safety cord before exercising. Some treadmills come with stop cords and no warnings. In this case, management should post signs around the area strongly recommending the use of the stop cord. Again, signs should only *recommend* the use of the stop cord. If people are *required* to use the cord, management is essentially responsible for having a staff member constantly monitor the area to make sure the cord is being used.

Group Exercise Area Safety

Risks in the group exercise area mainly come from user participation. In other words, most injuries range from sprained ankles to overexertion. It is still important for class instructors to inspect equipment daily—including steps, rubber bands, punching bags, and so forth. If defective equipment is discovered, it should be removed from use immediately and repaired or replaced. Signs should be placed in the area to help participants monitor their heart rates and rates of perceived exertion (RPE). Class instructors should be trained to spot participants who may be overexerting themselves.

Emergency Planning and Equipment

One of the key elements to having a successful fitness facility is an Emergency Action Plan (EAP). An EAP is designed to indicate duties to staff members when they are handling an emergency. An *emergency* is any situation in which a person is injured or lives are in danger. The emergency could be as simple as a sprained ankle or as complex as a fire evacuation. An EAP should address all possible emergencies.

An Emergency Action Plan should be developed one step at a time. Management must remember that it is planning for the unpredictable. The word *unpredictable* sounds like a contradiction, but there is no way management can know what type of accident will happen or when it will happen. Management must be prepared for anything. Management should keep its EAP basic because the simpler it is, the more likely it will be properly carried out. Management should remember that its EAP should be designed to save lives and/or reduce injuries. Developing an EAP should be an ongoing project. Management can always improve it. By practicing its EAP, management will improve it and keep it fresh—especially in the staff member's minds.

Before starting to develop an EAP, management should conduct a risk assessment to determine the most likely risks for the particular facility. There may be a greater risk of a fire than an earthquake, so management should be practical and determine what is more likely to happen in its facility setting and geographical location.

The following minimum requirements must be met in order to successfully implement an Emergency Action Plan:

- A CPR and first-aid certified staff member should always be on duty.

- A working and readily accessible communications system must be in place and available for use in contacting outside emergency assistance.
- Emergency telephone numbers must be posted beside all telephones.
- Detailed directions to the facility from the closest emergency service station must be posted beside all telephones. The complete address of the facility must be included, along with directions to it.
- First and second responders *must* be CPR/first-aid certified if the whole staff is not. The third responder must be designated to summon outside emergency help. The Emergency Action Plan must be rehearsed. Rehearsals must be documented.

First Aid Kit

Most of the time when an injury occurs, outside help is not needed. Sometimes all that is needed is an ice pack or Band-Aid. With this in mind, there must be at least one adequately stocked first aid kit on the premises. If an accident occurs calling for first aid, management must determine if the injured party can administer its own first-aid procedures or if it needs assistance from a staff member. If help is needed from a staff member, precautions should be taken. If blood is present, any staff member helping the injured person must wear rubber gloves to avoid possible contact with blood-borne pathogens (HIV, Hepatitis B, and so forth). If medical attention, such as CPR, is needed, the attending staff member may want to use a mouth guard. Such possibilities should be addressed in the Emergency Action Plan so that a quick decision can be made.

The following items should be available in the first aid kit:

- Rubber gloves
- Antiseptic spray
- Cotton swabs
- Band-Aids (various sizes)
- Gauze pads
- Cold packs
- First aid cream
- Blankets
- Scissors
- Current edition of a first aid manual

Automated External Defibrillator (AED)

A major issue for discussion today is whether or not fitness facilities should have an Automated External Defibrillator on the premises. An AED is a device used to administer an electric shock through the chest wall to the heart. Built-in computers assess the patient's heart rhythm, determine whether defibrillation is needed, and then administer the shock. Audio and/or visual prompts guide the user through the process. At the time of this printing, Arkansas, California, Illinois, Louisiana, Massachusetts, Michigan, New Jersey, New York, Oregon, and Rhode Island are the only states with laws that require fitness centers to install AEDs.

AEDs are important because they strengthen the chances of survival. They can restore a normal heart rhythm in victims of sudden cardiac arrest. The new portable AEDs enable more people to respond to a medical emergency that requires defibrillation. When a person suffers a sudden cardiac arrest, his or her chance of survival decreases by 7% to 10% for each minute that passes without defibrillation. An AED is safe to use by anyone who has been trained to operate it. Studies have shown the devices to be 90% sensitive (i.e., able 90% of the time to detect a rhythm that should be defibrillated) and 99% specific (i.e., able 99% of the time to recommend not shocking when defibrillation is not indicated). Because of the wide variety of situations in which it will typically be used, the AED is designed with multiple safeguards and warnings before any energy is released. The AED is programmed to deliver a shock only when it has detected ventricular fibrillation. However, potential dangers are associated with AED use. Consequently, training in its safe use and maintenance is essential.

Member Issues

Orientation/Supervision

All novice lifters should be required to undergo an orientation program to help them learn the basics of using exercise equipment. Learning simple tasks like seat adjustment, weight selection, accessory-bar selection, and so forth can be critical in providing a person with a foundation for safe exercise.

Personnel Qualifications

One of the most prevalent risks found in facilities today is the lack of qualified personnel. Qualified personnel are certified in safety techniques and procedures and, if applicable, in sport-specific instruction. Management should create a job description for each position in the facility. This description should indicate what certifications should be obtained to perform the job and should state time limits for obtaining these certifications.

CPR Certification

At least 50% of all staff members should be certified in CPR. If this percentage has not yet been obtained, at least one CPR-certified staff member should be on duty at all times. If an unforeseen situation arises calling for immediate medical attention, proper procedures can be quickly and correctly administered by a qualified staff member. CPR certification prepares staff members for dealing with heart attacks, strokes, diabetic emergencies, epileptic seizures, and complications arising from asthma.

First Aid Certification

At least 50% of all staff members should be certified in first aid, or at least one first-aid-certified staff member should be on duty at all times. If an unforeseen situation occurs calling for immediate medical assistance, proper procedures can be quickly and correctly administered. There is a high probability that first-aid techniques will be needed to correct the situation. First aid certification prepares staff members for bone, joint, and muscle injuries (very common in health clubs), for heat-related injuries, for bleeding, and for moving and rescuing victims.

Exercise Certification

All trainers and instructors should be certified in exercise instruction through a nationally accredited organization. An accredited organization is requires that an initial exam be passed (no take-home exams); then certification can be maintained only through yearly retesting and/or continuing education credits (CEC). Exercise certification provides trainers and instructors with insight into the different needs for different people, keeps trainers and instructors in touch with the ever-changing fitness industry, and teaches trainers the latest in techniques, nutrition, and so forth.

If they do not already exist, management should begin keeping personnel records that indicate what certifications are held by each staff member and that indicate the renewal date for each certification.

Facility Documentation

Record keeping is very important in day-to-day operations because it helps ensure that management strictly adheres to policies and procedures. Records should be kept for all activities offered at the facility and for any maintenance performed on equipment. If a lawsuit arises from an injury/accident, record keeping can be used as proof in a court of law that management acted responsibly in carrying out day-to-day operations. Documentation includes the following.

Liability Waivers

Liability waivers, if properly written, could release a facility from harm in the event an accident or injury has occurred and the facility has been accused of negligence in a lawsuit. Waivers must be created with the input of an attorney. More and more courts are upholding the validity of waivers today, but waivers must be written in favor of the facility and its staff. All new members and guests must be required to sign a waiver of liability before being allowed to use the facility. A waiver should be kept on file for at least two years after a member has left the facility.

Health History Form

Health history forms, or PAR-Q forms, are designed to discover any preexisting health problems or conditions experienced by new members prior to their use of the facility. Health history forms should require new members to disclose all known injuries and health-related conditions. These include any family health history conditions. If there is a suspect condition, a doctor's release note should be obtained before new members are cleared to exercise in the facility.

Incident Reports

Incident reports are a means of documenting the circumstances leading up to an accident or injury and the procedures taken by staff members to correct the situation. Blank, preformatted reports must be kept on file at the facility at all times. All managers must know how to properly fill out an injury report. The manager on duty must complete the incident report. If there are any witnesses to the accident, they should complete the witness report. A copy of the incident report should be sent immediately to the facility's insurance carrier.

It is imperative that all staff members understand the importance of reporting any incident, no matter how insignificant it seems. Even if the injured person says he or she is "okay," the incident must be reported anyway.

Maintenance Schedules

Maintenance schedules assign and explain duties to staff members involving basic cleaning and lubricating procedures on exercise equipment. Maintenance schedules should clearly state what pieces of equipment should be cleaned and lubricated and the frequency of such maintenance.

Equipment Maintenance Logs

Maintenance logs are a means of documenting major repairs performed on exercise equipment. Maintenance logs can help provide proof that management has followed the correct procedures in repairing equipment. The document should indicate who performed the work, what repairs were made, what type of parts were used (factory or generic), and what date the work was completed.

Equipment Maintenance

As advanced as today's exercise equipment has become, there is still a chance that a piece of equipment in the facility currently has some type of defective part. Whether the part was defective at the time of shipping or has become defective through heavy use must be determined by facility management. Maintenance logs and maintenance schedules are important because if management can prove that it inspected and serviced the equipment consistently and according to manufacturer's standards, it has a much better chance of being exonerated in the event an incident happens.

To get maximum results from exercise equipment, daily and weekly maintenance routines must be followed. The frequency of maintenance needed on exercise equipment is determined by factors such as the following: 1) temperature, 2) humidity, 3) use, 4) ventilation, 5) shielding, and 6) friction. Two types of maintenance must be performed on equipment: *external* and *internal* maintenance. One type is just as important as the other, so in order to ensure that neither type is overlooked, management should use maintenance schedules. Cleaning duties should be assigned to individual staff members through the maintenance schedules so that staff members will always know their responsibilities. The schedules should be posted on a wall or bulletin board or placed in a binder so that staff members can view them before beginning their daily maintenance duties.

Most equipment manufacturers today have some type of product liability insurance. Management should ask its sales rep if his or her company offers it. When a machine breaks down, management should immediately take it out of service. Management should move it off the floor if possible or, at the very least, put a sign on it: Out of Service, Do Not Use. A good way to check equipment for defects is for the facility manager or staff member to use it. Close attention should be paid to the heavily used equipment since these machines will break down the quickest.

Locker Rooms

Locker rooms have two high risk-areas that are often overlooked. They involve the following.

Nonslip Flooring

Nonslip flooring should be placed in each traffic area where water can wet the floor. Generally, such an area is the shower. Most people step out of the shower to dry off; as a result, water drips on the floor. Vinyl matting (waffle tile) is highly recommended for wet areas because it keeps a person out of direct contact with the tile floor and allows the floor to dry faster when water hits it. Vinyl matting also reduces the buildup of bacteria.

Ground-Fault Circuit Interrupters

Ground-Fault Circuit Interrupters (GFCI) are circuit breakers located on an electrical socket. GFCIs are designed to help prevent electric shock if a person is drying his or her hair and accidentally steps in a puddle of water. If the facility is less than five years old, GFCIs are probably already installed. If they are not, they should be installed in all areas having a potential mix of water and electricity. Ground-Fault Circuit Interrupters are inexpensive and easy to install, and their use could prevent a tragic accident.

References

Tharrett, S. J., Peterson, J. A., & American College of Sports Medicine. (1997). ACSM's health/fitness facility standards and guidelines. (2nd ed.) Champaign, IL: Human Kinetics.

Chapter 24

Risk Assessment and Reduction

Herb Appenzeller

As we enter the 21st century, litigation continues to plague the sport industry. Troublesome sport-related issues so common in the 1980s and 1990s continue to end up in court with enormous awards—and with damage to the reputation of an institution and its personnel. Today the issues are no longer just contract disputes or allegations of negligence in personal injury cases. There is a trend toward more diverse issues that have a tremendous impact on the multibillion-dollar sport industry and on all those who are associated with it.

Schubert, Smith, and Trentadue (1986) observe:

> One need look no further than the morning sports section to realize that law now has a rather profound influence on the world of sport. With labor law issues, contract issues, issues regarding the regulation of amateur athletics, antitrust issues regarding compensation for injuries and many other legal issues in the sport context, attorneys and judges are more than idle spectators at sporting events.

Sport litigation involves athletes, administrators, athletic trainers, physicians, coaches, equipment manufacturers, officials, facility operators, and even unsuspecting spectators. It seems that no one is immune from litigation today. It has been said that anyone can sue for anything. As a result of the escalation in sport-related lawsuits, the sport administrator (or manager) has added a new responsibility to a growing list of duties. The sport administrator is responsible for meeting the challenge of risk management and risk reduction. The most important task for the sport administrator may be the one most overlooked: legal management that involves the implementation of risk management strategies.

Risk Management Defined

Risk management has been described as asset management, asset protection, and asset preservation. For many years, it has been associated with business—especially the insurance industry. Before the 1970s, *loss control, exposure to loss, pre- and post-loss objectives, risk management strategies,* and *risk management techniques* were common terms in both the business and insurance industries. In the mid-1970s, and especially in the late 1990s and today's litigious world, risk management has become a "hot topic." Indeed, risk management has become a familiar expression for a program designed to meet sport litigation head-on.

In simple terms, *risk management* is the practice of assessing the risks inherent in a sport program by the implementation of a safety audit. After the risks are identified, the sport manager should correct or eliminate the risks that exist in the program. A final step is to transfer the risk by acquiring medical or liability insurance to protect the participants, the institution, and the personnel of the program.

Sport Publications That Reveal Trends in Litigation

The Society for the Study of Legal Aspects of Sport and Physical Activity (SS-LASPA), an organization of legal scholars, attorneys, and sport law professors, publishes a list of legal publications in the field of sports (Society for the Study of Legal Aspects of Sport and Physical Activity, 1995). The SSLASPA listed only five sport and law texts published in the 1970s. These texts included Herb Appenzeller's *From the Gym to the Jury* (1970), *Athletics and the Law* (1975), and *Physical Education and the Law* (1978); Lionel Sobel's *Professional Sports and the Law* (1977); and John Weistart and Cyn Lowell's *Law of Sports* (1979). These books were published in response to litigation in sport begun in the 1960s. In the 1980s, when the number of lawsuits increased dramatically, the number of publications in the field of sport and law increased to 43. In the 1990s, 38 additional texts were published in the field. From the 1970s through the 1990s, the number of authors increased from 4 to 117. Statistics from the SSLASPA reveal that by 1995, there were 7 sport law journals, 22 sport law newsletters, 12 professional periodicals, and over 18 videos on a variety of sport law issues. The growth of sport and law publications was an attempt to meet the escalating litigation. It was then—and is today—a desire to meet the needs of those associated with sport by reducing injuries and subsequent lawsuits against all who participate in the sport industry (Society for the Study of Legal Aspects of Sport and Physical Activity, 1995).

With the increase of risk management in the sport industry, risk management texts became a reality in the 1990s and appear to be on the rise in the 21st century. At the SSLASPA Conference in 2000, 80 presentations were scheduled, and the majority dealt with risk management issues. The increase of risk management publications is predictable and will continue to dominate sport and law publications in the 21st Century.

Importance of Risk Management

Risks are inherent in sport, and even the safest program will never prevent accidents and injuries. That someone is injured does not automatically mean that someone else is liable. The law does expect, however, that sport managers develop and implement loss control and risk management programs to ensure a safe environment for all who participate in sport activities.

Dr. Betty van der Smissen, a legal scholar and pioneer in sport law, explains the importance of risk management in the sport industry when she writes:

> It becomes imperative that managers and administrators as well as policy boards of entities offering leisure and educational services affirmatively and aggressively give attention to the management of financial and programmatic risks to effectively reduce costs and enable desirable programs and services to be continued (van der Smissen, 1990).

Risk management is as important as budgeting, financial management, eligibility, scheduling, equipment control, insurance coverage, contracts, transportation, medical services, due process, facility management, and other duties.

Ronald Baron, a sport law authority and Executive Director of the Center for Sports Law and Risk Management, sums up the importance of risk management when he writes:

> Risk management should help those who direct the sport program comply with their legal duties, provide safe programs and enable sport personnel to defend themselves and their programs in the event of a lawsuit (Baron, 1997).

What Is the Problem?

The maxim "An ounce of prevention is worth a pound of cure" still holds true, so people recognize the importance of implementing a risk management plan. However, despite the need for such a plan, sport managers too often assign it a low priority. For example, a facility manager admitted that the implementation of a risk management plan could reduce the cost of her insurance premiums and save a substantial amount of money. She stated that while such a plan is a good idea, she would not spend money to save money. Her response, unfortunately, is typical of others in the sport industry who understand the need and value of risk management but fail to develop a plan, thereby exposing their program to financial loss. In all too many instances, safety audits and risk management plans are put in place only after severe injuries occur or a damaging lawsuit is filed. We react to the crisis rather than being proactive or creative in preventing catastrophic injuries and subsequent lawsuits. The key is prevention.

Areas of Concern

John Weistart and Cym Lowell, in the *Law of Sports*, point out:

> The area of the law of sports which has received the most frequent analysis and which has received a correspondingly large body of decisional authority is the liability which may result from injuries sustained in sports activities. The issues that are raised by the liability cases are actually broad, and the question presented by any given case is likely to fall within a very narrow applicable legal principle (Weistart & Lowell, 1979).

On the basis of numerous cases, it is safe to conclude that areas of concern for the sport administrator are (1) a lack of supervision, (2) incompetent instruction, (3) defective equipment, and (4) unsafe facilities. Legal experts have added areas of concern since the publication of *Law and Sports* and consider the following as factors in risk management that involve litigation: (1) insurance, (2) medical procedures, (3) student rights, (4) constitutional issues, (5) transportation, (6) discrimination, and (7) employment.

Dr. Gary Rushing, a legal scholar and risk management authority, developed a legal liability self-appraisal instrument for sport administrators to evaluate their sport programs. Rushing comments:

[T]he purpose of this self-assessment is to provide school personnel with a means to identify safety and legal liability problems related to the operation of the school's athletics program (Rushing, 2000).

Furthermore, he notes:

[A]n auxiliary benefit is the act of performing the assessment that should make the evaluator aware of problem areas and therefore less likely to neglect them (Rushing, 2000).

The self-appraisal instrument with its 188 objective statements is designed to reduce the risks in a sport program. The instrument is available in Chapter 25 of Rushing's text and is a practical method for a staff to test its knowledge of the areas of concern in a sport program. It creates an awareness of problems and an opportunity to correct them.

Diversity of Lawsuits

A look at a few headlines of cases reported in *From the Gym to the Jury*, a sport law newsletter, indicates the diversity of today's lawsuits and the enormous awards.

Pool Drain Case Settled for $30.9 Million
College Student Rendered Quadriplegic Receives $9,000,000
Accident at Pool Results in Four Million Dollar Settlement
Fall off Jungle Gym: $500,000 Settlement
Deaf Lifeguard Sues for $20 Million
Failure to Warn Results in $3,500,000 Award
Defective Railing in Gym Results in Wrongful Death Award of $1,400,000
Collegiate Swimmer Crippled from Injury in Practice Settles for $7,600,000
Injury on Mini-Trampoline Leads to Award of $6,800,000
Jury Awards over $18 Million to Student Injured before Volleyball Practice
Injured Student Sues for $52 Million: Awarded $23 Million
(Appenzeller & Baron, 1997).

The suits are diverse and the awards have skyrocketed in the past few years. No one is certain how high awards will continue to escalate. A recent study of awards as reported in *From the Gym to the Jury* by the University of Houston Law School indicates that the average injury award is over $1.5 million (Fried, 1999).

Center for Sport Law and Risk Management

In 1987, I joined Ronald Baron and The Center for Sports Law and Risk Management as a special consultant. After 40 years of involvement in sport as a coach, athletic administrator, professor, and director of sport management, I had the opportunity to actively put into practice risk management strategies. This valuable opportunity to conduct risk reviews at all levels of sport gave me insight into the problems confronting all those who are involved with sport at every level. I now realize the importance of risk management at firsthand. The Center conducts risk reviews across the United States for elementary and secondary schools, colleges and universities, professional sports, venues, and municipalities. These clients have similar problems that we have seen over the years—such as the following:

- Exit doors locked in sport arenas while events are in progress.
- A lack of policy dealing with potential catastrophic events such as fires, tornadoes, earthquakes, or bomb threats.
- An absence of proper signs in swimming pools, weight rooms, playing fields, racquetball courts, bleachers, and other areas.
- A lack of informed-consent agreements for participants in many schools.
- A lack of emergency medical response plans for participants and spectators at sport events.
- Accident and injury reports worded in such a way that they cause problems in litigation.
- People with disabilities denied access to facilities in violation of federal law.
- A lack of expulsion policy for unruly spectators. Ushers, not security personnel, often mistreat spectators.
- Open drains and irrigation heads on playing fields.
- Participants playing on overlapping fields in sports such as softball, soccer, football, baseball, and track.
- Areas where water and electricity mix that lack ground fault interrupters (GFIs).
- Inspection of facilities and equipment often overlooked and not documented.
- Schools often lease facilities without requiring a certificate of insurance from the lessee. In many cases, the lessee is not required to indemnify the lessor in a facility-use agreement.
- Insurance contracts often contain exclusions regarding sporting events, resulting in the facility or program having inadequate coverage.
- Glass doors and windows located under or near goals.
- Lack of due process procedures.

These are just a few situations observed during risk reviews that can plague a sports administrator. A risk management program is necessary as well as essential in today's litigious society (Appenzeller 1993).

Five Steps in the Process of Risk Management

Concerning risk management, George Head and Stephen Horn II write:

Risk management occupies an important place in the broad definition of management—that devoted to minimizing the adverse effects of accidental loss on the organization. (Head & Horn II, 1994).

In addition, they list five steps in the risk management process:

1. Identifying exposures to accidental loss that may interfere with an organizations basic objectives.
2. Examining feasible alternative risk management techniques for dealing with these exposures.
3. Selecting the apparently best risk management technique(s).
4. Implementing the chosen risk management technique(s).
5. Monitoring the results of the chosen techniques to ensure that the risk management remains effective.
   (Head & Horn II, 1994).

Risk Assessment and Risk Reduction

United Educators, a risk retention group and a leader in risk management, have devised guidelines to reduce injuries and loss of property and have reasoned:

Safety risk and liability exposures are inherent in sports activities. Policies and procedures carefully communicated and enforced lessen the likelihood of injury and potential liability of the institution, faculty or staff. (United Educators, 1991).

United Educators write that attempts at managing risks often fail to meet our expectations because of the lack of "certain key components that are either not present or not totally integrated with the others" (United Educators, 1991). They list six essential components of a risk management program:

1. *Policies and Procedures.* Those in authority must provide policies and procedures directing and governing all activities sponsored by their athletic departments, including intercollegiate, intramural, and recreational activities. The guidance must clearly direct those who are supervisors to manage risks which are reasonable and foreseeable. Policies and procedures must be developed, codified, disseminated, and enforced with sufficient documentation at every step in the risk management process.
2. *Training.* Traditional ad hoc "on the job" training is no longer adequate. Some formal training should be given to all personnel, especially concerning the institution's policies and procedures. Substantive training must be given, and updated periodically for those assigned higher risk tasks like trainers and bus drivers. In each case, the institution should document the training.
3. *Supervision.* Every level of supervision must be actively involved in "looking over" rather than "overlooking" the actions of their subordinates. Failure to properly supervise should be treated as a serious shortcoming.
4. *Corrective Action.* When supervisors are aware that policies and procedures are not followed, the corrective action must be timely, relevant, and progressive. Some form of remedial training might be required; reprimands, suspensions, or possibly terminations might be necessary in the case of more serious performance shortcomings.
5. *Review and Revision.* Administrators must use the management data available to them, including: incident reports of injuries; deficiencies on

the part of staff; inspections and audits; possible claims or lawsuits; new statutes; and even court decisions that will affect the performance of duties. The review should be followed by consideration whether to revise policies and procedures or conduct training.

6. *Legal Counsel and Support.* To reduce the chances of lawsuits, corporation counsel must be actively involved in providing direction, reviewing policies and procedures, and giving proactive guidance to the staff. Thoughtful advice before the institution is sued is always superior to advice after the fact. (United Educators, 1991)

Risk Management Strategies for Sport Administrators

The athletic administrator should develop a risk management plan that assesses and reduces the possibility of risk. Implementing a risk management plan includes the following strategies:

1. Organize a risk management committee and appoint an assistant or associate athletics director as risk manager and chairperson of the committee. Add representatives for maintenance, security, finance, Title IX, ADA, student(s), and facilities. This committee can identify the risks of the program and accountability for the various areas of risk.
2. Implement an "agreement to participate" for all athletes that informs them of inherent risks of participation in sports and of safety measures to follow.
3. Develop an emergency medical action plan and put the plan in writing. Discuss the plan with the coaches and emphasize their role in the emergency plan. Have the coaches sign off that they understand the plan and their role in it.
4. Develop a catastrophic injury protocol to respond immediately to such an injury. Know immediately who informs parents, who becomes the point person, and who arranges travel, lodging, and meals for the parents on site. Know the proper procedure to follow in notifying the media, campus officials, athletes, the attorney, and the insurance carrier. Know the proper way to follow up with the injured athlete and parents and how to deal with a subsequent lawsuit.
5. Comply with Title IX and ADA mandates. Recent court decisions have clarified the position of the courts. An active plan must be developed to comply with the legislation, not to avoid it. Have the risk management committee assess Title IX and ADA compliance.
6. Implement procedures for transportation. Know how to write a contract with transportation carriers to ensure safety as well as economy.
7. Set up a regular routine of inspection of equipment and facilities. Devise forms that meet the needs of your program and document the inspections.
8. Review your insurance coverage to ensure proper coverage for your institution and personnel.
9. Make certain due process is extended to student athletes and other personnel in your athletics program.
10. Computerize your program so that equipment is not issued for practice or games until insurance, eligibility, and preparticipation physicals are checked and cleared.

11. Have a plan for student disruption that can go into affect immediately when a confrontation or protest occurs.

12. Check signage in all areas of the sports program, such as the weight rooms, swimming pool, stadium, field house, locker rooms, and gymnastic areas. Make the signs readable, attractive, and positive.

Trends in Risk Management

1. Today's average citizen is better informed than ever before of individual rights and the law. There is a prevailing attitude that every injury should be compensated by insurance companies, manufacturers, and school systems that society believes have endless financial resources. This attitude and awareness of the law leads to litigation and a future that legal authorities predict will be the most litigious ever.

2. Enormous damage awards are the rule today, and million dollar awards are common.

3. All 50 states have reportedly modified the doctrine of governmental immunity with exceptions such as insurance, tort claim acts, and claim procedures that do not go through the judicial system to resolve conflicts.

4. There is a movement toward the acceptance of the doctrine of comparative negligence rather than contributory negligence; most of the 50 states have adopted comparative negligence, and others are expected to adopt it in the future.

5. Lawsuits dealing with individuals with disabilities continue to escalate, along with cases based on race, religion, and sex.

6. Lawsuits for injuries involving alleged negligence continue to be taken out of the negligence area in favor of the constitutional law arena. Legal authorities report that lawsuits are now filed under the Civil Rights Act of 1871 when governmental immunity is claimed as a defense by state and local governments.

7. Sport managers will be held to a higher standard of care in the operation of their programs than ever before since the courts are placing additional responsibility and accountability on the sport manager.

8. More and more legal authorities, scholars, and practitioners are publishing books, periodicals, journals, and newsletters in the area of risk management. This information will be available to all who work in the field of risk management.

Summary/Conclusion: Recommendations for the Reduction of Risks in Sport Programs

1. Keep abreast of current trends in the law as they relate to sport. Attend workshops that deal with risk management, sport medicine, and injury prevention.

2. Organize a safety committee (a risk management committee) to address the problem of risk.

3. Designate a safety officer to conduct and assume the responsibility for a safety audit of the sport program. Develop a clear, written policy for identifying and correcting potential risks.
4. Transfer the burden and cost of risks in the program by acquiring medical and/or liability insurance to protect participants, personnel, and the program itself.
5. Know and obey the rules, the regulations, and the law as they apply to the sport program.
6. Do not wait for an accident or crisis to act. Act now and be prepared by careful planning and preventive action to provide a risk-free program.
7. Warn participants in the program of all potential dangers and risks.
8. Provide competent personnel to direct and supervise the sport program. Determine the number of supervisors by the activity, size, and age of the group. Work closely with inexperienced or less-qualified personnel. Eliminate high-risk activities until qualified personnel are available.
9. Consult with a qualified attorney in planning the operation of the safety audit and the overall program.

References

Appenzeller, H. (1993). *Managing Sports and Risk Management Strategies*. Durham, NC: Carolina Academic Press.

Appenzeller, H. and R. Baron (1980). *From The Gym To The Jury*. Greensboro, NC: The Center for Sports Law and Risk Management.

Baron, R. (1997). *Risk Management Manual*. Dallas, TX: The Center for Sports Law and Risk Management.

Burling, P. and G.P. Gallagher (1992). *Managing Athletic Liability: An Assessment Guide*. Chevy Chase, MD: United Educators Risk Retention Group, Inc.

Fried, Gil (1999). *Safe At First*. Durham, NC: Carolina Academic Press.

Head, G.L. and S. Horn, II (1994). *Essentials of Risk Management*. Malvern, PA: Insurance Institute of America.

Rushing, G. (2000). In *Successful Sport Management, 2nd Edition*. Durham, NC: Carolina Academic Press: *A Safety and Legal Liability Self-Appraisal Instrument for Athletic Programs*. Mankato, MN.

Schubert, G.W., R. Smith, and J.C. Trentadue (1986). *Sports Law*. St. Paul, MN: West Publishing Co.

Society for the Study of Legal Aspects of Sport and Physical Activity (1995). Terre Haute, IN.

United Educators Insurance Risk Retention Group, Inc. (1991). *Managing Athletic Liability: An Assessment Guide:* Chevy Chase, MD: Institute for Liability Management.

van der Smissen, B. (1990). *Legal Liability Management for Public and Private Entities*. Cincinnati, OH: Anderson Publishing Co.

Weistart, J. and C. Lowell (1979). *Law of Sports*. Charlottesville, VA: Bobbs Merrill Co.

Chapter 25

Title IX: Past, Present, and Future

Bob Malekoff

There may be worse (more socially serious) forms of prejudice in the United States, but there is no sharper example of discrimination today than that which operates against girls and women who take part in competitive sport, wish to take part, or might wish to if society did not scorn such endeavors.

—Bill Gilbert and Nancy Williamson, *Sports Illustrated*, 1973

No woman should be denied the opportunity to play anything on a college campus. But if there are fewer of them interested in playing, as I believe the evidence suggests, then the men who are playing shouldn't be punished.

—Mike DiMauro, *New London Day*, 2005

Some observers of the American sports landscape argue that no event has had a greater impact on sport in American society than the 1972 passage of Title IX of the Educational Amendments to the 1964 Civil Rights Act. Before this development, participation in girl's and women's sports was—to be generous—paltry. Today, more than 3 million high school girls and 165,000 college women benefit from the many opportunities associated with being part of competitive athletic teams, and elementary- and middle-school-aged children throughout the country happily participate in activities that were not long ago part of an almost exclusively male domain. But despite important gains since the law's adoption, interpretations of the legislation and the concept of this thing we call "gender equity" remain in many quarters shrouded in disagreement and controversy.

Title IX: The Basics

The crux of Title IX can be captured in one, brief sentence:

No person in the United States shall, on the basis of sex, be excluded from participation in, be denied the benefits of, or be subjected to discrimination under any education program or activity receiving Federal financial assistance.

While the interpretation and application of this passage has been the source of considerable and, at times, heated debate, there can be no question that the passage ultimately represents a legal mandate that educational institutions at all levels must take seriously.

From a compliance standpoint, Title IX can be broken down into three primary components:

1. Athletically related financial aid (i.e., athletic scholarships) must be awarded to a degree that reflects the proportion of men and women participating in the intercollegiate program.
2. Men and women must receive equal treatment and benefits in terms of various operational components of an athletic program, including, but not limited to, academic support services, coaching, locker room facilities, media services, medical care, practice and competition facilities, and travel accommodations.
3. The athletic interests and abilities of both men and women must be effectively accommodated so that equal opportunity in athletics is achieved for both genders.

It is important to note that in order for a school to be in compliance with Title IX, all three of these standards must be adequately met.

The first requirement lends itself to uncomplicated measurement. For example, in 2005–06, Vanderbilt University had 308 students participating on intercollegiate teams. Of these students, 182 (59%) were men and 126 (41%) were women. Therefore, in order to meet the athletically related financial aid standard, 59% of athletic scholarship award expenditures must be awarded to males and 41% to females.

The second requirement—while admittedly more complex than the athletically related financial aid standard—can also be evaluated for an appropriate level of equity without great difficulty. It is important to note that this "operational component" requirement does not mandate that an equal amount of money be spent in support of men's and women's sports. For example, in a high-contact sport like men's lacrosse, players wear helmets, shoulder pads, and heavily padded gloves—items that come with a healthy price tag. In terms of protective gear for women's lacrosse, players wear lightly padded gloves and protective eyewear. So while protective equipment requirements are far more expensive in men's lacrosse as compared with those of the women's game, the key standard is that levels of support for safety between the two sports must be *equal in effect*. Perhaps the best rule of thumb in terms of thinking about the "operational component" requirement is illuminated by the definition of *gender equity* as given in 1992 by the National Association of College Women's Athletic Administrators:

> An athletics program is gender equitable when either the men's or women's sports program would be pleased to accept as its own the overall program of the other gender.

So while most educators find the first two requirements somewhat straightforward, it is the accommodation of interests and abilities directive that has met with the most confusion, and even resistance, among athletes, coaches, athletic administrators, and college leaders. In 1979, the Department of Health, Education, and Welfare shared guidelines concerning how schools could demonstrate evidence of the provision of equal opportunity for both genders. Using what has become to be known as the "Three-Prong Test," educational institutions must satisfy one of the following standards in order to demonstrate compliance:

1. The number of athletic participants should mirror the number of undergraduate students from a participation percentage standpoint. For example, in 2005–06, 51% of the students at Wake Forest University were women. In order to be in compliance with the participation rate criterion, approximately 51 percent of the athletes at the university should be women. (There are cases where a very small variance is acceptable.)

If a school fails to meet the often elusive and controversial proportionality standard, there are two other compliance opportunities:

2. Schools may demonstrate that they have regularly added teams in an effort to increase opportunities for the underrepresented gender.
3. Schools may demonstrate that when members of the underrepresented gender have demonstrated sufficient ability and interest to warrant the addition of a new program and/or new participation opportunities, that interest has been met.

Stops and Starts: The First 20 Years of Title IX

In order to understand Title IX and the nuances surrounding its application to interscholastic and intercollegiate sports, it may be helpful to briefly consider the law from a historical perspective.

There is a common misconception that Title IX is a sports law. Ironically, when this legislation that calls for equality in all federally funded educational programs was being considered in 1970, there was some question as to whether or not Title IX would even apply to athletics. When it became apparent that some lawmakers believed the amendment should encompass extracurricular activities, including sports, the National Collegiate Athletic Association (NCAA) launched a forceful lobbying effort to defeat the proposal. Nonetheless, even after its passage, there was confusion and disagreement about how it might be appropriately interpreted and applied—disagreement that continues today.

While many educational institutions were dragged kicking and screaming into the Title IX "era," there were immediate signs of progress in terms of participatory increases. To wit, by 1977, over 64,000 women were playing on college teams, more than double the pre-Title IX participation rate. The impact at the high school level was in some ways more profound, even shockingly so, as interscholastic participation rates rose nearly tenfold—from 294,000 to over 2 million. But while some applauded that more girls and women were being afforded the opportunity to "get in the game," others—including some prominent politicians—seemed to be more concerned about the amendment's potential impact on the male stronghold over competitive athletics. In 1974, Texas Senator John Tower proposed an amendment that would effectively eliminate "revenue-producing" sports such as men's basketball and football from Title IX oversight. The proposal failed, but to this day, there are those who believe that schools sponsoring football teams are unfairly disadvantaged in terms of their quest for compliance.

While Title IX was officially signed into law in 1972, specific provisions prohibiting gender discrimination in athletics were not adopted until 1975, and only after great opposition from various members of the House of Representatives and Senate were overcome. At that time, educational institutions were afforded a three-year window to achieve full compliance. In the ensuing years, several unsuccessful attempts were made to weaken the amendment in terms of its oversight of athletics, and it was not until 1979 when the Health, Education, and Welfare Department (HEW) issued its final policy interpretation highlighted by the implementation of the Three-Prong Test. Five years later, Title IX faced its next big challenge.

Grove City College, a small liberal arts school in western Pennsylvania, purposefully did not seek federal funding of any type in order to maintain autonomy from governmental oversight in all institutional matters. However, Grove City students in need of financial aid did benefit from federally sponsored Pell grants. So when the school—on the basis of its "independent" status—refused to develop a gender equity plan, the Department of Health, Education, and Welfare considered cutting off the availability of Pell grants to Grove City undergraduates. This action prompted the college and four of its students to file suit. The Supreme Court heard the case in 1984 and ruled that Title IX should apply only to programs within an institution that directly receive federal funds. This meant that educational institutions were not required to offer equal opportunities for men and women in terms of intercollegiate and interscholastic sports programs. To some, the decision portended the beginning of the end for the gender-equity-in-athletics movement, and indeed many colleges chose from that point on to disregard Title IX. But in 1988, Congress passed the Civil Rights Restoration Act, mandating that all aspects of the educational program—whether curricular or extracurricular—be in compliance. In essence, Title IX was back.

Some argued that despite the restored inclusion of sports programs as part of the Title IX formula, the law still lacked the necessary clout to effect real change. After all, there were no meaningful consequences facing institutions that did not seek to achieve compliance in an intentional manner. While schools found to be in violation of the law could be required to address discriminatory policies and procedures, they did not have to pay compensatory damages. In 1992, however, this all changed. A suburban Atlanta high school student was allegedly sexually harassed and raped by a teacher/coach at her school. To add insult to injury, the school had a history of ignoring warnings about this teacher's illegal and harmful conduct. Because Title IX forbids sexual harassment, the student in question filed a complaint with the Office of Civil Rights and later sued the school district, drawing a connection between its inaction and the harm that she suffered. The Supreme Court ruled that compensatory damages could be applied in cases where intentional discrimination was established. Therefore, it was theoretically far more enticing to file suit, and schools had to take seriously the possibility that a failure to comply with the law could significantly impact the financial bottom line. At least in some people's eyes, Title IX had a resharpened set of teeth.

Seminal Cases: A Sampling

Cook v. Colgate

Colgate University, a highly selective liberal arts institution located in upstate New York, sponsored a men's ice hockey program that played in the competitive Eastern Collegiate Athletic Conference with Ivy League schools and other hockey powers such as St. Lawrence and the University of Vermont. The program met with reasonable competitive success and had a strong following among students, alumni, and townsfolk, many of whom viewed the team's games as highlights during the long, cold winter months.

In the mid-1970s a group of Colgate women who wanted to play hockey started a club team that subsisted with almost no support, financial or otherwise, from the university. In the ensuing decade, they applied for elevation to varsity status on a number of occasions, meeting with resistance each time. Before one meeting to discuss the possibility of elevation to varsity status, a member of the university-appointed committee charged with reviewing the proposal reportedly said, "I had better get comfortable, this one puts me asleep." After being rebuffed yet again, a group of players filed suit against the university.

During the trial, it was disclosed that the level of support for the men's and women's programs was alarmingly disparate. The men's team seemed to be equipped much like a National Hockey League franchise, while the women were required to purchase their own gear. Reportedly, some of the men sold their used skates for personal profit and simply reported to the equipment room for new pairs as needed. Practice time (the men got three hours of ice at peak times, the women 90 minutes during off hours), travel accommodations (the men traveled on charter buses and stayed in hotels, while the women drove vans and scrounged for lodging and meal money), and coaching support (the men had three paid coaches, while the women found part-time student coaches or volunteers), were first class for the men and almost nonexistent for the women. In the same year that the university turned down a relatively modest budget-increase request from the women because it was "too costly," it was revealed that $10,000 of the men's $238,000 budget was earmarked for the purchase of hockey sticks.

By even the most generous accounting, the ensuing trial proved to be an embarrassment to Colgate and a signal to colleges and universities throughout the nation that the all-too-common disparate treatment of men's and women's programs was against the law and would not be tolerated. Judge David N. Hurd sharply remarked that while Colgate was "treating its male players like princes," the females were dealt with like "chimney sweeps."

But the controversy did not stop there. Colgate officials elected to appeal the ruling on the basis of their belief that Hurd had erred in basing his decision on a direct comparison of the men's and women's ice hockey programs as opposed to the program-wide evaluation mandated by Title IX. In other words, the university acknowledged that it had to comply with the law but insisted that Title IX afforded greater flexibility than Hurd's ruling allowed. Colgate filed a successful appeal but facing the probability of yet another suit, chose to elevate the women's program to varsity status. So while the university may or may not have had a technical leg to stand on, many believe that the promise of more bad publicity in a new trial motivated campus leaders to become more serious about offering equitable opportunities to female athletes.

Cohen v. Brown University

While some colleges and universities were clearly threatened by the implications of Title IX, Brown University and some of its Ivy League brethren were thought to be comparatively proactive, even noble, in their efforts to create athletic opportunities for female students. Indeed, by 1993, one-half of Brown's 32 intercollegiate programs were dedicated to women. But in that same year, Brown's athletic director David Roach was instructed to cut $113,000 out of his department's budget as part of a university-wide belt-tightening directive. Roach chose to demote two men's sports (golf and water polo) and two women's sports (gymnastics and volleyball) from varsity to club status, a decision which, on the surface, seemed fair and equitable to many. But even though Brown sponsored the same number of men's and women's varsity programs, women—who comprised 51% of the student body—made up only 38% of athletic participants. Women athletes brought suit against the university for failing to effectively accommodate the interests and abilities of female athletes. They argued that not only did Brown not meet Title IX's proportionality requirement but also that the university had not added a varsity sport for women since 1982.

Brown replied that the variance between the number of male and female athletes was representative of the actual interests and abilities of the student body and that the equal-opportunity standard did not require numerical proportionality. In addition, the university argued that while it was true that no women's team had been added in eleven years, the school was being effectively penalized for its proactive support of women's athletics well before it was fashionable or mandated. Indeed, there was only one school in all of Division I that sponsored more women's varsity teams.

But a district court found that because there were members of the underrepresented gender interested in and able to participate in the two demoted women's programs, Brown was in violation of Title IX and was therefore required to restore the gymnastics and volleyball teams to full varsity status. Brown chose to appeal the ruling on the basis of their contention that fewer women than men were interested in playing sports, but in this case, it appeared that there were indeed two groups of women who demonstrated both the interest in playing sports and the ability to participate in them. And while Brown's lawyers went on to argue that the district court's decision served to equate Title IX with a mandatory—and illegal— quota system, they were defeated at the appeals level. Eventually, Brown—with strong support from other colleges and universities who feared the implications of a precedent-setting defeat—sought to take its case to the Supreme Court but was denied. Rightly or wrongly, the pressure to meet the controversial substantial-proportionality standard was stronger than ever and would dramatically impact the way athletic departments did business for years to come.

Mercer v. Duke University

Can a woman play college football? Heather Sue Mercer was a placekicker for her high school football team and decided to try out for her college squad, Duke University. In the spring of 1995, Mercer trained with the Duke team and even played in the annual spring intrasquad game where she booted the game-winning field goal. Duke coach Fred Goldsmith told newspaper reporters that Mercer's performance had earned her a spot on the team. But when the 1995 season rolled around, Goldsmith did not allow Mercer to participate in preseason training camp and allegedly suggested that she would be "better off focusing her attention on beauty pageants and boyfriends." It should be noted that Duke had a long history of not cutting football players on the basis of their ability. Unbowed, Mercer sought to join the team for winter-conditioning workouts, but Goldsmith would allegedly still not allow her to train with the team. When Mercer sought to meet with Duke officials about her situation, she was denied and chose to file a sex discrimination suit against Goldsmith and Duke—a suit she eventually won.

But was this result really a victory for women? Title IX supports the concept that educational institutions should support separate but equal athletic programs for men and women. But what if a school offers a sport for only one gender and what if it is a high-contact sport like football? Title IX guidelines mandate that if Duke had a men's soccer team and no women's soccer program (in fact, Duke sponsors a highly successful intercollegiate women's team), women may try out for the men's team. But this is not the case for football, ice hockey, and wrestling because they are legally defined as "contact sports." Indeed, Duke sought to have the suit thrown out on the basis of this interpretation, but the effort failed because once the university had permitted Mercer to try out for the team, Title IX protected her from being discriminated against on the basis of gender. But the longer-term concern may be that as long as certain contact sports are "protected" by the try-out "loophole," some coaches may simply deny girls and women an opportunity to make the team.

Jackson v. Birmingham Board of Education

Some may find it at least a bit ironic that one of the most important Title IX legal developments was brought on by a case of discrimination against a male coach. When Roderick Jackson was hired as the girl's basketball coach at Ensley High School in Birmingham, Alabama, in 1999, he was shocked to see the disparities between how his team and the school's boy's program were supported. While Jackson's team practiced in a dilapidated gymnasium with bent rims and no heat, the boy's team trained in a new facility. The school district chose to fully fund the boy's team but not the girl's, and while the boy's squad was able to retain revenue from ticket sales, the district seized any earnings associated with girl's games. When Jackson raised these concerns to the local school board, rather than seeking to correct the inequities, it chose to fire him. Having learned that Title IX did not provide protection for people who raised concerns about discriminatory practices, Jackson decided to sue the school board on the basis of his belief that he had been fired for speaking out. After suffering defeats at two lower courts (both ruling that whistle-blowers are not protected from retaliation under Title IX guidelines), Jackson found validation when the Supreme Court voted 5–4 that coaches and teachers who face retaliation for fighting perceived cases of sex discrimination can sue under Title IX. This ruling sent a powerful message to coaches that should they feel the need to speak to superiors about perceived inequities, they can do so without fear of reprisal related to job security.

Death Knell For Men's Sports?

While few would argue that Title IX has served as a much-needed catalyst in affording women a wide variety of opportunities both inside and outside the athletic arena, there remains in some people's estimation a dark side to what the amendment has wrought. Critics argue that if Title IX is supposed to create opportunities for both genders, how can we stand by while men's teams are eliminated in order to meet what some would decry as a quota system that negatively impacts male athletes?

Since 1972, hundreds of men's teams have been eliminated, and various men's sport associations—perhaps most prominently the National Wrestling Coaches Association (NWCA)—have taken issue with the alleged role that efforts to comply with Title IX played in the demise of these programs. In fact, the NWCA felt so strongly that it filed suit, albeit unsuccessfully, against the U.S. Department of Education on the basis of its belief that Title IX interpretation is harmful to male athletes. Specifically, the NWCA contended that the amendment relied more on a participation-formula/quota system than on some more realistic measurement of student interest. The association's executive director, Mike Moyer, argued that while Title IX did create needed opportunities for women, it also resulted in the roster capping and elimination of men's programs—almost always "minor sport" (read, not football or basketball) teams that did not produce revenue. The NWCA saw its suit dismissed when the presiding judge ruled that it had failed to demonstrate that men's programs were being eliminated because of Title IX, the implication being that there were other ways to comply with the law without reducing the number of opportunities for men.

It is accurate to say that some schools have chosen to eliminate men's teams—and therefore have denied participation opportunities to some males—in order to comply with the tenets set forth in Title IX and that some sports in particular have been disproportionately impacted. However, women's sport advocates claim not only that overall male-participation rates have continued to rise since the passage of the amendment but also that men's sports associations are unfairly laying blame at the doorstep of Title IX. They go on to argue that exorbitant expenditures on select male programs such as football and men's basketball are the real reason why some men's sports find themselves on the outside looking in. Insofar as the "major college" level is concerned, Smith College economist Andrew Zimbalist points to a lack of "financial discipline" by athletic directors, coaches, and conference commissioners and believes that a "paring down of unnecessary expenses" would allow for the retention of men's teams without impeding progress toward gender-equitable programs. The Women's Sports Foundation argues that the careful consideration of funding spent on football scholarships and on seemingly out-of-control football and men's basketball coaches' salaries could go a long way toward reducing athletic department expenditures and solidifying the future of both men's and women's programs.

The "Commission" Controversy

As controversy heightened surrounding Title IX interpretation and application and their perceived impact on men's sports, Education Secretary Roderick Paige formed the Secretary's Commission on Opportunity in Athletics. Paige, a one-time college football coach, was thought by some to be sympathetic to the alleged plight of men's sports like wrestling and gymnastics and to the arguments espoused by those who saw Title IX as discriminatory against certain men's sports. The Commission was made up primarily of Division I university athletic administrators and officials from groups such as the Women's Sports Foundation, as well as some representatives from the Education Department. Page charged the committee with, among other things, determining whether or not Title IX assessment standards and practices served to adequately promote opportunities for female *and* male athletes. This raised something of a red flag among staunch Title IX advocates in that the amendment had historically been applied to increase opportunities for the underrepresented gender, which, in terms of athletics, has always been girls and women.

The primary focus of the Commission's deliberations concerned the appropriateness of the Three-Prong Test. While some argued that an overdependence on the proportionality prong led to the elimination of men's programs, those in favor of the status-quo interpretation pointed out that the law could be satisfied through adding programs and opportunities. While such an approach might likely lead to additional expenditures, it could also result from a more balanced appropriation of existing funds.

One of the more controversial recommendations that emerged from the Commission's deliberations was a suggestion that in measuring for proportionality, the Office of Civil Rights (OCR) should count participation opportunities rather than actual participants. In other words, instead of simply counting the total number of men and women playing on intercollegiate teams, each roster would be assigned a designated number of opportunities. For example, let us assume that a soccer team has 24 designated roster slots but only 20 actual players. For Title IX measurement purposes, the participation rate could be calculated as 24 because the university has committed to supporting that number of athletes, with the four vacant roster slots resulting from a lack of interest.

Perhaps equally divisive was a recommendation that the OCR consider allowing institutions to demonstrate compliance with the third prong (the creation of opportunities based on demonstration of sufficient interest and ability by the underrepresented gender) through a study of youth/high school participation rates and/or results of interest surveys from prospective and current students. Title IX advocates — many of whom were understandably against any commission recommendations that might serve to weaken the amendment — reacted harshly, raising concerns that girls and women would be forced to demonstrate interest before they actually had an opportunity to play and that schools would be hard-pressed to develop and implement a reliable survey instrument and procedure.

Arguably bowing to fierce pressure from women's rights advocacy groups such as the Women's Sports Foundation and the National Women's Law Center, Assistant Secretary for Civil Rights Gerald Reynolds issued a letter to high school and college athletic officials that essentially stated there would be no changes in the application of Title IX and that emphasized the availability of any one of the three prongs as sufficient means for compliance. The letter was immediately endorsed by NCAA President Myles Brand as a victory for both male and female athletes. In the eyes of some, Title IX had dodged yet another bullet.

Frequently Asked Questions

What is the Equity in Athletics Disclosure Act? Is it an effective tool when trying to compare how various schools support men's and women's athletic programs?

In 1994, the Equity in Athletics Disclosure Act (EADA) was passed, requiring all coeducational colleges and universities that receive federal funding to report and make public information pertaining to their intercollegiate athletic programs. The reporting-requirement components include athletic participation, staffing, revenues, and expenses. Hypothetically, these data allow the public—especially prospective students and their parents—to gauge the level of support for men's and women's programs. But while these data offer a reasonable overview, they can sometimes be misleading because of inconsistent reporting practices. It may be illustrative to consider various different reporting procedures.

School A's and School B's Division III fall sport teams practice on campus before the start of the school year. Both schools feed and house 200 athletes during this period, and most of the cost is shouldered by men's sports programs because the football team has by far the most participants and the longest preseason period. School A calculates the costs incurred by men's and women's teams and includes these expenses in its EADA report. But School B sees the cost of housing and meals as internal paper transfers (the athletic department is budgeted for preseason expenses and simply pays the housing and food-services departments) and does not account for the expenses on its EADA report. Likewise, various schools have different budgeting procedures in terms of operational components such as telephone, computing, utilities, facility maintenance, and so forth. So until the EADA accounting requirements lead to greater uniformity in reporting, many "college consumers" will be comparing apples and oranges.

This is not to say that EADA reports do not provide a helpful snapshot. In addition, that colleges and universities know they will have to provide this information annually in a public forum leads to more thoughtful consideration of how existing resources are allocated and of the general support levels for both men and women.

Does Title IX legislation apply to middle schools and high schools as well as colleges and universities?

Perhaps because the media have focused on Title IX cases involving higher-profile colleges and universities, some believe that the amendment applies only to intercollegiate athletics. First, Title IX is not a "sports law" but legislation that applies to all educational programs at federally funded schools. And the amendment does apply to elementary schools, middle schools, and high schools. Indeed, one of the first athletically related gender discrimination cases involved a Minnesota high school tennis player who wanted to try out for the boy's team because her school did not sponsor a varsity girl's program. The court ruled that she was being discriminated against because the school did not provide a comparable athletic opportunity for girls interested in playing tennis.

When Title IX critics point to their belief that females are less interested in athletics than males, it may be instructive to consider where the seeds of this alleged lack of interest were sown. Before the passage of Title IX, the opportunities for grade school girls to participate in competitive athletics were few and far between, and when opportunities did exist, the level of support paled in comparison with benefits that boys took for granted. If disparate interest levels between men and women do exist, it is at least partly the product of decades of discrimination.

Is funding received from outside sources such as alumni and/or booster donations included in Title IX calculations?

Today, more than ever before, both interscholastic and intercollegiate athletic programs rely on various forms of external funding. Some believe that financial gifts from boosters can be earmarked as the athletic department sees fit without factoring in how any related benefits might impact compliance with Title IX. But while these gifts may be used to reduce or eliminate gender-equity-related disparities, they may not create a new inequity or exacerbate an existing one. For example, let us assume that a booster wanted to give a gift that would be earmarked toward building a state-of-the-art strength-training facility for an institution's men's athletic teams. If strength-training facilities for all women's teams were mediocre, it would be incumbent upon the school to provide facilities for the women's teams that were equal in effect to what the donor was pledging in support of the men's teams. One way to do this might be to encourage the donor to increase the gift in such a way that both genders would benefit. Ultimately, if there was no way to ensure equal effects for both genders, the gift might have to be declined. The burden falls on institutional administrators—especially the athletic director—to ensure that benefits and services are equivalent for both men and women.

Isn't it impossible for schools that sponsor football to be in compliance with the proportionality prong of Title IX, and therefore shouldn't the sport be exempt from substantive proportionality calculations?

Many athletic administrators see football as a unique, one-of-a-kind sport on the basis of the belief that the physical and specialized natures of the game call for extremely large rosters. They go on to argue that—from a Title IX compliance standpoint—there is no comparable women's sport that requires anywhere near the same number of participants. However, no matter how many times the issue of football and its impact on proportionality has been raised, no Title IX interpretation has suggested that it be treated differently from other sports. In other words, a football "opportunity" is considered the same as a soccer or golf "opportunity."

But is it possible to sponsor a large football roster and comply with the substantial proportionality standard? In a word, yes. Let us consider two Division I-A universities as examples. Women make up slightly over one-half of the student body at the University of Kansas, and almost 52% of the school's athletes. Likewise, 48% percent of Washington State University's students are female—a figure that matches the percentage of athletes who are women. Both schools have over 100 men playing football (Kansas, 134; Washington State, 117), but each school also sponsors varsity opportunities for women in the sport of rowing with participation rates that are significant (Kansas, 75; Washington State, 72). Detractors argue that in these two cases, the development of rowing programs represents an artificial effort to meet the required Title IX "quota." But supporters point out that women were essentially excluded from sports for over 100 years, and it is only right that educators proactively seek to create opportunities in whatever forms that might ultimately meet female interest and ability levels.

Looking Ahead

Gender equity does not lend itself to definition or measurement as easily as Title IX. The quest for gender equity is a far-reaching societal challenge that must be addressed from grade school through the level of higher education in an ongoing manner. Thirty-five years after the passage of Title IX, there are still girls and women participating in athletics who feel as if they are treated like second-class citizens. Some female athletes are stereotyped regarding their sexual orientation and are considered "different" by their peers. Indeed, some girls and women still choose not to participate in competitive sports because of their anxiety over being categorized. While female athletes make up more than 50% of all college undergraduates, they receive significantly less than men in terms of athletic scholarships and budgetary support.

But on the other extreme, while there may be an overall increase in the number of males participating in high school and college sports, some men are losing opportunities because administrators have chosen to meet Title IX compliance standards by dropping men's sports.

There can be no question that without Title IX, tens of thousands of opportunities available to girls and women—both inside and outside sports—would not exist today, and one cannot overestimate the amendment's far-reaching impact. But in a more ideal world, gender equity would not be about statistics and quantitative measurement. Rather, it would embody an important philosophical commitment to create an environment where equal opportunity exists because it is right and fair to each individual—and ultimately in the best interests of our educational institutions and society at large.

So how might we best proceed? One possibility is to commit ourselves to viewing interscholastic and intercollegiate athletics in an educational rather than an entertainment context. Before concluding that funding is not available to support new opportunities for women or before choosing to eliminate men's teams, educational leaders should ask themselves, "Are current policies, procedures, and expenditures in concert with educational goals? Or are spending patterns more influenced by the "keep-up-with-the-Joneses" mentality that, with each passing year, seems to be a more prevalent part of the competitive athletics landscape? And we should not lose sight of the possibility that the excesses we see in college athletics may be a reflection of what can be observed in other areas of higher education as schools fight fiercely to attract and retain the best students and faculty. This is not to say that decisions regarding resource allocation in the highly competitive sports world are simple and straightforward, and certainly there are potential pitfalls for any school that chooses to "go it alone" in terms of practicing a more balanced allocation of resources.

Perhaps we will know that we are on the road to gender equity when all concerned parties choose to prioritize an appropriate educational balance intended to benefit all students. Until that time, a continuing dependence on mandated, quantitative standards will likely rule the day.

References

Brand, M. (2003, July 11). Statement by Myles Brand on Title IX. National Collegiate Athletic Association.

DiMauro, M. (2005). I commend Title IX, but amend it! *New London Day*.

Gilbert, B., & Williamson, N. (1973, May 28). Sport is unfair to women. *Sports Illustrated*.

Lederman, D. (1993, February 17). Colgate U. becomes a battleground over equity in college athletics. *The Chronicle of Higher Education*.

Lipka, S. (2005, April 8). High court expands protections of Title IX. *The Chronicle of Higher Education.*

Lynch, M. (2001, April). Title IX's Pyrrhic victory: How the quest for "gender equity is killing men's athletic programs. *Reason Magazine.*

Office of Postsecondary Education (2007). Equity in athletics data analysis cutting tool Web site <http://ope.ed.gov/athletics/main.asp>.

Suggs, W. (2003, March 7). Cheers and condemnation greet report on gender equity. *The Chronicle of Higher Education.*

Suggs, W. (2005). *A place on the team: The triumph and tragedy of Title IX.* Princeton, NJ: Princeton University Press.

Sharp L., Moorman, A., & Claussen, C. (2007). *Sport law: A managerial approach.* Scottsdale, AZ: Holcomb Hathaway.

Szanton, A. (1993, October). On balance. *Brown Alumni Monthly.*

Women's Sports Foundation. (2000). Dropping men's sports—Expanding opportunities for girls and women in sport without eliminating men's sports: The Foundation position <http://www.womenssportsfoundation.org/cgi-bin/iowa/issues/rights/article.html?record=84>.

Women's Sports Foundation. (2002). Commission to recommend a weakened Title IX <http://www.womenssportsfoundation.org.cgi-bin/iowa/issues/rights/article.html?record=938>.

Women's Sports Foundation. (2002). Title IX and the Wrestling Coaches Association's lawsuit <http://womenssportsfoundation.org.cgi-bin/iowa/issues/rights/article.html?record=894>.

Wong, G. M. (2002). *Essentials of sports law.* Westport, CT: Praeger Press.

Zimbalist, A. (1997). *Unpaid professionals: Commercialism and conflict in big-time college sports.* Princeton, NJ: Princeton University Press.

Chapter 26

The Americans with Disabilities Act and Sport Facilities

Gil B. Fried

In a watershed event for millions of Americans, President George H. W. Bush signed the Americans with Disabilities Act (ADA) into law on January 26, 1990. The new law promised millions of Americans the opportunity to receive equality in ways never before experienced by some and long forgotten by others. The ADA has been dubbed the Emancipation Proclamation and the Bill of Rights for individuals with disabilities (Schneid, 1992). Approximately 45 million individuals benefit from protections provided by the ADA (Schneid, 1992).

The Civil Rights Act of 1964 is considered a sweeping legislative enactment entitling women and minorities the equality they need to be gainfully employed. The ADA is even more sweeping because while it is unusual (or even sometimes impossible) for someone to change sex, nationality, race, or religion, it is not uncommon for a healthy individual to be suddenly stricken by heart disease, diabetes, arthritis, or a variety of other maladies. These unwanted maladies can become the basis for potential discrimination or exclusion. One of the primary purposes of the ADA is to ensure that facilities and organizations that provide public accommodations are usable by all people. It requires that any recreation/sports provider must make "reasonable accommodations, for participants who have a disability."

Nowhere can the ADA's effect be seen more prominently than in facilities. Sports and recreational facilities are especially prominent in ADA coverage because of the publicity generated by such facilities and the number of individuals who attend events or engage in activities at such facilities. Sports facilities have become the target for such organizations as the Paralyzed Veterans of America—a group which has engaged in a concerted effort on behalf of its 17,000 members to challenge new sports facilities which do not meet ADA requirements. The group has filed suits against several arenas, claiming that while spaces are available at each site for wheelchairs, most seats do not offer a clear view of the action when surrounding fans stand up. Regulations under the ADA require all wheelchair seats to be designed so that the wheelchair-using patron is not isolated and has the choice of various seats and ticket prices. Furthermore, in places where fans are expected to stand, facilities must provide a line of sight "comparable" to the view from seats provided to other spectators.

Specific ADA rules are being proposed by other groups for various sports facilities. Indeed, the United States Architectural and Transportation Barriers Compliance Board has proposed recommendations not only for sports facilities but also for places of amusement; play settings; golf; recreational, boating, and fishing facilities; and outdoor development areas. The Board's sports facility recommendations are set forth in over 200 pages, describing the layout of baseball dugouts, entrance turnstiles, and other sports facility components (see Exhibit A). It is obvious that the ADA does not operate in a vacuum regarding sports facilities.

Other laws work with the ADA to create a complete compendium of laws covering all sports facilities. The Architectural Barriers Act of 1968 and the Rehabilitation Act of 1973 provide an extensive regulatory framework for sports facilities. State and local laws can also affect facility design, construction, and renovations. Building codes determine specific issues such as how many steps can be built without requiring a handrail, the number of inches required per person and per seat in bleacher seating (usually 17–20 inches allocated for each seat), and the number and size of exits based on the number of individuals expected to use each exit.

These laws are all coming into play in a variety of sports facilities, ranging from stadiums and arenas to schools and bowling alleys. The scope and applicability of ADA facility requirements are best understood when analyzed in light of the express purpose of the ADA.

Purpose of the ADA

The underlying principles of the ADA entail the equal opportunity for individuals with disabilities to participate in and benefit from programs and facilities in the most integrated setting possible. The goal of the ADA is "mainstreaming"—that is, allowing individuals with disabilities the opportunity to mainstream into American society. To help bring about mainstreaming, facilities and programs must integrate individuals with disabilities to the maximum extent possible, must provide separate programs when required to ensure equal opportunity, and must not exclude individuals with disabilities from regular programs (unless there is a significant injury risk).

ADA Requirements for Sports Facilities

Title III of the ADA covers places of public accommodation and commercial facilities. For a facility to be considered a place of public accommodation, the facility's operation has to affect interstate commerce. Public facilities which meet this test include, but are not limited to, any establishment serving food and drinks; entertainment facilities (movie theaters, concert halls, and so forth); public gathering places (auditoriums, convention centers, stadiums, arenas, and so forth); public transportation centers; places of recreation (parks, zoos, bowling alleys, and so forth); places of education (private schools); and places of exercise or recreation (gymnasiums, golf courses, and so forth). The only exceptions from Title III coverage are private clubs and religious organizations.

Under the ADA, a place of public accommodation is required to remove all architectural barriers to access if such removal is "readily achievable." When an architectural barrier cannot be removed, the facility must provide alternative services. However, any new construction or facility alteration must comply with all ADA accessibility standards. New construction is required to be accessible and usable unless it is structurally impracticable to accomplish.

EXHIBIT A

ASSSEMBLY SPACES

UNIT 5: Technical Information Modifications to Spaces

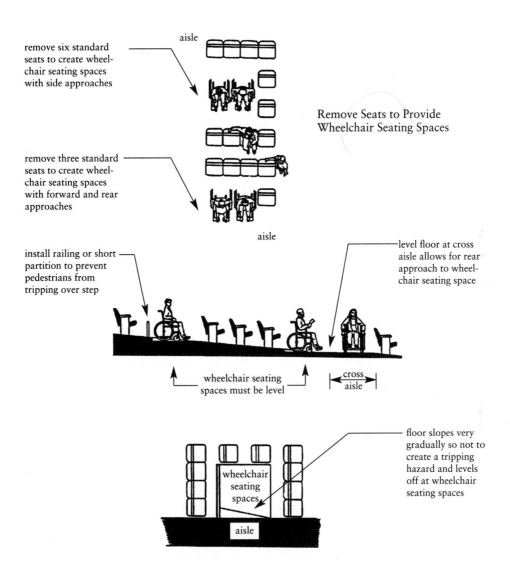

remove six standard seats to create wheel-chair seating spaces with side approaches

aisle

Remove Seats to Provide Wheelchair Seating Spaces

remove three standard seats to create wheel-chair seating spaces with forward and rear approaches

aisle

install railing or short partition to prevent pedestrians from tripping over step

level floor at cross aisle allows for rear approach to wheel-chair seating space

wheelchair seating spaces must be level

cross aisle

floor slopes very gradually so not to create a tripping hazard and levels off at wheelchair seating spaces

wheelchair seating spaces

aisle

Modify Floor to Create Access Route from Aisle to Seating Space

Commercial facilities are facilities not intended for residential use and whose operation affects interstate commerce. Examples of commercial facilities include factories, warehouses, and office buildings. Existing commercial facilities are not required to remove architectural barriers even if the removal is readily achievable. Commercial facilities are also not required to provide alternative services. Only newly constructed commercial facilities and alterations to existing commercial facilities need to meet ADA requirements.

The primary focus in analyzing sports facilities revolves around the public-accommodation requirements. Places of public accommodation may not discriminate against individuals with disabilities. Disabled individuals cannot be denied full and equal enjoyment of the "goods, services, facilities, privileges, advantages or accommodations" offered by a covered facility. The ADA applies to covered facilities whether they are owned by the private, nonprofit, or government sectors.

Full and equal enjoyment covers more than just facilities. It also covers programs held within the facilities. The landmark case setting forth ADA requirements for sports programs under Title III is *Anderson v. Little League Baseball, Inc.* (794 F. Supp. 342 (DC. Ariz 1992)). Little League Baseball adopted a policy in 1991 that prohibited wheelchair-using coaches because of potential collisions that could occur between a player and coach. Anderson, a wheelchair user who also was an on-field coach, contended that the policy change was instituted to prevent him from coaching during a 1991 season-end tournament. The local Little League office refused to enforce the rule and Anderson's team was eliminated early in the tournament. The issue arose again in 1992, when Anderson coached an all-star team.

The court questioned whether Anderson posed a risk to other participants. The court also examined whether Little League's claimed "direct threat" (to others) was based on generalizations or stereotypes about the effects of a particular disability. The court held that each coach had to be individually assessed. There was no evidence that Little League Baseball, Inc. undertook any type of inquiry to ascertain the nature, duration, and severity of risk; the probability that injury could actually occur; or whether reasonable modifications of policies, practices, or procedures could reduce the risk. Thus, any rule developed by an organization (that utilizes places of public accommodation) must provide the opportunity to evaluate each program participant on his or her own merits. Any policy that results in an absolute ban on any handicapped individual(s) will always be struck down if there is at least one person who does not pose a "direct threat" or prove that he or she does not epitomize a generalization or stereotype.

The unfair and indiscriminate application of stereotypes has resulted in several successful suits against sports facilities. A California ski resort violated the ADA with its policy that prohibited persons in wheelchairs from riding cable cars to the resort's recreational facilities. The court concluded that the resort's policy responds not to an actual risk but to "speculation, stereotypes, and generalizations." The resort was forced to modify its policies. A Philadelphia gym facing significant legal fees agreed to pay $35,000, to adopt a nondiscrimination policy, and to provide its staff with mandatory AIDS/HIV education to settle an ADA (Title III) lawsuit. The suit was brought by an AIDS victim who claimed that the gym owner had publicly humiliated him, thrown him out, and told him never to return to the gym because he had AIDS.

What Disabilities Are Covered by ADA?

The ADA employment provision clarifies what constitutes a disability under the ADA. Individuals covered by the ADA include those with *significant physical or mental impairments*, those with *a record of an impairment*, and those *regarded as having an impairment.* A person with a record of disability is protected even though he or she might not currently experience any impairment. Thus, a cancer patient in remission is still covered by the ADA. Furthermore, those regarded as having an impairment are protected even if they never had an impairment.

Not all physical or mental impairments constitute a disability. The impairment has to be *significant.* To help determine significance, the following factors are examined: the length of time the impairment has existed, the number and types of life activities affected by the impairment, the extent to which the impairment limits opportunities, and whether the impairment is medically diagnosable.

Common examples of protected disabilities include the following: paralysis, diabetes, arthritis, cancer, epilepsy, asthma, vision impairments, hearing impairments, speech impairments, learning disabilities, muscular dystrophy, heart disease, and manic depressive disorder. Conditions commonly regarded as impairments include dwarfism, albinism, cosmetic deformities, controlled diabetes, and visible burn injuries. The ADA specifically excludes homosexuals, bisexuals, transvestites, transsexuals, pyromaniacs, kleptomaniacs, and compulsive gamblers. Other conditions that are not covered by the ADA include the following: colds, broken bones, appendicitis, hair color, hair type, and left-handedness.

Disabled individuals are not the only ones protected by the ADA. The ADA prohibits discrimination against individuals or entities because they have a known relationship or association with persons who are disabled. Thus, the roommate of a disabled participant cannot be excluded from attending an event at a facility. This does not mean that the roommate can get into a stadium free. If the roommate and the disabled patron both have tickets, they should be allowed to sit together. Furthermore, individuals who exercise their rights under the ADA or who assist others in exercising their rights are protected from retaliation.

The physical attributes and conditions enumerated above present a complicated list of potentially disabled individuals. Unfortunately, most of the disabilities covered under the ADA are not readily visible. Thus, the notion that one can see a person's disability when that person uses one's facility is a fallacy. Therefore, one must prepare one's facility for all potential users. The hallmark for proper preparation entails providing reasonable accommodation.

What Constitutes "Reasonable Accommodation"?

"Reasonable accommodation" means correcting both architectural and program-related barriers. An architectural barrier is a building's physical characteristic that impedes access for disabled individuals. Examples of architectural barriers include the following: steps and curbs rather than ramps; unpaved parking areas; conventional doors rather than automatic doors; office layouts that do not allow a wheelchair to move through an office; deep-pile carpeting, which is difficult for wheelchairs to traverse; and mirrors, paper towel dispensers, and sinks that are positioned too high on a bathroom wall.

All facilities covered by the ADA must reasonably modify their policies, practices, and procedures to avoid discrimination. Modifications do not need to be undertaken if they would fundamentally alter the nature of the goods, services, facilities, privileges, advantages, or accommodations. A perfect example of this rule was seen at the inaugural Disney World Marathon. One disabled participant, a motorized wheelchair user, sued, claiming that the race organizers were not reasonably accommodating his needs. The race organizers replied that if the disabled individual was allowed compete, the race would be fundamentally altered. The court agreed with the race organizers. The judge concluded that the race organizers were providing reasonable accommodation to disabled individuals through the running of a wheelchair-user division in the race. However, the disabled prospective participant who filed the claim was no ordinary wheelchair user. He used a motorized wheelchair. The court reasoned that the use of a motorized wheelchair would significantly alter the nature of the event. If the court had allowed a motorized wheelchair, it would have opened the door for a disabled person to claim, next year, that he or she wished to participate while driving in a customized van. The court was unwilling to let the law go so far as to alter the very nature of the event.

There is no need for a public accommodation facility to provide individual prescription devices that must be customized for individual use — such as eyeglasses, wheelchairs, or hearing aids. Neither is there a requirement to provide individualized assistance for activities such as eating, dressing, and using the toilet. Thus, while it is fairly easy to determine what accommodations do not need to be provided, it is much more difficult to determine the appropriate level for achieving reasonable accommodation.

Do I Have to Prepare for All Potential Handicaps?

Most facility operators when faced with possible access barriers often struggle with a prioritization process. Which repairs should be completed first? Which repairs or changes can be implemented over time? In order to provide guidance, the Department of Justice has made suggestions for removing barriers in order of priority. First priority is to remove all barriers that would prevent individuals with disabilities from entering the facility. Second priority is to provide access to areas where goods and services are made available to the general public. Third priority is to provide access to restrooms. Fourth priority is to remove all barriers to using the facility by making modifications to it. Such modifications can include adding floor-level indicators in elevators, lowering telephones, and lowering paper-towel dispensers in bathrooms. These modifications should be made only to areas that are not exclusively used by employees as work areas.

Reasonable accommodation for ensuring equal communication can include many auxiliary-communication aids, such as the following: qualified interpreters, transcription services, audio recordings, speech synthesizers, telecommunication devices for the deaf (TDDs), telephone handset amplifiers, video text displays, written material (including large print), note takers, assistive listening devices, closed caption decoders, and materials in Braille. Besides the purchase of needed equipment, all equipment must be kept in accessible locations and in working condition. Most auxiliary aids are relatively inexpensive, such as amplifiers for telephones. However, purchasing and maintaining a significant amount of auxiliary equipment can become costly for smaller businesses.

How Much Will It Cost Me?

Places of public accommodation are required only to remove barriers when such removal is "readily achievable" (ADA, Section 302(b)(2)(A)(iv)). "Readily achievable" means that repairs or modifications can be made without significant difficulty or expense (301(9)).

Several factors influence the costs associated with barrier removal. These factors include the nature and cost of needed remedial action, the financial strength of the facility or organization required to provide the accommodation, and the relationship of the facility in the overall financial picture of the parent company. Companies with significant capital will be held responsible for undertaking more repairs than a financially strapped business.

Cost is only one factor to be considered when attempting to make a facility barrier free. An *alteration* is defined as any physical change that affects facility usability. Such changes can include remodeling, renovations, rearranging walls, and other changes that affect a facility's use. Any alterations begun after January 26, 1992, must be useable by disabled individuals to the maximum extent feasible. An example of an unfeasible alteration can be demonstrated by analyzing a renovation project for a facility entrance. While performing renovations, the facility manager is told that the only way to increase the doorway size to accommodate a wheelchair would affect the building's structure. Thus, it would be technically unfeasible to widen the entrance. Only that portion of the accommodation plan can be avoided. All other ADA alteration requirements have to be followed.

Traditionally, landlords are responsible for facility repairs and modifications. Thus, landlords are typically responsible for financing required renovations or repairs. Lease agreements can provide the tenant with a right to modify a facility. If a lease agreement specifically allows a tenant to renovate a facility, it will be the tenant's responsibility to pay for ADA-required modifications. If a lease is silent concerning responsibility for required repairs, the Department of Justice could force both the landlord and tenant to pay for them.

While some accommodations might seem impossible for a company to afford, tax benefits can make such improvements attainable. Internal Revenue Service (IRS) Code, Section 190, specifies that up to $15,000 of allowable expenditures for ADA-required compliance can be deducted rather than capitalized. All expenditures over $15,000 constitute capital expenditures. Furthermore, under IRS Code, Section 44, eligible small businesses with sales of less than $1 million and with fewer than 30 employees can receive a credit equal to 50% of the expenses for accommodations that exceed $250, but do not exceed $10,250, in any tax year. This credit applies to expenditures that are both reasonable and necessary. These tax benefits are best discussed by means of an example.

Sam Jones is the owner of Health-T Fitness Facility. Jones employs 15 people and has sales of $400,000 per year. After hiring an ADA-compliance consulting company, Jones discovered that he needed to modify the facility's front entrance so that a wheelchair could enter through the front door. The consulting company also concluded that a ramp had to be built to provide access between the aerobic area and a soon-to-be-built tennis playing area. In year one, Jones spent $18,000 to modify the front entrance. Jones took a $15,000 tax deduction and capitalized the remaining $3,000 expense. In year two, Jones spent $12,000 on the required ramp. The amount by which $12,000 exceeds $250, but not $10,250, is $10,000. Fifty percent of $10,000 is $5,000. Thus, Jones was eligible for a $5,000 tax credit on his next tax return.

What Will Happen If I Just Do Nothing?

The ADA is enforced through several means. Private citizens can file their own ADA claim in federal court. Private claims are only entitled to injunctive relief and attorney's fees. Thus, if a bowling alley does not provide any reasonable accommodation, a patron can sue to force the alley to build a ramp so that a wheelchair user can reach the lanes, but the patron cannot sue for monetary damages.

A private citizen can also file a claim with the attorney general. After receiving a complaint, the attorney general can then sue the facility owner and seek injunctive relief. The attorney general can also recover monetary damages and civil penalties.

Practical and Inexpensive ADA Solutions for Sports Facilities

The purpose of this chapter is not to scare facility administrators. However, they should note the Justice Department's clear indication that the days of ADA education are now over and the days of ADA enforcement have begun.

There are numerous ADA solutions that can be implemented with little or no cost. While facility renovation and repair costs are hard to reduce, it is much easier to implement program-wide attitude changes, which can significantly reduce the chance of incurring an ADA complaint, and to provide evidence that ADA compliance is being developed and fostered throughout the organizational staff.

For extensive repairs or renovations, facility operators can hire an ADA consulting firm to determine what repairs need to be made. Another option involves performing a complete facility review and program review to discover firsthand what potential problems exist. The first step necessary when facility operators undertake their own ADA review is to designate one individual within their organization as the ADA expert. This "expert" will have to review literature in the field, become familiar with ADA regulations and specifications, and listen to the needs of employees and customers.

The second step involves the undertaking of a comprehensive facility audit. All facility components should be analyzed and evaluated for accessibility. A written evaluation should be prepared to track needed repairs, facility evaluation dates, repair dates, repair costs, priorities, and similar concerns. Such documentation is critical when facility operators face an ADA investigation.

A convenient approach to conducting a facility audit entails working from outside to inside a facility—following the same travel path a disabled person might use. The following list of questions represents specific concerns that should be examined. This list is not an exhaustive one, but a framework for further analysis.

Parking Area

Does the facility have an adequate number of parking spaces for individuals with special parking needs?

Are international symbols for the disabled used to identify parking spaces?

Is there adequate spacing between a disabled individual's potential parking space and other spaces so that a wheelchair can easily be moved around the side of a car or van?

Are there directional signs indicating the entrance to the facility?

Sidewalks/Ramps

Are sidewalks at least 68 inches wide so that two wheelchairs can move simultaneously past each other on the sidewalk?

Are ramps clearly set apart with colored paint and the international handicapped symbol?

Can the ramp or curb be reached easily by someone parking in the handicapped-parking space?

Is the slope of each ramp easy for any handicapped person to negotiate?

Entryways

Are entrance doors/paths unlocked and accessible?

Is there a minimum of 60 x 60 inches of level space in front of the entrance door to allow for maneuvering?

Are doors easy to open? "Push" or "pull" doors require less than 8.5 pounds of pressure to be opened. Sliding doors and interior doors require less than 5 pounds of pressure. Fire doors require at least 15 pounds of pressure.

Are doormats no more than one-half inch in height? Are they located in the proper place in order not to obstruct access?

Can doorknobs and door handles be grasped with one hand without the need of a tight grip or a turning of the wrist?

Are automatic doors set to open only when someone is less than two feet away from them? (This maladjustment could cause an individual in a wheelchair to be hit by them.)

Are there accessible doors located beside revolving doors?

Is there any metal or wood plating on the very bottom 7½" of a glass door?

Is the door threshold flush with the floor or entrance surface?

Are interior floors covered with a nonslip surface?

Is high-plush carpeting used in transit areas?

Stairs

Are the treads at least 11" x 11"? Are they covered with nonslip material?

Are the stairs risers? Do they have a uniform height?

Are the nosings abrupt? Do they extend past the lip over 1 inch?

Do the handrails extend at least 12 inches past the top stair and the bottom stair?

Is the height of the handrail between 34 and 38 inches above the stair treads?

Is the handrail grab bar less than 1½" in diameter and easy to grip?

Are there tactile designations at the top and the bottom of the stair run?

Elevators

Is an elevator required for accessibility to all facility levels?

Is an audible and visual signal provided to identify the elevator's travel direction?

Are elevator call buttons located no more than 42 inches above the ground? Are they without any obstructions, such as ash trays?

Are Braille or raised/indented floor-level designation buttons within the elevator?

Do the elevator doors open at least 32 inches? Do they provide ample wheelchair accessibility into the elevator?

Does the elevator stop flush or within ½ inch at each floor level?

Is the elevator equipped with an automatic bumper or other safety closing mechanism?

Does the elevator have handrails mounted 34 to 36 inches above the elevator's floor?

Is the control panel located no more than 48 inches above the elevator's floor?

Should an elevator's automatic doors not function properly, is there a maintenance plan in place to make immediate repairs?

Public Restrooms

Is an accessible restroom available for each sex?

Are restrooms and appropriate stalls clearly marked with international symbols?

Are restrooms identified with Braille or raised/incised lettering on the door or beside the door frame?

Are mirrors and paper dispenser mounted within 40 inches from the floor?

Is the toilet placed at the right height and distance from any hot plumbing fixtures?

Is an area of at least 30" x 48" provided in front of the toilet for a wheelchair to move around?

How are faucets activated? By levers, handles, or motion detectors?

Does the handicapped stall have a door that swings out and provides at least 32 inches of clearance?

Are handrails appropriately placed in the stall?

Are toilet paper and seat covers within easy reach of a person on the toilet? Are flush controls mounted lower than 40 inches from the floor and easy to grasp?

Is there unobstructed access to the restroom?

Telephones

Are the telephone touch-tone buttons and coin slots no higher than 48 inches above the floor?

Is the receiver cord at least 30 inches in length?

Are the telephone directories usable at wheelchair level?

Is the handset equipped with an amplification mechanism?

Are usage and payment instructions available in Braille?

Water Fountains

Is the fountain at least 27 inches high and 17–19 inches deep?

Are there easy-to-control buttons, levers, or motion detectors?

Is some signage available showing how to operate the fountain? Are drinking cups available for fountains that are too high?

The third step involves evaluating facility policies, procedures, and practices. All policies, procedures, and practices that may affect individuals with disabilities need to be addressed. These can be modified with little cost or effort. For example, a receptionist could be asked to answer all telephones in a loud voice while clearly enunciating the company's name. Waiters could be instructed to ask each party being served how they can accommodate any special needs that any patron might have. The key to such an effort is to co-opt all employees into the process with the view that they should not be afraid to ask how they can help or what they can do. For example, a sporting goods store's normal practice might be to require a driver's license when accepting a personal check. If someone does not have a license, the sales clerk should not automatically reject the check. The sales clerk should ask for other pieces of identification or ask why the customer cannot produce a driver's license. Many individuals with disabilities do not have driver's licenses.

The fourth step involves acquiring, and maintaining in readily usable fashion, any necessary auxiliary aids such as interpreters, taped text, Braille text, and assistive listening devises, to name a few. There is no requirement that the most expensive method of accommodation should be pursued. Any method of accommodation or auxiliary aid needs to be effective for its intended purpose.

The fifth step involves following up to make sure the plans are acted upon. In one case handled by the author, an individual with a disability defecated on herself in a restaurant even though the restaurant had accessible restrooms. The individual sued the restaurant for violating the ADA. While the restroom did indeed meet the ADA requirements, a food shipment had been received earlier in the day, and the only place the employees thought about putting the boxes was the hallway to the restrooms. While there was a wide enough path for a person to enter, there was no room for a wheelchair to fit through. Constant vigilance is required to insure that changing circumstances do not render a facility inaccessible.

Last, facility owners should always check with their accountant to determine if they should receive a tax break.

There are numerous solutions to ADA-related compliance problems. Only technology and ingenuity limit the development of solutions that create accessibility. Assistive listening systems and devices present a perfect example of methods that can be used to provide accessibility.

Hear This

Under the ADA, integral components of an event or facility need to be accessible. Of special concern for sports facilities are sound-related issues. If sound, music, or other auditory components of a program constitute an integral component of an activity, the facility needs to provide assistive listening devices. For example, an integral component of an aerobics class is music. Auditory-related issues are also a key concern under the Architectural Barriers Act and Title V of the Rehabilitation Act of 1973 since the United States has over four million hearing-aid users and fifteen million others with hearing losses requiring additional hearing assistance.

There are four different assistive listening services (ALSs) that utilize input from existing public address (PA) systems to distribute sound. An FM system uses sound from a PA system fed into an FM transmitter to transmit sound to individual FM receivers. An FM system produces excellent sound quality, is highly reliable, and allows listeners to choose their seating locations. Furthermore, installation and operating costs are fairly low. A typical system costs about $1,500. However, the FM system transmits sound through walls, affecting listeners in other rooms, and access is restricted to those with FM receivers. Similar to the FM system is the AM system, which produces sounds that can be received even with small AM portable radios. However, AM systems often have poor sound quality, and the sound may be especially poor in steel-reinforced buildings. AM transmitters cost from $350 to $1,000.

Sound can also be distributed through an induction loop. This system involves a wire loop around a room that receives input from a PA system and retransmits the sound through a magnetic field within the loop. The receiver is equipped with an amplifier that allows the listener to control the sound level. Individuals with hearing aids can use their aids without any additional devices. This system is also easy to install, inexpensive, and portable. A loop receiver costs about $75, and a typical complete system costs about $1,000. Its major disadvantage is that amplification occurs only when someone sits within the loop. Additionally, sound quality is often uneven and fluorescent lights can interfere with sound transmission.

An infrared system uses invisible, harmless infrared light to carry information from the transmitter to a special portable receiver worn by the listener. The system is easy to operate, is not subject to electrical interference, and provides the best system for transmitting confidential information. A typical infrared system costs about $2,000. The major drawback of an infrared system is that the listener must be within the transmitter's sight line to receive the transmission.

Summary/Conclusion

The Department of Justice is past the stage of ADA education and is now aggressively pursuing ADA violators. Sports facility administrators have to develop a mind-set (and co-opt other employees into accepting the mind-set) of providing all potential facility and program users with reasonable assistance. The key to ADA compliance was recently highlighted in a youth league baseball case in Hemet, California. The national governing body for the baseball league backed the youth league in its refusal to allow an athlete to play — in part, to prevent the athlete from "embarrassing himself." The choice of whether or not a person might be embarrassed is solely up to that person, not others. Facility administrators and program coordinators cannot exclude a person from participating just because that person might be embarrassed. Participants should be provided the opportunity to determine if they, in fact, will be embarrassed. This is the mandate of reasonable accommodation.

References

Bureau of National Affairs, Inc. (1994). *Americans with Disability Act manual* (Vol. 3). Washington, DC: Author.

Bureau of National Affairs, Inc. (1995). *Americans with Disability Act manual* (Vol. 4). Washington, DC: Author.

Schneid, T. D. (1992). *The Americans with Disabilities Act: A practical guide for managers*. New York: Van Nostrand Reinhold.

United States Architectural and Transportation Barriers Compliance Board. (1991). *Assistive listening systems*. Washington, DC: Author.

Part 7

Job Search Strategies

I firmly believe if you commit to your dreams and working hard that you can enjoy success in sports and find true happiness.

Adonis Jeralds

Chapter 27

Defining Your Destiny

Adonis Jeralds

Often we hear the phrase "climb the ladder of success." With the competition for jobs in the world of sport, that ladder becomes a mountain for many young professionals. With over 25 years in the sport and entertainment business, I have developed the following steps that will allow you to climb that mountain and reach your **D-E-S-T-I-N-Y**.

Dream Big Dreams

When I finished speaking to the sport management class at the University of South Carolina, a young lady named Susan walked up and introduced herself. After telling me a little about herself, she confidently stated that one day she would become the Commissioner of the National Football League. Why would I doubt her? Billionaire Donald Trump once said, "You have to dream, why not dream big?" Dreaming "big" allowed an inexperienced former lifeguard to become manager of the largest public assembly facility in the country at the age of 30. *I* was that former lifeguard. Another of my favorite quotations is, "Nothing comes to a dreamer but sleep." The message from that quotation is clear: no matter how big your dreams are, you must initiate some action in order to make them come true. The action which ignites our dreams is called "setting goals." There are four major components to a successful goals program.

1. Goals must be **Personal**. I came across the following quotation several years ago: "My worst fear is that I would have come to the end of my life and realized I had lived someone else's dreams." All of the people that love us can support and encourage us, but we have to make sure we are living our own dreams.
2. Goals must be **Specific**. It is important to be as specific as possible when developing your goals. Therefore, you should not say, "I want to land a job in sport." A clearer goal would be to land a job as marketing representative with the Charlotte Bobcats.
3. Goals must have a **Timetable**. It is important to establish a time frame for reaching your goals. For example: "I want to land a job as a marketing representative with the Charlotte Bobcats *within three months* of completing my undergraduate degree."
4. Goals must be **Written Down**. By writing your goals down, you plant seeds in your subconscious. So write your goals down and place them on your nightstand, in your wallet, or in your desk at work. It is then very easy to move toward reaching your goals.

Exceed Expectations

Colin Powell rose to the rank of four-star general and became Chairman of the Joint Chiefs of Staff. When asked how he was able to become so successful, he affirmed, "I worked like a dog for 28 years."

Spud Webb is another example of the value of going the extra mile. At 5'7" he was one of the shortest players in the National Basketball Association. In his book *Flying High*, he writes that during his summers in high school, he would begin playing in the morning and often played through lunchtime. He would always come home for lunch and watch an hour of TV. Then he would go back to the courts and practice until dark and, and on some evenings, come home and put flashlights in the trees in order to keep shooting baskets.

Spud's story emphasizes that it takes more than talent to make it to the NBA. Such an accomplishment also requires hard work. Basketball legend Magic Johnson summed it up nicely: "Talent is never enough. With few exceptions, the best players are also the hardest workers."

If you are to be successful in sport management, you must be willing to do more and to work harder than your competition. It may mean taking an extra assignment, working weekends, or taking a computer class. The sacrifice involved in reaching the top is not easy, but if it were easy, everybody would be making the sacrifice.

Stay Positive

One of the cornerstones of success in any business is a positive attitude. The competition for jobs and promotions makes a positive attitude even more important in the world of sport management. Low salaries and long hours make the initial glamour of working in sport wear off very quickly.

A study by Harvard University revealed that 85% of the reasons for success, accomplishments, promotions, and so forth come from a positive attitude and only 15% from technical expertise. Charles Swindoll, author and pastor, once wrote: "The longer I live, the more I realize the impact of attitude on life. Attitude to me is more important than facts. It is more important than the past, than money, than circumstances, than failures, than successes, than what other people think or say or do. It is more important than appearance, ability, or skill."

Knowledge, experience, education, and job skills do not mean anything if an employee cannot get along with others, is a chronic complainer, and is generally unpleasant to have in the workplace. The person with a positive attitude and a few technical skills is likely to get a job or promotion because skills can be taught while a bad attitude is very difficult to change. In short, attitude is more important than aptitude.

Take Responsibility

As a kid, I vividly remember the neighborhood baseball games. All the small kids would stand on the sideline dying for an opportunity to play. On those rare occasions when there were not enough big kids, the small kids would be pressed into service in order to make the teams even. In order to make the games as competitive as possible, the small kids were allowed only two strikes when batting. To avoid a strikeout, one of the bigger kids would "pinch-hit" for the small kid on the last strike. If the big kid hit the ball, the small kid still got to run the bases.

Unfortunately, there are rare occasions in real life when we are allowed pinch hitters. How simple life would be if we could have a person with our talents stand in and do the work for us in pursuit of our dreams. However, only you can study and prepare for the graduate school admissions test. Only you can research the sport organization and apply for positions with it. Only you can apply for the loan and start your small business. Only you can use the talents you have. Make up your mind today that you will take responsibility for your life.

Integrity

My friend Michael is without question the smartest person I know. He is well read and the depth of his knowledge on such subjects as physics and African American history is astounding. Imagine how intrigued I was when he posed this simple question: "What is the hardest thing in the world to do?" First, I suggested brain surgery. No. Then I offered rocket science. No. Finally, I said, "Climbing Mt. Everest." After chuckling for a moment, Michael shared with me that the hardest thing in the world to do is *to do the right thing*. I have thought of that interchange often as I am faced with issues related to integrity.

In 2006, integrity was the most looked-up word in the dictionary. Certainly, that speaks volumes about our society. With political scandals, corporate misconduct, and cheating in college and professional sport, Americans now, more than ever before, want to know what it means to be a person of integrity. For young professionals in sport management, it is important to commit to uncompromising values.

Senator Alan Simpson once said, "If you have integrity, nothing else matters; if you don't have integrity, nothing else matters."

Never Stop Learning

Early in my professional career, I remember having a discussion with my mentor. He said, "If you're green, you're ripe, and if you're red, you're rotten." I reflected on that a few minutes but could not quite figure out what he meant. He explained that as an apple ripens, it is green in color. At some magical moment, it will be red—and perfect for eating. The problem is that magical moment lasts just a short period of time, and after it has passed, the apple stops growing, deteriorates, and is no longer desirable for eating.

The illustration applies to us as well. As we go through school, accept our first jobs, climb the career ladder, and become professionals, we must never forget that there is always more to learn. We should view each day we are blessed with as a school day—another learning opportunity.

If we ever feel we have grown as much as we need to, we will surely deteriorate and become rotten. It is important to make a personal commitment and a conscious effort to grow a little each day and never be satisfied.

Y Not You?

In 2006, there was a very funny film entitled *Phat Girlz*, which starred comedienne Monique. The movie revolves around her character and her trials and tribulations as she finds true love. One of the costars of the movie is a young lady named Kendra C. Johnson, who plays Monique's best friend.

In 2001, Kendra was working as part of my staff at the Charlotte Coliseum. She worked in the Human Resources Department, although with her effervescent personality, you would have thought she was part of the Marketing Department. One day, Kendra came into my office and stated that she wanted to go to Hollywood to become an actress. Without hesitation, I asked her, "When are you leaving?" With the challenge of my question, Kendra began planning for her move. A few months later, without knowing anyone there except a cousin, Kendra moved to Hollywood. Over the next three years, she worked several jobs, found an agent, and secured several body-double roles for Queen Latifah, which eventually led to her big break in *Phat Girlz*. Now, the sky is the limit. I am thankful that I had the wisdom on that day to ask Kendra, "When are you leaving?" Without that challenge, she may have become one of the millions who never really purposefully pursue their dreams. You, too, can reach your dreams, no matter how far-fetched they may seem to other people.

Although Kendra's experience relates to the entertainment industry, it parallels what most young people experience in the world of sport management. As in the entertainment industry, the road to success in the sport industry is not easy. That is why so many choose not to pursue a career in the industry or give up after only a few months or years in it. Career, by definition, implies longevity. You must pack your bags and prepare for a long journey.

I purposely used **D-E-S-T-I-N-Y** as an acrostic as I worked through my seven steps for success in the sport industry. The dictionary defines *destiny* as something that is to happen to someone in the future. I firmly believe that if you commit to your dreams and work hard, you will enjoy tremendous success in sport and find true happiness. **Your Destiny Awaits!**

Chapter 28

Student Professional Development

Calvin Hunter

Introduction

The question is, "What are you going to do the Monday after graduation?" Many students respond to this question by saying, "I'll be looking for a job." Much student success after graduation depends on the student's professional development during his or her time as an undergraduate. Time spent as an undergraduate, beyond an internship or practicum, can be vital to the student's professional development. A student's professional development should begin early. Time and effort while an undergraduate are key components to shaping the student's professional success. Here are some points to help the student develop professionally.

Work with Your College's Athletic Department

As a sport management major, the student has a great opportunity within walking distance on his or her campus. The athletic department can be a great training ground for sport management majors. Although the focus is athletic administration, the experiences can involve a variety of areas such as the following:

- Sport Marketing
- Facility and Event Management
- Communications
- Game Operations

Your college's athletic department can be an oasis of opportunities. It is up to you to take advantage of this oasis by getting involved in it.

Volunteer at Sporting Events

As an undergraduate, I had many opportunities to volunteer at sporting events involving college basketball, professional baseball, professional golf, NASCAR races, professional tennis, and NBA basketball. Depending on your location, you may be exposed to the same types of opportunities. Maybe there are professional events happening near your institution. For example, professional golf tournament officials are always looking for volunteers to aid in the operation of a tournament. Opportunities like this can often provide valuable and rewarding experiences you can obtain only by being a part of an event. You may feel that volunteering at a sporting event is a waste of time, but you should remember that the time you spend now will help you in your professional development for the future.

Shadow Someone in the Field

According to the *American Heritage College Dictionary*, the term *shadow* can mean "one that follows or trails another." As part of your professional development, seek out someone performing a job you are interested in obtaining. Many professionals are willing to share some of their time to enlighten you about the sport management field. I remember being interested in intercollegiate athletic administration, and I wanted to shadow an athletic director. I called Nelson Bobb, athletic director at the University of North Carolina at Greensboro. Mr. Bobb was very accommodating and allowed me the opportunity to spend the day shadowing him throughout his schedule. I was thankful to Mr. Bobb for giving me a glimpse into the world of a college athletic director. I had the opportunity to ask candid questions about athletic administration. But more important, I received sound advice from an outstanding professional in the field.

Join Professional Organizations

Professional organizations can provide tremendous opportunities for students to grow and develop as professionals. These organizations provide opportunities for students to hear from and network with professionals in the field as well as to network with other student sport management majors. Most professional organizations provide a discount membership fee for students, and many provide students with leadership opportunities. Being involved in professional organization conferences can even afford students the opportunity to present their ideas in the form of lectures or poster presentations. Here are some examples of professional organizations:

- North American Society for Sport Management (NASSM)—www.nassm.com
- American Alliance for Health, Physical Education, and Recreation (AAHPERD)—www.aahperd.org (AAHPERD may also have a state chapter.)
- National Intramural-Recreational Sport Association (NIRSA)—www.nirsa.org
- Sport and Recreation Law Association—http://srlaweb.org/
- National Recreation and Park Association (NRPA)—www.nrpa.org

There are also many opportunities to attend sport management conferences hosted by different institutions around the country. Remember that your success will depend on your level of involvement. Getting involved in your program's student majors club will provide you with a great opportunity in professional development. Student majors clubs afford students opportunities to develop their leadership skills and provide students another avenue to develop professionally through networking and hands-on experiences.

Prepare to Market Yourself

Ultimately, student professional development is about preparing yourself for a career. Most sport management program directors will cover important preparation concepts such as résumé writing, interviewing skills, and communication skills. Listed below are a few ways to enhance each of these concepts:

- Résumé Writing
  - o Decide on the type of résumé—either chronological or functional. A chronological résumé is the most common. It lists education and experience in reverse chronological order.
  - o Your résumé should communicate two significant aspects:
    - What you have done.
    - How you can fit the employer's needs.
- Interviewing
  - o Practice, practice, practice.
  - o Go to informal interviews. Ask potential employers what they are looking for.
  - o Job fairs present an opportunity to get general, on-the-spot practice in interviewing.
- Communication
  - o Always proofread (and allow someone else to proofread) any information you will be sending out—whether it appears on a cover letter or a résumé. In addition, accurate information is a must.
  - o Be professional.
    - Provide a professional e-mail address on your résumé.
    - Arrive early for interviews.
    - Always send out thank-you notes.

Summary/Conclusion

The Pareto Principle suggests that 20% of your activities will account for 80% of your success. It is important for you as a student to take control of your time investment. How you develop professionally is due in large part to the actions you take while you are an undergraduate. Take advantage of your situation and use those things you have access to in order to legitimize your efforts to become the best sport management professional possible.

My will shall shape the future. Whether I fail or succeed shall be no man's doing but my own. I am the force; I can clear any obstacle before me or I can be lost in the maze. My choice; my responsibility; win or lose, only I hold the key to my destiny.

—Elaine Maxwell

Chapter 29

Preparing for a Career in Sport Management

Art Chase

My good friend and longtime college athletic administrator Andy Solomon says, "Jobs are like buses. They come around every so often and you just have to know which one to get on."

Job opportunities are everywhere, but finding the right fit may come easier for some than others. Seeking job openings is quite simple with today's technology, since Internet-based job postings are the norm.

One thing that has not changed in the world of employment is the concept of networking. Networking requires the effort of establishing relationships with others. For individuals attempting to break into a field such as college athletics, the network is crucial: it can have a bigger impact on your ability to obtain a job than your set of skills. If candidate A and candidate B have the same marketable skills, it is only human nature that the employer would choose the individual with a larger and better-known network of people supporting him or her.

My first "networking" experience came when I was a student in college. The time had come for me to choose an internship to complete my degree requirements, and my search was dragging without success. Two classmates of mine had work-study positions in the school's sports information office, and I asked them to introduce me to their employer. They did, and after a 20-minute conversation, I had secured a semester-long internship.

Generating connections can be that uncomplicated.

Networking and Résumés

Some time ago, the old adage "It's not who you know, it's who knows you" turned into "It's not who knows you, but who knows who you know." When we have an opening at Duke University, hundreds of résumés will come into the office. When reviewing them, I look at the list of references and the places the applicants have been and ask, "Who do I know that might know this applicant?"

My theory is that references will generally say positive things about applicants. In order to carry the process one step further, I like to talk with someone who has an association with the applicant but can give a more objective view than a reference sometimes offers. Not to discount references, I will contact references for feedback and information on a candidate.

The concept of networking plays a vital role when you are searching for employment. The more people you know—or who know you—in a professional discipline, the better are your chances for connections.

After you apply for a position, there becomes a fine line between appropriate actions in terms of networking. The usual questions revolve around having references or other individuals call the prospective employer on your behalf. How many calls should be made? On what timetable should they be made?

As a manager, I welcome these types of calls or e-mails. But I prefer to receive communication from references and others on behalf of a candidate after getting the résumé but before an interview. This allows me time to digest the information before talking with the candidate. I do not believe there is a magic number of calls, but more than four would be overkill.

The two rules of thumb I use when offering advice on preparing résumés are first, keep it simple and concise, and second, always include references. Two pages should be more than enough space for anyone to list his or her education, experience, and references. As for references, the last thing a job-search manager wants to do is contact a candidate for his or her reference list. Just list the references in the first place.

Interviewing

Interviewing for a job can be gut-wrenching—but only if you allow it to be.

A mentor of mine—Josh Baker, former sports information director at The Citadel—told me when I was in line for an interview: "Be prepared and be yourself."

Preparation is crucial. Here are a few guidelines:

1. Anticipate questions—especially the difficult ones. Make a list of questions you think the potential employer will ask—and answer them.
2. Do research. Most employers will provide an itinerary with scheduled meetings. Determine whether you have connections with anyone you will be talking with. Take advantage of your "who-knows-who" network.
3. Be ready to ask questions. Create a list of questions regarding the job, the working environment, the social scene, the quality of life in the area, and so forth. You want to find out as much information about your potential employer and new location as you can.
4. Seek help. Before the interview, sit down with some interview "veterans" you know and pick their brains. What advice can they offer?
5. Obtain directions. If you are responsible for transportation to the interview, not only obtain directions but also—if time permits—practice getting to the location. You do not want to be late.
6. For telephone interviews, make sure you are at a location where *nothing* can interfere with the session. It is inappropriate to interview over the phone with distractions. A potential employer will not be impressed if he or she hears a dog barking or another telephone ringing in the background. Being in a secluded environment will also allow you to focus on the interview.
7. Be prepared to talk about yourself during an interview. This does not come easy for some individuals. If you meet with several different

people during an interview, the chances are that the first interaction with all of them will be, "Tell me about yourself." Well-phrased answers will come from practice.

Internships

The concept of internship runs high in the world of college athletics. Many—if not all—intercollegiate athletic departments rely heavily on interns each year. An internship is the perfect two-way street—free or cheap labor in exchange for entry-level experience necessary to advance in the field.

Internships allow individuals to discover information about a profession with on-the-job training. Prospective employers everywhere look for experience, and the internship is generally regarded as the first step in gaining that experience.

I do not hesitate to say that most men and women working in the field have at one point in their careers served an internship for little or no money.

First and foremost, choosing an internship should be based on your field of interest. You should not choose an internship because it makes your schedule more convenient or because your best friend will be working in the same building.

For an intern, the experience can be equated to a first impression: you get one chance to make the most of it. Your actions and work ethic will be evaluated by your employer, who will most likely serve as the top reference on your résumé in the future. When new interns arrive in our office, I offer four concepts that I believe will enhance their experience.

1. Work extremely hard. A strong work ethic is the number one quality in college athletics. The hours of the job are usually odd and long. No prospective employer will continue to look at a candidate once a reference says, "Johnny's work ethic is average."
2. Be a sponge. Learn as much as you can about the operation. Ask questions. Ask more questions. Take notes or keep a journal.
3. Ask for more. An internship is only as good as the intern makes it. Do not be satisfied with doing only what is asked of you. Go above and beyond. Seek out additional responsibilities.
4. Have fun. Internships—like all jobs—are meant to be challenging. If you do not enjoy what you are doing, however, you should probably be doing something else.

On many occasions, an internship will allow you to determine whether or not you want to remain in college athletics or in the specific field you have worked in. So use the internship experience to gauge your interest in the discipline.

Luck?

Is there luck involved with getting a job? Certainly.

In the spring of 2000, I applied for a job in the sports information department at the University of North Carolina, but I was not hired. Later that summer, Duke's Jon Jackson telephoned me and said, "I know you don't know me, but I got your name from Steve Kirschner at North Carolina. We have a job opening here that you may or may not be interested in."

That afternoon, Jon and I talked for several hours, and the next day I traveled to Durham to meet with him and members of the staff. Two days later, I accepted the position.

Before the telephone call, I had never met Jon Jackson or even known that Duke had a vacant position. Jon had asked Steve about other candidates from the search at North Carolina earlier that year, and my name was passed along.

You never know whom you might make a positive impression on—so do so on everyone.

Chapter 30

Job Search Strategies

Joyce Richman

What does it take for prospective employers to recognize your potential and grant you an interview? Essentially, you either look like a match or you don't. How do they know? Either you tell them personally or your résumé does the job for you.

Résumés that land in the employer's "yes" box are those that are objective-based, match the employer's stated requirements for the job, and are written in a succinct, focused-on-accomplishments style with a legible font.

Match Your Objective with the Employer's Need

Résumés should begin with a clearly stated objective that corresponds to the employer's clearly stated need. For example, if the employer's job posting describes the company as a fast-paced production facility seeking an experienced production manager with strong leadership capabilities and X, Y, and Z experience; the résumé's objective should be an action statement that reads the same way: "Energetic production manager with strong leadership skills and X, Y, and Z experience seeks challenging opportunity with fast-paced production facility."

After the objective comes the experience section of the resume: the section that reinforces the job applicant's objective. It states when and where the job seeker helped bring about change while working in a demanding and fast-paced environment—change that met and exceeded the company's goals.

A list of the job applicant's accomplishments follows the experience section of the résumé. The list should be bulleted and should provide quantitative evidence of the applicant's proven ability to drive top-line results or to protect bottom-line results.

Résumés that end up in the trash get there because of a mismatch between the applicant's objective and the job posting; a mismatch between his or her experience and the job posting; or a discrepancy between the applicant's objective and his or her experience.

Take Time to Tailor Your Response

You'll need to tailor your response, which includes your résumé as well as your cover letter, to each job opening, using the key words in the advertisement as your guide.

Proofread Your Résumé

Résumé readers have little tolerance for spelling errors (which show carelessness about details); for sweeping generalities (which indicate that the applicant plays fast and loose with facts); for overstatements, exaggeration, and hype (which indicate that the applicant oversells and underdelivers); for "The Great American Novel" (which indicates that the applicant takes too long to say too little); and for font size that resembles ants on parade (which indicates that the applicant is unaware of needs of others).

Leave Out Unnecessary Information

Leave out information about why you left your last job, why you aren't working, or what happened the last time you worked. Leave out your age, where you were born, your marital status, kids, pets, and hobbies. Leave out your religious preferences, spirituality, and political affiliations. Leave out the names of organizations or memberships that conjure images of polarization or division. Leave out high school activities and pictures of you while your were performing them.

Format Your Résumé Simply, Use the Preferred Kind of Paper — and Be Concise

Résumé readers prefer résumés printed on 8½" x 11" white, cream, or gray paper. They like black ink, 12-point type, readable fonts; they don't like italics; they want it all said in two pages or less; and they're put off by anything snazzy, jazzy, or razz-ma-tazzy.

Tell the Truth

Résumé readers expect applicants to tell the truth. No matter how competitive you are, how badly you need work, or how much you lust for the job, you'll only succeed if you stick with the basics: who you are, what you know, and what you do best. Regardless of how tempted you are to tweak the truth a little, or tweak it a lot, doing so is not worth it. If you lie to land an interview and fudge the facts to get the offer, you'll hedge and dodge while on the job, and you'll be found out. You'll lose your job and your reputation, and it will be even harder to get a job the next time you try.

Use the New Three R's As Your Guide

Just when you thought the three R's were Reading, 'Riting and 'Rithmetic, I have three more for you: Résumés, References, and Research.

Résumés

The key to writing an effective résumé is to focus on your objective.

When you figure that out, everything else falls into place. What's your objective? It describes the job that you do most naturally, that dedicate your free time to, and that requires the least amount of energy from you. The job should be personally gratifying and financially rewarding, and it should benefit those who profit from your endeavors. When you nail down your objective, you simplify your search, because you know what to say to the networking contacts and prospective employers who make such statements as: "Tell me about yourself"; "Tell me about your strengths"; and "Describe what you're proud of having accomplished." Align your work experiences with your objective (the job that benefits both you and the employer). For each job you've held, list three or more accomplishments that support your objective by demonstrating ways you've made a quantifiable difference in verifiable ways.

When responding to openings that you find in print or online, focus on the key words that appear in the ads. Include those words in your objective as well as in your job descriptions and accomplishments.

The more frequently these key words appear, the more likely your résumé will be retained for further consideration.

References

Once you've specified your objective, you know whom to contact for references: former customers, clients, and owners or managers who have benefitted from what you do best. Be considerate. Not everyone wants to be a reference or is obliged to agree with the direction you would like your career to take. If you would like to get a candid reaction and at the same time save face (yours and theirs), say something like this: "John, I've learned a lot working for you over the last few years and I value your perspective. I'd like to get your reaction to a job I'm considering." Then describe what job you're looking for and give John time to respond. If he is supportive and encouraging, ask if he would be willing to serve as a reference for you. If he sounds hesitant or says the job is not a good match for you, brace yourself and ask him to give you some honest feedback about what you are missing or are failing to consider. Listen to his take on what he thinks you need to do going forward. Be respectful. Don't argue, explain, or defend your position, and don't ask John to be your reference. Contact others you know and trust and pay attention to the sum of what they're telling you. If they're in solid agreement that you're on the right road, sign them up: they'll be good references.

Research

Prospective employers expect you to do your homework before you pay them a visit. Learn who they are, what they do, where they do it, and how they add value to the marketplace.

You'll find almost all you need to know from the company's Web site.

Download the information, review it, use it like a study guide, and prepare questions based on it.

While you're online, search for additional information about the company: articles that have appeared in the press and in trade magazines that reference recent changes in leadership and direction, expansions and acquisitions, downsizing and layoffs.

If you're interviewing with retail or service businesses and want to know their track record with the consuming public, check with the Better Business Bureau.

The bottom line: look for a match that satisfies what you want and do best and what the company values and needs most.

The better informed and prepared you are, the more successful you will be.

So You Got an Interview? Now Visualize Perfecting It

You just received your message marked "urgent." You have an interview tomorrow morning, you want to know what to do, and you want to know it now.

For starters, relax.

If you're so uptight, you're likely to shut down the interview, along with the interviewer. Go for a walk, jog, or swim, and think about the impression you want to make during that interview.

Imagine your calm, cool, and collected self driving to the meeting, knowing where you're going, with plenty of time to spare, wearing clothes and shoes that fit you well and comfortably.

Then picture yourself parking in the visitor's lot, walking to the building, greeting the receptionist, providing your name, along with the name and title of the person you've come to see.

And see yourself sitting patiently as you wait however long it takes for the interview to begin.

As the interviewer approaches, imagine yourself naturally extending your arm for a firm, warm, dry handshake and upon entering his office, waiting to be seated until he or she gestures you to the appropriate chair.

You sit comfortably; you're alert, tilted forward ever so slightly, your arms uncrossed, your feet on the floor.

You picture the interviewer as your equal, as interested as you are in finding the right match. You notice how the meeting begins conversationally, with small talk about having a fine weekend and an easy time finding the office.

He or she begins by making the statement you've most looked forward to: "Tell me about yourself." So you describe why you are interested in working with the company and what you believe you can do to contribute to its success.

As the interview progresses, you delight in how your earlier practice sessions have paid off, how easily you respond to open-ended questions about your strengths; skills; and abilities to overcome business challenges, to be a team player, and to attain individual as well as team goals.

You let the interviewer set the pace, the tone, and the atmosphere for the interview.

You focus on why you want to be there and why you were invited to be there.

Your style is pleasantly upbeat and optimistic as you describe your experience through a perspective of authenticity, curiosity, and consideration.

You obviously enjoy the opportunity to learn about what is important to this company and its leadership team.

You're pleased that you took the time to study the company's Web site, particularly when the employer referenced it, asking questions about it. You seemed to surprise him or her with your level of understanding of his or her business and market strategy.

He or she didn't realize that you had also gone online to read some recent articles published about the business in newspapers and magazines.

Your listening skills are at their very best. You take in what the interviewer is saying and when you're unclear of his or her meaning, you ask for clarification before responding. You're able to connect his or her comments to your experiences, demonstrating your knowledge and ability to add value to the company.

You ask open-ended, exploratory questions about the company's direction and its strategy to get there; its culture; what management and personnel expect of one another; what the boss will expect of you; and what it will take to demonstrate success.

The conversation moves effortlessly. The interviewer says he or she will be in touch, and you confirm your interest in the job.

You know that the interviewer will draw conclusions, as will you. He or she will make comparisons, as will you. And he or she will come to a decision.

As will you. And that is as it should be.

So are you ready?

Conclusion

During our years teaching courses for sport management on both the undergraduate and graduate levels, many students and former students have sought advice. Many have had questions regarding résumés, interviews, job searches, feedback, and, on occasion, how to handle downsizing.

We have a tremendous asset in Joyce Richman, a noted speaker and career coach, who conducts seminars and workshops throughout the United States. She is the author of *Roads and Ruts, a Guidebook for Career Success*, and she is often called upon to answer career questions. Her column in the *Greensboro News-Record* and her appearance on local television are extremely popular and helpful.

When people need career help from us, we invariably recommend a meeting with Joyce Richman for guidance. She has agreed to share some of her columns with us for our readers. This act of kindness and professional courtesy is a significant contribution to readers of this text who ask common questions regarding their careers.

Part 8

The Future of Sport Management

The changes in literacy and technology will enable persons from the early years to death to communicate effectively with people all over the world. Computers will translate messages such that no effort will be needed to learn the language of the person with whom you are working. Thus, the potential for a global economy will be in place.

Annie Clement

Chapter 31

The Future and the Sport Manager

Annie Clement

Introduction

It is the year—2020, a little over ten years from today.

If you view the world as an optimist, you are vacationing in space. The space station has replaced Disney World as the number one vacation destination for family fun. If you are a pessimist, you are fleeing your home and/or the country because of terrorist activities, an economic crisis, a failure of municipal infrastructure, or hazardous weather conditions. All these events could occur in the year 2020.

The optimist and the pessimist are playing with predictions, the generation of ideas about the future. And what are the chances of a prediction becoming reality? Let's look at a few past predictions. In August 1948, *Science Digest* reported that landing and moving around on the moon would offer so many serious problems for human beings that it would take science another 200 years to lick them. Neil Armstrong walked on the moon on July 20, 1969—less than thirty years later. And when television first appeared, some predicted that after about six months, people would tire of staring at a box every evening. Today, watching television is a major pastime. In 1990, Clement predicted that office buildings would have health spas, that hospital wellness centers would open their doors to the public, and that robots would be the tennis partners of choice by the year 2000 (Parks & Zanger, 1990). Health spas and hospital wellness centers flourished in the 1990s. Robotic tennis partners never became reality. However, "Japanese scientists have invented a soccer playing robot called VisiON; they claim a team of such robots will win the World Cup by 2050" (Brown, 2006, pp. 51–52).

Daydreaming Is Thinking

Contemplating the future is a creative venture that challenges the imagination and frees the mind to dream. It forces one to ignore concerns of daily life; it makes daydreaming legitimate. We tend to clutter our time with tasks that demand that work hours produce something for which we are accountable. We fail to daydream and use our imagination for the joy of thinking. Seldom do we engage in lateral thinking, the transfer of known ideas to solve new problems (DeBono, 1970). Remember that as a "future sport manager, you are limited only by the extent of your imagination" (Parks & Zanger, 1990, p. 257). The purpose of this chapter is to enable the reader to put contemporary concerns aside and follow futurists toward the years 2020, 2030, and 2050.

The Journey

In 1980, Toffler (1980) explained the impending crisis in our country as the death of industrialism and the rise of a new civilization, a civilization he called "the third wave," or "the information age." Waldrop (1992) states that the "linear, reductionist thinking that has dominated science and research since the time of Newton is no longer capable of addressing modern work problems" (p. 13). He sees today's systems as spontaneous, disorderly, and alive. Waldrop (1992) believes: "[C]omplex systems have somehow acquired the ability to bring order and chaos into a special kind of balance. This balance point—often called the edge of chaos—is where the components of a system never quite lock into place, and yet never quite dissolve into turbulence.... The edge of chaos is where life has enough stability to sustain itself and enough creativity to deserve the name of life" (p. 12).

Pink (2005) suggests that we are in a period of movement from the Information Age to the Conceptual Age. He states: "We are moving from an economy and a society built on the logical, linear, computer-like capabilities of the Information Age to an economy and a society built on the inventive, empathic, big-picture capabilities of what's rising in its place, the Conceptual Age" (p. 2).

Aburdene (2005) describes society's massive change as a move from the information age or economy to social responsibility. She envisions the demise of "business as usual" to the birth of Conscious Capitalism. "Creativity and innovation are the name of the game" (p. xv). For Aburdene (2005), "consciousness, the prime ingredient in creativity, represents a higher intelligence than the mind" (p. xvi).

Aburdene's focus on spirituality, the greatest megatrend of contemporary society, is driven by the current threat of manmade and natural disasters or terrorism, contemporary wars, and lost savings. Her purpose is to dispel the notion "that free enterprise is rooted in greed." (p. xxii). She goes on to state: "Conscious Capitalism isn't altruism, either; it relies instead on the wisdom of enlightened self-interest" (p. xxii). She disagrees with the idea that the sole purpose of a for-profit business is to make money for the shareholders. Her thesis is that the business, while trying to make a profit, must be concerned with the needs of society. In addition, Aburdene suggests that many of the recent illegal actions of major businesses were prompted by the need of executives to find more ways of unscrupulously improving shareholders investments. Had CEOs held a sense of corporate social responsibility, these problems would not have occurred.

Change

Our only guarantee for the future is that things will change, change rapidly, and change continuously. What changes are we currently experiencing? Service organizations have replaced the steel and coal industries; as a result, intellect or knowledge possessed by the work force has replaced the physical labor required of those who worked in the past. People, capable of planning, thinking, and implementing, have become our primary economic asset. People are important to the world economy; they are more important than buildings and factories. Ideas and the resolution of complex problems, rather than the speed in which an object can be manufactured, commands success today and will command success in the 2020 economy. Reorganization and reconfiguration of existing technologies and ideas, many that have been invented and patented but have not been mainstreamed, will be used by a wide range of consumers.

Planning, as a concept, will take on new meaning. We will look to the future attempting to accurately predict events, needs, and services essential to success in that future. Less time will be dedicated to analyzing the success of earlier achievements, and greater effort will be placed on creating alternate futures. While history will continue to be cherished and used to examine events in the context of success and failure, future thinking will guide the growth and development of our businesses.

How will you and I know that it is 2020? Technology will have so taken over our daily needs that a person will rise to a breakfast prepared by an appliance and live in a home, office, transportation vehicle, and other environment preprogrammed to personal specifications. When the cost of the refrigerator that inventories food and orders replacements has come within the reach of the masses, few grocery stores, as we know them today, will exist. Massive food warehouses will satisfy our needs for groceries; a few stores will be available to those who consider shopping a hobby. Household chores and the cleaning of our dwellings will be the job of programmed appliances and robots. Engineer futurists envision that these appliances will orchestrate our daily requirements and cater to our needs, while biologist believe that chemical changes and other changes in the air will be the answer to cleaning. Although not all of the processes are clear, we will have eliminated general household chores.

Our homes will have comprehensive work environments for each inhabitant, thus making them much larger than they are today. In a paperless, or near paperless, society, the space once dedicated to libraries will be comfort zones for effective work and leisure. Computers will be small and often worn as jewelry.

We will be in the beginning of the genetic revolution. Parents will determine their offspring's genetic makeup prior to birth. As a result, a coach, for example, may face serious problems with parents whose children were engineered to be outstanding athletes when the coach fails to see the child as an accomplished performer.

Research Charting the Course of Predictions for the Years 2020, 2030 and 2050

Research dictating societal change will be addressed in this section—which will focus on energy, health and longevity, food, life style, manmade and natural disasters, literacy, and education and employment. Emphasis will be placed on sport, leisure, and tourism. Globalization, technology, and creativity will influence these topics and will propel us into the future.

Energy

Energy, or power, is a main source of our economy. Societies' needs for transportation, air conditioning and heat, electricity, and other forms of energy are beyond necessity; many feel they could not survive without them. In order to provide these services in the future, new sources of energy will be identified and developed. Advancement toward that goal can be seen in the projects at Fraunhofer Institute in Germany and in Hanoi University of Technology that convert rice husks into electricity (Tomorrow in Brief, 2007; Fraunhofer Institute, http://www.fraunhofer.de). At the same time researchers at Florida Atlantic University in Boca Raton, Florida, are harnessing the Gulf Stream as a source of power to generate electricity (Environment, 2007).

Recently, light fixtures have seen radical change toward efficiency. The compact fluorescent light is about four times as efficient as an incandescent bulb. The Ostar LED, a mercury-free light that will glow for 60,000 hours, is ready for market, and professionals predict that by 2010, glowing walls lit by sheets of organic light emitting diodes (OLED) will illuminate our homes, businesses, and community facilities (Bright lights, big savings, 2007), Batteries have also changed and are predicted to continue to increase the number of hours of service. Home design and construction professionals will make use of nature's light and energy in future living quarters.

Health and Longevity

Life span to one hundred and one hundred and twenty years will be reality in the next thirty to fifty years. Genetic engineering, bionics, stem cell science, and pharmacology will enable people to lead productive lives into their 90s and 100s. Zey (2005a, 2005b) calls this change in longevity "super longevity" and defines it as the "radical extension of the human life span accompanied by improved health and vibrancy at all ages" (Zey, 2005a, p. 1).

Two factors that will play an important role in longevity are the replacement of body parts, a phenomenon of today's medical environment taken many steps forward, and the replacement of body organs, including lungs. Swansea University in Wales has developed an artificial lung (Tomorrow in Brief, 2007; Swansea University, http://www.swansea.ac.uk). The genetic engineering of children will also play a significant role in the extension of life into the 100s. "Health-enhancement rights fueled by the wealth of aging baby boomers and the fusion of nano, bio, IT and neuro innovation, will become a fierce social issue" (Canton, 2006, p. 118).

Food

Diet, exercise, and life style influence health and longevity. Water is a primary concern of contemporary and future societies, since potential shortages are a reality. Efforts by researchers throughout the world to convert salt water to potable water may ease the shortage. Health will be improved through the use of new laser-based technology for detecting food-borne pathogens and through chemical-based technology for killing pathogens on fresh produce—both recent accomplishments of a Purdue University food scientist (Tomorrow in Brief, 2007; http://www.purdue.edu/UNS).

Food shortages will be a concern in the United States because of the elimination of vast farm lands. Farms in sky scrapers, according to Despommier (2007), will leave the green fields of the Midwest and move to thirty-story buildings in urban centers. He envisions abandoned buildings in urban areas retrofitted for hydroponics. Irrigation would come from desludged sewage filtered through nonedible barrier plants and zebra mussels, resulting in pristine water. In addition, NASA is currently working on a wide range of products that can be grown indoors for use on Mars and on Earth (Despommier, 2007).

Lifestyle

Lifestyle will under go the greatest change, as virtual reality is incorporated into daily, leisure, and business activities. For example, most of our household products will be ordered from a wireless television or handheld devices. As soon as the order is placed, money will be deducted from a bank or a special type of account to pay for the order. Some predict that a new form of credit will eliminate cards and bank accounts. Today's problems with privacy, security, and counterfeiting of paper currency will result in a cashless society (Kupetz, 2007). The order will be delivered by a flying drone.

Before this chapter goes to press, wireless telephones will have TVs. Shortly, the telephone will begin to control household appliances. Security systems and strategically placed cameras will monitor activities in the homes and workplace. Telephone, television, and the Internet will be fully integrated by 2020.

In 2050, roads and highways will no longer exist, as travel will be conducted by helicopter-type vehicles, some controlled by humans and others manipulated by drones or robots. These machines will be stored in the out of doors or in special housing, with two or three portal landing strips accompanying each living quarter.

Today's robots are vacuum cleaners, machines that enter places unavailable to humans, or assembly lines. Tomorrow's robots will serve the evening cocktails, locate the newspaper, input computer data, and alert owners to danger.

As space travel becomes popular, people will choose to live on the moon or on space platforms. *Wired*, in July 2007, provided pictures of homes or lunar habitats planned by NASA contractors for living on the moon. The structures will accommodate daytime temperatures of 250 degrees Fahrenheit and nighttime lows of minus 450 degrees Fahrenheit. NASA reports that these homes will be operative by 2020 (Kuang, 2007).

Manmade and Natural Disasters

Among the disasters faced today and projected for the immediate future is the manmade disaster of terrorism. Privacy (or lack of privacy), a national security issue, accompanies many of the terrorism solutions. Another issue is the relationship between terrorism and oil. If the need for oil is substantially reduced, could the threat of terrorism be reduced? The aging of the United State's infrastructures: highways, bridges, power plants, water systems, and so forth is a potential manmade disaster.

Natural disasters such as hurricanes, tornadoes, floods, mountain slides, and fires will cause damage and change. These changes will be geographic, financial, and related to lifestyle. Global warning is predicted to eliminate much of today's Atlantic and Pacific residential coasts. Taxes and insurance may also erode the value of coastal dwellings. Should disasters, manmade or natural, continue at the pace of the recent past, economic structures will change.

Literacy

Futurists predict the end of the written word and the rise of visual culture. Video and video games are the choice of today's youth; newspaper purchases are on the decline. Text messaging is in; written notes are out.

Crossman (2007) states that by the year 2050, "talking computers incorporating multisensory, multimodal technology will make written language obsolete and all writing and reading will be replaced by speech and multisensory content, recreating a world wide oral culture" (p. 27). He further believes that the "three R's—reading, riting and rithmetic—will be replaced by the 4 C's, critical thinking, creative thinking, computer skills, and calculators."

Crossman's (2007) logic for the change to an oral culture is based on four factors he identifies as engines. First, biology and psychology directs us to use speech-based methods. Second, written language is a form of technology, and like all technologies, it can be replaced. Third, youth are rejecting the written word for verbal and visual relationships. Letters are being replaced with telephone calls. And fourth, language and communication barriers will be removed as people will be able to communicate with the 80% of adults who are functionally nonliterate (Crossman, 2007). "The voice recognition technology that allows simultaneous translation of spoken language from one language to another is in place. And the software that translates speech into on-screen 3-D sign language is here" (Crossman, 2007, p. 9). These changes will enable all humans to communicate with one another and to enjoy the culture of all parts of the world. The technology, available within the next ten years, will change the course of social interaction around the world.

Naisbitt (2006) confirms Crossman's views, stating: "a visual culture is taking over the world" (p. 113). His rationale includes the decline of newspapers, the value of pictures in advertising, upscale design, fashion, architecture and art, music, video and film, the changing role of photography, and the availability of museums. Naisbitt mentions design and creativity as key elements in the economy, thus supporting the view of Pink (2005).

Education and Employment

Although predictions were made that by now schools would no longer exist, these predictions have not occurred. However, elementary schools, middle schools, and high schools have changed radically in delivery systems over the past ten years and are expected to continue to change. Higher education has taken the giant leap in altering the learning environment through online or distance learning. It is anticipated that this higher education model will be the model for all forms of education. Within the immediate future or by 2020, higher education students will acquire all factual knowledge online. However, they will continue to attend interactive seminars to share ideas and sharpen social skills. Elementary schools, middle schools, and high schools will follow the college model but will continue to include face-to-face social interaction.

The changes in literacy and technology will enable persons from their early years to their old age to communicate effectively with people all over the world. Computers will translate messages in such a way that no effort will be needed to learn the language of the person with whom you are working. Thus, the potential for a global economy will be in place.

Increased longevity, with the masses living to over 100 years, will be accompanied by changes in careers. The life work sequence of forty to fifty years will change to seventy to eighty years. These changes will enable or require people to plan for four, five, or six different careers during their lifetimes. New skill sets will be necessary for each career and within many of the careers. A difficult change will be the loss of seniority as a value in the workplace, with success based principally on current skill capacity. This change is influenced by the speed with which technology renders work skills obsolete.

Employment will be global, with various parts of the world known as the leaders in certain industries. If one wishes to be employed in a particular field, it may require study and employment in the country that specializes in that field. Those changes will create common wage and working conditions across boundaries, thus eliminating today's outsourcing of labor to countries that pay low wages.

Project manager specialists will replace many of today's CEOs in the business world; the specialists will hold key roles in business and industry and will be independent contractors. They will move from one business to another while carrying out major projects. Project managers, as a result of technology, will be international. Naisbitt (2006) suggests that as business, industry, and education become global, we will move toward a world government.

Changes in Sport, Leisure, and Tourism

Global

International globalization and technology will have a profound effect on sport as we know it today. Naisbitt (2006) notes that today, sport permits the United States to lead in globalization. He credits sport's sharing of talent as being what puts sport way ahead of most other sectors of the United States. "Embedded in the sports model is a preview of what will happen in the economic domain" (p. 174). Sport team member selection and employment is international. At the same time, nearly all of professional sport franchises have a physical presence, playing games and holding championships in countries throughout the world. Individual sport athletes in tennis and golf often study with people around the world, while athletes from all over the world come to America to train and live. The Olympics and regional competitions require sports to use common rules and strategies throughout the world. Television and technology bring new games and contests to the viewer every day. For example, fifteen years ago, the U. S. Olympic basketball team was seen in 180 countries. Chuck Daly, reporting this event in the June 21, 2007 issue of *USA Today*, mentioned that a native of Sudan, Chicago Bulls star and former Duke player Luci Deng, an NBA professional, witnessed the basketball games and switched from soccer to basketball. Recently, the author saw a piece on television introducing cross-country walking as a new fitness activity.

Cross-country walking was a popular pastime thirty years ago, when she studied in Norway. In addition, sport has been instrumental in achieving unity throughout the world, even in troubled times.

Visual

Sport and entertainment bridge the gap to the visual future. Although many people who continue to read the newspaper check the sport page carefully and others read concert programs, most sport and entertainment spectator time is spent in the visual culture. Intellectual property knowledge, currently advanced by the sport and entertainment community, will become the model for intellectual property in all visual business sectors.

Fitness

Future sport and physical activity will be fitness for all, career-focused, ultimate personal goal achievement, or social. Sport management personnel will oversee or manage all of these areas. Within each of the physical activity areas, physiologists, biomechanics (skill specialists), medical personnel, athletic trainers, and strategy specialists will play a role in helping people achieve their objectives.

Technology has had a tremendous impact on sport at all levels. The computer and sophisticated programs enable coaches to use biomechanical analysis in the coaching of skills and strategies. The same equipment is a must in observing game play and strategy for opponents and team members. Technology has revolutionized stadiums and arenas—from the scoreboard to seating and storage. Games and computer programs have generated considerable revenue for sports figures and agencies and promise to provide new and exciting experiences. Virtual reality sports are big business for participants and spectators.

The design of sport programs to meet the needs of people with free time will be the responsibility of the sport management professional. The literature on the future suggests that people will have more free time as a result of reduced work hours per week and reduction in time required for household tasks, personal responsibilities, and education; however, none of the authors consulted for this chapter stated such as fact. If many of the tasks and jobs that consume our time today are eliminated, new recreational, leisure, and spectator activities will need to be designed. These activities will be discussed under the headings "participant" and "spectator."

Participant

Many people within sport believe that the greatest change will be found in society's desire to participate in sport and physical activity. Fitness, prompted by the obesity epidemic of 2000 to 2015, will become a part of everyone's life. The desire for longevity will also fuel the fire for fitness, and business and industry will reward those who remain fit. Fitness centers will exist for people from three-years-old to over eighty. Participation in team, individual, extreme, and new forms of sport, yet to be named, will exist. Competitive and social experiences will be provided for common skill levels in each sport or activity. Play will resemble the type of play provided today in adult tennis, golf, and skiing. Those wishing to compete at their ultimate personal skill level will have ample opportunity to achieve their goals. Those using sport as a means of meeting people and socializing will have many opportunities to satisfy their desires, while those wishing to engage in human movement for the joy of moving will be offered a full range of activities. Programs to simulate weightlessness will be popular among those planning short- and long-term trips to the moon and the planets circling Earth.

Sport specialists will manage massive fitness enterprises designed to measure fitness using medical-stress and space-age technology. Computer-generated personal fitness scores derived from health, nutrition, and genetic composition will be scanned by a computer from a bar code on the nail of the fourth finger of the person's left hand and will be available free of charge to everyone. Facilities or rooms of capsules will house simulation laboratories designed to develop personal human movement basics and sport skills. Camera and movement film streams embedded in the individual learning capsule will enable participants to understand the quality of their over arm throw or their capacity to move upright after using a commode, whichever skill the person wants to learn.

Pictures from the capsule camera will automatically be digitized, sent to a database reference of efficient skill for the movement and the size of the individual, and within seconds, the performer will have a readout of the quality of his or her performance and the next step in improving that performance or in bringing it in line with the perfect form according to principles of anatomy and physics. Therapists and sport skill specialists will be available to guide individual skill development. Those aspiring to game play will receive information as to whether personal skills are beginning, intermediate, advanced, or expert (Clement & Hartman, 1994) and which game-play simulators will provide them with skills specific to a particular sport.

Sport and game virtual-reality capsules will simulate position and game play from partner play to small-group play and, finally, to full-team play. Virtual reality will enable the athlete first to mimic his or her role by using rules and strategies; then the performer will actually move in response to those with whom he or she is playing in the virtual world. When the performer has achieved intermediate skill and strategy levels, he or she will leave the learning capsule and enter the gymnasium to begin to play with humans.

In competitive sport, capsules will be programmed to simulate real competition. Physical-skill level, nutrition, and genetic background of players will be one of the most guarded secrets and will be covered by contemporary privacy law. Technology will have made this information valuable to opponents.

An advantage of the above approach to the acquisition of skill, knowledge of rules, and game play is that the mental components of rules and strategies will be acquired in virtual reality, thus eliminating the overuse injuries that occur among athletes who spend too many hours playing to acquire game knowledge and strategy knowledge. Even though nanomachines will repair and replace joints, tendons, nerves, brain cells, and other body parts, athletes will want to conserve body structure in the hope of remaining competitive in senior events for as long as 125 to 130 years.

Swimming and gymnastics will be coveted by the masses these activities will be essential to successful space travel. This assumes that scientists will not have overcome the problems of weightlessness; thus, the space station will necessitate that persons learn to move in a weightless environment. Trampolines and thick bouncing mats will be used to assist people in the first stage of overcoming weightlessness. The practice of underwater aquatic movements taken from water polo and synchronized swimming will enable persons to move efficiently and socially in the space village. Knowledge of placement from indoor soccer, ice hockey, and billiards will assist performers in applying their bodies' force against firm structures as a means of moving in space. Once these skills are acquired, space athletes will attend workshops using discarded astronaut simulators. NordicTrack, Nike, and others who have survived the economic crises will market simulators for home use.

The physically challenged person will seldom exist, as technology will have repaired limbs and organs. Mentally challenged persons will be fewer in number than they are today as a result of genetic engineering and the replacement of brain cells. The role of stress, drugs, and other psychological factors in the future is unclear, as is the potential for personal hazards that cannot be identified. All of these changes will have an impact on the human body and personality and could result in problems.

Should worst-case scenarios of terrorism play a role in the immediate future, the population will be prepared, physically and psychologically, for disaster. And that preparation will have been accomplished through adventure education — knowing how to function in the wilderness. The acquisition of camping, hiking, climbing, nutrition, and health skills in the wild will be as important as knowing how to effectively brush one's teeth.

Spectator

At the same time, a wide range of sport entertainment will be provided for spectators. With three hundred to five hundred television stations available, networks will be dedicated not only to traditional sports but to dance, synchronized swimming, diving, fencing, and field hockey. This change will open employment to a far greater number of athletes than that which exists today.

As schools and colleges began to disappear in 2020, scholastic and collegiate sport in the United States will move to the club model popular in the rest of the world. Special clubs will be established to meet the needs of the much larger population of athletes who will aspire to professional sport as a career.

John Sweeney (2007), founder of the University of North Carolina Sports Communication Program identifies ten key trends that will shape the future of the sports industry. The first key trend is branding, with a recognized unifying logo. He points out that the "future belongs not just to those who understand branding, but to those able to achieve the enormous political discipline necessary to make it work" (Sweeney, 2007, p. 35). The second key trend is a need to change the media, while the third trend will be what women's sports will bring to the media. The next trends are the changes that will occur in viewer attention once there are a hundred TV stations; the value of wealth; the replacement of participation by spectatorship, primarily on TV; the influence of environmental change; engineered athletes; global change; and moral connections (Sweeney, 2007). Sweeney has challenged the career-focused and spectator-sport industry in these words. Branding, along with the elimination of the written word, will place responsibility on tomorrow's sport management professionals to understand and achieve success in the area of preservation through intellectual property law.

Leisure and tourism, in conjunction with sport, will make use of the forms of transportation essential to short- and long-term space travel and periods of living on space platforms or villages and the moon. One of the new sports proposed is "dive from space." People will ride a rocket into space, abandon the rocket, and jump or dive from about 60 miles above Earth. The dive will be used as a safety device for persons facing problems while touring outer space and for those who intentionally enter outer space for this new sport. Sophisticated space suits will enable the body to withstand the heat of reentry and will provide oxygen to the diver (Weed, 2007).

International travel will be commonplace since people will wish to visit with those with whom they have been communicating for years. Camping and outdoor adventures will become important, as people shed the fear of terrorism but wish to use the well-honed skills acquired for long-term survival in remote areas.

Sport managers will play the lead role in the entertainment industry as they meet the needs of spectators and will lead amateur sport organizations in the provision of opportunities for all. The proliferation of television stations will enable the viewer in 2020 to watch only those sports of interest. Viewer selection will drive sports virtually ignored into mainstream entertainment.

Scenarios Specific to the Future

Characteristics of 2020

- Agriculture waste and wind will convert to electricity; all power will be electric or solar.
- Efficient light in homes and offices will be provided by windows and open spaces.
- People will live to 90 to 100 years of age and will work until 70 to 75 years of age.
- Technology, research, fitness, and nutrition will make longevity possible.
- Extended life span will require learning for multiple careers.
- Conversion of salt water to drinking water and laser-based technology for detecting and killing food-borne pathogens will increase longevity.
- Household needs, including groceries and other items, will be ordered from hand held devices and delivered to homes.
- The vehicles will be created but will not be owned by many.
- Television, telephone, and the Internet will be fully integrated.
- Robots will do general household chores.
- People will be prepared for natural and manmade disasters.
- Cell phones and other social devices will put people in close touch with a small but intimate group of their selection. Families and friends will be able to maintain close contact even though they are miles apart.
- Athletes will use virtual reality for practice and skill development.
- Robots will become practice partners in sport.
- Personal skill levels of the average population will be elevated.
- A high level of fitness will be rewarded by employers.
- An increase in jobs for professional athletes and sport media/communication specialists will occur in a wide range of sports to meet the expansion of television stations.

- International sport competition will increase.
- American sport franchises at home and abroad will be at their peak, with spectators frequently traveling to other parts of the world to see their favorite teams.
- New stadiums will be surrounded by shops, housing, and popular tourist attractions.

Characteristics of 2030

- Cars will be replaced by flying machines, either person- or robot-powered (drones).
- Homes and businesses will be redesigned to use natural power more efficiently.
- All energy will come from wind, water power, and the efficient use of light.
- Oceans will provide drinking water.
- Life will extend to 100 to 120 years, with most people working until 80 to 90 years of age.
- People will plan for a number of careers and will continuously update employment skills to be competitive in the workforce.
- Extended life will be the result of genetic engineering and the replacement of body parts, particularly organs such as lungs. Diseases will have been eliminated.
- Agriculture will have moved from farmlands to urban high-rise buildings.
- NASA technology will be commonplace and used by everyone.
- Money, as we know it, will no longer exist. New, global financial plans will guide people in saving and purchasing on the basis of life styles.
- All transportation will be by air. Roads and highways will become urban walking trails.
- No motorized vehicles will be used on these paths.
- Housing will continue to be individually owned but will favor group-oriented living before marriage and after child rearing. With changes in health and longevity, child rearing may last for a far longer period of time, with couples averaging 6 to 8 children.
- People will have moved inland from the coasts of oceans, rivers, and the Great Lakes; portable structures on water fronts will become prime vacation property.
- Planning for international sport will be massive.
- Camping, hiking, and so forth will be global.
- New sports will be invented.
- Events will be planned for all people, with the wealthier engaging in the most international travel.
- Sports will be club sports; intercollegiate and interscholastic sport will have disappeared.
- Space travel will be available for the masses.
- Space diving will be an important sport.

Characteristics of 2050

- Government and society will be global.
- Transportation, by air, will occur around the globe and to the moon and space platforms.
- Vehicles for short trips will be personally owned and will be launched from home or business; a number of different kinds of vehicles, yet to be designed, will be used for various types and lengths of travel.
- Sun, wind, and water will provide all necessary power.
- Living quarters will store energy from one season to the next. Oceans and winds will supply remaining needs.
- Persons will live to 120 to 130 years of age, working until 90 or 100 years of age. The change in longevity will be attributed to planned genetic sequences of individuals before birth, the eradication of diseases, and improved nutrition and emotional controls.
- Nutrition will change, with food, as we know it today, used only for festivals.
- Should urban farms succeed, food may remain as is. Urban farm failure may mean that people will eat nutritional pills instead of food.
- Sport events will be global, with levels of competition provided for both advanced and expert athletes, from youth to seniors.
- The global economy will enhance global travel for business and pleasure.

Preparing for the Future

Pink (2005) emphasizes the change that will occur with respect to right-brain people, who will become "creators and empathizers ... meaning makers ... and big picture thinkers" (p. 1). The Information Age rewarded the left brain, or rational, analytic, and logical minds. The Conceptual Age will reward nonlinear thinking, intuitiveness, empathy, and joy. Pink notes that the ability "to combine seemingly unrelated ideas into something new" will be highly rated (p. 2). More information about combing unrelated ideas can be found in DeBono's work on lateral thinking, a must-read in this area (DeBono, 1970).

According to Pink (2005), the six senses are *design, story, symphony, empathy, play,* and *meaning.* Concerning *design,* he states that as a result of contemporary affluence, today's society wants products, services, and experiences to be beautiful or "emotionally engaging" (p. 65). Examples are the wide range of decorated cases available for cell phones and the decorated flip-flops found in our department stores. What was once a mere product for the beach has become a fashion statement. Furthermore, he believes that the ultimate form of persuasion and communication is the use of a *story* to make a point.

According to Pink (2005), *symphony* means synthesis, or seeing the big picture. It is this skill that will be most valued by sport specialists employed to design facilities and implement events. The planner who visions the finished product before placing the first word on paper has that "big picture" mind. *Empathy,* or the ability to walk in the shoes of another, is another of Pink's senses. Pink defines *empathy* as the "ability to understand what makes their fellow women tick, forge relationships, and to care for others" (p. 66). Sport marketing professionals need to examine *empathy* and place that quality high on their list of skills and attitudes.

Play, a historical characteristic of the profession of sport, is another of Pink's six senses. *Laughter* and *humor* are among the characteristics he recommends that one acquire. Pink (2005), who often uses play, extends the concept to spontaneous nondirected goal activity. It is childlike movement and thinking. It is the freedom found in dance, gymnastics, and synchronized swimming.

Meaning, what we do and what we provide for others, is the sixth, and last, of Pink's senses. By *meaning*, Pink (2005) means that vision which remains with us. For example, contrast your memories of walking through the gate at Daytona, sitting in the Super Bowl, yelling at the Orange Bowl, freezing in the lounge after dark at the Salt Lake Olympics with similar television events. According to Pink, attending an event provides lasting memories seldom achieved by watching an event on electronic media.

From all of Pink's work, the statement to take with you is: "Anyone can master the six Conceptual Age senses. But those who master them first will have a huge advantage" (Pink, 2005, p. 67). To be first to master these senses, or to find a niche, will be one of the most important achievements of the future.

Futurists tend to agree that in order to succeed or to plan for the future, one must change the way one thinks. Kida (2006), for example, cautions that we need to understand statistics, particularly probability theory, and use research rather than stories in making decisions. He notes that the ability to question an idea is more important than to merely confirm the idea. In addition, he suggests that we sometimes misperceive the world around us, oversimplify our thinking, and have faulty memories. In planning for the future, he recommends "strategic foresight."

Gardner (2006), in *Five Minds for the Future*, presents the following:

The *disciplined mind* has mastered one or more scholarly disciplines. Without at least one discipline, persons will be restricted to menial tasks.

The *synthesizing mind* gathers information and research from a wide range of sources, analyzes the information objectively, and fashions the results into a coherent idea or statement. Without synthesizing skills, people will be overwhelmed by information.

The *creative mind* generates new ideas, asks questions, and gains acceptance for the new ideas. Computers will replace all but the creative minds.

The *respectful mind* appreciates and respects all forms of diversity and enjoys working with others. Those without appreciation and respect will harm the work environment.
The *ethical mind* is empathetic to the needs and wishes of others. Those without ethics will harm the employer and coworkers. (p. 18–19).

He notes: "With these minds ... a person will be well equipped to deal with what is expected, as well as what cannot be anticipated; without these minds, a person will be at the mercy of forces that he or she can't understand, let alone control" (p. 2).

Gardner (2006) makes the point that one cannot be creative in a subject until one knows the subject. In the following description of the creative emphasis in the

United States in the 1980s, he states: "Everyone wanted to be creative; too many persons believed they were creative, even though they had scarcely begun to master a domain and even though no expert in the field would have judged them as creative.... Only through the honing of discipline would genuinely creative options ultimately emerge" (p. 85).

Naisbitt (2006) provides guidance in how to think. He mentions two important factors. First: "Understand how powerful it is not to have to be right" (p. xix). Doing so enables one to be creative—to retain a childlike approach to life. Second: "Don't get so far ahead of the parade that people don't know you're in it" (p. xix). In other words, work with others by using their familiar territory. He also recommends that when "looking for the shape of the future, look for and bet on the exploiters of opportunities, not the problem solvers" (p. 81).

According to Lombardo (2006), future consciousness "improves higher-order thinking abilities ... expands mental and behavior freedom ... can work against depression, fear, apathy and perceived helplessness ... and brings greater self-control over one's life" (p. 49).

Sport managers need to know that Gardner (2006) predicts: "Design and creativity are one of the key competitive advantages companies in developed economics can have—probably the only one they have left.... Fifteen years ago companies competed on price, now it's quality. Tomorrow it's design" (p. 124). Gardner (2006) goes on to quote Scott Morrison: "The aim today is to create products and services that 'look sharp, function intuitively, and wake some sort of positive emotional response from the consumer'" (p. 124).

According to Canton (2006). if you want to be proactive rather than reactive you can influence your future by adopting the following:

1. A future vision—clear vision.
2. A sound strategy to get there.
3. Tools to persuade key people—colleagues, teammates, family members, and so on—to commit to a shared vision and strategy.
4. Effective execution.

To be ready for the future, Canton (2006) recommends the following future-ready skills:

1. A positive outlook on the future.
2. Family and community involvement: a commitment to values.
3. Higher education.
4. Science and tech skills.
5. Financial awareness skills and personal money management.

Hines (2006) suggests six phases to be used in any order that seems appropriate to the leader or visionary. These phases will, hopefully, lead to clarity, creativity, and confidence. One phase is a comprehensive approach to problem identification and alternative scenarios. Here, objectives and outcomes are identified. Much of this phase is typical of existing planning systems; however, emphasis is placed on many alternatives rather than one path. Scanning, for example, in the organizational context, is the internal and external forces that fit an organization into the world in general. The remaining phases are as follows: 1) envisioning alternate futures; 2) identifying those preferred; 3) bridging the gap between the vision and action; 4) tailoring tactics and strategies to the organization; and 5) outlining the action phase, or how to carry out the vision (Hines, 2006). In addition to being a great planning process, the Hines system appears to engender employee loyalty. This method expands today's planning process to incorporate the culture of the business—to require all in the business to envision the future of the company and each individual's role in the company.

Conclusion

Hopefully, this chapter enabled you to dream and to think of how the future will affect your life. Prediction, as you will have noticed, becomes more difficult as the distance grows. The successful sport management professional in the year 2020 will be sensitive to people, welcome change, anticipate the needs of society, and be quick to bring new programs into reality. He or she will not only welcome and embrace change; he or she will also recognize the merits of timing—the timing of program delivery—as an element of the change process. Sport management professionals will have challenging and exciting careers if they have the following characteristics:

- They are sensitive to people and the world around them.
- They are eager to dream.
- They are diligent planners.
- They are able to make thing happen.

References

Aburdene, P. (2005). *Megatrends 2010*. Charlottesville, VA: Hampton Roads.

Bright Light, Big Savings. (2007). *Popular Science, 271* (1), 28.

Brown, A. (2006). The robotic economy, Brave new world or return to slavery? *The Futurist 40* (4), 50–55.

Canton, J. (2006). *The extreme future*. New York: Penguin Group.

Clement, A., & Hartman, B. (1994). *The teaching of physical skill*. Dubuque, IA: Brown/Benchmark.

Crossman, W. (2004). Voice in, voice out. *The Futurist, 41* (2), 27–28.

Crossman, W. (2007). *Voice in, voice out (VIVO)*. Oakland, CA: Regent Press.

Custer, K. J. (2007, Winter). From mice to men: Genetic doping in international sports. *30 Hastings Int'l & Comp. L. Rev.* 181.

DeBono, E. (1970). *Lateral thinking: Creativity step by step*. New York: Harper & Row.

Despommier, D. (2007). The vertical farmer. *Popular Science, 171* (1), 45–46.

Environment. (2007). *The Futurist, 41* (2), 8.

Gardner, H. (2006). *Five minds for the future*. Boston: Harvard Business School Press.

Hines, A. (2006). Strategic foresight: The state of the art. *The Futurist, 40* (5), 18–21.

Kida, T. (2006). *Don't believe everything you think: The 6 basic mistakes we make in thinking*. Amherst, NY: Prometheus.

Kuang, C. (2007). A giant leap for housing. *Wired, 15* (7), 76.

Kupetz, A. H. (2007). Our cashless future. *The Futurist, 41* (3), 36–40.

Lombardo, T. (2006). Thinking ahead: The value of future consciousness. *The Futurist, 40* (1), 45–50.

Naisbitt, J. (2006). *Mind set.* New York: Harper/Collins.

Parks, J., & Zanger, B. (Eds.). (1990). *Sports and fitness management, career strategies and professional content.* Champaign, IL: Human Kinetics.

Pink, D. H. (2005). *A whole new mind.* New York: Penguin Group.

Science Digest, August 1948.

Sweeney, J. (2007). Sport cast, 10 controversial issues confronting the sports industry. *The Futurist, 41* (1), 35–39.

Toffler, A. (1980). *The third wave.* New York: Bantam Books.

Tomorrow in Brief. (2007). *The Futurist, 41* (2), 2.

Waldrop, M. M. (1992). *Complexity.* New York: A Touchstone Book.

Weed, S. (2007). High dive. *Popular Science, 271* (1), 52–57, 97–98.

Zey, M. G. (2005a). *The ageless society.* A power point presentation (zeywfs05).

Zey, M. G. (2005b). The super longevity revolution. *The Futurist, 39* (6), 16–21.

Recommended Reading

Sterling, B. (July, 2007). Dispatches from the hyperlocal future. *Wired, 15* (7), 161–166.

DeBono, E. (1970). *Lateral thinking: Creativity step by step.* New York: Harper & Row.

The World Futures Society Publications

Recommended Exercises

1. Picture yourself at 100 years of age.
2. Describe sport in the global economy in 2030 by using only the visual culture.
3. Defend the use of video games to sharpen your intellectual skills.

Part 9

Career Opportunities

The concept of networking plays a vital role when searching for employment. The more people you know or who know you — in a professional discipline only increases the chances for connections.

Art Chase

Chapter 32

Career Opportunities

Herb Appenzeller
Tom Appenzeller

Herb: We started the sport management program at Guilford College as an interdisciplinary venture in 1980. Our department taught courses such as Introduction to Sport Management, Sport Philosophy, Sport Psychology, Legal Issues in Sport, and Sport Finance. Courses in computer science, business practices, financial management, sport sociology, micro/macro economics were taught by the various departments on campus. The arrangement worked well because all departments cooperated to make the sport management major work.

Our students responded well to the challenges offered them and soon received respect for their determination to succeed and their ability to handle courses offered by the various disciplines.

After 28 years, our students have achieved success in the sport industry. Our graduates have gone on to earn master's and doctorate degrees in sport administration. Because the students majored in sport management, they routinely chose advanced degrees in such fields as business administration (the MBA), political science, and sociology. In addition, many entered law school.

We can now give an accurate picture of our former undergraduate students and list some of the jobs that currently relate to their majors.

Some of our former students are athletic directors, business managers of athletics, equipment managers at large universities, facility managers, golf professionals, managers of golf courses, promoters of major golf tournaments, and teaching professionals. (One former student is the Director of the Nationwide Tour, and another is the Director of the MCI Heritage Golf Tournament at Hilton Head Island, South Carolina.) Other former students are tennis professionals, teachers, publishers of tennis magazines, and country club tennis professionals. Several operate major sport facilities such as the Greensboro Coliseum Complex. Many are in professional sport, such as baseball, basketball, golf, tennis, and football. Many are sport information directors at colleges and universities, while many are involved in sport marketing and sport television. A number of our former students entered the sport industry and later changed careers in jobs that required management and leadership skills. A number of our former students have become interested in the law after courses in legal issues in sport and are in the legal profession with law degrees. Still others became interested in risk management and now have their own companies that conduct risk assessments of facilities nationwide. The list goes on, but one thing is consistent among our graduates: those in the sport industry love their work and look forward to work each day.

Tom: Our sport management program at Wingate graduated its first major in 1994 and became a nationally approved program in 2001. Over the last 14 years, we have been very pleased with the success of our former students. One is assistant athletics director for North Carolina State University, and another was the youngest Division I equipment manager in the nation at Appalachian State University. Currently, two are in ticket operations for Virginia Tech and the University of Miami. A number of graduates have pursued master's degrees, with graduates holding jobs in professional football, professional basketball, professional ice hockey, NASCAR, golf course management, YMCA administration, health clubs, recreation management, sales, and coaching at the high school and college levels. Others are involved in media and communications (one is a television sport reporter in Charlotte, North Carolina).

In this section, a group of sport management majors tell the stories of how they entered the profession after graduation. Some changed directions in their careers but utilized the training they received in the program.

Athletic Administration

Mike Waddell, Associate Athletic Director,
University of Cincinnati, Cincinnati, Ohio

Since you were a sport management major, I have several questions for you.

1. Were your major courses helpful in your job? Which course would you recommend to other majors?

The mixture of business courses such as microeconomics, macroeconomics, accounting, and, of course, marketing have been vital to my career in college athletics. My career path of one day becoming a Division I director of athletics is more about fiscal responsibility, revenue generation, and personnel management than anything to do with a ball or bat. As such, I would be lost without the foundation of my business professors.

Looking back to my time in college, the most important courses to my eventual career path were the lecture classes which included guests from the real world of sport management. Having an industry leader as an advisor made every class that he taught the very best of the Guilford College classes I completed. His combination of professional experience on many levels merges well with his truism that we would all "change directions at least five times" during our career. If only I was so lucky!

Some of the guest lecturers who visited our sport management classes included Bernie Mullin, Debbie Yow, and Peter Roth, all of whom I have interacted with since graduation. I have also worked hard to maintain a network of alumni since having a sincere trust in the folks I hire is essential to our management team's success.

2. Where did you do your internship? Was it helpful and did it lead to your job?

My internship was spent with the Greensboro Monarchs of the East Coast Hockey League, and it was a great introduction to a variety of potential career paths. During my time with the franchise, I worked with media relations, corporate sales, multimedia broadcasting, player personnel, arena management, licensing and merchandising, ticket sales, human resources, as well as marketing and promotions—and the obligatory bailing minor league hockey players out of jail. I have used the experience from that internship in performing my professional duties over the past 17 years. Having the chance to work at the lowest of levels in the internship for no pay other than a $25 watch and a $100 Christmas envelope made me realize that working in sport management was not all glitz and glamour—it was hard work and it was performed during the times that many of my friends were off having fun.

This is the leisure entertainment business, and you have got to realize that we have jobs, not hours. If you approach the business in terms of 9 to 5, then you should choose another field because you are only going to get frustrated and eventually burn out. If you love adrenaline rushes, working 20-hour days half the year, and accomplishing team goals with interesting people in some fun (and not so enchanting) places, then this is the career path for you. And one last word to the wise, if you have never worked an "un-paid" internship, then please do not waste my time in applying for a job with any search I am connected to, because you will not last very long in the pool. Select your internship based on what opportunities you will be assigned and what other duties you can make for yourself within those which you are given. This will make you valuable to your internship mentor, and in the end you will more than likely either be offered a job or have a strong recommendation from the person for whom you have performed.

3. Explain your job description.

Workaholic ... problem solver ... rainmaker ... human resources expert ... conflict/resolution counselor ... in loco parentis ... insomniac—oops, too honest on that first description.

I am now in my 17th year working in sport management. I started as a radio and television broadcaster, as well as a graphics designer; then, I performed a combination of on-air work and broadcast sales: finally, I entered the administrative world of college athletics.

Since 1991, I have worked at Delta State University as a graduate assistant and assistant director of athletics; for the University of North Carolina Tar Heel Sports Network as a broadcaster and designer; at the University of Virginia as a broadcaster and broadcast sales manager; at Appalachian State University as a broadcaster, sales manager, and marketing director; at the United States Military Academy as the director of sports marketing and broadcasting; at the University of Akron as the associate director of athletics (and later as the interim director of athletics; and now at the University of Cincinnati as the senior associate director of athletics.

My day starts at around 5 a.m., with a wake-up call followed by a morning workout. I always beat my boss into the office, when I get there around 7 a.m. I try to be the last person to leave the office, but that has been harder since I need to be at home for dinner with the family as often as I can.

My present job oversight portfolio includes managing all external aspects of the UC Department of Athletics, including corporate sales, ticketing, marketing and promotions, game day operations and development, licensing and merchandising, media relations and multimedia development, information technology, along with sport oversight over men's soccer, men's and women's swimming and diving, and women's and men's golf. Add some civic boards, volunteer work, time with my staff for professional development, and attending most home and away football and men's basketball games, and the plate is getting a little crowded. But I love it and I cannot imagine doing anything else. It certainly beats tending a crop or loading a truck, neither of which I could do with any success.

4. How do you feel about your job? Positives and negatives.

Obviously I love my job, or I would not still be following this career path. I could make much more money by working in an advertising agency in New York or Los Angeles. As corny as it may seem, I really enjoy the fact that I have never spent a day since 1974 out of school. I like the interaction with the kids on campus since it keeps me thinking young, although my body keeps reminding me that I am no longer 21.

Here is a short list of positives and negatives.

+ I work with passionate, creative, and positive people on a daily basis and enjoy the ability to constantly be challenged mentally from some outstanding young people as student athletes and young professionals.

I have been exposed to some of the best people who have walked the face of the earth—some famous and others not so much, who give more of themselves than they take, a rarity.

I sit in better seats at sporting events than people who make $1,000,000 running Fortune 100 corporations—Ha Ha Ha!

I get to see young people come to college and witness their transformation into the best of the best that our nation produces.

− I work closely with the print media, which continue to amaze me with their lack of civility and respect for human decency. Unlike television and radio, the print media are generally some of the most miserable people I have encountered. This is more of a reflection of living in the 21st century, I suppose.

Our family has moved more than I care to put onto paper, which makes it hard for those around me. I have incredible support, and I appreciate that support more than I can state.

College athletics at the Division I level is becoming more about facilities and cash flow than about the welfare of the student athlete. The national leadership says one thing when the cameras are on, yet governs in a manner that defies common sense. There is no reason why the NCAA manual needs to be thicker than the Manhattan phone book or why we need two different three-point lines for men's and women's basketball. Title IX issues pressure some schools to add sports which make no sense, only to comply with participation numbers which were decided in a board room, and the inclusion of football into the equation leaves many Olympic sports on the cutting room floor. When you need to hire several attorneys to assist in the day-to-day management of a collegiate department of athletics, the intent has somehow gone astray. Money rules the day, in college athletics as in everyday society in modern-day America. There is no other example clearer than Division I college football and the lack of a playoff system because of supposed academic issues for the student athletes.

Athletic Administration

Brad Fisher, Assistant Athletic Director,
Reynolds High School, Winston-Salem, NC

After earning my undergraduate degree in sport management, I pursued my master's degree. While the work was more challenging, the rewards outlasted the extra effort. With my graduate degree, I began teaching and coaching at a small country school in central North Carolina. While there, I did an internship with the athletic office and learned the ropes of local and state high school rules. While interning, I worked with eligibility, scheduling, parent/coach relations, and, most important, time management. In teaching a full course load, coaching a sport, and being an athletic administrator for other sports, time is of the essence.

Since my internship ended, I have been named assistant athletic director at a 4A school in the 5th largest school district in the state. I represent the school at conference and county AD meetings. I am the director of the regional tournament and serve on the committees for three other tournaments. Of the 36 varsity and junior varsity sports we offer, I am the administrator for 18. I am in charge of the eligibility rules, physicals, schedules, transportation, booking of officials, and staff assignments to work the gate or clocks; also, I have many other responsibilities.

Without the help of my professors and classmates, I would not be where I am today. I hope to be an athletic director of my own school in the near future and owe all my hope to my classes in sport management.

Athletic Business Manager

Jeff Blythe, Georgia Southern University, Statesboro, Georgia

Sport management is a growing field for those who want to have a career in sports. It's a very important part of my life, and I hope that my story will help inspire those who want to enter the realm of sport management.

My life has always revolved around sports. In high school, I played on the tennis team. In order to help my parents pay for lessons, I received a job at the local country club working at the tennis pro shop. It was a great job. I learned how to string racquets and taught tennis clinics to area children. Part of my responsibilities were to reserve courts for club members, maintain the courts, buy and sell tennis merchandise, and help the manager with balancing the petty cash account at the end of each day. It was called a job, but I never considered it real work because I had a lot of fun. I did not know it at the time, but that job helped me understand what I really wanted to do as a career.

After high school, I went to the University of North Carolina at Chapel Hill. UNC was the only university I had ever wanted to attend. I worked extremely hard during high school, and my dream turned into reality when I enrolled at UNC during the fall of 1998. Entering college, I wanted to become a doctor. During my first year, I took a lot of math and science classes so that I would be on track for medical school.

Also during my freshman year, I worked with the North Carolina basketball program. My responsibilities included attending all practices for the junior varsity and attending all home games. We would set up the locker rooms and make sure everything was lined up correctly so that the coaches and players didn't have to worry about anything. It was a lot of fun, and I met some great people. It was hard work, but because I was living a dream, I never thought twice about it.

During the fall semester of my sophomore year, I met with my advisor. He looked over my course schedule and asked me how I was enjoying the chemistry and biology classes. I answered him honestly and told him that I was not passionate about them and thought it might be best to look for another career path. He smiled, and his response I will never forget. He told me that with my grades, there would not be a medical school in the country that would accept me and that I should reexamine my career choice. Obviously, I was disappointed, but I later told him that that was the best thing that could have happened to me.

Working at the country club and working with the Carolina basketball team was preparing me for my future career without my knowing it. I had no idea that there was a field called sport management and that you could do those sorts of jobs as a profession. I looked over all the majors at Carolina and noticed that there was one called Exercise and Sport Science. I then looked at the courses within that major and saw several classes that I might enjoy. During the spring of my sophomore year, I took a class from Professor Ron Hyatt entitled "The History of Sport." I absolutely loved everything about the class. Dr. Hyatt and I formed a friendship, and he told me about the world of sport management. He told me that with an advanced degree, I could work for any sports entity, including the athletic department at Carolina. From that moment, I knew what I wanted to do with my life.

For the next two years as an undergraduate, I took as many sport management classes offered and worked extremely hard so that I could attend graduate school. I was offered a paid internship with the North Carolina High School Athletic Association (NCHSAA) (located in Chapel Hill) that oversees all the high school athletic programs in North Carolina. The internship was a great learning experience for me because I saw firsthand people working within sports full time. The internship also reassured me that I was on the right track.

I earned my master's degree in sport administration at Appalachian State University in a program designed to give an individual a broad spectrum of choices into the world of sport management. I took classes such as sport law, facility management, and sport finance. I worked in the Holmes Convocation Center for my internship and saw how the event staff prepares for different kinds of events as well as how a box office operates. I worked closely with my professor on many research projects. I was very impressed with how dedicated he was, and still is, to the field of sport management. He has been a great mentor for me, and I continue to lean on him for advice to this day.

As I was finishing up my course work, I started to send out résumés and applications to different universities. I was due to graduate in December of 2003 and had no job lined up. Two weeks before graduating, I was starting to get desperate, and Dr. Hyatt from UNC called me and told me that he had a job lined up for me at the North Carolina High School Athletic Association (NCHSAA). A point to remember in this profession is that it is who you know, not what you know. I immediately called and put in my formal application, and I started working for the NCHSAA in January 2004.

My job at the NCHSAA was a great experience. I loved the people. I worked with the sports department and helped run high school state championships and helped sanction tournaments. I also updated the tournament brackets on the Web site—and basically carried out whatever other office chores needed to be done. During the spring, I was assigned to help with the high school state tennis championships. I was at one of the tournament sites and started talking to one of the volunteers who was the assistant tennis coach at Elon University. Elon was one of the places to which I had sent my résumé, but Elon did not have any job openings at the time. The tennis coach and I started talking about Elon, and he told me about a job opening in its athletic department. I was immediately excited about the opening, but I was uncertain about what to do with this potential job change. I had been working for the NCHSAA for only six months. A lot of people had helped me get the job, and I felt that if I left after working there for such a small amount of time, I would burn bridges and upset these outstanding individuals. I knew that eventually I wanted to work in college athletics, but I didn't know if Elon was the right fit. I spoke with many people about what do and finally decided that it would be best for my career if I left the high school ranks and started my career in college athletics. It was one of the hardest decisions I've ever had to make because I left some really good people, but deep down, I knew it was the right thing to do.

My official title at Elon was the Assistant Business Manager and Ticket Manager. I learned quickly that at the smaller schools, athletic department personnel do many different things. I came to Elon in the summer of 2004, and because I was the ticket manager, I had to immediately learn how to operate the ticket software and print and mail season football tickets. I worked very closely with the development office in making sure the Elon donors had the correct tickets and parking passes. I was thrown into the fire, but I adapted quickly. Once you begin your job in athletics, you will learn what you like to do and what you dislike to do. At Elon, I learned that I enjoyed the business side of sports. I enjoyed helping coaches and staff with the internal operations of running an athletic department. Taking care of budget reports and financial data was fun to me. I was very content with my position at Elon; however. there was no opportunity for advancement.

After three years at Elon, my supervisor knew that I was growing uncertain about my future. He knew that I wanted to concentrate my efforts on the business side. In the spring of 2007, he told me about a job opening at Georgia Southern University as the Assistant Athletic Director for Business and Finance. I knew about Georgia Southern because GSU and Elon are in the same athletic conference. I had a lot of reservations about leaving Elon because of its location and the comfort level I felt. My wife and I are both from North Carolina, and for us to move to Georgia would be difficult. We had just bought a home in Elon, and financially it made no sense to move. But after much internal debate, the GSU opening was an opportunity that I could not pass up. Sometimes in life, you have to take a gamble and a leap of faith.

I took the job at Georgia Southern in April 2007. I oversee all the business operations in the athletic department. I am about to finish up six months on the job and have loved the responsibility as well as what the position entails. This position has more responsibility in the human resource side of athletics, which is fun to learn. After taking this job, at the age of 26, I found out that I am one of the youngest assistant athletic directors in the country for a school the size of Georgia Southern. I've had to leave two great places to work and I've had to make some very difficult decisions in the process. I still have the goal of going back to Chapel

Hill and working for my alma mater, but I am in no hurry. I am very eager to see where this road is going to take me. I feel very blessed and very fortunate to have gotten where I am. Many people have helped me along the way, including those that I mentioned and many more. My wife and my family have been by my side through this entire process, and I owe a lot of my success to them. I am always learning new things and meeting new people and want to help those that want to get their career started in sports. It's a fascinating field. You have to put in a lot of hours and a lot of hard work, but if you love sports, it's definitely worth it.

Cheerleading Coach

Elizabeth Appenzeller

I decided that I wanted a career in sport management after my first year in law school. Law school was great, but I missed classes that had a direct focus on sport. I left law school and went on to obtain a master of science degree in sport studies. While I was working toward my master's degree, I discovered that I enjoyed working with college athletes, and I began to focus on collegiate athletic administration. I set a career goal for myself to work in college athletics.

There are many different areas of collegiate administration, including compliance, business management, and academic advising. I have been open to trying a variety of areas in athletic administration in the hope that I will discover an area that I am truly passionate about.

Currently, I am a collegiate coach. College coaching for me has been an opportunity to learn how college athletic departments really function. I have learned about home game event management, budgets, the Champs Life Skills program, fund-raising, and so forth. I believe that my time as a college coach will better prepare me for a job in collegiate athletic administration. College coaches have unique job needs, and it is important that administrators know how to work with coaches to maximize the success of each individual sport in their department.

Through my cheerleading coaching, I am the coauthor (with two other risk management experts) of the book *Cheerleading and the Law: Risk Management Strategies*. The book became available February 2008. I have also been a consultant for cheerleading at several universities.

Professional Soccer

Emily Ballus, MOJO Sports Event Solutions, California

Childhood memories of attending games, my passion for team play, and the joy of being around sports propelled me to choose sport management as a major. That was over twenty years ago. Today, with hundreds of sports event productions behind me, a BS and MS in sport management, and a doctorate in the works, I run my own company. My collective experiences, affinity for challenges, and ongoing sport management education prepared me for this entrepreneurial leap.

For years, I made other people's ideas a reality or turned their visions into success. Working as an agent of change or start-up authority, I participated in the launch of Major League Soccer, contributed to the single-sport attendance record-setting 1999 FIFA Women's World Cup, played a part in the launch of the women's pro soccer league, WUSA, and developed other national and local community sports events. Fortified by this experience and anxious to develop my own shows, I formally launched my company in 2003—MOJO Sports Event Solutions, LLC—which assists companies, leagues, and nonprofits with sports event organization and execution.

Additionally, MOJO Sports is a vehicle for hands-on learning and instruction for entry-level sport management graduates. Through MOJO Sports, I continue to leverage existing sport relations to place high-caliber sport management graduates in positive sports environments, to lobby sport management programs to align with their business schools to strengthen the program in the corporate realm, and to foster support from the professional leagues to hire sport management majors first on a consistent basis.

Years of study in the practical sense have made me a field expert. But sport management programs have provided me with the foundation and opportunity to gather best practices and ideas of dedicated and experienced faculty and career sports executives, to study the current trends of the business, to learn from fellow classmates, and to participate in courses that are stimulating and relevant.

In their book *Successful Sport Management* (1st edition), Drs. Guy Lewis and Herb Appenzeller state: "As the body of information on sport management increases, the arrangement of that information can become increasingly precise through conferences and additional publications. When this happens, sport management will take its place as an appropriately recognized branch of the management field."

What Drs. Lewis and Appenzeller could add today, almost 20 years later, is that sport has evolved into a fiercely competitive, research driven, results-oriented, technical, and savvy multibillion dollar industry that increasingly requires expertise in contract law, finance, facilities, marketing, management, and human resources and that demands the specialization which sport management programs offer. Sport management coursework is on target for issues relevant today and key in the future. There are the proliferation of multimillion dollar player contracts; scandals surrounding corporate America's ethics generally; fast launches or quick demises of emerging sports leagues; the prevalence of sports litigation; labor relations and work stoppages; and the enormous amount of money and broadcast exposure driving the industry. Therefore, courses such as Ethics in Sports, Legal Aspects, Labor Relations, Sports Entrepreneurship, Facility Management, and so forth are meaningful career-oriented courses that guide professional and ethical executives. The pedagogic diversity, the national and international business scope, and the hands-on opportunities afforded reinforce the major's mission to educate the world's next sport executives through instruction, study, and opportunity.

The sport management major provides the finest technical tactics and academic strategies to do original and noteworthy research and to cultivate innovative and progressive business. As sport management *is* taking its place as an established genre of management, sport business programs will and must emerge to provide sport executives continued intellectual involvement and sophistication in the study of the field. Following this example, I continue to take classes while I build my company. But more important, I keep adding to my twenty-some years of fun, thanks to my sport management vocation.

Risk Management

David Harlowe, The Sport Management Group

I graduated from college in 1991 with a BS in Sport Management. I was working as an assistant football coach at the time. I thoroughly enjoyed coaching, but I knew it was not going to be my livelihood. From coaching, I moved into the field of personal fitness training. I worked at a local health club for a while until I decided that I wanted to concentrate solely on personal training. I started working at a personal training studio and initially liked the work. My greatest love in the business was working with athletes. Unfortunately, at that time the personal training business centered on nonathletic individuals. I was also quickly learning that not everyone in the business was properly trained in good business practices. So I decided to venture out on my own.

I put together a business plan, got a loan, and started my own personal training studio. I liked having my own business, but I still had the desire to work in athletics—the field for which my sport management degree had prepared me. After about a year of running my fitness center, I could see that I was just not where I wanted to be. I began talking to people about what I should do, and I decided to point myself in the direction of a risk management career. About three months before I shut down the fitness center, I started another company that was completely based on risk management in the fitness industry. I realized that there was a need for people in risk management in fitness just as in any other industry. So I began cold-calling insurance companies to see if they were interested in my new services. I found my first client in Pennsylvania and began building my company from there.

In the 12 years since I started my company, I have performed over six thousand inspections on health clubs around the country. It was not easy in the beginning, because I was my only employee, which meant I had to travel all over the country performing inspections for my clients. It's a hard life traveling all the time, but the results have been worth it. While my company was slowly growing, I still had the desire to work with athletic programs. I had built my own Web site and stated on it that I could perform inspections for high schools and colleges. One day, I received a call from a potential client in New York. It was a small college that was looking for someone to identify risks within their athletic and intramural programs. It was the break I was looking for. I had plenty of experience with the inspection process, but I wanted to make sure I knew as much as I could before visiting the campus. I began studying NCAA rules, Americans with Disabilities Act laws, and so forth. It was quite exciting to expand my knowledge in the field. I was awarded the contract and went to New York. For such a small school, it had an outstanding athletic and intramural program as well as some rather large facilities. I was finally getting to do what I had always wanted to do.

One of the most rewarding parts of working with an athletic program compared with a health club is that when an athletic administration brings you in, it is going to listen to you. One bad thing about the fitness industry is that many naysayers don't believe in what I do and have the attitude of "that's why we have insurance." Do not get me wrong: there are a lot of good people who try to comply with industry standards and guidelines, but as a whole, the industry needs a lot of help. That attitude lets me know there will always be work for me in the fitness industry. If you ask me though, athletics is where it is. It is such a great feeling to visit a campus, make recommendations, and then go back later to see that what you told the administration has been put into place. And the perks are wonderful, too. I have walked the sidelines of professional football teams, brushed shoulders with major college coaches, and have been included in longtime college traditions (some of which I had to recommend stopping).

Because I was able to major in sport management, I have countless opportunities to provide a service to the sport industry that can make a difference in the lives of many people.

Sport Insurance

John M. Sadler

The nonprofit and for-profit organizations that conduct sports and recreation activities rely heavily on the sports and recreation insurance industry to provide essential risk management and risk transfer services that allow the games and fun to go on. Quite simply, without these essential services, the very real threat of litigation arising from participant injury and spectator injury would provide a powerful disincentive and the resulting cessation of activities. Within this context, the sports and recreation insurance industry can provide career opportunities that are challenging, rewarding, exciting, and of vital importance to society.

The sport and recreation industry is vast, and it includes amateur sports, professional sports, Motor Sports, extreme sports, amusement parks, concerts, camps, events and attractions, venues, gaming, fairs, festivals, arenas, community centers, sportsplexes, fitness centers, outfitters and guides, hunting and fishing, and gymnastics/martial arts/dance studios. Each of these areas have its own unique exposures to loss and relies on insurance professionals in the fields of underwriting, claims adjusting, risk management, loss control, actuarial analysis, regulatory compliance, automation, and marketing.

Most professionals who are currently employed in the sports and recreation insurance industry are educated insurance veterans who ended up in the sports and recreation niche by accident. However, a growing number of employees have actively sought out career opportunities in this niche to match their passions for sports and recreation. Many have come from backgrounds in amateur sports, professional sports, or the amusement industry.

The sport and recreation insurance industry is estimated to encompass $3 billion to $5 billion in premium volume, which consists of many different policy types, including General Liability, Directors' and Officers' Liability, Business Auto, Workers' Compensation, Property, Inland Marine, Life, Disability, and Health. This niche employs approximately 3,000 employees nationwide, who are primarily employed by insurance carriers, managing general agencies, insurance agencies, claims administration firms, loss control firms, and consulting firms.

Most of the key employees in this niche have college educations as well as special professional designations such as CIC, CPCU, ARM, JD, CLU, and CPA. Many of these designations can be earned at the expense of the employer while working full time. A college degree in insurance and risk management is a plus but is not a requirement of most employers. On-the-job training and in-house education are still the best source of essential skills. Many employers actually prefer to hire new college graduates with good people skills and to train them through a combination of in-house education and special outside courses.

Those who have a passion for sports and entertainment should strongly consider a career in the insurance industry to maximize their potential job satisfaction. By doing so, it is possible to mix business and pleasure.

Sport Television Leads to Career Changes

Rob Goodman

From the time I was a child, I wanted to be a sportscaster. If given my choice, I wanted to be one of the walking commentators for CBS Sports' coverage of the PGA TOUR. That was it; there was no other career for me, and I was certain of it. While attending Guilford College, I learned of a major called "sport management." I really did not know what it was, but it revolved around sports, so I figured I would at least be headed in the right direction to reach my television goal.

As I got into the major, I realized that these courses were more about the law and business aspects of sports than I wanted, but it was interesting, so I stayed with it. That decision would pay off many years down the road when I started my own business. My school advisor and the head of the major worked with me to craft my own little television portion of the sport management program. After my junior year in college, I started an internship at the CBS television affiliate in Greensboro, North Carolina.

After a successful summer internship, I continued working with the sports department at this station, and as time passed, I began covering and reporting on sports events for the station. Throughout my senior year of college, I continued at a local station and gained additional experience and confidence. My advisor arranged for me to get college credits for my work at the TV station because I was learning so much in that environment.

Upon graduation with a BS in sport management and a minor in political science, I was hired at the local television station as a part-time sports producer. The more experienced I became, the more confidence I gained. A short time after graduation, I was named the sports producer at WFMY-TV. Then, I had to work my way into an on-air position, which would be much more difficult. Conventional wisdom suggested that aspiring young television professionals needed to start in a very small market to learn the business. That route generally requires a two-year stay in a market, followed by a two-year stay in a bigger market, and so on.

I was not interested in small-market television because from the time I started my internship, I was covering the nation's best college basketball in the Atlantic Coast Conference, as well as NASCAR and the PGA TOUR. I had it all right here, and I was determined to make it to an on-air position in the Greensboro-High Point-Winston-Salem market, which at the time was the 46th largest market in the country.

It was not long before the sports director at the local station allowed me to do a story for air. When that worked out, my job responsibilities changed to include both sports producing and sports reporting. What started with stories making the air turned into brief anchor appearances and occasional live shots from sports events. Later, I was named the weekend sports anchor. As the sports anchor, I was telling stories of games, but I was often tossing the broadcast to someone who was reporting live from the game. I missed being at the game. If I was to attain my childhood goal of a becoming a walking broadcaster on a network of golf broadcasts, I needed experience at the game; I did not need to be chained to the anchor desk. As fate would have it, I was moved to the position of sports reporter so that I could provide live reports from sports events.

In this phase of my television career, I reported on the NCAA Basketball Tournament, the Atlantic Coast Conference Basketball Tournament, NASCAR events, PGA TOUR events, as well as local events such as community swim meets and minor league baseball. Our station decided to start a weekend morning show, and I was chosen to anchor the morning sports. That meant arriving at work by about 5 a.m. to prepare for a 6 a.m. broadcast on Saturday and Sunday of every week. It was great exposure for me and a great opportunity, but it was not what I wanted to do.

A few months later, I began looking for another job in another city because I had advanced as far as I possibly could at the local channel. The right television situation never presented itself, so I decided it was time for a career change. I had enjoyed covering NASCAR a great deal and put the word out that if the right NASCAR media-relations job came along, I would be interested. My broadcasting career would have to wait.

About a month later, I was covering a golf tournament near Winston-Salem, North Carolina, called the Vantage Championship on the same weekend a NASCAR Winston Cup (now NASCAR Sprint Cup Series) race was being run in nearby North Wilkesboro. The sports marketing department at R. J. Reynolds Tobacco Company was running the golf tournament and activating the sponsorship of the NASCAR race. I had a conversation with the president of Sports Marketing Enterprises (SME) about a job opening in his department. Two interviews later, I was making my first major career change. After seven years in television, I was moving to the corporate world to be a part of a behemoth of a sport called NASCAR. I was excited and scared at the same time, and it turned out to be a fantastic career move.

Working at a tobacco company was not easy because the tide of public opinion was beginning to turn against tobacco sponsorships. I was now a media-relations person for R. J. Reynolds' sports sponsorships, and there were definitely challenges. I had no idea how many government restrictions had already been placed on the tobacco industry regarding how it could market its product. Almost everything we did had to be approved by the legal department to ensure that it was within the guidelines.

Upon starting at SME, I was one of the team public relations representatives for the Camel-sponsored Smokin' Joe's Racing Team. Our NASCAR entry was driven by Jimmy Spencer. Our two NHRA Winston Drag Racing (Now NHRA PowerAde Drag Racing) entries were driven by Top Fuel Dragster driver Jim Head and Funny Car Driver Gordie Bonin. The team also included an Unlimited Hydroplane Racing Association boat and four American Motorcyclist Association motorcycles. My primary responsibilities were in NASCAR and NHRA, but I made multiple visits to the boat and motorcycle events, too.

In addition to my Motor Sports responsibilities, I took over as the director of media relations for the Vantage Championship, the Senior PGA TOUR event (now the PGA TOUR's Champions Tour). A couple of years later, I began working with the media representative for the NASCAR Winston Cup Series as well as the Smokin' Joe's racing team. Eventually, the Camel brand marketing group decided to get out of Motor Sports, so the NASCAR and NHRA teams took Winston sponsorship. At that time, I became the media contact for the NHRA Winston Drag Racing Series, but my responsibilities also included the Team Winston Top Fuel Dragster, the Team Winston Funny Car, and the Team Winston Pro Stock Motorcycle.

It was a delicate balance because I was the media representative for the series as well as for these Winston-sponsored teams. Each week, I distributed news releases about both the teams and the series. I had to work very hard to show the other drivers that while I represented Team Winston, I could also be objective and represent them, too. To that end, I never wore a Team Winston shirt at the race track. All of my shirts said NHRA Winston Drag Racing to help show that I represented the entire sport, not just one team. It seemed like a small thing, but it made a huge difference.

Standard operating procedure at SME was to switch people around to different programs every couple of years. So after my two amazing years in drag racing, I was moved back to the NASCAR program as an assistant manager of media relations for the NASCAR Winston Cup Series. A short time later, I was promoted to manager of media relations.

My last five years at SME were also the last five years of Winston's NASCAR sponsorship. After signing a five-year extension to the sponsorship, the dynamics changed in the tobacco industry, and R. J. Reynolds decided to end its NASCAR sponsorship after 33 years. I believed it was a short-sighted decision because I was confident the company could weather the storm. When NASCAR signed Nextel Communications as their next title sponsor, it was clear my job would terminate at the end of 2003. RJR was disbanding its sports marketing department after 33 years of unparalleled success.

I interviewed with Nextel, and it appeared I would continue my current responsibilities with a new company. Things changed, however, and Nextel decided to fill their media relations department with people who had not been associated with the Winston sponsorship. I interviewed with several great companies, and I could have had my pick of jobs if I had been willing to move to either the Charlotte area or Indianapolis. I had been married for one year, and I had made a commitment to stay in Greensboro, North Carolina. In my job search, while I was up for some very good jobs that required moving to a new city, many people told me that they needed me for a certain project, event, or period of time but that they did not want to add a position. So since no jobs felt right and I was not willing to move, I thought I could work part-time for a bunch of different companies and have the equivalent of full-time work. I started my own business in March of 2004.

3-G Sports, LLC was designed to be a multifaceted business focused on media relations and sponsorship management. I set it up with a generic name because I did not want to be known as a sport-marketing company or a media-relations company. One of the great things about working in sports marketing at RJR was that we were all involved in many different aspects of the sponsorships. So while my title always said media relations, I also dealt with signage, sponsorship issues, VIP hosting, and just about every aspect of sponsorship operations. Since the majority of my relationships were in Motor Sports and golf, I thought my business would be heavy in those two areas. I had done more Motor Sports than golf, so I figured I would be very busy in NASCAR-related business, and I thought it would eventually be great if there was some golf business, too.

The first year was predictably slow, but because of the amazing severance package from RJR, I was still being paid my normal salary for most of the year. That guaranteed income allowed me to start a business without fear of money issues. I knew I could pay my bills whether the new company made any money or not. I had one major client in Texas during that first year. I served as a NASCAR consultant for this company that was considering a major jump into NASCAR. I was their conduit into the sport to determine if the project they wanted to do was possible. After several months on this project, it became apparent that it was not possible, so the consultancy ended. However, since I was still being paid by RJR, all of that money went into the bank, which meant that year two was possible.

Also during that first year, I met a man named Mark Brazil, the tournament director for the PGA TOUR event in Greensboro, North Carolina. Mark agreed to meet with me, and I told him I wanted to be his director of media relations since he did not have anyone in that capacity. He was interested, but he was not in a position to hire me at that time. I told him I was certain my contacts at the PGA TOUR would write him letters on my behalf. He told me he did not need such references, because my contacts had already been calling him to ask why he had not hired me yet. Hearing that was very nice and a huge confidence boost. Later that year, 3-G Sports was retained to manage media relations for the FootJoy Boys Invitational, a major American Junior Golf Association tournament held in Greensboro, North Carolina, on the same course the PGA TOUR used.

After a successful run in the AJGA event, 3-G Sports was retained as a media consultant for the PGA TOUR event so that I could determine what needed to change and what needed to stay the same within this tournament's media-relations area. While I was just a consultant, I served as more of a media-relations director. This tournament was in the very early part of a complete change in the way it operated. For more than 60 years, the Greensboro Jaycees had run the tournament, but now the PGA TOUR was mandating that every tournament be run by professionals in every area.

Under the old business model, a different person would manage the media effort each year, meaning there was no continuity in the effort. Members of the media did not have a consistent contact because it changed every year. In early 2006, I became the director of media relations for this PGA TOUR event, and in just its third year, 3-G Sports had its first base client. The income from the Wyndham Championship would pay the bills, meaning that income from the remaining clients would allow the company to grow. Other clients followed, and while 3-G Sports has had a consistent Motor Sports presence since its inception, more than half of my business was then golf-related, which was definitely not what I expected. Landing the Wyndham Championship as my base client was the key that unlocked the growth potential of my business.

Now, in 2007, 3-G Sports, LLC is in its fourth year, and I am close to signing two new major golf clients. One of them is a golf course, and the other is a business that provides a service for the PGA TOUR. While I am confident both of these new clients will come through, until both parties sign the contract, there are no guarantees. If both of these agreements are signed, 3-G Sports will have reached, in just four years, the level at which it can sustain itself for years to come.

And if both of these agreements are signed, 3-G Sports will be about 90% golf and 10% Motor Sports, which is just about opposite of what I expected when I started the company in March 2004. Running a company is also very different from my original career goal. When I was growing up, I always wanted to be a golf commentator on network television, but as years pass, things change and priorities evolve. Now my priority is to make 3-G Sports the best company it can possibly be so I can be in business for myself for a very long time.

So why have I been successful? What made it possible for 3-G Sports to experience slow, steady, healthy growth? It started with my decision to major in sport management. I could not possibly have known at the time, but the decision then to learn about sport management made it possible for me to be running a successful business now. It is also the relationships I have had over the years.

I operate 3-G Sports with the same philosophy. I learned my priorities are to create and nurture the relationships that allow me to do my job, pay close attention to detail, and leave nothing to chance. Strong relationships are vital to the success of any venture. The 3-G Sports philosophy couples strong relationships with flawless execution to help clients achieve their business objectives. I believe in investing time to understand each client's concerns and goals. At the end of the day, a successful event, project, sponsorship, or marketing venture is determined by the bottom line, and there's only one true measure of success: Did my business accomplish my client's stated business objective? 3-G Sports is still a very young company, but I truly believe that my business philosophy will make my business successful over the long term. For additional information on my business and a client list, please visit www.3-gsports.com.

Director of Athletic Annual Fund

Michael Roach

I graduated from college in May 1994. While majoring in sport management, I learned from my advisor a number of tricks of the trade, such as never to say "no comment" if I was asked a question. As I came to the end of my collegiate career, I did not know what I was going to do. I played basketball in college, and as just about anyone who knew me could tell, I loved college sports. I knew that with my love of sports and my degree in sports management, I wanted to work in college athletics.

My first year out of school, I was fortunate to find an assistant basketball coaching position at Presbyterian College in Clinton, South Carolina. It was the second assistant position, and I thought it was a great opportunity for me to see if coaching was what I really wanted to do. I stayed at Presbyterian for two years and really enjoyed my time there. It gave me great insight into how the coaching world worked and how much time the profession required. While I was at Presbyterian, it won the South Atlantic Conference Tournament and received a bid for the NCAA Division II Tournament. At the end of my second year, I made a tough decision to leave the coaching business, because I felt it was too time-consuming and not as fulfilling as I had hoped.

After several years in corporate America, I missed working in higher education. I started networking and was offered the job of Assistant Director of Alumni Relations at my alma mater. This was a great way of getting back into working at a college. I did many things while there: I worked on setting up alumni events, working with the Alumni Board, heading up the Family Leadership Council, sending out e-mails to recent alumni, and planning events for Homecoming. While I was there, I realized that my long-term career goal was to work in college athletics, and I knew that for me to reach my ultimate goal, I must move on.

Again, through networking, I found a job at Wake Forest University in the development office for the Law School. I was the Assistant Director of Law Development and Alumni Relations. I took this job because I thought it would help me reach my goal of working in athletics. While I was at Wake Forest, I had a couple of charges. My most important charge was to raise money for the annual fund. This was done with individual calls on alumni of the school, and then I put together fund-raising events at law firms where a certain number of alumni were working. I also worked closely with the director in organizing agendas for the Law Alumni Council and the Law Board of Visitors. Also during my calls, I sought individuals who would be candidates for either of these groups. Wake Forest was a great institution to work for, and after three years for working there, I finally returned to athletics.

I was offered a job in the 49er Club as the Director of the Athletic Annual Fund at the University North Carolina at Charlotte. I was excited about being offered a position at a Division I institution that was in a well-known conference, Conference USA. As my title read, I was in charge of raising money for the Athletic Annual Fund. I made individual calls on alumni and friends of the university, asking for money from first-time donors and for increases in gifts from previous donors. While at Charlotte, I started a telethon using the Student Athletic Advisory Council to call on former student athletes. My goal was to lay the groundwork to educate current and former student athletes about the importance of their involvement in fund-raising. I also started a fee-based student booster group for current students who were enthusiastic supporters of athletics. In the first year, we had over 120 members. Again, I was trying to lay the groundwork for future donations by introducing the 49er Club to students while they were in school so that when they graduated, we could continue our relationship with them and would have a strong basis for asking for fund-raising dollars. Two other jobs I had were overseeing a hospitality room we opened before all home men's basketball games and obtaining trade-outs and organizing rooms and meals for athletic teams while the university was not open.

After a little more than two years at Charlotte, an opportunity presented itself at the University of North Carolina at Greensboro. The position of Director of the Spartan Club opened up, and I decided to submit an application. Because of the excellent experience I had gained at Charlotte, I felt I had an opportunity for the job and was thrilled when it was offered to me. At UNCG, I oversee all fund-raising for athletics, which includes annual-fund and endowments gifts. There is great potential for the Spartan Club to be very successful, but it is going to take much work from me and my staff. We need to work diligently to get alumni, friends of the program, and community leaders involved in Spartan athletics. One of the first things I did upon taking the job was to make changes to our executive committee by adding more members. The main goal of the executive committee is fund-raising. Previously, there were only 10 members, and I did not think this was an adequate number of members for a school that has around 100,000 alumni. I am also trying to upgrade the golf classic fund-raiser that the Spartan Club holds every year by moving it to a country club, where most people would not be able to play. Another one of my main focuses is to improve and maintain good communication with former student athletes. There are many challenges that face me in my current position, and I welcome them as I grow in my career in college athletics. I look forward to my time at UNCG, and when I leave, I will be able to say I have left a positive mark on the Spartan Club.

My career path has been somewhat circuitous, but I feel that my sport management degree has been at the foundation of all of my jobs. I have a passion for sports and specifically college athletics. My degree has allowed me many experiences and many career opportunities, and I am enjoying all of them.

Golf Management

Greg Lewandrowski, Teaching Professional,
IMG at El Conquistador Golf and Country Club

After a successful high school athletic and academic career in upstate New York, I escaped to a warmer climate to play golf and pursue a higher education. I thought North Carolina would be the perfect state to do so. After applying to Duke, North Carolina-Chapel Hill, and Wake Forest, I finally decided to attend Guilford College, mainly because it was the only school of the four to offer a sport management major.

Under the tutelage of my professors in the classroom and my golf coach, my future eventually began to take shape. I eventually became the Outstanding Sport Management Major of the Year award winner and started on the college's nationally ranked golf team.

I also became a student intramural director, eventually winning a Student Life Service Award. In addition, I became a sport studies departmental assistant.

Within the sport management major, I was required to serve two internships. My first was as a golf club assistant at The Cardinal.

While there, I worked under the supervision of PGA Professional Rick Murphy. I believe this is where I got the golf teaching bug while working on my own game. I also learned the idiosyncrasies of the entire golf club operation.

My second internship was as the athletic director's assistant. I shadowed Guilford's athletic director. It was very exciting to see how all the different coaches interacted to make up a successful Division III athletic department. It was also an eye opener to see the huge responsibility the athletic director had overseeing the entire program.

Nearing graduation, I decided to pursue a graduate degree. After applying to North Carolina-Chapel Hill, Georgia, Georgia Southern, and Miami, I finally decided to attend Florida State University (FSU), again pursuing the sunshine, more year-round golf, and a higher education.

While at FSU, I majored in physical education, specializing in athletic administration and coaching. I also had a graduate assistantship teaching golf. In addition, I had an internship as the assistant golf coach for neighboring Florida A&M University (FAMU). It was a fantastic time to be there because Florida State's football team won the national title, and Charlie Ward won the Heisman Trophy, under the tutelage of the all-time winningest coach, Bobby Bowden. FSU also made it to baseball's College World Series.

The basketball team had made it to the Elite Eight of the NCAA Tournament the year before as well. This was my first taste of big-time Division I athletics. I also coached National Minority Champion Robert Ames of FAMU to the title that year of my internship.

Upon graduating with my master's degree from FSU, I decided to get into the PGA's Golf Professional Training Program. I had to pass the PGA's Player's Ability Test and 21 academic courses about the people, the business, and the game. Four years later, I was elected as a class "A" member of the Professional Golf Association.

Soon after, I applied to IMG to be a golf professional at its David Leadbetter Golf Academy (DLGA) in Bradenton, Florida. I was honored to be hired there because David is renowned as the #1 golf coach in the world. Also, I found it ironic that I was working indirectly for Mark McCormack's world famous International Management Group.

I really felt at home at DLGA using all of my former training on golf mechanics, golf course management, sport psychology, physical fitness, and nutrition. I taught many of the top juniors in the world there, including Michelle Wie. The golf academy is intertwined with the Nick Bollettieri Tennis Academy, as well as many other sports, including football, baseball, basketball, soccer, hockey, and even fishing.

Recently, IMG invested in the nearby private El Conquistador Golf and Country Club. This led me to an opportunity to become the club's teaching professional, where I teach the members, run tournaments, and help run the everyday operation of the club. This seems like the perfect culmination up to this point of my career.

I now look forward to passing on my knowledge to future sport management and golf management students and professionals. Several Professional Golf Management (PGM) programs have sprung up around the country, including Florida Gulf Coast University in nearby Fort Myers, Florida. In addition, the University of South Florida, in nearby Tampa, Florida, has an excellent physical education and athletic program. I plan to offer my services to these universities if the opportunity presents itself.

The Legal Profession

Randy Stowell

"Go get 'em," my law partners say to me each time I head off to trial.

To this day, every time I sit in the cavernous, stately appointed courtrooms, I wonder to myself how amazing it is that I am about to do what few people ever get the opportunity to do. I know that a jury is waiting for me to hear what I have to say, to present my case, and I know it will then render a verdict.

At times, I still marvel that national insurance companies entrust the defense of their cases, sometimes worth seven figures, to me, Randy Stowell from Guilford College, class of '83.

The root of my interest in the law was born in my college days. I went to college for the wrong reason—to play football—and wound up getting an education and a foundation for my future.

Although I was not a very good student, my major in sport management, my class work in Business Law and Sports and the Courts, and my extra curricular work on the newsletter *From the Gym to the Jury* planted the seed for my career in the legal profession.

I did not immediately go to law school, partially because I did not feel I had the grades to get in. Then, one day, I decided to listen to the voice that had followed me since college and make the legal profession my career.

I went to the Stetson University College of Law and sat with an admissions faculty member and explained my background. His response was, "Don't bother applying." Undaunted, I applied, was accepted, and even had that same professor for Contract Law! I graduated with honors and never looked back.

Under the mentorship, guidance, and friendship of my professors, I acquired perseverance and a steady work ethic, and I learned that, while grades are important, who you are and how you go about doing things will determine your success in any career you choose.

Whatever the career choice, my advice has been and always will be:

"Go get' em!"

Motor Sports

Heidi Mowrey, BrinksRacing, Inc.

BrinksRacing, Inc. started with one man's dream and vision and my ability to utilize the solid foundation that I was taught during my years of sport studies. Michael Anthony "Mike" Brinkley (president and CEO of BrinksRacing, Inc.), Heidi Brian Mowery (vice president and CMO of BrinksRacing, Inc.) crossed paths in November 2006. It was like those stories you hear about people stumbling on the "vintage Corvette" that the widower has covered up in the old tobacco barn on what once was a thriving farm—except in this case, it was a 260 Dragster, and it was carefully housed in Mike's garage. Mike had always said he had a "rail" he raced for fun, but then in North Carolina, doesn't *everybody* have some aspiration to be a race car driver? After all, the state is known as "the Motor Sports state." So naturally, I dismissed Mike's comments. But the old adage Seeing Is Believing became a reality. I looked at this dragster, looked at Michael, and said, "Can you really drive this thing?" (I was silently thinking, "This is at least two thousand horsepower, he's bluffing. I'm going to call his bluff!"). We met at a professionally sanctioned quarter-mile track, and all I remember was the smell of raw hydrogen burning and he was gone. Shortly after that, we founded BrinksRacing, Inc.

Michael's vision and our vision at BrinksRacing is to be the first Top Fuel Operation in North Carolina, complete with fabrication, all facets of machine work, producing complete operating, state-of-the-art Top Fuel Dragsters. These Top Fuel Dragsters reach an average of 330 mph in approximately 4.6 seconds. Launch acceleration is close to 8 G's. We are fortunate to have the equipment to do everything in-house. Even so, each run costs BrinksRacing, Inc. $1,000,00 per second to operate. The Dragster has reached over 330 mph by the time you just read this sentence. It's intense, but then again so are all facets of Motor Sports.

When we hear of Motor Sports or racing, we automatically think of oval-track racing (NASCAR), but often drag racing is not mentioned as a professional sport. This is getting ready to explode. Today, there are sanctioning bodies in this Motor Sports field. We, at BrinksRacing, Inc., are sanctioned by the International Hot

Rod Association (IHRA). The IHRA is specific to the East Coast, Canada, and the Deep South. Twelve events are scheduled for the 2007 season, and IHRA is adding more for 2008. According to the IHRA, some of these recent events have been "standing room only."

The key to success in sport management in Motor Sports is being able to "wear many hats" and having an inherent passion for what you do. The management process encompasses everything—from development and implementation to marketing objectives and business strategies. I have already touched on ownership and foundation. Doing your homework is key to a successful business start-up. You must have a plan for participation and administration as well as for budget and finance.

It is imperative that you have knowledge of sport marketing and public relations and the awareness that without these, successful sports management is not possible. You must be prepared for anything that will be asked of you.

My knowledge has been tested—from statistical information to household viewership per televised event. Even though marketing is a "sales job," you cannot bluff your way through. I, especially, being a female in what is virtually a male-dominated sport, have had to work twice as hard. I am fortunate that I really do not have to keep a team owner satisfied since Michael states that we at BrinksRacing, Inc. *are* a team. Being the second in command and the chief marketing officer, I have the responsibility to know the venues (race tracks) we will be running and the protocols and operations, as well as supporting the suppliers. Promoting IHRA-sanctioned events is fortunately done for us. The IHRA (our sanctioning body) does an excellent job of advertising via television, film, and radio, as well as via the Internet. The IHRA removes an enormous burden from us and allows us to concentrate on the motor sport itself, providing hospitality for fans/spectators. Sponsors are probably the most challenging aspect of my duties. Not only am I responsible for acquiring sponsorship; I am equally responsible for securing it.

This leads me to the topic of legal aspects in sport. There are many contracts involved—from sponsorship contracts for upcoming seasons to employment contracts with crew members. An awareness of risk management must be present, as we have been faced with many challenges from a safety and environmental standpoint in the shop as well as during our travels and at the events. It is unfortunate, but we live in a very litigious society, and any potential lawsuit must be handled before it begins.

There are always new obstacles to overcome. Motor Sports managers should be able to cover all bases—from copyright and trademark infringement (people always want to borrow materials—e.g., photos and quotations) to moral and ethical issues. We have a responsibility to society in multiple environments.

I strive every day to achieve successful sport management by using the foundations I learned as tools to set objectives to maintain. The contacts and friends I have made along the way have been vital resources to success. To quote from my very first Introduction to Sport Management class, "I cannot stress how important it is to keep a paper trail!" Remember those words. Etch them in your brain if you must, since my "paper trail" has been a key in asking for help along the way and in always thanking everyone involved. As Michael always said, "Heidi, it takes a complete team to make a winning circle." The only thing better than achieving success is sharing it with others.

Professional Baseball

Tony Womack

It has been said that a good education not only never dies but also takes one to places far from the outstretched minds of many in order for it to become a reality in one's career. I have been playing professional baseball for 15 years. I signed a professional contract with the Pittsburgh Pirates during my junior year in college, and this prohibited me from participating in football and baseball during my senior year. With the cooperation of my college and the Pittsburgh Pirates, I was given permission to take an independent sport law course and do an internship in sport management to complete my degree in sport management. At the same time, I was playing for the Pittsburgh Pirates in the National League.

My goal was to win a championship, and I accomplished this with the Arizona Diamondbacks in 2001 after I had been traded from the Pittsburgh Pirates. We defeated the New York Yankees in the World Series, and I was fortunate to play a major role in the championship. In 2004, I was playing for the St. Louis Cardinals in another World Series against the Boston Red Sox. Today, major league baseball appears to be on its way out for me, and my career in sport management is about to begin. I now want to fulfill my responsibilities to the sport industry by utilizing my training and preparation in the sport profession. I am eager to receive accolades in the field of sport management just as I did in professional baseball. I am grateful that I have a rock solid background in sport management and look forward to a second career in sport.

Ticketmaster

Kristen Faris, Ticketmaster

One of the most important things in sport management is an internship. During my senior year in college, I held an internship with the Greensboro Coliseum. I worked with the special projects manager and with Laura Smith, the business manager. An internship provides you with real-world experience as well as contacts in the sport management field. You are able to get an idea of the way the business works in a way that you cannot get in a classroom setting. You can begin to make local contacts in the sport management field that you can draw on when you begin your job search after graduation. An internship gives you something to put on your résumé under "Work Experience," which is often the weakest section for a new graduate. My first position at the Greensboro Coliseum as assistant box office manager was a direct result of my internship.

As Client Services Manager of the Carolinas at Ticketmaster, I am responsible for all of the clients in our market. I have one client rep and three event programmers who report to me, and we handle about 40 clients, which include two 20,000-seat amphitheaters, six major arenas, a NASCAR motor speedway, an NFL stadium, an NHL team, an NBA team, and other auditoriums and various smaller venues. I am responsible for making sure that all the clients have manifests for their various venue setups, whether it is a concert, a basketball game, or a rodeo. I am responsible for making sure that all of the events are conducted with the correct prices, the ticket text, and various promotions which are submitted to us from the client. My department is also responsible for all the training of each box office and box office staff. I help introduce new products to each client, including access control, which allows the bar codes on each ticket to be scanned upon entrance and ensures that counterfeit or invalid tickets do not enter the building.

I really enjoy my job, although it can be stressful at times. It is certainly a job that requires strength in organization and time management as I am constantly under deadline pressure. Venues always find out about events at the last minute, and I am under pressure to turn them around for quick sales. I do enjoy the fast paced atmosphere. It is a job that changes from day to day, so there is no time to get bored or do mundane tasks. I get a chance to work with all kinds of clients who have all kinds of events at their venues.

About the Authors

Herb Appenzeller has been a faculty member at Guilford College since 1956 and has had varied responsibilities, including teaching, coaching, dean of students and, for 31 years, athletics director. He is known as one of the most distinguished athletic directors in the nation for his dedication to individual development and team cooperation in his student athletes. His accomplishments as an administrator are a matter of record. He is responsible for turning unsuccessful programs around at four schools. He guided Guilford College to national titles in men's basketball and women's tennis and instituted a sports management program that has received national attention and acclaim. He capped his athletics career with the teaching and research responsibilities of an endowed professorship to become Jefferson-Pilot Professor of Sports Management. He is a respected consultant in sports management throughout the United States.

Appenzeller has worked as a scholar in the field of sports law. He has been a board member of the National Association of Sports Officials, the Sports Medicine Foundation, and is a special consultant for the Center for Sport Law and Risk Management. He has been honored with membership in the Athletics Hall of Fame for the National Association of Collegiate Directors of Athletics and the National Association of Intercollegiate Athletics. In 1988, the Safety Society of the American Alliance for Health, Physical Education, Recreation and Dance awarded Appenzeller its Professional Service Award. In 1993, he received the Distinguished Service Award from the North Carolina High School Coaches Association, and Guilford College recognized his career contributions to the college with its Distinguished Service Award. Herb received the Leadership Award from the Society for the Study of the Legal Aspects of Sport and Physical Activity (SS-LASPA) in 1999, the Simon Terrell Director's Choice Award in 2001, the SS-LASPA President's Award in 2002, the Guy M. Lewis Academic Achievement Award from the International Conference on Sport and Entertainment Business in 2002, the 2004 Outstanding Achievement Award, Sport Management Council of the National Association for Sport and Physical Education, the George Whitfield Baseball Clinic Honor Award in 2005, the 2006 Presidential Award from the Safety and Risk Management Council of AAHPERD and on September 30, 2006 Guilford College dedicated its football field to Herb Appenzeller. He was inducted into the Wake Forest University Sports Hall of Fame in January 2008 and the Guilford County Sport Hall of Fame, 2008.

Tom Appenzeller is an Associate Professor of Sport Management at Wingate University in Wingate, North Carolina. Author of *Youth Sports and the Law*, Appenzeller is one of the leading authorities in the United States on the topic of

Legal Issues in Youth Sports and has been a featured speaker on the international, national, regional and state levels on sport law. Co-author of *Sports and the Courts*, Appenzeller received his bachelor of science degree in history education from Presbyterian College and a masters of education degree in history from the University of North Carolina, Greensboro. A second masters degree in sport management from the University of Massachusetts was followed by a doctorate in physical education from the University of North Carolina at Greensboro. As a teacher and administrator, he has been involved in education for the past 35 years on the high school, junior college, and university level and has been a coach or athletic director for 30 years. Appenzeller has been a professor at Wingate University for 19 years.

Art Chase joined the Duke University athletic staff in August 2000 and serves as the department's Sports Information Director. After graduating from Guilford College in 1991 with a bachelor of science degree in sport management, Chase served two years as an assistant sports information director at The Citadel in Charleston, S.C. After a three-year stint as the SID at Presbyterian College, he returned to The Citadel as SID, holding the position for four years until accepting a position on the Duke staff. A native of Chapel Hill, N.C., Chase is married to the former Kaye Watts of Mayesville, S.C., and the couple has two labrador retrievers, Moses and Goliath.

Annie Clement, joined the faculty at the University of New Mexico in 2008 and is best known for her texts: *Law in Sport and Physical Activity, Legal Responsibility in Aquatics, and Teaching Physical Activity.* Twenty-five book chapters, 75 articles, and over 150 presentations are among her achievements. While her research and writing cover many areas, among her in-depth studies are the topics of intellectual property, disaster and risk management, futures, aquatics, and gender equity.

Clement holds a bachelor's degree from the University of Minnesota, Duluth, and a master's degree from the University of Minnesota, Minneapolis. Her doctorate is from the University of Iowa and her juris doctorate is from Cleveland State University. She has studied at Cambridge University and the University of Oslo. Clement has held teaching or management positions at the University of Iowa, Ohio State University, Florida State University, Bowling Green State University and Cleveland State University.

In addition to her role as the distinguished speaker at fifteen different universities, Clement has been awarded numerous honors, including Fellow, American Bar Foundation; Nonprofit Lawyers Award (ABA, Section of Business); President, National Association for Sport and Physical Education (NASPE); President, Ohio Teacher Educators; American Alliance for Health, Physical Education, Recreation and Dance, Honor Award; Aquatic Council Merit Award and the NASPE Joy of Effort Award. She also received the Sport, Recreation, Law Association Leadership Award; the Ohio AAHPERD Honor Award; Tsunami Spirit Award from the Aquatic Therapy and Rehab Institute; the Susan B. Anthony Award from the Ohio National Organization for Women; and Honor Award from the National Cooperation in Aquatics.

Gil Fried is a recognized expert in sport management. He is a tenured professor at the University of New Haven where he teaches sport law, finance, facility management, and management related classes. He is a lawyer by training and has represented numerous sport organizations over the past fifteen years and has served as an expert witness in several major sport liability cases. He regularly speaks at professional and academic conferences throughout the world and writes a number of industry articles. He has written five textbooks currently used in the industry. In his "spare" time he is a competitive badminton player.

Jerald D. Hawkins is Professor Emeritus and the former Monica Martin Stranch Endowed Professor and Director of Sports Medicine Education at Lander University where he taught for twenty-one years. He holds degrees from Carson-Newman College, the University of Memphis, and the University of Georgia. A Fellow of the American College of Sports Medicine, Hawkins is a certified athletic trainer with broad expertise in exercise science and sports medicine. The author of five books and numerous book chapters and articles, Hawkins is an active writer, speaker, and consultant in the areas of wellness, exercise science, legal issues in sport and physical education, and sports medicine. During his 34-year career, Hawkins has taught kindergarten through graduate school, been department chair at two colleges, and served on the sports medicine staff of numerous international sports events including the 1990 Goodwill Games, Junior World Luge Championships in Italy, Germany, and Japan, and two U.S. Olympic Festivals.

David Harlowe graduated from Guilford College with a degree in sport management. He has vast experience within the athletic and fitness industries. Harlowe was an intercollegiate athlete, coached on the college level, and was a strength & conditioning coach for a minor league hockey team. In addition, he has worked in the front office of a minor league baseball team and has been a fitness facility owner. Harlowe has now become one of the industry's leading experts in risk management and the many fields that make up sport management. He has personally performed over 1,600 risk reviews on fitness and athletic facilities nationwide and currently writes a risk management column for a nationally published magazine and is an expert witness for the fitness and athletic industries.

Calvin Hunter is a professor in the department of physical education and recreation at Catawba College. He coordinates the undergraduate sport management major and advises the department's Student Majors Club. He received his bachelor of science degree from Guilford College, master's degree from Georgia Southern University, and doctorate from the United States Sports Academy. Hunter has worked with the Greensboro Coliseum Complex, YMCA, and the Equestrian Park during the 1996 Summer Olympic Games in Atlanta, Georgia, and was a 2006 Athletic Hall of Fame inductee at Guilford College.

John Horshok has worked with a variety of significant business entities in his career in the area of business, sports, entertainment and non-profit. He has been the Chief Operating Officer/ Managing Partner of five professional sports teams and was the first Executive Director of the Major League Baseball Players Alumni Association. He has represented various sports properties internationally and was the original person hired by Coca-Cola USA to expand support for the International Special Olympics with Eunice Kennedy Shriver. Horshok has won many awards for writing including National Sportswriter of the Year (Joseph P. Kennedy Foundation) and the Understanding Through Sports Award from the U.S. State Department for his work in Latin America. Currently representing

Siemens in development, Horshok is involved in several sports properties includ-ing serving on the Board of Directors for the Harmon Killebrew Foundation. He graduated from Eastern Michigan University and was President of the Michigan Collegiate Press Association.

Adonis "Sporty" Jeralds is a native of Fayetteville, North Carolina. He gradu-ated from Guilford College with a degree in criminal justice and holds a master's degree from UNC Chapel Hill in public administration and a second master's de-gree from the University of Massachusetts in sports management. He started a ca-reer in public assembly facilities management at the Hampton Virginia Coliseum in 1983. In 1988 he accepted a position at the Charlotte Coliseum as Assistant Manager. In 1990 he became manager of the Charlotte Coliseum, a position he held for fifteen years. He is a certified facilities executive, one of only 200 in the world. In his career, he has coordinated such internationally recognized events as the Men's and Women's Final Four, the NBA All-Star Game, a visit by Mother Teresa and the Rolling Stones. He currently works in the Marketing and Events Department with the new Charlotte Bobcats Arena.

He is the author of the highly successful book, *The Champion in You*. Com-mitted to education, he is currently an instructor at Johnson and Wales Univer-sity. In 2005 he was recognized by the Charlotte Regional Visitors Authority and *Trip Magazine* with a scholarship named in his honor. In 2006 he was awarded the Harold J. Vanderzwaag Distinguished Alumnus Award from the Sports Man-agement Department at the University of Massachusetts—Amherst. In 2006 he also visited Asia, teaching sports marketing to the Taiwan Society for Sport Management.

Dennis A. Johnson is the Assistant Dean of Education overseeing the sport sci-ences department at Wingate University. He teaches several sport management courses (e.g., sport psychology, sport philosophy, and internship) and is the men's and women's cross country coach. Prior to coming to Wingate University, he taught public school physical education and coached high school wrestling for 23 years in the Warren County, Pennsylvania, school system.

Debra Korb opened the Monroe (N.C.) Tourism & Visitors Bureau in Septem-ber 2004. She is responsible for promoting tourism and attracting visitors to Union County. During the process of researching the assets in the community, she found that many of the community's needs were untapped: parks & greenways, horse & bike trails, sidewalks, downtown shopping experiences, museums, art galleries, etc. By serving on boards throughout the county, Debra often has the opportunity to help people and business opportunities connect. Korb has more than 20 years of marketing and sales support experience from a variety of indus-tries and locations across the country. Most recently, she was marketing manager, coordinating national events and handling promotion for American City Business Journals, the parent company of the *Charlotte Business Journal*.

Nancy L. Lough is an Associate Professor at the University of Nevada Las Vegas, where she is the director of the Athletic Administration Graduate Program in the department of Sport Education Leadership. Dr. Lough has worked in sport extensively, with experience as a collegiate coach, athletic administrator and con-sultant. Prior to assuming her position at UNLV, Dr. Lough served as sport man-agement faculty at the University of New Mexico, Iowa State University and Kent

State University. Her years of experience in the sport management field have also included coaching and administrative roles in NCAA Division I and II programs in California, Texas and Colorado. Dr. Lough's research has focused primarily on marketing of women's sport and leadership development for women in sport as evidenced by numerous national presentations and publications. She is currently the associate editor for *Sport Marketing Quarterly* and the director of the Center for Sport Education at UNLV.

Tim Lynde has held a variety of positions in the sports marketing industry since 1995, including those on different sides of the sponsorship table—agency, property and corporate. His corporate experience includes two of the most recognizable and respected brands in the U.S.: The Coca Cola Company and The Home Depot. With The Home Depot, he has worked in various aspects of sponsorship management including leading the company's negotiations, strategic planning and activation of the following properties: NFL, MLB, US Olympic Committee, ESPN College GameDay and numerous deals such as the Atlanta Braves, Boston Red Sox and Chicago Bears. Some of his prior experience includes the international sports marketing agency Advantage International (now Octagon), Chick-fil-A Bowl and the NCAA's Corporate Marketing Group. Lynde is currently Vice President for Television for ISP Sports in Winston-Salem, N.C.

Bob Malekoff is an assistant professor of sport studies and director of the sport management program at Guilford College. Malekoff served as head coach of women's soccer and assistant coach of men's lacrosse at Princeton University before embarking on a career in athletic administration. He served as Associate Director of Athletics at Harvard University, Director of Athletics at Connecticut College, and Director of Athletics at The College of Wooster. Malekoff also served as the Director of Research for The Center of Sport in Society at Northeastern University and is presently a member of the coordinating committee for the College Sports Project, an Andrew W. Mellon Foundation initiative aimed at ensuring the educational value of intercollegiate sport. He was recently named to the Advisory Committee of the College Sport Research Institute at the University of Memphis. Malekoff has written extensively about issues germane to sport in society, and is the co-author of *On the Mark: Putting the Student Back in Student-Athlete.*

David R. Maraghy is CEO of Sports Management International, LC (SMI), a professional sports management and marketing firm located in Richmond, Virginia. He has been a successful sports attorney for more than 20 years (Williams College, BA, 1974; Wake Forest University School of Law, JD, 1977). Maraghy began his sports career by serving as general chairman of the 1986 Greater Greensboro Open on the PGA Tour. For the next 10 years he was a principal in Pros, Incorporated where his clients included such PGA Tour stars as Tom Kite, Lanny Wadkins, Davis Love, III, Justin Leonard and Steve Pate. During that time he also produced and televised the State Open of Virginia and the Crown Royal Golf Championships. In the mid-90s Maraghy created two significant golf events in Korea: The Hyundai Motor Golf Classic (on ESPN) and the Ssangyong Securities Challenge. For those events he brought to Korea some of the biggest names in golf: John Daly, Tom Kite, Corey Pavin, Tom Watson, Curtis Strange, and Justin Leonard. In 1996 he created SMI and presently represents PGA Tour players John Rollins, Daniel Chopra and Omar Uresti. SMI also manages and markets the

PGA Tour's Nationwide stop, The Henrico County Open, and for the LPGA Duramed FUTURES Tour the Greater Richmond Duramed Futures Tour Challenge. In 1999 Maraghy co-founded the Virginia Commonwealth University Sports Center, a unique graduate program in sports leadership, and served as Executive Director until 2002.

Kenny Morgan is the Account Manager for the Charlotte Bobcats and Charlotte Bobcats Arena for Show Pros Entertainment Services of Charlotte, N.C. He held the same position for the Carolina Panthers and Bank of America Stadium from 2003–2005. In addition to his work with the NFL and NBA, Morgan has been a part of management teams associated with the 2005 Greater New York Billy Graham Crusade, the PGA's Wachovia Championship and Greater Greensboro Open, multiple ACC and NCAA Men's Basketball tournaments, Division I and I-AA College Football, and over 200 concerts and special events. He has previously authored a chapter in *Managing Sports (2004)*. Morgan earned his bachelor's degree from the University of North Carolina at Chapel Hill and a masters degree in sport management from Appalachian State University.

Charlie Patterson has been in college fundraising for almost 40 years. He has been directly involved in eight capital campaigns, planned giving and annual funds at five different colleges/universities. He has been a pioneer in planned giving, assistant to the President, and Vice President of both public and private universities, as well as Associate Athletic Director at Wake Forest University. At Wake Forest, Patterson planned and directed two major capital campaigns to fund a basketball/entertainment coliseum, soccer stadium, baseball stadium, golf practice complex, football fieldhouse including athletic offices/entertainment facilities, track & field facility, and both indoor & outdoor tennis complexes. He also led the effort to establish a significant athletic endowment at Wake Forest. Patterson has been an active member of CASE during his career and was an original member of NADD, receiving the 2001 Athletic Fundraiser of the Year award. He has also received Lifetime Achievement recognition from the Association of Fundraising Professionals.

Joyce Richman is a career counselor, consultant, and coach. She is a National Certified Counselor, Licensed Professional Counselor, Certified Personnel Consultant and has a masters degree in counseling from the University of North Carolina at Greensboro. In addition, Richman is a graduate of Harvard University's Program On Negotiation. Joyce appears frequently as a guest on Greensboro television, is a regular columnist for Greensboro's *News & Record*, and is the author of *Road, Routes, and Ruts: A Guidebook for Career Success*. A popular lecturer, Richman has conducted seminars and workshops throughout the United States and has consulted in Belgium, Canada and England. She also serves as an Adjunct to the Center for Creative Leadership, an international management and leadership development organization.

Frank Russo serves as Senior Vice President for Global Spectrum, where his responsibilities include worldwide development of private management contracts for civic and convention centers, arenas, stadiums and other public assembly facilities. Russo brings to Global Spectrum over thirty years experience in the fields of municipal and facility management. Prior to joining Global Spectrum he held the position of Vice President of Sales and Client Services for

Ogden Entertainment. Russo also served simultaneously as Ogden's Vice President of International Operations with oversight responsibilities for venues in England, Germany, Belgium and Australia.

Russo was designated by the International Association of Assembly Managers (IAAM) as a Certified Facility Executive (CFE) in 1979. Currently, he serves as Chairman of the Body of Knowledge Task Force and the IAAM Board of Education Committee. An educator, author and public speaker, Russo has shared his considerable knowledge and experience with diverse audiences. He taught a course in public assembly facility management as an adjunct professor for the department of sports studies at the University of Massachusetts. He has also provided consulting services to several cities and civic centers on downtown economic development, market studies and surveys, construction and renovation, and the overall operation, management and organization of public assembly facilities. Russo earned his bachelor of arts degree in history from St. Michael's College and his masters degree in public administration from the University of Connecticut.

David K. Scott is an associate professor for sport administration and has recently been appointed Associate Dean for Research and Information Management in the College of Education at the University of New Mexico. He received his bachelor of science degree from Texas A&M University, his master of science degree from Midwestern State University and his doctorate from the University of Northern Colorado. He taught sport management at Southern Illinois University in 1997 and then moved to the University of New Mexico, where he taught graduate courses in sport administration from 1998–2005. He became department chair for Health, Exercise and Sports Sciences at UNM in 2005. Throughout his academic career, his research focus has primarily been in leadership and organizational behavior for sport organizations. He additionally enjoys consulting and conducting workshops regarding culture management and leadership development for coaches and athletic administrators. He is currently a member of the North American Society for Sport Management and the American Alliance for Health, Physical Education, Recreation and Dance.

Todd Seidler is currently professor and coordinator of the graduate program in sport administration at the University of New Mexico. He received his bachelor's degree in physical education from San Diego State University and earned his master's and Ph.D. in sports administration from the University of New Mexico. Prior to returning to UNM, Seidler spent six years as the coordinator of the graduate Sports Administration program at Wayne State University and then was the coordinator of the undergraduate Sport Management Program at Guilford College in North Carolina.

Seidler is a former President of the Sport and Recreation Law Association, a professional organization for those interested in teaching sport law and risk management. He has also served on the Executive Board and as Chair of both the Sport Management Council and the Council on Facilities and Equipment within the American Alliance for Health, Physical Education, Recreation and Dance (AAHPERD) and is an active member of the North American Society for Sport Management (NASSM). Seidler is President of Southwest Sports Management, LLC, a consulting firm specializing in sport safety and risk management as well as planning facilities for sport and recreation. He frequently presents, publishes, and teaches classes on risk management in sport, sport facility planning and design, facility and event management, and legal aspects of sport.

Robert Taylor is an associate professor of sport management at California University of Pennsylvania. He earned his bachelor's degree in physical education from San Diego State University, a master's degree from Frostburg State University, and a doctoral degree in human performance from the University of Southern Mississippi. He has held teaching positions at numerous schools and universities, including his three alma maters. Taylor has coached men's and women's collegiate basketball teams and camps, is the owner of a fitness training business, and organized sponsorship opportunities between California University of Pa. and the Ironman Triathalon series. His research interests include marketing sport, recreation and fitness to "baby boomers."

Travis Teague has served in many capacities related to teaching and research in higher education. Currently the Program Coordinator of the Motorsport Management program at Winston-Salem State University, he has served in leadership positions with the Society of Manufacturing Engineers, including being the Chair of the national Motorsports Education Advisory Committee. Teague also serves as the President of the Sport Management Association of the North Carolina Alliance for Athletics, Health, Physical Education, Recreation and Dance. Teague's primary areas of research and scholarly activity focus upon workforce development and diversity within motorsport, as well as crowd dynamics and risk management. Teague has taught and led experiential learning trips for students in numerous international venues including Italy, Germany, and Venezuela. He will also co-lead a collaborative contingent from WSSU and Western Kentucky University to China during the 2008 Summer Olympic Games.

Index